JOHN KELLY (1931-1991) ed   1 St. Conleth's College, Glenstal Abbey,
University College, Dublin,   delberg and Oxford. Former Professor of
Jurisprudence and Roman Law   university College, Dublin. Member of Dáil
Éireann 1973-1989. Serve   amentary Secretary to the Taoiseach and as
Attorney G   alition Administration 1973-1977 and as Minister
for Trade, Commerce and Tourism in the Government of 1981-1982. His
publications include *Fundamental Rights in the Irish Law* and *Constitution, the
Irish Constitution* and the recently published *Short History of Western Legal
Theory*. He is author of a number of works on Roman Law.

Belling the Cats
SELECTED SPEECHES AND ARTICLES OF JOHN KELLY

Belling the Cats

SELECTED SPEECHES AND ARTICLES OF JOHN KELLY

Edited by

JOHN FANAGAN

MOYTURA PRESS • DUBLIN

in association with
FINE GAEL

This book was typeset by Gilbert Gough Typesetting
for Moytura Press, Ormond Court
11 Lower Ormond Quay, Dublin 1.

A catalogue record for this book
is available from the British Library

ISBN 1 871305 08 X

First published May 1992
Reprinted May 1992
Second edition June 1992

Printed in Ireland by
Colour Books Ltd, Dublin

Contents

Foreword — by Liam Cosgrave

These speeches by John Kelly were delivered in Dáil Éireann or at meetings. They reflect his views and comments on matters before the Dail and give examples of his thinking on particular issues as well as criticism of certain proposals or policies. However, these interesting speeches only give a partial indication of his remarkable talents.

He was an academic who was practical, a lawyer, a linguist, an orator, a writer and a politician. All these attributes he possessed to a high degree.

He practised at the Bar and was later Professor of Jurisprudence and Roman law at U.C.D. He edited the New Series of the Irish Jurist. As well as his book on the Irish Constitution he wrote Princeps Iudex (Weimar 1957), Fundamental Rights in the Irish Law and Constitution (Dublin 1961), Roman Litigation (Oxford 1966) and Studies in the Civil Judicature of the Roman Republic (Oxford 1976).

He had an excellent knowledge of Constitutional Law. The writing of the Irish Constitution was a remarkable achievement as he did so while he was actively engaged in political work as a member of Dail Eireann. In this work he dealt with the Constitution where he emphasised the continuity in many respects of the 1937 Constitution with the 1922 Constitution, often with a commentary Article by Article.

In 1969 he entered the political arena where he displayed that steadfast loyalty which was to shine like a beacon from then onwards. He showed in his political work a flair that in many ways marked him out as outstanding. While he was responsible for arranging Dail business the sitting hours were extended and the 20th Dail sat on more days than any other Dail since the foundation of the State and worked almost 30% more hours than the longest other Dail. This dramatic reform was conducted against continuous opposition even when contrary to the national interest. He was quiet about his work in this area but spectacularly efficient. As these speeches clearly show, he had a great gift of speech, eloquent, witty and delivered with good humour. He was a clear thinker and speaker. Forthright in his views. Perceptive in his vision.

When his colleagues embarked on a line of policy that was wrong or flawed he expressed, and vigorously, his dissent. When he saw monumental political incompetence or danger ahead he said so with compelling accuracy and clarity. Welcome or unwelcome he spoke the truth. He did not pose, he had no need to. He was no political surf rider propelling himself forward on the labours of others.

In financial and economic affairs he had a great sense of realism about the

Nation's economy although he would not claim to be an economist. He did not try to create any myth. He did his duty. The nation benefited greatly from his selfless dedication to his work.

In his dealing with Deputies he was sympathetic and considerate with a great feel for the problems and difficulties of each individual. His intellectual brilliance did not prevent him having a genuine rapport with people less gifted than he, but who appreciated his concern for their welfare.

He was a most accomplished linguist fluent in Irish, English, German, French, Italian and with a profound knowledge of Latin. What a combination.

While his writings and speeches give a good idea of his extraordinary versatile ability and career, he had to be known in person to understand his merit and sterling character. He had intellect, courage, kindliness and loyalty. In a great many respects he was in a class by himself.

April 1992

Acknowledgements

Thanks are due to many who helped in the preparation of this book. Gerard Arthurs and Paul Malone made initial assessments of all the Dail speeches. Enid and Eric Dunlop and Margaret Hogan also made assessments of material from different sections. Particular assistance at the outset came from Garret FitzGerald and encouragement from Deputies Tom Enright and Ted Nealon; also from Marie Gillman and David Fitzgerald. A huge debt is owed to Angela Edghill for giving so much of her scarce time and organisation in putting the speeches on to computer; her assistants, particularly Deirdre Chambers, Ruth Lawlor, Edel Flanagan, Mairead Hassett, Mary Farrelly, Clare Fallon and Mary O'Connor worked against seemingly impossible deadlines at times.

The Kelly family, especially Delphine, provided limitless help and encouragement and our publisher, Gerard O'Connor of Moytura Press, gave a commitment to the work beyond the professional call of duty. The final selection remains my sole responsibility and I am sorry if I have omitted (as I am sure I have) particular favourites.

Motivating all of us has been the memory of John. I hope that these speeches and articles will help keep our memories of him fresh and introduce him to a generation not fortunate enough to have known or heard him.

J.M.F.

SECTION 1

Life in Irish Politics

50th Anniversary of First Dáil, Hibernia, 3 January 1969

1969: the fiftieth anniversary of the First Dáil; also, probably the last year of the Eighteenth Dáil and of the Fianna Fáil administration. A time, in the idiom of a retreat preacher, for taking stock; for looking back before again going forward; for renewal of our faith. A time for looking at the State's baptismal vows and for seeing how well they have been kept.

This metaphor is not a mere literary contrivance. It is seriously intended to express a mood which can be vaguely felt in the air at the beginning of this year.

Two very different politicians on the Fianna Fáil side have helped in creating this mood; Mr. Lenihan, by his interview with the Daily Telegraph in which he said that national independence wasn't everything; and Mr. Colley with his call for a "winter of debate" and a re-appraisal of our national aims. Political capital was, naturally, made by their opponents out of these utterances, because they came from a party which, with unbearable arrogance, has always pretended to an infallible understanding of the Irish soul and destiny; and yet, both Ministers have done us a service by speaking their minds. If the Legion of the Rearguard are searching their hearts, it is certainly high time for the rest of us to do so.

Very grave material for recognition of this kind is provided by the recent events in the North, in particular by Captain O'Neill's successful appeal to moderate Unionism and by the apparent shift of feeling on the Nationalist side. It seems that a 32-county State is not now by a long chalk the main objective of the Nationalists, and that there is a good chance of their settling permanently for a separate North, provided that official discrimination ceases. What this boils down to is that Dublin has become nearly irrelevant even to the Nationalists of the six counties over which our Constitution still implicitly claims jurisdiction. This is a real disaster for which all political parties in the Republic must bear some blame; and which might in turn lead us to go further than the hints of Messrs. Lenihan and Colley and to ask, has it all been worth while?

What, as a State, have we achieved in nearly half a century of self government that we would not equally have got if we had stayed in the United Kingdom? The disparity in social benefits between here and the North can be left out of the reckoning, as being purely a question of money; if we had it, we too could pay it out. But is our loss of population any less than it would have been? Has the Irish language fared any better? Is our educational system any more advanced? Have we made innovations in democratic government, in administration, in law reform, in the treatment of delinquents and dropouts, that vindicate our separate legislature? Have we been more imaginative than the

English in improving our physical environment, or even in preserving the urban and rural amenities which we still had in 1922?

If the answers to these questions are disappointing, they do not point to any going back on, or surrender of our independence. On the contrary, they point in just the opposite direction; if we have done less than well, it is because we haven't acted independently, because we haven't struck out for ourselves often enough and far enough.

It is a curious thing that wherever we have struck out for ourselves it has mostly worked well. Take the courts, the judicial arm of the State. On the surface, indeed, these are still of an English pattern; wigs, gowns and so on. But, in fact, the whole standing and structure of the court system here is very different from that of England, thanks to the radical reorganisation of 1924 and to the entrenchment of court independence by the Constitution of 1937; and though there is plenty of room for improvement, it could be reasonably claimed that we have in many ways a better administration of justice than we would have had if we were still in the U.K.

On the other hand, where we have stuck closely to the old British pattern, the results are bad. The closed, cautious, secretive approach to administrative government; the wide sphere still accessible to patronage and private intercession; the cops and robbers atmosphere of the Parliament (as a contributor to Hibernia called it recently), are all suggestive not of a dynamic young people given their head at last, but of a society left over from the Britain of 50 years ago and frozen in the conventional wisdoms of Asquith and Lloyd George. These are exactly the things that have produced the public cynicism and alienation from politics of which those who are themselves most at fault sometimes complain.

The future of this country, the justification of its independence, and the prospect of its unity, depend on two things.

Firstly, on greater use of our freedom, not less; which means making promising experiments rather than sticking to old precedent; bold innovations rather than cautious imitation; willingness to admit mistakes and start again; indifference to prestige and publicity; the humility to seek good advice wherever it can be got.

Secondly, on some one political party convincing the people that self sacrifice, frankness and fair play are its absolute principles of conduct; because nothing else will recreate the true unity of national purpose of which the First Dáil was an expression.

Serious faces, stiff collars, buttoned boots; a glum lot they look in the old photograph. But they had the people behind them: because the people thought they meant what they said about a new and different Ireland, because the people never heard them promise jobs to their own supporters "all other things being equal," because the people never saw them paying themselves 60% salary increases. The party that can think itself back into the spirit of the First Dáil is the party that will rule the next one.

4

TD's Duties, Dáil, 2 November 1977

The other thing I want to mention is the question of the burden of ministerial office, which is central to this Bill. The Leader of my party, Deputy FitzGerald, who as, I have said, has the constitution of three horses and any number of men, spoke about this burden. I thought he was the only man I had ever met who never seemed to feel such a burden. There were times when it could be seen from his demeanour and in his person that he must have been fatigued but he never seemed to realise that he was fatigued. It was very impressive to me that even that man, who I am certain even his political foes as well as his political friends will admit is unique in everyone's experience, feels that he has to speak about the burden of ministerial office. Sometimes he seems scarcely flesh and blood at all, his energy is so superhuman.

I want to say something about flesh and blood office holders. I was never a member of Government and was only very briefly at the end of the last Government in an office senior to that of Parliamentary Secretary. Before I say anything that might be interpreted as making an excuse or a begging-off from the performance of duties commonly expected of office holders, I want to say a word in regard to press reaction on issues of this kind. I have noticed with pleasure that on a couple of occasions when there has been a conspicuous death in ministerial ranks here or across the water the press have tended to react by saying "They ought to look again a bit more carefully at what they expect our public men to do". I recall that at the beginning of this year when the British Foreign Secretary had a stroke and died within 24 hours the papers all printed an account of the way he had spent the last week of his life. This was a man certainly not in his first youth, neither was he an old man. I suppose he could be described as being in the late prime of life. The description of the last ought to be asked to bear. Even some of the Irish papers said that perhaps we should look again at what was expected of public men and see whether we are not expecting too much from them when a thing like this can happen, when this brilliant man, a member of his own Cabinet, nearly the most senior man in his own Government, a possible contender for leadership of the Labour party who possibly would have been Prime Minister , was struck down by overwork. The same thing was said here nine years ago when the late Deputy Donogh O'Malley dropped dead in the middle of a by-election campaign. The *Irish Times* printed an editorial which said: "We have seen this week that politics is literally a killing occupation."

Against that background which I am not ashamed to evoke, I may be allowed something additional to what Deputy FitzGerald said about the burdens of ministerial office and not be accused of being lazy or unwilling to pull my weight or do my share in or out of Government. The description which Deputy FitzGerald gave of a Minister's week I thought was fairly mild. He left out of the description many of the minor things which can get in a man's way. An ordinary man who is flesh and blood has a wife and family and perhaps problems with neighbours and financial worries and so on. Deputy FitzGerald spoke about a ministerial meeting on Monday morning with the central advisers of his Department. That is all very fine, but he has forgotten that on the odd Monday morning something happens which leaves one late for the office. Some problem, something about the children, something in one's constituency which cannot be neglected, cuts the tripe out of one's morning. In his case as Minister for Foreign Affairs he had to escort an ambassador to Aras an Uachtarain. That could destroy his morning. It is not always possible to arrange these things for some morning when he does not have a ministerial conference. Please do not believe that the relatively civilised description which the leader of my party gave of a Minister's Monday is a universal one. It by no means is so, as I know from my limited experience. Any number of things will come in and torpedo your morning. Some of them are domestic. Others are of a political kind which cannot be avoided. There is no use in saying that you are not paid to do that, you are paid to do the other and so you must do the other. That is not the practical response to the problem.

The average Minister or Parliamentary Secretary or whatever he is going to be called, and to a very large extent the average Deputy, lives an existence which is at times not the life of a dog. The fact that the public complain about their performance in their office I take for granted. That is part of the game. If you do not like it get out of it. If you are not able to put up with that you ought not to be in politics at all. They are treated not so much by the complaining members of the public but by the relatively indifferent or perhaps, friendly members of the public with a total lack of understanding in regard to what they are physically capable of. No professional association feel that their annual occasion or even their twice or three times a year occasion is complete these days without the attendance at least of a Minister, if at all possible the Taoiseach, failing him the Tanaiste and failing him a Minister. Some of them will turn quite sour if they are fobbed off with a Parliamentary Secretary. Possibly this is one of the reasons for the improvement in the title of the seven junior colleagues of the Minister.

Employment, Dáil, 14 May 1978

I do not admire the Fianna Fáil Party. I do not believe in their programme. I think it is a fraud and a sham but they should be given a chance to put it into effect. They should not be battered into the ground by being given an average of five or six hours' sleep a night and only one weekend in every four which is common ministerial experience. They should be given the chance of living as ordinary human beings with an ordinary amount of rest, an ordinary amount of relaxation, an ordinary amount of time to see their families and their friends, and to pursue their hobbies if they have any outside politics. That sort of thing should be as much the entitlement of a Minister as of anybody else.

Those functions are a severe burden, but I want to advert to another function which Ministers sometimes accept voluntarily, but which is not necessary. It is nothing to do with the kind of functions I have been talking about. That is, what I would call ministerial skites or trips. Perhaps I should not have used the word "skite". It has another meaning which I do not intend. I should like that word blotted from the record. I do not mean a skite in the sense of a binge. I mean a ministerial trip.

I do not hold this of one party more than another, but I think Ministers, possibly because their own organisms scream for relief, for just a few days, relief, from the crushing burdens and sequence of work in their Departments, work in this House, constituency work, going to functions, reading scripts, always being on their best behaviour, take the opportunity frequently, and I mean frequently, of going on absolutely indefensible, idiotic, exotic trips around the world. I do not say Fianna Fáil are any worse than we were in that regard, but they are shaping up, and may get more worse quickly.

I will give the House an example of the kind of thing I mean. This is an accidental example of the kind of thing I mean. I want to emphasise that I produce this example for another reason than that it came into my post from the GIS yesterday. It concerns the Minister for Defence. I want to ask the House to believe that in no sense do I intend this as an attack on Deputy Molloy. If this debate had taken place next week I would have had another example. If it had taken place the previous week I would have had the example of Deputy Barrett, Minister for the Environment, who was then in Japan, Japan if you please.

On 26th, 27th and 28th October, 1977, according to the GIS, the Minister for Defence was, if you do not mind, at the colloquy on the conservation of the living resources of the seas held in Valetta, Malta, under the auspices of the Council of Europe. There were three sitting days. The Minister for Defence has nothing whatsoever to do with the conservation of the resources of the sea except for patrolling it. He and his Department know as much officially about the conservation of the resources of the seas as the Department of Education.

Please believe that I do not mean this as an attack on the Minister for Defence. It is a pure accident that this came out this weekend. These things are out every weekend. This is the most recent one. There is absolutely no excuse or defence in the wide world whatsoever for that attendance. The Minister more nearly apposite would have been the Minister for Fisheries for whom he was standing in. Even his attendance would have been indefensible. At that kind of colloquy held by the Council of Europe, although they invite ministerial participation, I know from experience they do not really expect it. No one would have known or cared if Ireland had been represented there by some political personage other than a Minister or perhaps by no political personage at all but

7

merely by an official. Although I have not done any research on this, I defy the Minister for Finance or anybody else to tell me which other Minister for Defence from all the other Council of Europe nations spend three days in the middle of the week plus a day at either end for travelling there and back, in Malta, at a conference on the conservation of the resources of the sea.

Nomination of Taoiseach, Dáil, 11 December 1979

There is a strain in the Irish temperament, and I suppose in the genetic mix of the Irish people, which guarantees there will always be a proportion who are irreconcilable and unwilling to abide by the rules. In a sense I suppose there will never be an end to some kind of civil dissension here. There will always be a turbulent and impossible section of the people. I do not flatter myself that we will ever seriously and finally do what John Costello once thought we could do: take the gun out of Irish politics for good.

I wanted to say to Deputies who are distressed at what is happening here today that on this side of the House, in saying this I do not compromise one iota of the principle which we have tried to stand for, there is a feeling among us of a kind I never saw in my party before, a feeling of compassion and an anxiety to see if something good can come out of this, an anxiety which stretches out hands to pass over things and to say sorry for the things we regret.

I mean that for several other people as well. I want to ask them, not overnight or on any particular date, if they can look at this situation objectively and ask themselves whether we could at last take out of politics the awful carping, the infantile sneering and trying to pretend you are responsible for the sun coming up in the morning and your opponents to blame for it going down in the evening, that awful infantilism which has dogged Irish politics since the beginning as a pure consequence of the division between these two parties. If there are enough of these people here, and if there is the will, I would like to ask them to re-establish in this House and in this country unity of purpose which the civil war shattered, but which corresponds to a whole range of sensations and beliefs which is alive in the heart of everyone on this side of the House, and I believe is equally alive in the hearts of many on the other side.

Ministers and Secretaries Bill, Dáil, 5 March 1980

I agree I have been going far afield. This Bill fits into the pattern of the public service reform which the last Taoiseach on forming his Government held out to the Dáil as being a first priority. What happened? He upgraded the title of Parliamentary Secretary, which had been good enough for all his predecessors because the neighbours did not understand it. Where did he get the title "Minister of State"? Where did he run to for that? Was it to the Italians, Russians, The Chinese? No. He did not run further than London for it. He made ten of them while he was at it, not seven.

We have been told here again, with unparalleled impertinence, by the Minister who spoke a few moments ago, that the new office created in 1977 would be "an office with greater responsibility". I defy Deputy Calleary opposite me to tell me what greater responsibility does a Minister of State in the Office of Public works or elsewhere have than the corresponding Parliamentary Secretary had under Deputy Liam Cosgrave's Government. I have no personal spleen about this, but I have a general anger about the way the country is being run, not only by this Government but by their predecessors in some respects. I have a particular anger about the sham and the cod and the loping after the English. However, it is not any personal experience of mine that adds to my sense of outrage about this.

As a Parliamentary Secretary for four years in the office of the Taoiseach and simultaneously in the Department of Foreign Affairs for two years according to Deputy Lynch I had a title which was misleadingly modest I was paid only half what either Deputy Lalor or Deputy Andrews were being paid when they were upgraded. It took the two of them to do the job that I did. Deputy Bruton for two years was simultaneously Parliamentary Secretary to the Departments of Education and Industry and Commerce. Deputy Bruton has an even harder case than I. I do not mean a hard personal case I am sure it would not cross his mind to make this calculation I am trying to put into perspective what are supposed to be the "greater responsibilities" of these Ministers of State.

The responsibilities carried by Deputies Lalor and Andrews, two decent gentlemen and, I should like to think, two friends of mine, were roughly half the responsibilities I carried and approximately one third of what Deputy Bruton carried. He had Education and both sections in Industry and Commerce which were given to Deputy Geoghegan Quinn and Deputy Ray Burke. Where is the "greater responsibility"? There is not any. The sections which were assigned to me in Foreign Affairs are the same as those assigned to Deputy Andrews when he was Minister of State.

In other words, the workload has shrunk: less work is expected from more

9

office holders, at least less work of the kind they are paid to do. But of course that is not the whole story, because to the extent that their load is lighter in their Departments they have more time for other things.

Again, I want to mention a Deputy against whom I have no personal spleen although I have, on a couple of occasions, asked questions about him in the House. I think he resented and felt that I was in some way out to do him down. I was not. I give the House my word that I have absolutely no reason to persecute this Deputy, now a Minister, personally in any way at all. But the conspicuous manner in which he seemed to restrict his public duties to his own constituency struck me time and again. I asked questions about it, not because I had anything against him, but because he seemed to be a particularly flagrant offender of in this regard. I call it an offender, because he is not a Minister of State or Parliamentary Secretary for one county, or one and a half counties, but for the whole State, if the title means anything at all.

"Piglets" Speech, Claremorris, 16 August 1981

This State has reached a turning point of which its present financial difficulties are not a signal. That crisis has arrived because, after 60 years of adding continually to its own burden, the State has finally begun to sag under the weight.

Undoubtedly the decisive moment in this development occurred ten years ago, when for the first time it became accepted that annual budgets need not balance, and that the year's current expenditure need not necessarily be paid for out of the year's taxation. But deficit budgeting was only the last stage in a process to which our form of democracy "demand democracy" has lent itself all too easily.

Since there was always a political party or group willing to take up and amplify any demand, however little justified according to earlier standards, the habit grew of looking to the State or a State agency for everything.

A simple example among many is housing. Once upon a time people regarded their house as something they had to provide for themselves; and so they saved, if necessary postponing marriage, until they had themselves put together enough of the purchase price to support a mortgage for the rest. But over the years the State has seemed to assume a growing liability in this area, even for people far above the economic level for which the public authority might naturally be expected to provide. This same development has been seen in health, in education, and most recently in employment, where the State is now expected to "create" jobs, even if the job involves no work that anyone would pay for in a free market.

Any reluctance by Government to collaborate in this demand democracy instantly evokes a righteous clamour from Opposition. Has the Government "turned its back" on the homeless? Is it "downgrading" this county or has it "abandoned" that town? Is it indifferent to dental health? What is it doing about road safety? Does it expect people to live on only £x a week? Will it leave school leavers with no job? What is it doing about the crying scandal of ground rents?

The consequence after 60 years is a little like the reverse of Joyce's ugly and cruel image of Ireland as an old sow devouring her young. If there must be a sow in the simile, she is lying, panting, exhausted by her own weight, and being rent by a farrow of cannibal piglets.

Perhaps this is a morbid perception, and certainly it is true that other Western States suffer in some degree from the same complaints. But here we have reached a point at which the mere interest payments on our national debt consume nearly the whole of what the State takes in through the P.A.Y.E. system; or 31p in every pound of total State revenue.

It is in this perspective that the importance of local structures such as Chambers of Commerce and Community Associations becomes evident. We need such organisations and we need them very much strengthened, not as mere loudspeakers for the articulation of yet more demands, but as the elements of a truer, more self-reliant democracy, in which all communities will provide first, to the best of their ability and resources, for their own future and their children's, and in which a leaner, more modest State can retreat in the direction of the original elementary functions which alone justify its existence.

Cavan Monaghan By-Election, Dáil, 26 January 1982

I want to tell the House briefly a couple of things about the holding of by-elections seen from the point of view of trying to organise Government business. Perhaps we might have looked a little further than the British in constructing the form in which our parliament works. Perhaps we might have looked to countries which I hope Deputies Haughey and Wilson would acknowledge are equally parliamentary democracies, but which do not regard it as necessary to go back to a particular constituency in order to fill a casual vacancy. I do not offer any judgment on that now but we have that system for better or for worse. When we have a contest, it is asking too much of flesh and blood that the people most prominent in the contesting parties will not go out and take sides in it. Although we all deplore the waste of time and of life and effort which goes into by-elections, that has been done since this State was founded.

It is nonsensical to suggest that the business of the House can continue here at what one might call a normal tempo when a by-election is in progress. If it were possible to scan, by something like the last 60 years, one would find that the vibrations sank almost to a horizontal level at certain points. If one were to plot against that graph the times when by-elections occurred one would find that those horizontal patches corresponded exactly.

I can tell the House that a Government which is a lazy Government, which has no particular plans, which does not mind going out for three weeks, slogging it out in the depths of Winter, what is more with the other side in any particular constituency, would have no problem about going out and fighting a by-election. But a Government who have a problem such as we have, namely, that we have a programme to get through, one made all the more necessary by the era of misgovernment which preceded us, realise that it simply cannot be done.

I can recall by-elections being held during the term of the Twentieth Dáil. I can recall one in the constituency of Monaghan, another pair held on the same day in East and West Galway, another pair held in Dublin South-West and in North-East Donegal on the same day, and one in West Mayo also. I think those were the six by-elections held during the term of the Twentieth Dáil and, on each occasion, the House was in session. I then had the job Deputy Fergus O'Brien now has and essentially, the House's pulse not through any fault of mine but simply because I could not put business through without a full House behind me slowed almost to a standstill. We had Estimate debate after Estimate debate. Occasionally, when we could not and did not wish to avoid a Private Member's Motion, a vote had to take place on Wednesday evening and Deputies were whipped to come up. A minimum amount of pairing only took place. Perhaps there might have been one vote in the week. As soon as that vote was over they scuttled off, paying perhaps a quick call on their constituencies, otherwise getting back to the scene of the conflict.

It is not reasonable to accept that anything except a sort of free wheeling debate — in which one can predict the time of the vote — can take place on a Tuesday or on a Thursday, and perhaps even on a great part of Wednesday, in conditions like that. That being said, I hope the House will see the point that, if there were no other element to be said for the point of view the Taoiseach has expressed, this one must carry very powerful conviction.

I want to offer the House a much smaller and humbler argument in relation to the time of year. I know we are all great democrats. Perhaps we like to see ourselves cast in stone with a toga and a loving inscription on the plinth. It may be that Members of this House will in due course so qualify. Perhaps gems from Deputy Wilson's speech here this afternoon will be engraved on his plinth. But let me put before the House the humble consideration that we are in the depths of one of the bitterest winters this country has had in 20 years. We do not know when the weather is going to turn bad again.

Evening begins, Sir, practically at 4 o'clock or 4.30 in the afternoon. And anybody over there who pretends that that is a matter of indifference to him is simply pretending. I remember 1974 and 1975, before the temper of the House improved with the new sitting hours. We were under fire here right through the end of June into July, and on one occasion into the first week into August. The noises made in the House over here by the people now in opposition at the time were: "We will sit here right through the recess; we will not bother with the recess at all; we will sit here until we have thrashed out this business properly and we will not submit to time allocation motions or anything else of that kind". That was the public face they presented here but that was not the face presented to me in the corridors outside when I went up to talk to the Fianna Fáil whips.

Then it was a case of: "When in the name of God are you going to let us off?" When I finally went up to the Fianna Fáil Whips and announced, in 1974 and 1975, that we had been reluctantly compelled to decide to put down time allocation motions, I did not see any long faces up there; no, there were smiles from ear to ear at the news that their hours were going to be cut short. That was simply a question of their Summer holidays, and they did not put it as anything more important than that; but it is a simple, human consideration. I think this House must contain a lot of solemn asses if we are too solemn to admit that the time of year is also a consideration of some small human, and perhaps even other, importance in the context of a by-election.

National Enterprise Agency, Dáil, 13 May 1982

All I hoped was that the Minister this morning, having signalled this enterprise agency, would tell us what it is going to do. Having listened to his speech and re-read it, I find that there is not a single clue in it. No businessman in the wide world would lend him 6p on the intentions and waffle and flummery — I say that with respect to his Department, whose officials have no option but to follow political directions which are given, even though they may not believe in them. There is not a businessman or private concern in the world unless constrained politically — and that is what is bringing us down — by the necessity to keep alive by scrounging votes off people and swindling them out of them, who would advance 6p on the security of the promises and the proposals made by the Minister this morning. They would not know what they were. It is not simply a pig in a poke, because at least while you cannot see the pig, you can see there is something wiggling in there. This is a poke with nothing in it but air, so far as one can judge. There is no sign of life at all in it.

I suppose I have long enough experienced this sort of thing from both sides of the House to say that I very nearly could have written this speech for the

Minister myself. I very nearly could have predicted what he was going to produce this morning and certainly would have predicted that the speech here this morning would include the fact that this would be the only concrete operation to be funded out of the £5 million — the recruitment of a chief executive and of staff. He might have added premises, auditors and cute little graphic designers to do the annual report cover, I have no doubt at all about the State's capacity to throw money away on these things. First get your chief executive, set him up with a suite, wall to wall bureaucracy, a stainless steel plate on the front with cute little logograms of the National Enterprise Agency and someone to translate it into Irish. That is the primrose path down which hundreds of millions of hard earned Irish pounds have marched over the last decades. That is the only concrete project so far that we are getting for the 5 million which the Minister mentioned here this morning — to recruit a chief executive. I have no doubt the head hunters are doing it at this minute; they will also want their pound of flesh. When they have the stock and the premises it is only then they will think of something to do.

The chief executive's first idea will be to hire a firm of outside consultants for them to tell him what to do. They will also want their pound of flesh. If I am doing the Minister an injustice, he will be able to reply here today — although I hope he will not take it as a discourtesy if I am not there to hear him as I have to go very shortly when I conclude my speech. I will be reading, with great interest, what he says in reply. If I am doing the Minister an injustice and if he has got up his sleeve some details of the concrete projects that this agency will be either itself initiating, collaborating in or supporting, please let us have the details, not just to satisfy the Opposition but to discharge our duty as that House of the Oireachtas which controls the disbursement of public funds. Our duty to the people is not to spend their money and put it into the hands of a Minister who can do what he likes with it,without knowing what it is going to be spent on.

Deputy Power, Minister for Defence, seemed to be reading over the speech for his own Estimate, which now looks as though it will not be reached for a while. I have no doubt that Deputy Power's Estimate for the Department of Defence will contain details of engines of destruction and warlike stories of all kinds which he wants us to invest in. I have no doubt that there will be details in it of salaries, renewal of barracks and grandiose infernal machines of all kinds which he wants us to lay in a stock of. Whether one disagrees with that or whatever one's view of neutrality, whether it is of the old kind or of the kind we have heard enunciated for the first time in the history of the civilised world the other day, does not really matter. At least one would be able to see in one's mind's eye the range of hardware, extra salaries or extra barrack accommodation which this money is going to be spent on. It may perhaps be a fishery protection vessel, I do not know. Perhaps I should have read the Estimate. But we have no idea what this £5 million will be spent on or — I will stake my solemn oath on it — the Minister opposite has not got a clue either. I also say

14

with the greatest respect to the officials who serve him, and I know they do it loyally and well, that not one of them has an idea either. They are going through the motions because they have to, under political orders of producing a speech and an ostensible excuse for spending £5 million. I do not blame them for that, but we already have a very complete apparatus of State bodies for doing all kinds of functions with an economic purpose, many of which are commercial enterprises of a sort in which there is a saleable end product. I can well see that a man might be put to the pin of his collar to see what else was left for an agency of this kind to do, if there was some serious project that it could undertake I do not want it defined in terms of "co-ordinating" this and "liaising with" that. I want to know if it is going to turn out bricks or mortar or both? Is it going to turn out tin cans or the labels for tin cans? The Minister will have a chance to tell us that. I hope we will not be told that he is afraid of having his thunder stolen by the private sector. I hope we will not be told that there is up the sleeves of the IIRS, the NBST or An Foras Talúntais some project for extracting wealth from some new process or exploiting some new form of natural resource which the private sector does not yet know about and which, if it did, would be falling over itself to get into. That is the duty and the job of the IIRS or the NBST or An Foras Talúntais, not to be keeping secrets up their sleeves because they too are funded by public money and subscribed for by the tax-payer. If they have suddenly thought up some process or some possible product which is worth something or which somebody not constrained by public necessity would pay good money for, they have a duty to let it out to the world and let the private sector get into it if need be. Let the people of Ireland avoid the millstone of risk which the super-imposition on this process of a bureaucratic machine inevitably will bring with it.

On page 8 of the Minister's speech he paints on a broad canvas the object of the agency. He told us this should facilitate more effective "co-ordination" of the work of the various State agencies involved in industrial promotion and development. I would associate with that a reference from page 13 in which the Minister mentioned the IDA in connection with the National Enterprise Agency. He said a representative of the Department of Industry and Energy is on the board of both bodies and this should reinforce "liaison" arrangements between them.

Could we lay aside our party uniforms and imagine that he and I are having a drink or out having a walk in the country, and could the two of us just sit back and have a good laugh at the idea of a country of this size, barely three million people, having so many barriers and distances between the various elements of the State apparatus that their activities have to be "co-ordinated", that there has to be "liaison" between them, if you please?

The word "liaison" in modern usage — I am only saying this from the top of my head — goes back to the First World War when, because of ethnic and cultural differences, the Serbian Army had to have a liaison officer with the Belgians, or the Germans with the Bulgarians, or something of that sort. There is every excuse for liaison there because people might have come to blows otherwise. Here we are talking about a limited number of officials, the important ones of whom all know each other by their first names. They are well able to lift a phone and talk to one another. They read the newspapers. They all know what the others are doing and they are not so prodigal of the State's resources or so neglectful of their duties as to be deliberately going in for something that would wastefully duplicate what other agencies are doing.

These scripts I see every other day from Ministers — the same was true of us — includes such things as "to co-ordinate this" or "to identify that", to "monitor", to "evaluate", or to "promote". This is all aimed at stringing out inordinately a series of simple intellectual functions which are natural to anybody engaged in ordinary business. For instance, a shoemaker naturally co-ordinates this and that: he actually liaises with this and that, naturally identifies opportunities. It would never occur to him to put big words on them because they are natural, instinctive, an intuitive part of every business project and of every administrative project if it is being conducted properly. It is ridiculous that we are to have a special agency of this kind to co-ordinate and set up a liaison, if you please, between Pat this and Tom that, both of whom were at school together and have known each other for 30 or 40 years, live in the same suburb, play golf with one another and, if they are not on friendly terms, they are well able to phone one another. They are not at the same distance as the Bulgarians or the Serbians in 1914 or 1915. We do not need an agency for liaison. We are all in the same boat together and it has been springing many a leak, and if the boat sinks we will all go down. We are all keen not to waste the State's money. We are all keen to get value for what we put into projects. That goes just as much, if not more in my experience, for public officials as it does for the rest of us, and they do not need a special agency to co-ordinate or liaise them. If they are doing their job properly that would happen automatically.

P & T, Dáil, 22 June 1982

I am speaking from memory but I think it was a Deputy Ahern I am sorry I do not know his first name, who said that when Deputy Reynolds was Minister for Posts and Telegraphs we made terrific strides, that everything went forward with great alacrity and that there was improvement upon improvement. He said that when the Coalition Government got in we dropped back again but now, with Fianna Fáil back in power, it is full steam ahead again for the telephone service. That is the kind of primitive brontosaurus kind of politics that I would like to kill in this House. You should not be able to say this sort of thing without the House telling you to grow up, that in the course of eight months, merely because your political opponents are in power, the posts and telephone services show a deterioration. The Minister is too civilised to say such a foolish thing except in moments of excitement, to which he is no more immune than I am but he would not be capable of saying it in cold blood. He knows it is not the case and he knows also that, as far as Deputy Reynolds is concerned I will not fall into the same brontosaurus trap as Deputy Ahern the message that the telephone service here was under capitalised only percolated through to Government level in the term of the national Coalition Government of 1973 to 1977. It had percolated through to a Fianna Fáil Minister a couple of years before that, I think Deputy Gerry Collins was Minister at the time.

I remember Dr. Cruise O'Brien, when he was Minister, playing a very dirty trick, as it was painted by the Fianna Fáil Deputies of taking out of his bag a long plaintive letter written by Deputy Collins in 1971 to the Minister for Finance of the day, warning him that unless massive funds were made available for the telephone service, we were going to find ourselves back at Somerville and Ross levels compared to the rest of Europe. He said it would be the kind of the tinker's level of service here if we did not get a massive injection of funds, but nothing happened. If I may blow the trumpet of my own friends for a couple of minutes, I shall resume my ecumenical habit after that, it only happened when the Coalition Government came to power and put more in four years into the telephone service than had previously been put into it in the 55 years since the foundation of the State. I can see Deputy Harte nodding, I would not expect him to contradict me. He knows that is the case and I am sure he will be saying it with much more force and conviction, authority and detail when he rises to speak. That is the reality. That heavy investment programme was continued by Fianna Fáil when they got in in 1977 and I do not begrudge them the credit for it. I would not be so childish as to pretend it got any worse. It did not get any worse under the short period of the second Coalition Government either, but it is still far behind European levels.

Many of us live and die without ever requiring to make an STD call to Moscow or Hong Kong but the ordinary dialling service in the city of Dublin is fit to drive a man out of his mind. You lift the telephone and you dial 789911, the number of this House, and you could get no tone three times in a row, not the engaged signal, not the out of order signal, not the service suspended or they have not paid their bill signal, but no tone at all. That just does not happen in other countries. I said I would not make a meal out of the telephone service but I suddenly find I have done so. I want to tell the Minister, in case his Department have any illusions, that with the exceptions I have conceded of the continuing level of installations and the trunk dialling system, if he thinks that the level of service at the ordinary domestic level is getting any better or the level of frequency with which people complain about delay in repairs to the system is getting better, he is deceiving himself.

There are other things I should like to see in the telephone system here which I think is a stick-in-the-mud system. I say that with regret and I should like the Minister to hear this: over the years, in and out of office I have had a very happy relationship with the staff of the secretary's office who have provided me with the most courteous, careful, friendly and speedy service. I have very often been able to help constituents as they say, of whatever political persuasion. In parentheses, may I say that it is a curious tribute to say of a politician that he never discriminated, that he was willing to help somebody on the other side of the fence. So well he might be; it is the best of his play; if he can get that man to vote for him it is as good as two of his own. With regret I have to say that I think the attitude of the Minister's Department by and large has been somewhat stick-in-the mud when it comes to devising means of making the service more popular or getting the people to like it and use it more.

Last year when Deputy Killilea was Minister of state I asked whether he would consider introducing a system whereby subscriber trunk dialling to the Continent on Saturdays and Sundays and off peak hours could be at a cheaper rate. This country does not spend its life dialling Munich or Montparnasse and I think the volume of traffic to Europe would be modest from here but the people who need it are inclined to be business people and it is a very heavy item to them. Many are business people who do not mind working and whose second nature it is to work Saturdays and Sundays if need be and it would be a considerable asset to them to be able to use the telephone at weekends at a reduced rate in the manner which is customary in a very large part of the European Community.

There is a reciprocal system in operation between the German Federal Republic and all its neighbours which means that it operates between Germany and Denmark it stretches into the Eastern Block, Czechoslovakia; I am not sure about Eastern Germany but there subsidised rates for that in any case in Denmark, Austria, Switzerland, France, Belgium, Holland and Luxembourg. All these countries have reciprocal arrangements with Germany, so that we are talking of the large bulk of telephone consumers in the European Community, whereby telephone calls out of peak hours are made at a privileged rate and on Sundays I think at something like half rate.

The suggestion I made here was made little of by Deputy Killilea but I believe it would relieve pressure on the trunk lines at peak hours and the cost to the State, taking into account the reduced exasperation of people who cannot avoid using the phone on weekdays, would be extremely small. It is a typical reflection of the way we do business that we are very willing to cut all kinds of corners in order to treat this country and Britain as one. I never tire of complaining about that. We look over our shoulder to England for everything. We have the same postal rate for posting to England as inside the country; the same telephone regulations, cheap rates and so on but when it is a question of going as far as Ostend, the curtains come and the niggers begin there just as completely as they do for the English.

I am sorry that I have spent far too long on this matter. I believe that the Minister — not himself personally but the persona which he has the honour to carry — is under an official illusion if he supposes that the public are satisfied or within an ass's roar of being satisfied with the level of postal and tele-communications services: most certainly they are not. I am sorry to give voice to such an unworthy suspicion but I think the real reason behind the creation of these two boards except for the "Paddy" reason that the English have two such boards, which I suspect is the most basic reason, God help us apart from the fact that we still have to copy the English whatever they do. We never would have thought of An Bord Poist and An Bord Telecom if the English had not had such things for the past four or five years.

When did we invent something here, let alone a major structural admin-istrative reform in which the English had not preceded us? Let the Minister name one. It is shaming and I should expect the Minister to be foremost in being ashamed about it. We were long enough learning about other countries. We hardly know where they are. It is enough to have An Bord Poist and An Bord Telecom so that Pat can traipse after them.

The real reason next to that and the real reason they said in the Post Office that it might not be a bad idea to have these two boards, is that they would take the political heat off whoever is Minister for the bad service which the public are getting. It will now be possible for the Minister to say or, possibly, the Ceann Comhairle to say in an expression which I get in my daily communications from his office: "The question is out of order because the Minister has no responsibility to the Dáil for this matter." Certainly, when the postal service is under an Bord Poist and when telephone, telex and so on are under An Bord Telecom the Minister will be able to decline all responsibility. He will not have to answer questions about it any more than as Minister for Transport he will have to answer questions about why it is that four No. 7 buses arrive at a bus stop within three minutes and that another 40 minutes can go by before another one is seen. He will be able to dismiss questions in the House about the abominable working of these services in the same way as the Minister for Transport cannot be called on to answer here for the condition of CIE.

That is the real reason, apart from the fact that we have to stay near the English it could be dangerous to depart in any way from the pattern which the English have laid down, keen though we seem to have been for 800 years, if I understand my mythology correctly, to get clear of them and do things our own way. That fine enthusiasm evaporated quickly; it lasted about ten years while William Cosgrave was in power and that was the end of it. In fairness I must say, I think it extended into the first few years of Mr. de Valera's regime also, but for the last 25 or 30 years very little of it was seen. Any innovation in this State was done in the first 15 or 16 years or was not done at all, any independent innovation that was worthwhile.

I hope we shall not find that the establishment of these two boards will make the cost of the services worse instead of better. Perhaps the Minister is not aware of the degree to which the people have to carry this taxation on their backs. Of course it is a form of taxation because one is as much dependent in the late 20th. century on posts and telegraphs as one is on every public service. One cannot do without it and so a telephone or postal charge is as much a form of taxation as income tax or VAT. It is no use telling somebody not to use the postal service of telephone. People must use them. Only hermits or members of enclosed orders, of which there are fewer and fewer and they are becoming less and less enclosed, are in the situation of not being dependent on these services. People are dependent on them and the charge for them is as much a form of taxation as VAT.

The Minister may again be looking over his shoulder no further than England and I suspect I do not mean Deputy Wilson, who I know is a man of individuality and character who is not so base as to be this in his own right, but the ministerial persona, a sort of man in the iron mask, the man being switched out through a kind of zip in the back with every change of Government. Therefore the Minister for Posts and Telegraphs may not be aware of the gross disparity which exists between the level of these charges here and those that obtain in most of Continental Europe. When I was a student in Germany as long ago as 1954 the cost of a local telephone call was 20 pfennigs. In those days, because the German mark was worth less that it is now, 20 pfennigs was worth about four old pence. It was a somewhat dearer local call than the Irish one which in those days was 2d. The cost of a local telephone call in Germany today, 27 or 28 years later, is still 20 pfennigs. You can still ring up and talk your head of to somebody in the same city or postal district for the same 20 pfennigs, the same two coins which you could have put as a lucky charm in your wallet. When I qualified in 1956 I could have put 20 pfennigs in my pocket, come back 28 years later and put them into the same telephone and I would have got the same service for them.

What has happened here? The 2d have gone by the board. We now have new pence honoured with the dignity of designs personally approved by the present Taoiseach without competition or consultation with man, woman or child, let alone anyone who knew anything about it. Those 2d amounted to less than 1p. The cost of a local telephone call now is 10p, two shillings in old money or 24d. In other words the cost of a local telephone call here in the span of time which I am talking about 28 years, has risen 12 times, that is when you can find a public telephone that works, that has not been vandalised, or, having been vandalised because Ireland has no monopoly of vandalism, has been repaired.

If I may use the same comparison, I would like to recall that when I first went to Germany as a student in 1954 I could write a letter to my mother at home for 40 pfennigs. In other words, that was twice the cost of a local telephone call or about 8d. in those days. The cost of a letter in the other direction, from Ireland to the Continent, was 5d. What is the situation now? In Germany the cost of a letter to elsewhere in Europe has advanced from 40 pfennigs in 1954 to about 70 pfennigs in 1982. I am not absolutely certain of that and it could be 80 pfennigs, but I believe it is 70. What has happened here? If I write to someone in Germany from here I am not paying 5d any longer. I am not even paying 5p. I am paying 29p. How about that for an increase? That is damn nearly 6s in the old money. It is not far off half of the week's pocket money that I got when I was a student, and that is the cost of posting one letter.

I could multiply these examples in other European countries, not with the same accuracy or recollection naturally, but I want the Minister to understand that it is not simply a question of people who do not do very much writing of letters, of some old lady or gentleman who neither gets nor sends very much post. It affects people in business who are attempting to run their lives in dependence on a postal or telephone service. It is extremely expensive and unless An Bord Telecom can provide a cheaper service they will avoid giving us a great deal of the benefit that they might give.

I must apologise to the House for going on so long on these two topics, the quality and the cost of these two services. I have dined out on them to some extent and I did not mean to do so. I will do penance for that by being quick in the rest of the points I want to make. The Minister proposes in section 61 to confer immunity from liability on An Post. We can discuss this in greater detail on Committee Stage, but I ask the Minister if he has got the Attorney General's Office to consider if in this country immunity from suit can be conferred legally on anybody and whether it is possible to discriminate between citizens or between citizens and the Administration in such a way as to make one sort of person immune from being sued for an act which would be actionable if committed by somebody else. The section related to An Bord Poist and reads:

> (1) Subject to subsection (3), the company shall be immune from all liability in respect of any loss, damage or injury suffered by any person by reason of—
> (a) failure, neglect or delay in providing operating or maintaining a postal service.

There may be a mistake, an accident and nobody is making any fuss about that, but suppose there is widespread neglect, carelessness, indolence, indifference in the postal service and people are damaged in their business as a result. It is to avoid that very thing that we find the courier services, document exchange and so on springing up all around us. Why should this board be exempt from suit? Why should they be feather-bedded, cushioned against their own neglect by such a provision?

My memory is nearly as bad as that of former Deputy Lynch. I am never entirely sure when I am talking about something that happened a few months or some years ago that I am recollecting it accurately and very often I make serious mistakes in the way that he did although never about anything quite so serious, but I feel for him because I know what it is to have a bad memory. I will not swear to this, but when we were in government six months ago I too had a persona, a kind of man in the iron mask outfit. I climbed into it after Deputy O'Malley left it and I restored it to him in good shape when I left by decree of the sovereign people. At any rate, the Department over which I presided felt — and I agreed with them — that there was no justification for exempting An Bord Poist from having actions taken against them for neglect and if my recollection is correct I do not quite know why this provision is back here again. There were one or two other provisions on which I will not waste the House's time now of which the same could be said in which at my instance objectionable provisions were removed but I suppose the absence of a Fine Gael Minister allowed the people to feel that they could be safely reinstated in the Bill before it reached the Dáil. Such an immunity may not be constitutional. I recognise that the Constitution, in Article 40, permits discrimination, to take place where people's social function differs. Of course, there is a clear distinction between a State board with a public task to perform on the one hand and an individual on the other, but is the difference one in respect of which it can be said there is any material element justifying this discrimination? I cannot see that there is. The Minister will do himself a service by asking the Attorney General to advise him about this and any other similar provision which there may be in regard to An Bord Telecom.

Section 63 has a provision about the inviolability of mail. I have nothing to say about that. Naturally I agree that mail should be inviolable except under the familiar conditions relating to security, but could the Minister find out, even as a matter of reference or information for himself and his Department, whether there is a legal view as to who owns a letter or postal packet — a grand Victorian name for what you and I would call a letter — when it is in transit? That is a serious legal question and I spent some hours vainly trying to get the answer during the limited postal dispute affecting the Blackrock delivery area when I was consulted by people who were desperate because their remittances, pension payments or some money they expected, a postal order perhaps, were, they knew, locked up in Blackrock Post Office and they could not get at them. They had no money and were destitute until the expected money arrived. Luckily the dispute ended before it came to a final point, but it was a serious question, leaving aside the sacredness of industrial disputes, as to whether it would be possible or advisable to sue the Minister for Posts and Telegraphs in respect of withholding or the physical detention or possession of an item which did not belong to him. After all, the Minister is the carrier and the person in possession of the letter in transit. If it happens to be in the bowels of the Blackrock post office at a time when the industrial curtains come down in the course of a dispute, the Minister is still the possessor. I presume he does not own it. Who owns it? Is it the sender or the recipient? If it is either of them, one or the other must be entitled to recapture the letter from him. If not, why not? That is a point my own legal expertise was not able to surmount in the time available to me. But it would be well worth the Minister's while, and it would be in the public interest, if he was to inquire about that and find out what his legal situation is where he finds himself involuntarily in control of a postal packet which is inaccessible and incapable of delivery because of an industrial dispute. It may well be that the High Court would pay no attention to an industrial dispute and would simply say: "John Wilson, Minister for Posts and Telegraphs, hand out that letter this minute and no more old talk out of you about industrial disputes". I hope there is enough freedom and law in the country that there would be that effect, particularly in the situation where an old widow or a remittance man is left destitute because a money order or draft which is destined for him cannot be got at as it is in the bowels of a strike-bound post office.

Deputy Cosgrave mentioned sub-post offices and paid tribute to the services they have provided. I support him in that and praise the Minister for taking the trouble to say something to the same effect in his speech. The State would suffer a great loss if it sacrificed the unique network of potential public facility which the sub-post offices represent. I am not putting in a plug for them or for the people who work in them or whose business is associated with them. In this immense network of post offices the State has a means of communicating with the people and a means of providing facilities for them which is established and understood and used for a range of purposes which have nothing to do with the strict postal service.

I can imagine many situations, even of national emergency, where it might be necessary to expand the range of services provided by the post offices. In the seventies we had a series of incredible bank strikes. The last one in 1976 or 1977 lasted for six months or more. It was a mammoth strike and business was paralysed. People, as Deputy Colley used to say, wrote their own credit because they were not within reach of their bank manager and there were IOUs flying around. Bank notes were such that one could almost see the cultures of vermin growing on them. The country was in a situation of severe commercial handicap. I repeatedly questioned Deputy Colley when the strike was over about what contingency plans he had for providing for a further bank strike. The State, with all due respect to the sanctity of industrial dispute, must have emergency plans up its sleeve for dealing with a protracted bank dispute. What would Deputy Colley have done if the banks had never re-opened? Did he ever think about that? Surely there must be contingency plans, whether in the Department of Defence in Parkgate Street or elsewhere, for an endless bank strike. My suggestion is that if such plans were drawn up they could be based on the post office and sub-post office structure. I am not suggesting that one can turn a country sweet shop, a Ballyscullion operation, into something which is capable of handling a large cash flow overnight. However, some thought ought to be given to the possibility of saving the economy and commercial life of the country in the event of a prolonged bank strike by having a contingency system which will depend on and be operated by the sub-post office network.

I should like to draw the attention of the House to the suspect nature of the State monopoly in the postal and telephone service which the Minister proposes to confer on these two bodies. These monopolies are constitutionally defensible only as long as they serve the public interests. Once the time comes when, because one or other falls victim to industrial unrest or for some other reason, it fails to provide a reasonable service the constitutional basis for the monopoly drops away into the sea. When that moment comes there will be a free for all situation just as free as in the selling of sweets or ice cream so far as the provision of telephone, telegraph, postal or broadcasting systems are concerned. The Minister or his predecessors have never taken that point of view as seriously as they ought, not because it is mine but because it is staring everybody in the face. There is no reason why there should be a postal or a telephone monopoly unless it serves the public interests. When it ceases to do that, the legal basis for having a monopoly disappears. When that happens there must be a free for all. I do not think the Department or any Minister under any administration ever really faced up to that situation and asked themselves how they would deal with it or, less frequently asked, how the interest of the people require that it be dealt with.

Adjournment debate, Dáil, 16 July 1982

Let us suppose that after the next election Fine Gael have got 75 seats or 80 seats or 85 seats, and suppose the Fianna Fáil seats around the country fall like ninepins, Fianna Fáil would not be destroyed. As Deputy Lenihan said once in one of his inspired, unforgettable phrases — not forgotten by me anyway — "you can shift us but you can't shunt us", or it may have been "you can shunt us but you can't shift us". In other words we can put Fianna Fáil out for a time, perhaps for a long time, but for the reason, the irremovable reason, that they represent very much the same kind of people that we do and in roughly comparable volume, the political element which Fianna Fáil represents can be extinguished only by a miracle. The very same is true of my party and, for so long as that competition between similar parties continues, cowardice will be the first instinct to be consulted by either Government.

That was not always the case. It certainly was not the case in Willie Cosgrave's time; it was not the case in Mr. de Valera's time; it was not the case in John Costello's time, and it was not the case in Sean Lemass's time. These four Taoisigh never heard of a current budget deficit. They most certainly never heard of the kind which in 1977 provided a milestone for disaster, a major turning point in this country's history. I am not saying this with hindsight, because we say it clearly then and we have been saying it ever since. They never heard of such a thing. But in those seventies and since, cowardice is the first emotion or instinct consulted by the Government now in office, and we ourselves could not claim to be free of it either.

I really see no long term way of belling all the cats I have mentioned, not for their own sake, but in order that some financial sanity will return to this State and that we will be able to do the things we are always talking about in regard to providing a proper infrastructure and a proper stream of investment money.

24

I see no other way of doing it than for the two parties that are most heavily represented in this Dáil to put behind them — and I know that I have been a major offender and still am every day of the week — the bitterness and the hard words that are increasingly disgusting the people, particularly the younger generation, and to see whether it would be possible, even if only temporarily, for five or ten years, — we can resume the fighting where we left off in five or ten years time when things are back to normal — to agree. We do not need to live in one another's pockets; we do not need to go to one another's dances; we do not need to take in one another's social washing. But we could see whether, even at arms length and with no more than a modicum of civility, we can agree on a programme where we will not be under the fear of losing seats, or not enough seats to make any difference, and which will pull this economy and the finances of this State around to where they should be. Afterwards, let us go our own way again. No doubt splits and personality differences will develop and it might be natural to let the ordinary play of political forces take over again. But that is the only way I see to bell, quickly and fearlessly, all the cats which are going to require that obscure operation if this State is to be rescued from the disaster which is now so plainly ahead of it, and which even ordinary people, whatever their political affiliation, can see staring them in the face.

I have met plenty of Fianna Fáil voters in the East Galway by-election, just as I met them in West Dublin. I do not make any silly predictions about one by-election any more than I did about the last one. These people, for all I know, are probably still going to vote Fianna Fáil. But they are all wagging their heads sadly and saying they do not know where they are going. They do not know where we are going. They do know the State is in deep trouble, and I do not believe they will thank a party or a government that conceals that from them, and cods them along until they wake up one morning and find that Fine Gael, Fianna Fáil and all that are swept into the dust bin, and they are being run, if not directly by the Cubans, by people who take their line from them and resemble them in style of management.

Politicians and Lobbies, Macroom, 20 May 1983

In a country like this, no one can stand altogether aside from the political process. Naturally, we do not expect churchmen or vocational leaders publicly to take sides in the party-political sense; but they cannot wash their hands of large issues of State policy, when these issues are in course of decision, and then complain if the decision or its consequences are not to their liking.

Having said this, I admit that those of us in active politics must offer an unlovely spectacle to the public and one which we in Fine Gael, and our long separated and estranged Siamese twin Fianna Fáil could do a lot to improve.

The bragging and boasting we were taught as children to avoid, but constantly indulge in as adults; the mean belittling of one another's efforts and achievements; the easy way we condemn that which, when on the other side of the House, we proposed or advocated that which we formally avoided doing ourselves; the reach-me-down verbal republicanism; the bogus fury, the sham sorrow, the cheap compassion; these things, at the best of times, bored the public, but now, with economic hardship so widespread,they positively disgust them.

In this month, exactly 60 years since the civil war ended, surely we in these two parties could ask ourselves if the people who founded our organisations really intended their efforts to end up like this? If they really would have seen a point in perpetuating the split which, even after 60 years, has still not developed an ideological or other base than personal rivalry sustained by group ethos no more profound that that which sustains football teams? If they would really have fought the burden of public debt, the constriction of national development, the fatuous nationalist convulsions, over constitutional formulae equally redundant, the disgust and despair of youth and their alienation from the state, a small price to pay for the vindication of their opinions on transient and forgotten issues?

I am glad to say that these days there are signs from the other side which, like the dove returning to the Ark with an olive leaf in her beak suggest that the sour flood-waters of unreason and ungenerosity are at last beginning to recede. Deputy Mary Harney has the courage publicly to doubt the necessity of her party's position on the amendment; Senator Hanafin has the decency publicly to acknowledge that Fine Gael's embarrassments on the issue do not mean that anyone in the party is pro abortion.

Out of these small things and out of this whole humiliating episode, perhaps some new and better chapter will emerge: an awakening of both parties to the losses and absurdities which tribal animosity has brought upon the country.

I hope that, when that process gathers momentum among Fianna Fáil's real republicans, we in our equally republican party will go out to meet them, if necessary, more than half-way.

Judicial Offices Bill, Dáil, 3 November 1983

The idea that the long recess in the Summer is in some way a holiday for Deputies is absolute moonshine. I am amazed that the press should perpetuate that, as they sometimes do, when they have members in their press lobby who can see what goes on here and know that the business brought up at Question Time, or in some other context, by Deputies is not thought up on the spur of the moment on the train to Dublin, but reflects the grinding drudgery they put in because their constituents want it of them during the rest of the time. The vulgarity and ignorance of this point of view about the holidays of Deputies is, I am sorry to say, not corrected by the press. We have all seen cartoons of a couple of Deputies — their facial characteristics about as hateful as could be contrived within the parameters of what is possible in a Hibernian countenance — on the beach on the Costa Brava with their trouser bottoms rolled up, paddling in the wavelets, and their suitcases behind them marked "TD", with some cynical remark passing from one to the other about it being "great to have three months of this ahead of us, Mick". That is a bit of a laugh, but it is a grotesque misrepresentation of the reality of life for most Deputies, certainly for most rural Deputies.

I must admit that my own existence is nothing like as tough, and I do not get the same demands made on me, for geographical reasons and other reasons, but many of my colleagues do. I have seen the demands made of them ; and the patience with which people who do this job for whatever motive — sometimes the motive may not be very respectable — bear misrepresentation and lampooning of that type is admirable. I should like to protest about the ignorant idea that the only work done by people elected to Dáil Eireann is during the sitting hours of the House. It is done from one end of the week to the other and in hours that nobody else would tolerate, with the exception of a priest or a doctor.

That leaves out of account the office-holders — I think there are too many office-holders — who number 30, not counting the Attorney General who is not a Member of the House. They do not get three months' holidays. They do not have free weekends, they have to look after their constituents and attend to their Departments and do a back-breaking round of Government meetings. At certain times of the year, such as when Estimates are being discussed, they have to work hours that would kill a horse. Office-holders have not got to that level of office merely to make money: I do not think anyone has made money out of politics, certainly not regularly. The burden that office-holders bear is a very heavy one and I say that about both sides of the House, and to include them in the general jibe about free weekends and long holidays is outrageous. I do not blame some simple person who has never had an opportunity of seeing how matters work here; but the press, who are good in general about enlightening people on matters that otherwise would remain closed to them, are not good about correcting the balance in this regard.

The Minister and Deputy Ahern might have said more about the expenses many Deputies have to bear. I do not carry as much in the way of expenses as do many of my colleagues. Deputy Ahern mentioned by-elections. I do not think the public realise what happens during a by-election. Personally I think the system could be looked at; I do not think it is necessarily a vital exercise in democracy that whenever a Deputy dies or resigns instantly all work should be suspended here, most work suspended in the Government, and every Deputy and Senator should have to down tools in his own constituency and go to some remote part of the country. They should not have to spend three long weekends fighting a by-election. We might reasonably look to see if casual vacancies in this House might be filled in some other way. The Constitution does not prescribe that casual vacancies must be filled by by-elections. I could think of other ways of doing that that would be less disruptive to public business, and less exhausting and exacting on the people who, by convention, take part in by-elections.

The expense of by-elections, which Deputy Ahern mentioned briefly, is something the public do not understand at all. Many Deputies who take their Party's work seriously put nearly as much of their own money into a by-election campaign in a distant constituency as they would into an election in their own constituency. The last country by-election in which I took part— I did not play as extensive a role as did many of my colleagues — was in east Galway in the Summer of last year. I do not think I had any change out of £300 or £400 after spending a few weeks in Galway; and many of my colleagues put far more work into the by-election. That is the same as writing off nearly £1,000 gross from their salary for one by-election that is over and forgotten in three weeks.

Neither the Minister nor Deputy Ahern mentioned the private telephone accounts the country and city Deputies have to pay. I am not making a complaint on my own account; most of my own telephone calls are in the city, and I do a great part of my work in here anyway. However, once country Deputies go home on Thursday they have to pay their own telephone bills. I remember one of my colleagues, now a Minister, who lives in a distant constituency telling me in 1978 or 1979 — and the matter is much worse now — that his telephone bill was roughly £400 per quarter. That Deputy will not get any allowance from the State for that. It is part of the expenses for which the tax-free element of his salary is supposed to compensate. The notion that these expenses are trivial, or that Deputies do not have to pay them out of their own pocket is quite wrong.

Entertainment is a subject on which one could be facetious, and for that reason I will not spend any time on it. Entertainment, whether in the constituency or in Leinster House, is a not inconsiderable item. I am probably one of the Deputies least hit by this. However, many country Deputies receive deputations here. I can see them bringing such deputations into the restaurant and paying for a meal for five, six or seven people out of their own pockets. Such is the admittedly rather lovable Irish characteristic, which despises meanness and which admires generosity, that a Deputy would be regarded as a gortachan if he did not put his hand in his pocket.

In the same way every public representative is the first target for charitable appeals, not just in his own constituency but throughout the country. Everyone has to subscribe to charity; no one should belittle charities, or say anything that would discourage the enormous amount of voluntary effort that goes into organising them. It is a dreadful drudgery for private charities to try to raise funds. I have no doubt it goes much against their grain to have to seek subscriptions; but it has now become the fashion that the first person they turn to is their elected representative. Some of them are quite shameless about it — Saint Francis may have been shameless in collecting alms for the friars mendicant for a good purpose. I do not make these remarks in a critical sense. I say this as I might have said it over a mendicant friar or nun. It cannot be denied that charities are shameless in intensifying the level of appeals, particularly at election times, with the hidden suggestion that the news that the public representative involved has failed to respond to the appeal will not remain private. I wish to repeat again that this is not intended as an attack on charities, far from it; I support them and I agree they have to be shameless in their approach. I am merely pointing out that in this way of conducting their affairs Deputies are in the front rank as their target.

Country Deputies get an allowance for travelling to Dublin. I am in a favoured situation because I can walk to Leinster House and I usually do that when the weather is fine. In fact, if I wanted to I could almost walk from one end of my constituency to the other without much difficulty. However, there are several country Deputies whose constituencies are nearly 100 miles in length and they have to travel through that area at their own expense. That is not an inconsiderable item with a car that might do from 28 miles to 32 miles to the gallon when one considers all the stopping and starting of the vehicle that would be necessary. Many Deputies write off their car after a year. I have been able to observe they are not the most careful drivers in Ireland. Many of them change their car once a year because they have driven the guts out of the first car. That money must come from their own pockets.

Country Deputies are obliged to advertise in the local press their availability in their clinics to constituents and that cannot be done for nothing. I was speaking to a Deputy yesterday who said that his bill for inserting a couple of small advertisements in two local papers stating where he would be on a certain day in the month comes to about £30 or £40 per week. That is £2,000 a year before he starts to feed his family, to pay for his petrol, to treat his constituents and to fight by-elections.

The Minister dealt with this matter with dignity, and so did Deputy Ahern, and I do not want to be dramatising the thing because we are living in times when many people would be very glad to be able even to muddle along in the way Deputies do.

Deputies who rely completely or largely on a Dáil salary must get this increase. Indeed I would have supported a somewhat larger increase. Deputies who rely solely on their Dáil salaries cannot do their jobs properly with less than this increase, unless they cut corners with either their constituents or their families. This morning I overheard a radio report of the statement of the Comptroller and Auditor General in which he said that he had discovered a couple of instances of persons in the Public Service who in one year made, in overtime alone, more than a Deputy's salary will now be.

The press, who provide a platform for the public, have been opening their reports by referring to a "flood of rage" which has swept the country and with "anger spreading last night" as the news spread. You would swear the newspapers' telephones were choked up with angry calls; whereas, more probably, they may just have been having a word or two with one another. "Anger may have been spreading" last night among student leaders who may have been telephoning in to say, "My people are fit to be tied". That is far from being a wave of anger among the people of the country. I do not intend to fall out with the press or anything like that, I depend on them the same as anybody else, but in so far as Deputies who are full-time TDs are concerned, this increase is the least that could have been given.

I do not know what the figures are in relation to part-time and whole-time Deputies. We are all whole-time in the sense that nobody would accept from us, nor would we offer as an excuse for not doing our job as Deputies, that we have other occupations. A man who may have a business, or another job as I have, or a farm, will never offer as an excuse to his colleagues or his constituents that he has some other interests.

Nevertheless, the fact is, and it cannot be denied, that some Deputies — I will not put a figure on it — have other sources of income. The Minister dealt with this matter very fairly. I do not know about the private affairs of most of my own colleagues on this side, never mind on the other side of the House, but there are people here who have other sources of income. I am one of them. This is certainly a ground for public annoyance at a time like this; I will not become rhetorical about it or overstate it but I think the public who hear appeals being made on all sides for moderation, and who expect leadership and example from the top, have a point in this instance, but only in this instance. They have a case in respect of Members who do not need the extra money.

I do not know how many there may be. If I put a figure on it it would be only a flying guess. Rather than involve the whole body of Deputies and Senators in odium which ought to be directed only towards this single area, it would be wise for the government to consider if there is some way of showing recognition of the fact that some people here will be getting money which they do not need out of the public pocket — in other words, money provided by the taxpayers — and that therefore the level of benefits to social welfare recipients and others will be diminished because of the contribution of more money towards people who do not require it.

I do not think there could be any such thing as paying differential salaries. I am not recommending that people here should be paid according to their needs — if everyone here is doing the same job he or she should be given the same at the payment end. If some of them are doing it badly the constituents will no doubt take it out on them later on. But it could be deducted back again at the tax end; and therefore I should like to see the Government consider putting right the only thing that needs to be put right as far as this is concerned, by means of what I will not call a "penal" level of tax — because "penal" suggests that somebody has done something wrong, and nobody has done anything wrong

30

in this regard — but we might have a particular heavy system of tax on Oireachtas allowances, so that people who move with their general income into a very high tax band, people paying 65p in the £ on the upper part of their incomes, might pay, on the increased Oireachtas allowances part, 80p or 85p. There could be some debate about that.

It is a pity that this measure, which is fully justified, and which does not even go as far as could be justified in respect of many Members, should drive the Government and the Legislature on the defensive publicly, and that they should be lambasted in the public prints because of this one area in respect of which criticism can fairly be made. There should be some alteration of the tax structure which would effectively claw back most of the increase given to Deputies whose other situation is such that they do not need it. That would be justifiable, and it would completely deprive the critics and the leader-writers of their ground for complaint.

There are other matters which I will not go into now, but which would stand scrutiny, such as the practice which, I am sorry to say, the Minister yesterday inadequately defended in a few words in reply to Deputy Mac Giolla. I refer to ministerial pensions, tiny though they are, paid to people who are still Members of the House. That system could be looked at, and I do not think it is unreasonable for the public to complain about it. I get a small ministerial pension. It is so small that it is not worth having to carry that much odium for receiving it — I would prefer to do without it and be clear of the odium. I do not think there are many other ex-office holders sitting on the back benches on this side, but I suppose there are a few on the other side. That would bear examination, and I think this would clear up these marginal dimensions of the whole delicate problem of paying ourselves salary increases. It would then be possible to defend with a whole heart everything the Minister is doing, or something that might have gone a good deal further.

Financial Resolutions, Dáil, 13 February 1986

I could scarcely believe my eyes when I read in the papers the day after Deputy Haughey spoke here that he had said — I think it was even given the status of a saying of the week somewhere — that "what we needed to get away from here was not civil war politics but Victorian economics and financial precepts". If Mr. Gladstone could be recreated and brought back to earth and given a look at what this State has been doing with itself for the last 17 years, since I first came into Leinster House and before that, would he recognise any similarity between the philosophy underlying our activities and those which guided him?

What would Mr. Gladstone have said about a State which annually runs a colossal deficit on current account and has been doing so increasingly since 1972?

I will go further and leave Mr. Gladstone and his whiskers out of it. What would Deputy Haughey when he was Minister for Finance have said about that? Deputy Haughey was Minister for Finance for a couple of years up to 1970. He never produced a budget here which provided for a current account deficit, and he would not have been let do so by his party as they then were, even if he had wished to do so. We do not need to go back to Mr. Gladstone for the days of a bit of rectitude in these matters. We do not have to go back beyond 1972.

What would Mr. Disraeli have thought of a country like this with £20 billion of a national debt? Is that Victorian? Where are the heavy tasselled plush curtains and horsehair sofas behind the philosophy which ran up that kind of public debt here over the last half generation?

Where is the Victorian philosophy in the near-doubling of the numbers of the Civil Service in the last 30 years? These 30 years started out with the old post office pen rusting on the blotting paper and ended up with the micro-chips. These 30 years have seen service employment shed, halved, decimated in every other area which was private, but not in the State which, until the Minister, Deputy Boland, got his axe to it, kept expanding the workforce as though it was a galactic explosion somewhere out in the universe. It appeared to be expanding at a colossal speed in all directions simultaneously for no visible reason. There were all kinds of office aids, calculating aids and computerisations available to the public service in the eighties which should have made additional recruitment redundant. I do not mean that people should have been made redundant, but according as people retired the slack could have been taken up by all these glittering machines. Of course, they have the glittering machines anyway, because the poor old State can pay for them. There is no shortage of glittering equipment; but the people working the equipment have not reduced in number, at least until Deputy Boland got to work, for which no doubt we will pay a political price — I have no doubt that there are many in my constituency who voted for me last time who will not do so next time because of the Government's approach to the Civil Service — I cannot see anything too mutton-chop-whiskery about that development.

What is Victorian about the shape of our health services? The institutions themselves, in some cases, may be Victorian alright, but the central feature of our health service here is the presence of a large number of relatively inefficient hospitals providing nothing except ease of access for visits for relations at the expense of better services in fewer locations, at an immense public cost. What is Victorian about that? I cannot see that any niggling Victorian miser has been at work there. There is no Scrooge in a stovepipe hat behind the design of our present health services.

What about the wild reckless waste around us every day of the week — as though the State were an ill-designed robot filled with some kind of fluid, leaking at every step as it clanks across the floor?

I use this only as a symbol for other things — I am perfectly certain that there are white elephants to be accounted for on all sides; we have a culpable part in the history on one thing, too — but about the Knock Airport syndrome? Was that Victorian? What about the huge overruns on projects like NET and public building? What about the fact that there is no proper financial management, no proper criterion of value for money in the individual Departments? The accounting officer has remained, as he was before 1922, secretary of the Department. Once upon a time he might have been able to keep an eye, in the humble days of the twenties, on whether too many public servants were going with the Minister to a conference or something of that kind. It is now completely beyond such a man, who is burdened by all kinds of other business to keep an eye on whether the offices are unnecessarily ordering new equipment or unnecessarily expanding into a new building. Where is the Victorianism there?

What about the local government councillors paid for — in spite of all the bleating of Ministers for the Environment, largely or mostly if not always — out of the public purse on their expeditions to international conferences on this or that subject at which the Irish contingent not infrequently outnumbers the rest of the world put together? It was possible for one of my colleagues to report to me on his return from one such conference that the centre of Oslo, the night before the conference was to open, presented the aspect of O'Connell Street on the night before an All-Ireland Final. That is not my image — I do not want to be accused of colourful speech in this regard — that is the image of one of my colleagues, sitting at table with me in the restaurant, describing where he had just come from. On my oath, he so described the centre of Oslo on the evening before a conference on high rise buildings or something of that kind. There was a genial Irish presence, courtesy of the Irish taxpayer.

What about the Talbot deal and these election-time strokes? Is there any chance that the dear Queen might have authorised such a thing, or any of her Ministers from first to last — Lord Melbourne, Lord Palmerston, Lord Salisbury? Deputy Haughey and his team will need to think up a few more homely epithets before they will make an accurate point along those lines again.

Review of Stephen O'Byrnes's Hiding Behind the Face, Sunday Tribune, 19 October 1986

Perhaps the explanation is that the party's rapid growth both in Dáil and grass-roots membership — rather as with a child that shoots up at an unusual speed — has imposed a strain on the party's constitution, and ethos, if I may put it so, which has not really yet been digested, or adapted to. The party leadership, having been involved in Government now for more than half of the period since 1977, has not given itself the time or leisure to think through what we are about, apart from the crude but important task of staying in office.

There seemed to me in the pre-1977 Fine Gael party to be still a strong strain of Arthur Griffith and Sinn Fein, a deep reserve (contrary to Fianna Fáil propaganda) about the British (more than once expressed very bluntly by Liam Cosgrave). There was also — and here is the point in which we most differed from Fianna Fáil — a contempt for sham and for the bloody old nonsense (the "old foolishness" as Patrick Kavanagh's weekly called it, or the "verbal patriotism", in Liam Cosgrave's phrase) which seemed as inseparable from the guff-republicans as a skin.

These elements of the Fine Gael ethos, no doubt not, always lived up to either then or now, are still present under Garret FitzGerald; but an emphasis on social reform, even at a pace faster than the public will wear, which is so important to many newer deputies, and above all the grinding, distracting problem of grappling in government with economic nightmare while tied to a Labour Party whose pace is dictated by competition from further Left, have somewhat overlaid them.

I think the party should reflect on its roots, on what Sinn Fein was about, on what Cumann na nGaedheal too was about, which ran the state during the most radically innovative ten years of its history; even on what de Valera's Fianna Fáil was also about, once the Civil War issues had disappeared.

The proudly national and innovative spirit seems to have left all parties entirely. The freedom which was supposed to let us do things for ourselves in our own way, has been used in recent decades to copy, timidly and belatedly, British patterns in nearly everything.

Apart from the era between 1922 and the Second World War, as I recently heard a friend saying, Ireland's political and official rulers have largely behaved like a crew of maintenance engineers, just keeping a lot of old British structures and plant ticking over.

The fundamental challenge before Fine Gael is not just to contrive some way out of chronic budget deficit and chronic unemployment. Problems like that, though defeating, so far, both us and our opponents, are inherently of an order capable of solution even by officials — witness the impact of the 1958 Programme for Economic Development, the sole work of a gifted civil servant, whom Gerard Sweetman had spotted and promoted during the second inter-party government, and Sean Lemass had backed after Fianna Fáil returned to office in 1957.

The challenge is rather to evolve structures within which the people can be drawn into individual and community responsibility for their own development. It is to motivate a population towards excellence, towards being the best in the world, and to cast behind them the indifference and lack of pride in work which is all too Irish.

The people, especially young people, need to be re-oriented towards an understanding of, and familiarity with, the civilisation and the standards of the larger Europe, not just of the U.K. The party that succeeds in doing these things will, I honestly believe, also achieve Irish unity as a by-product, as the rise of this republic to something that the rest of the world can envy destroys the deepest psychological barrier which repels the unionist from us.

Naturally Stephen O'Byrnes did not set out to write a political manifesto or tract, merely a slice of political history. In this, he has succeeded very well.

I only wanted, in advancing the reflections above, to regret that he stopped short of a conclusion at which I am more or less arriving: that Garret FitzGerald's greatest achievement would be, not even the success of the Hillsborough pact, but the elaboration and selling to his party of a re-launch of the republic around the lines I mention, and around the kind of ideal which 70 years ago made Irish public affairs seem worth devoting one's life to.

Electoral Bill, Dáil, 11 December 1986

Let me ask in a couple of words what is the point of this panoply of the register of political parties? Why do we need a register of political parties? Is the entire paraphernalia of a register seriously necessary? If somebody wants to call themselves the Freedom from Mozambique or the Integrated with Taiwan Party and who do not mind making fools of themselves for three weeks and ending up with 12 votes let them do so. God knows, there are enough potential ones around but are we so solemn that the State feels affronted if an eccentric inserts himself into its machinery in this form? I cannot see the reason for it.

The register of political parties has no function in the law whatsoever except to the extent that it permits people to add if they are on the register, the name of a party after their names. That is its only function and it is very frequently understood as being in some way a guarantee of constitutionality. It is very frequently misunderstood by people as meaning that the Clerk of the Dáil has certified the party as being somehow morally OK. It means nothing of the kind and there is no such discretion in the Clerk of the Dáil. All he has to do is be satisfied of these minimal requirements. What is the point of a register? It is a piece of gratuitous State busybodyness.

Elections on Sundays, Dáil, 3 June 1988

The estimates contain a reference to the cost of conducting elections. I should like to say a few words about the system of holding national elections here and the expense attached to them. The expense of a national poll nowadays — the Minister will correct me if I am wrong — is approaching £3 million, no matter what the issue is, whether a referendum, a Dáil election, or anything else. It may be that there are minimal differences in the cost as between a referendum and a Dáil election, no doubt the count does not take so long and probably is not as expensive from that point of view, but all the other expenses, payment of the returning officers and staff, Garda overtime and so on tot up, every time we hold a national poll, to about £3 million. That is not chickenfeed. We ought not to despise money like that. We should try to economise on these outings. We had a terrible rash of them over the last five or six years, more than we needed.

There is also the disruption of the school week when the holding of polls in the middle of the week, on a Wednesday or Thursday, causes. I know perfectly well that sooner or later we will get around to having national polls at weekends, on Saturdays or Sundays, but that day will not come until the British do it. As soon as they do it, there will be somebody in here within a week asking why could we not have legislation of the same kind. Since the people across the water are seen now to have satisfied themselves that the reasons for it are not good, we too must do the same thing, although the reasons that speak in favour of that change now are just as visible, as loud and as cogent for us at this moment as they would be across the water. We should make that change now. There are very few Sabbatarians left in the country so strict that they should imagine that exercising their political duty in the shape of putting a ballot paper in a box would breach proper observance of the Lord's Day. Although, I respect anybody's opinion, no matter how much in the minority it is, there is a limit beyond which minorities' susceptibilities ought not to be a bar to what most of us would regard as a rational reform. It may be that the implications of a financial kind are greater than I have taken into account, possibly overtime problems would be greater at a weekend than during the week. Admittedly, I have not reckoned that up. It may also be that a day would be required on either side of the polling day for cleaning the place up. I cannot believe that it really takes 72 hours, not just the polling day itself, but the day before and the day after, to rearrange the school desks and sweep the place. It could be done far faster than that. A poll could be held on a Saturday or Sunday and the children could still have their schoolday up to ordinary closing time on Friday and be there again on Monday morning. It is not beyond human wit or capacity. Just because a different system still obtains across the water is no reason why we should not make the change, at least experimentally. If it turns out to be a disaster, we can go back to the old system and I shall not have any further complaints about it.

SECTION 2

Fianna Fáil and Charles Haughey

Put them out, 1968

No one looking at the Government's behaviour could doubt that it had lost all trace of a philosophy or purpose other than keeping itself in office by all or any means. Frantic efforts were being made to improve Ministers' "Images" and to get them to behave themselves so that the public might think them worthy of the positions they held, but every now and then the mask slipped, and Ministers used language, in Dáil Éireann and elsewhere, which showed the real ugly nature lurking beneath the painfully built-up "personality".

The Minister for Local Government had had the insolence, when a television programme was not to his liking, to refer to the priest chairman as "a so-called cleric"; the Minister for Education had not been in office a week before he was talking about using "the big stick" on the universities. How dare they behave as if the country and everybody in it were there own private property? Under the smooth covering of mohair and suede the Government were, with few exceptions, a collection of contemptuous bullies, whose effect on the Irish people had been nearly to destroy their belief in decent standards of government. They had been so often caught out in lies, in jobbery and incompetence that public faith in Irish democracy was seriously shaken. It was enough to make a cat laugh to hear them complaining of cynicism about politics among ordinary people, when it was their own arrogant and self-interested behaviour that had created and fostered that cynicism.

Fianna Fáil had been in office for 30 of the last 36 years, and had quietly dumped, one after the other, all the main planks of their original platform. How many Ministers really cared two straws about the ending of partition? or about saving the Irish language from extinction? or about maintaining a stable rural population? Everything that once quickened the hearts of the Irish people was gone, flung to the winds in exchange for the prospect of being allowed to creep into a kind of half-prosperity through association with other, larger nations. This might be good enough from a party which had never preached anything but pragmatism and materialism; but from the "Soldiers of Destiny" it was shameful. The Irish people must realise that Fine Gael were now the only heirs of the tradition of Irish independence who really cared about it and were determined to translate it into the terms which those who fought and died for it would understand.

In this year 1968 the final value of Fianna Fáil to the Irish people might be judged by the fact that their main energies were being devoted to changing the voting system so that they could stay in office even in the face of a large hostile majority. The time had come for Fine Gael to repeat the crude and simple slogan of 1948, and to repeat it with the confidence that, in 1968, Fine Gael alone could form a strong alternative Government: "Put them out!"

Adjournment speech, Dáil, 26 June 1978

We make all allowances for election time. At such times and at other times we may not mean everything we say and we would regret if people took seriously 100 per cent of what we say, but the performance of Fianna Fáil has been cynical and dishonest from beginning to end. If a Green Paper of this kind was introduced by the Coalition or even by the Government that preceded the Coalition or by any other government headed by Mr Lynch, by the late Mr Lemass or by the late Mr de Valera, it would not deserve the same kind of niggling examination that it is receiving now; but this Green Paper is a product of the party who had all the answers, who laid down in black and white that there were "tens of thousands of jobs only waiting to be created", with the implication, which did not lurk too far beneath the surface, that nothing but Coalition stupidity, malice, envy and dissension prevented those jobs from being pulled out of the air. That is the background against which the Green Paper is being examined, and I do not apologise for adding my voice to that of my colleagues.

When I read this Green Paper with its promises of sacrificial times to come, of options that will not be easy, I am reminded of a story I heard as a child. It was one of the Brother Grimm's stories — a very apt name for the author. This story concerned a widower who had a beautiful daughter and who, for the daughter's sake, was anxious to remarry. When he put the matter to the woman of his choice she, being very anxious for a man promised him faithfully that the daughter of whom he was so fond would have wine to drink and milk to bathe in. Bathing in milk may sound disgusting now, but it must have sounded fine to a sixteenth century peasant audience in Germany. The marriage took place; and on the first day the girl had wine to drink and had milk in which to bathe, but on the second day there was no wine so that she got only milk to drink although she had milk in which to bathe. On the third day she had milk to drink but only water in which to bathe; while on the fourth day it was water all the way.

That is an analogy not too far removed from what we are discussing today. I make allowances for the weakness of politicians. I have these weaknesses in full measure. Sometimes we promise more than we can fulfil. A politician may suffer from some personality defect which forces him into public life — that goes for everybody in this House and for everybody in every county council, too — in a sense it is a disease and I make all allowances for it, but the Government's performance tops all. I have never known anything else to come near what they have done. The Government of Deputy Cosgrave would have been ashamed to have been associated with a performance of this kind in order to get into office.

Twelve months after being returned to office on a set of promises the Government produce this document that is of stupefying banality. The

Taoiseach said yesterday that we were "stunned" by the Green Paper. He is right so far as I am concerned, because I cannot understand most of it. Never before have I seen a document that is so slovenly, so badly written, which is so full of jargon and which, in the matter of using words that are not understood outside the Department that put them together, is a sure sign that the man who put the document together does not know any better way of putting across what he is trying to say.

The Green Paper contains words that have never before appeared in print in this country in the sense in which they are being used now. For instance, there is talk of a "secular trend" in agricultural employment. The word "secular" had two meanings in ordinary Irish speech. It is used in the ecclesiastic sense as opposed to priests in regular orders, and it also can mean secular as opposed to clerical or professional in a general sense. But perhaps because I have the remains of a classical education, my guess is that the word is being made to bear the meaning "characteristic of the age". We know there is a trend in rural dis-employment that is characteristic of the age, but why can the man who wrote the document not say that rather than use a word that the people cannot understand and which takes me all my time to try to disentangle?

There is another reference to increases being merely "incremental" increases in employment. I know what an increment is. I was on an incremental scale for a long time before reaching a maximum, but that is not what the genius means in this document. Neither is it what is meant by the genius who presides over that genius in the Department of Economic Planning and Development. What is meant here by an "incremental" increase in employment is merely a slight increase, an increase that is so small as not to be worth talking about, but why cannot the author of this document say that? The Green Paper reflects the belief that we are all Paddys. Indeed we are paddywhacks of the deepest dye when we can have the wool pulled over our eyes in this way.

Having said that about the Green Paper I must confess that it contains a good deal with which I agree, and I do not wish to appear to devalue those parts of it that are useful and which I am glad to see included in it. However, before going on to that I wish to make the Press and the people a present of my own conclusions about the way in which the document was put together. The Department who launched it were idiotic enough to give a clue as to the dissensions in the Government by issuing an errata slip setting out a list of misprints, seven in all, and each one of which one would flash past without having to be told what was intended. We are told by way of erratum, for instance, that the word "married" is spelled in the document with only one "r". We do not need an errata slip to tell us that these were the parts of the Green Paper which reached completion last, but it tells us that these were the parts which came back from the printers and were rehashed. This slip indicates those parts of the document that were put together fleetingly. It is obvious that there was not sufficient time to read the proofs. The reason I am sure about this is that on my first reading of the document I found a further nine misprints and if the Minister wishes I can send him a list of those. The misprints mean that the document was so speedily put together that there was not time to correct it properly and this errata slip indicates the sections — one of which deals with health — about which there was the most contention, which were completed at the last moment which had to be recalled from the printer and re-set but without time to proof read before the document was bound. I will give that as a present to some other Sherlock Holmes to see what he can make of it, but that is my belief.

This is a Government of softies. They do not know what it is to govern. They are unwilling to incur any unpopularity. I worked within the National Coalition for four and a half years and I know what it is to see people doing things they knew will bring the house down around their ears, but they did it because it was their duty to do it. The Fianna Fáil manifesto played a substantial part in the Fianna Fáil victory but in hindsight the National Coalition had become unpopular for reasons which the manifesto merely built on. One of the reasons was that the people simply had not the stomach to be governed in the way that we thought it our duty to govern. This Government are running away from difficulties. They are faced with a population which is becoming more and more ungovernable, in common with many other populations in the western democracies, because of the essence in western democracies whereby competing parties offer more and more cake and jam and the people vote for whoever offers the most.

I could not believe my ears yesterday morning when I heard the Taoiseach say that he "wished to thank the people for their support given last year". Of course they will support a Government who do nothing only give hand outs. They will support any Government like that. If there was an election tomorrow, except for the fact that fishermen and various other groups would not vote for Fianna Fáil, the result might be the same as the one last July. If that is true, it is true for the reason that the Taoiseach intimated yesterday. The Taoiseach has the people's support in good times, but fair weather support is not worth anything and there is not much fair weather left ahead, as everybody knows. We had to fight through horrible external circumstances and horrible internal circumstances and naturally we trod on toes and made enemies when doing so. We have paid the penalty and I have never been heard to squeal about it. Unless this Government use their enormous majority to do these things now they will be in deep water in a few years time.

Muppet Show, Dáil, 13 March 1979

I do not want to offend the Minister personally. On the personal level I have a genuine regard for him, but when I find myself and his Government, whom I believe he has the considerable honour of leading in matters of this kind, conducting their affairs in such a way that their strategy is sending them further and further away from that stated objective, he reminds me of a figure like the scientist in "The Muppet Show", Dr. Bunsen and his experiments. They never work, as can be seen within a very short time and it is not at the expense of Dr. Bunsen, who is still looking out through his rimless spectacles, that they have not worked and have left everybody in the laboratory worse off than when he started, but at the expense of his wretched assistants. That does not faze Dr. Bunsen; he is back again next week with another plan which produces equally negative results.

Professor O'Donoghue: It was nice to know that the Deputy has the leisure to see this. When is he on?

I do not mean to offend the Minister. I sometimes regret that so much of the bitterness has gone out of public life here because occasionally I find it hard to speak as I really think for fear of hurting someone on the far side for whom I have a genuine regard.

Professor O'Donoghue: I promise not to be hurt. Please feel free.

However, when I find a measure of this kind defended by the Minister for Finance by reference to a speech made by the last Taoiseach four years ago, I ask myself if he has his feet on the ground at all. Does he realise where this is tending in regard to the Government's general economic policies, strategies and philosophy, if I may use a word with which they mantle themselves from time to time? Going back to 1975 as the Minister for Finance does, let me remind the House that food subsidies in those days were only part of a packet. In those days the then Government introduced that packet in order to knock four percentage points off the CPI and the rest of that package included the removal of VAT from clothing, footwear, electricity and gas, and the institution of the employment premium scheme.

Does the Minister know the kind of world he is living in? The kind of world which the Fianna Fáil Party have created is one which is not going to change any more. They have created expectations and mentalities in people which are not going to change even if the Fianna Fáil Party disappear tomorrow from those benches and into thin air. Whatever Government comes after them will have to deal with those attitudes and mentalities which their way of running the country has produced.

Finance Bill, Dáil, 2 May 1979

The policy of the State in regard to advertising benefits seems to be obscure. A benefit not just to the individual but to the whole economy, such as I recognise this to be, ought to be properly advertised. Money should be spent on it and I will come back to that point later in a different context. One must contrast the somewhat neglectful and sloppy approach of the State in telling people about the sums available to them with the enormous sums of money pumped into advertising campaigns, in some cases of a shaming absurdity and futility, such as the unspeakable campaign to persuade us that a few scraps of kitchen Irish — that is all they are — are part of what we are. They may very well be part of what Fianna Fáil are with the self-satisfaction induced by being able to speak three or four words of Irish that everybody's granny knew even though she knew nothing else. About 95 per cent of people in this country have spent long years learning Irish at school and we are asked to pat ourselves on the back and regard ourselves as something special if we understand three or four phrases in regard to which hundreds of thousands of pounds are being spent. This is a shaming campaign.

I agree, but I want to draw a contrast between the brazen absurdity of this campaign, which is only at home in the leprechaun mentality which the party opposite have displayed since the day they were founded, and the possibilities in a modest improvement which has been introduced by the hero of Deputy Andrews. Let us see some money being put into that; I will not begrudge it. However, I very much begrudge the hundreds of thousands of pounds being spent to persuade me that it is part of what I am if I am able to say "la brea" and "An mbeidh cupán tae agat?" Having spent 12 years at school learning this language, just as Deputy Andrews did, I am supposed to think more of myself if I speak a few phrases which are less than my granny knew.

An Ceann Comhairle: The Deputy is going into detail on the matter.

I am sorry. These things get under my skin and they should get under your skin as well. With respect, you should throw up as well when you see that kind of advertising being conducted at public expense. It is a shame and a disgrace.

An Ceann Comhairle: The Chair may not take part in debates.

You are a highly regarded Member of this House in your own right, even though you are sitting in the Chair, and since I address my remarks through you, allow me to draw you into the web of my own rhetoric in this matter. I appeal to you to ask yourself whether you have stomach for that advertising campaign. I do not believe you have.

The burden of what Deputy Andrews said was rational and temperate enough and I do not find fault with most of it. In relating the Finance Bill to the over-all approach of the Government towards their professed targets and towards the desire of the Government to secure full employment, he is not standing back and looking sufficiently closely at what is being done in his name.

The Government are having difficulty even in finding new words to describe agreements. They have tried words "contract", "compact", "harmony", and "concord" and now we have a "national understanding" in the vain hope that this will suppress everybody's cupidity and everybody's anxiety to get as much as they can. The Government feel that this "understanding" will defuse this cupidity or relegate it to a neutral area. That will not happen.

If there has been up to this point a reasonable degree of peacefulness and reasonableness in industrial relations and a willingness to settle for, perhaps, a good deal less than one originally set out to seek, it is because until lately the feelings of greed and cupidity, so roundly castigated by Deputy Andrews, were not triumphant. They were suspended like a chemical element in a solution in which ordinary Christian charity and neighbourliness played a part, but in which a part was also played by a kind of muddled conviction that the Government, even though one might not have actually voted for it, were in a kind of way doing their best to play fair with all sides.

That kind of muddled conviction was part of the elements which kept the cupidity and greed suspended. But, if I am making chemical sense, those feelings of greed and cupidity have now been precipitated into a thick and bloody-minded sludge at the bottom of the metaphorical container I am talking about. The agent which has precipitated them is the realisation that we are now being ruled by a Government who have not made a fair effort to maintain fairness between all sides and to show responsibility, even at the cost of popularity and votes in distributing benefits and imposing burdens. Visibly they have not made that effort. They created a mood during the election campaign and immediately afterwards which guaranteed, as the present Opposition said it would, an absolute intransigence on the part of the very sectors now being ticked off so roundly by Deputy Andrews. One cannot tell an industrial worker to moderate his wage demands when all he has to do is look around and see, as The Irish Times said yesterday, the people with tans in the middle of the winter.

Financial Resolutions, Dáil,
27 February 1980

Mr Killilea: Deputy Kelly is all blunder and bluff. He should get himself back on the rails.

Mr Kelly: I am not sure if it was Deputy Moore or Deputy Killilea who threw in that interjection. A party who went around talking about the real Taoiseach, as though it were Deputy Lynch in the years when he had been thrown out by the people and not by his own party, are the last party who can complain about soubriquets being applied to them; and I will not respect conventions which they contemptuously threw aside when they were out.

An Ceann Comhairle; The Deputy will obey the Chair's ruling.

Minister for Foreign Affairs (Mr Lenihan): Hear who is talking. It is all blunder and bluff. The Deputy has gone gaga.

Mr Kelly: That Minister over there is the thirteenth stroke of the clock in the Irish political system. He is the one who invites doubt not only about his own authenticity, but about the authenticity of all the other 12 as well. He is a national institution, and I would feel a pang if he lost his seat. He belongs up there at the Hyde Park Corner of the Dáil where the odd bods come in. That is where Deputy Lenihan belongs. A leader of a Government-------

An Ceann Comhairle: Would Deputy Kelly refer to him as the Minister for Foreign Affairs?

Mr Kelly: I have no spleen against Deputy Lenihan: I like him. I cannot resist liking him. But a man who thinks that in Deputy Lenihan is seen, for the outside world, the acceptable face of Ireland, is up a gum tree. I do not want to hold the House up, and I am not going to speak much longer, but I am perfectly entitled to talk about the impact which this measure will have on the tourist business. I am not going too far out of the way in recalling what happened to the tourist business in 1979 in consequence of the mishandling of the petrol business by Deputy O'Malley and the Department over which he then presided. Personally, I do not entirely blame Deputy O'Malley because he was badly advised — indeed he was not advised at all. He did not have enough people who were oilmen or knew anything about the business. He thought he would strike a posture; and the Government and Deputy Haughey thought they could join in the praise and share the applause for striking the posture of "standing up to the multi-nationals". They are a long way from that now, with petrol going to be almost twice the cost that it was in April of last year, and the multi-nationals only laughing up their sleeves at them. Deputy Killilea is very quiet up there, laughing behind his paper handkerchief. What has he to say about that now? The multinationals were going to be whipped by little Dessie, but he did not succeed in whipping them. He would not pay the going rate, and so they did not sell him the petrol. The result was that bookings were lost by the thousand. Hotels closed down because of the ruin of the tourist season. We have now got the system under this resolution in which the tourist season for 1980 will go under again.

I have not looked very much at television this evening or listened to radio. I suppose I spent about half an hour at it, and I have not yet heard the tourist industry speak their minds about this. They may have done so, but I will be very surprised if they welcome an extra 20p a gallon on petrol. It is a very undifferentiated 20p. Strangely enough, there are countries in Europe — Italy for one — in the EEC, subject to the same rules as we are, that are able to make special rates for tourists. Why do we not do that? Why is that never thought of? I will tell you the reason. It is because the English do not do it. That is the real reason, and the Soldiers of Destiny over there who think that they have not produced a budget until they have thrown in a paragraph of kitchen Irish about camáns are too much in the Paddy mould to strike out and do something for themselves. Because the English do not have special concessions on tourism it is more than good enough for us not to have them.

Haughey's new Ministers, Dáil, 16 December 1980

I would like to add my good wishes to those which have already been expressed to the three Deputies whose positions are about to be changed this afternoon. I do not know Deputy Smith very well but I wish him success and happiness in his job. I know Deputy Nolan a little better and have always found him a pleasant and agreeable colleague, although on the opposite side, and I wish him well too.

I also wish well Deputy Fitzgerald about whom I have somewhat stronger feelings. I remember his conduct when he was in opposition and I can say now that this is a big day for him. In turn, I hope he will be big enough to endure patiently the few things I may say about him which will not be very severe. He will not deny, perhaps he even takes pride in the fact that he was the noisiest and most obstructive member on the Opposition benches. He roared and bellowed so loudly when the National Coalition were in power that he could be heard — and I believe frequently was heard — on the street.

I never noticed in his attacks on the Coalition Government any special subtlety or any special grip on what government was all about, least of all on what the financial direction of government was all about. He seemed to be happy to have a crude figure, like the unemployment figure, add 60,000 and then beat us over the head with it. That was his style of debate. I hope he will not be hurt when I say that nothing has happened since then which has led me to form a better opinion of the grasp he has of the country's affairs.

He clearly has a grip on the affections of his constituents, to judge from his enormous vote on which I congratulated him after the last election, but his performance in this House does not lead me to be much impressed with this appointment, which is not just to any old Ministry but which is the nearest thing we have to a super Ministry. It is the Ministry on which all others depend. It is the Ministry from which all others have to get permission before they get a box of paper clips.

Deputy Fitzgerald is a convivial and nice man personally. When I got to know him better my feelings about his Dáil performance subsided. I accept he has very good personal qualities and for that reason I wish him the best, but I cannot pretend to be impressed by his appointment. I do not want to hurt his feelings, although I am sure he is tough enough to withstand a few words from me, but he is not the best man on the Fianna Fáil benches for this job. He may be the best man for some purposes which have not been disclosed to the House or which the House has not had an opportunity of debating; it may be that the elements that went into the decision to appoint him are valid for some people and for some reasons, but I think that there are at least three Fianna Fáil Deputies who would have been better suited because they have a better grasp of the economy, of large amounts of money, what they mean, how hard it is to collect them and how carefully they must be spent. I hope he will not be offended by that because I would not take it as an insult if somebody said the same — as they might have only too much ground to do — about me in making a disadvantageous comparison with some of my colleagues.

Deputy Colley should not have been moved from the portfolio he held and he should be put back there. Failing him, Deputy O'Malley should have received this post. Deputy O'Malley is no charmer and I had many a hard word with him and I do not suppose we have heard the last of them. Both Deputy Colley and Deputy O'Malley — despite the fact that they have the black mark of taking the benefit of a dishonest manifesto and of successive Government statements and policies which only made matters worse, and naturally must share in the collective responsibility for these — seem to be men who are more inclined than many men in their party to put the country first. I do not say that is an entirely unmixed sentiment because unfortunately as we have seen here only too often in lobby votes with the party opposite the party tends to come first and everything else tends to come last even if the devil is breathing down the back of its neck. It did seem to me over the years — though I do not especially admire either of them — that Deputy Colley and Deputy O'Malley have this quality, have a certain willingness to take unpopular decisions, to put up with hard words and severe criticism and to withstand the wind in their faces. I do not think Deputy Fitzgerald has this to the same degree.

I have noticed that at serious moments on the industrial relations scene he has tended over the last three years to lie low and say nothing. I remember the two months during which the country agonized over Ferenka when Deputy Fitzgerald was to be seen opening bull fights in Sligo, cutting the tape in Dunmore East, things like that. But as a factor in the developing Ferenka situation — I have said it to him before so he will not mind my saying it to him now in the hour of his triumph or promotion — he simply did not exist or, if he did, the activity of himself and his Department was kept well below the parapet; it could not be seen so it could not be criticised except for its low visibility. In general I must say that over the three years in which he has held the office of the Minister for Labour, augmented in the last year by responsibility for the public service, the performance has been fairly poor.

No, Sir, Deputy Fitzgerald already is a member of the Government and the statement which inaugurated this debate expressly referred to him as being the person to whom the Department of Finance was being assigned. I think I am the first Deputy who has spoken here today who has been pulled up on this point.

Moreover in the area of public service reform — I acknowledge that Deputy Fitzgerald has not been in charge of that for very long, for little less than a year — I should like to remind the House that there was no subject to which the Government, so far as it spoke through Deputy Jack Lynch, attached more importance in July 1977 than this. In the Official Report of 5 July 1977, Deputy Jack Lynch had this to say:

"I consider public service reform to be of fundamental importance for the effective discharge and implementation of the programmes of the national renewal and development upon which we are now embarking".

When Deputy Fitzgerald gets over his understandable elation at his new appointment I should like him to take a serious look at himself and the Department over which he presided until now, whose function he is now bringing back with him to finance, and ask himself what has been done about public service reform over the last three and a half years. We have asked questions about it from these benches occasionally when we have been met with a cataract of waffle. One was stunned and stupefied by the load of stuff about interdepartmental committees, ongoing reviews, escalating reappraisals and so on. But when the smoke is all cleared away the net result is that there are just 7,000 or 8,000 more people in the non-industrial Civil Service, and nothing else that I can see. I cannot see that anything is being done to ensure that the State gets better value for the public sector employment, that its work is better organised, that any effective redistribution of a kind that makes useful sense has taken place.

These are all areas in which between them Deputy Fitzgerald and Deputy O'Kennedy have had the prime responsibility over the last three years. I must say that to find one being replaced by the other at the helm of the economy awakens in me — I do not want to bring levity into this — no very serious sensation of respect, particularly when there exist on the other benches people who, whatever party differences there may be, are more accustomed to and I believe have the will to handle large issues of a financial and economic kind than is Deputy Fitzgerald. It is not being offensive to him to say that; they are much more accustomed to doing so. Nobody doubts their patriotic commitment, flavoured I am afraid, diluted, perhaps polluted, by a large element of mindless party loyalty. Nobody doubts their ability whatever relations one may have had with them personally. It is right to temper one's congratulations and good wishes by saying these things and I hope Deputy Fitzgerald will forgive me for saying them.

The circumstances which led to Deputy Fitzgerald's assignment to this Department are of an unprecedented kind. No Minister for Finance was ever appointed in this country since the State was founded on a caretaker basis. It is only because that happened that we are debating Deputy Fitzgerald's reassignment here today. There never was such a thing before and the very idea that it would cross a Government's mind, or its leader's mind, to make such an appointment only shows the depth of the reckless arrogance which possessed them. This country, by all the economic indicators — even the ones to which Deputy O'Kennedy was obliged to confess today, simpering as he handed out the answers — is in a recession far more serious, far more directly attributable to the Government's own acts than it was in the middle of the seventies, and it is at that time that the Government chose to acquiesce, and the party acquiesce, in a stop-gap appointment, a conacre Minister, on the 11 months system. That is a disgrace. I should like to know what would have been said if Deputy Liam Cosgrave had appointed Mr. Dick Burke as Minister for Finance at the end of 1975, in the depths of that recession, knowing full well that he would send him to Brussels at the end of 1976. What would have been said about him had he done that?

The Taoiseach: As he appointed Deputy Kelly Attorney General.

Mr. Kelly: I know what would have been said because I can remember the kind of criticisms which came from the Fianna Fáil Party in those days. If there were so much as a flaw in the printing of the Order Paper, if Deputy Lynch did not get the report of the bagpipes commission with his breakfast, there was a row about it here on the Order of Business. We were watched like hawks by the media and everybody else to see how we were doing the business — was it orderly or was it a shambles? So far as it was less than orderly, it was as a result of the constraints which the small majority imposed on us, as I was never tired explaining. Had Deputy Cosgrave done what I am talking about, and appointed on a stopgap basis somebody to the Department of Finance, whom he knew would be going in 11 or 12 months time, the roof would have fallen in on us. Of course he was not a showman. He had not spent 20 years assiduously slapping backs and buttering up people whose opinions are important at junkets like that. He did not do any of these things and so, of course, he did not enjoy the same immunity from critics.

Financial Resolutions, Dáil, 4 February 1981

I have often protested about budget debates, this ritual ding-dong which becomes progressively less interesting to the public. As I once said, it is like Japanese ritual fencers with their padded staves beating one another — predictable speeches coming from both sides. I have a recollection of budget debates in the last Dáil and Deputy Richie Ryan meant the stuff in his budget speech and I suppose he enraged people by apparently not only meaning it but feeling it. I have no doubt that Deputy Colley and Deputy O'Malley meant their stuff but there is an unreality about what is happening now because the Estimates are, to a very important extent, bogus Estimates. The budget speech, because of the features I have mentioned, (a) relying on the bogus Estimates and (b) gratuitously making allowances from the expenditure side in respect of sums pulled out of the air, is an unreal budget speech. What is the exercise all about?

I am not really sure that there is much point in this budget mystique, the big occasion of the year with everyone trying to get more than his fair share of tickets from the unfortunate Superintendent, the ladies coming in and having their dresses described in the papers the next day. All that mystique is, naturally, borrowed from the British, Paddies that we are: the battered dispatch box which even a republican Minister for Finance does not distain, holding it up in ridiculous foreshortening — I suppose he is the one who is foreshortened — to the camera as he sets out from Government Buildings.

I object to all that reach-me-down British mystique, not just for that reason but also because it builds up this false occasion and that false occasion puts a Government and a Minister under a strong subconscious pressure to produce some kind of nosegay or little bouquet of measures which will be cosmetically acceptable. He should not have to do that. He should not have to go through this rigmarole. He should be able to fine tune the economy. I do not mean monthly budgets in the sense of a monthly imposition of taxation but the economy and the fiscal mechanism which operates should be at the Minister's command all the year around. It was in our time when we put 15p on a gallon of petrol in a single measure. This Government have done equivalent things and, no doubt, will again. It should be accepted that that is the way to run an economy which can suffer shipwreck from some single event happening in the middle of the year in which no budget is in sight. There is something really meaningless about debating what we are debating today. Everybody knows, inside and outside the House, that these Estimates are going to be miles overshot by the end of 1981.

I have spoken for my full hour in a debate which I characterise as fairly meaningless for the reasons I have given. I cannot sit down without making a comment — I do not want to be hurtful — about the demeanour of the Minister for Finance when he was reading the budget speech here last week. He seemed to me to be a man with his back to the wall. I do not know how it struck other Deputies or other people who were watching him. He looked like a man absolutely with his back to the wall, and I do not mean merely exhaustion at having to read through 60 pages of typescript. He knew that he was presenting a document which did not even rest on sand. It was resting in the air in so far as it reposed on figures plucked out of the air. I think that I have never seen a weaker or more lamentable budget performance in either the statement itself or the way in which it was delivered.

Forgive me, Sir, for ending on a trivial note. I do not want to make a meal of it, but it intensified the weary feeling I get on listening to contributions on

53

occasions like that. He could not make a budget speech without saying cúpla focal as Gaeilge at the end. Listening to those words in Irish that he used at the end, I can say honestly that I never heard that Deputy use a word of Irish in this House before. Now he has to thrust in, or get some unfortunate public servant to sit down and spend 20 minutes writing out a paragraph of Irish for him. I am not going to go into this in detail, but I do not think that he even looked at what was being put into his hand. He said:

Ba mhaith liom focal scóir a rá as Gaeilge.

He followed with four or five sentences of platitudes, and he said:

Ní gá ach earraí déanta in nÉirinn a lorg go dúthrachtach sna siopaí. . . .

He said that all we had to do was look for goods made in Ireland in the shops. Not one word of his speech in English up to then had been devoted to the question of the "Buy Irish" programme which was supposed to produce 10,000 jobs. This is only one aspect of economic and financial management and it is put in here in a throw-away sentence that you might use in closing down a feis or opening a fleadh ceoil. It has as much relevance to the main thrust of the budget debate as if he was to sing the National Anthem and throw in a few bars of "Hello Patsy Fagan" when he had finished. It is pitiable. It is very often in these trivial touches that you see the spirit of the whole thing. It is pathetic. That is not parting words in Irish. Those types of parting words are parting words to Irish.

Gene Fitzgerald's hard neck, Dublin, 6 April 1981

The world will have been astonished by the news, contained in an official G.I.S. release on Friday, that Mr Gene Fitzgerald, Minister for Finance, was going to Holland to a meeting of his E.E.C. colleagues in order to "warn" them against "over-restrictive policies" and to "stress the vital importance" of sustaining investment. He was also due to make a "determined plea" that member States should make "every possible effort" to solve the unemployment problem.

By what right does Mr Fitzgerald issue "warnings" to Europe's Finance Ministers? You would swear he came from the strongest, most dynamic economy of the West, a kind of Celtic Japan, instead of representing a Government which, by a combination of electoral greed, incompetence, and its leader's massive conceit, has reduced the country to near-indigence.

I doubt if the Finance Minister of Holland, say, will submit patiently to lectures about "over-restrictive policies" by a Government which by enormous cash hand-outs had simply pushed up consumer imports, and with them the trade deficit, right to the threshold of exit from the E.M.S.

And I imagine the Finance Minister of Germany will resent the "determined plea" about action to solve unemployment, coming from a Government which, by adding several percentage points to the inflation rate by additional taxes, had wrecked the national wage agreement and put even more jobs in jeopardy.

And the Finance Minister of Denmark will hardly be receptive to Mr Fitzgerald's emphasis on the "vital importance of sustaining investment", if he knows that this Government, by running majestic Budget deficits in order to pay for the over-swollen public service, and to pay the interest on the staggering State debt, has absorbed most of the funds which more prudent management would have left available for ploughing into productive capital programmes.

Any friend of Mr Fitzgerald's ought to offer him two alternative pieces of advice — apart, that is, from counselling him to stay at home and spare Europe any more of his impudent warnings. One would be to resign. The other — assuming he insists on staying in office for the fag-end of this flickering, dying Government — is to take out and dust off the first Programme for Economic Expansion compiled in 1957-58 by T.K. Whitaker. Let him study its calm, jargon-free assessments, devoid of political trumpeting; its statement of priorities, not all of them popular; its setting of simple, modest, credible targets.

The spirit of this document — so far from the vapid waffle of recent Green and White Papers — can be easily adapted to the needs of 1981. The only doubt must relate to the capacity, and will, of the present Government to learn from it.

Finance Bill, Dáil, 8 April 1981

How pathetic can a speech and a Government be? He is not the only one. I am sorry to say his speech and that of another Fianna Fáil Deputy last night also contained the first promise that the Fianna Fáil election campaign will be so desperate that they will not even stop short of smearing candidates' characters. Deputy Andrews gave the clearest possible notice of that. So too last night did Deputy P. J. Morley. It is not so much these straws in the wind but, when the Government get to the point of threatening that when an election is called they will look into the ideological credentials and personal beliefs of every candidate, and make damn sure that the public know about them, the comparison I make is the legend about when Cromwell was besieging Clonmel and he was being held up by the gallant defenders for longer than his plan or, if the Minister wishes, his strategy required.

He was walking around the fields in gloom one day when what did he find only a silver bullet. He said to himself: "Begob, these fellows must be really down on their uppers when they are melting silver plate to fire it out of guns, and when the only metal they have left is silver". There are many items in that little historical parallel which I would not wish literally transferred to the present situation; but when I find Deputy Andrews and Deputy Morley insinuating that we can expect that kind of character-smearing of our candidates, or the candidates of the Labour party, in the next election I say to myself that these are the silver bullets of which any decent man or decent woman should be ashamed.

I remember that image of human life — an old Anglo-Saxon poem — about the little bird which flies out of the dark into the lighted hall, flits through the lighted hall, is seen and sees for a little while, flies out of the hall at the end once more into the darkness. This is a very touching and beautiful allegory of human life. I am sorry to have thought of it off the top of my head in comparing the passage of Deputy O'Kennedy through the Department of Finance with that image. But, in a sense the speed of his arrival and departure — mind you, not caused by any accident but utterly predicted and known to the man who appointed him — is the single greatest disgrace in the economic management of this State in the last four years, and it is against heavy competition that I am awarding that palm.

Deputy O'Kennedy, having been in the Department of Finance for a year, left it to go to Brussels, which the man who appointed him knew he was sending him to a year previously. His opinion of his own conceit was so high and his opinion of his own mastery of those details was so great that it did not really matter who he had in the Department of Finance; he was only a cipher, easily manipulated, a pawn that just with the press of a switch on the intercom he could put right if he got a couple of hundred million pounds wrong in a calculation on the morning. He might easily do that because Deputy O'Kennedy, by training, education and background had no greater competence to fill the Department of Finance than Deputy Dick Burke would have had at the end of 1975. What would have been said had Deputy Liam Cosgrave sent him to the Department of Finance for a year, knowing that he would be going to Brussels a year later? The roof would have fallen in on him; and every criticism spoken about him would have been correct.

A lot of us are lucky with the kind of jobs we have. I have always recognised that I am very privileged in my job outside the House. I believe one of the worst jobs is that of somebody in the public service who has to write a Minister's speech. For all I know he comes in in the morning with the same kind of bothers at home we all have, with screaming children and so on, and he groans to himself: What will I put in this man's mouth ? I had better fire in something about the cost of oil. He gets a few words down. I always find that is a help. "There is a growing realisation" is always a great start to a sentence. It carries him through a line and it gives a bit of bulk to the speech.

Would the Minister for Finance tell us something that we do not know, for a change? It is incredible that a Minister for Finance could tell us this. I hope Deputy Corish will not mind if I mention the name of his distinguished predecessor in the leadership of the Labour Party. I remember the late Myles na gCopaleen making unmerciful fun of the late Deputy Norton when he was Minister for Industry and Commerce, because on a couple of occasions he said, which was not such a very odd thing to say in 1948 or 1949, that air transport was here to stay. Deputy Norton used often say that in his speeches. The late Myles na gCopaleen used make unmerciful fun of him for that. I feel that to be told in this day and age by a Minister for Finance that "there is a growing realisation" is as though the thing is only still dawning, that there are corners the dawn has not yet reached, even in this House, if the Minister's implication is to be taken seriously. The Minister apparently realises that dear oil is a fact of life. Has he asked himself what the Government or the people in his own Department are doing in response to that new fact of life other than whingeing about it and complaining about it? What have the Government done, in concrete terms, as distinct from talk, by way of trying — I do not mean tinkering with the problem — to produce alternative energy sources and wind down our oil consumption and demands?

Rommel and Gene Fitzgerald, Dáil, 22 July 1981

The reason Deputy Kemmy spoke this morning was that I let him in when I should have been speaking myself. I do not regret having done so, because I had the benefit of listening to his remarks. I felt a little saddened, as I have heard such remarks before, and I have even said such things myself when I was talking about the quality of the debate here on one of these stock occasions such as a set of budget resolutions. He complained, with a lot of justice, about the way he had heard Deputy Gene Fitzgerald speak. He complained about his routine aggressiveness. He complained also about Deputy Flor Crowley for a slightly different reason. If Deputy Kemmy thinks he has heard the limit of Deputy Fitzgerald's range he is in for a surprise. If Deputy Fitzgerald reverts to the form he showed in the Twentieth Dáil, he will make the acquaintance of Deputy Gene Fitzgerald's ranting and raving up and down the scale, like a coloratura foghorn, which could be heard out in the street. No matter what the occasion or how little the excuse, it will be sufficient for that Deputy to behave in the way I have described. However, he was quick to take the point about Deputy Flor Crowley's interventions last night. They came as a surprise to myself. I had lost sight somewhat of Deputy Crowley over the last few years. He was in temporary eclipse in the Seanad; but yesterday, like a very full moon emerging from behind a bank of cloud, he was back here again with his usual jovial malignance, peppering speakers on this side of the House with what were intended to be unhelpful interruptions. That is the form of the two gentlemen whom Deputy Kemmy heard last night. They are not alone. None of us is perfect in regard to decorum in debating here, but the two he mentioned are particularly obnoxious offenders. However, I am afraid the Deputy is only starting to hear what they are capable of.

It is always a pleasure to listen to Deputy Lenihan. Really he ought to be somewhere in Bord Fáilte's portfolio of attractions. His irrepressible style, his all purpose shamelessness _____

Mr Lenihan: You are not bad yourself

Mr Kelly: _____ to deliver at any notice or at none___

Mr Gene Fitzgerald: Keep in line with it, Professor.

Mr Kelly: I hope that nobody on that side of the House thinks the word "professor" is in any sense a gibe or a jeer. I remind them that their own party was founded by a professor, or if it was not I am not aware that he ever had any other form of profession.

Mr Gene Fitzgerald: There were some differences all the same.

Mr Kelly: There were, but not necessarily to his advantage.

An Ceann Comhairle: The Chair would like to have the Minister without interruption. The Chair would ask the Minister, Deputy Kelly, to address himself to the Chair.

Mr Kelly: Deputy Lenihan here this morning, followed after a short interval by Deputy Flynn, gave a marvellous impersonation of a man genuinely indignant. He was indignant, as was Deputy Flynn almost speechless with indignation, about the "savagery" — the word "savage" was the most over-worked word in his vocabulary — of our impositions and about the limited and modest scale of benefits which the budget announced here yesterday contained. Nowhere in the speeches of these two Deputies was there the slightest sign of recognition that it was their own profligacy, and that of their party, that has left us in a situation that a Government here have no option but to produce a budget which we know is going to be unpopular.

Deputy Flynn asked rhetorically if when I was walking around my constituency — I have not had much chance to do so since late last night — I ever thought of stopping ordinary voters and asking them what they thought of this budget, because if so I would get a very unpleasant answer. I do not need Deputy Flynn to teach me that truth. I accept that if I stop the next ten people I meet in my constituency I am going to get sour looks from seven or eight of them. Everybody on the side of a government who have tried to rescue this country from a swamp into which it was plunged is going to get that sort of treatment. I have no doubt that it was in large part a similar effort which put out the first Government we had in 1932: and I have no doubt that it was an effort, very lacklustre but of a similar kind, which put Fianna Fáil out in the

58

General Election of 1954, when they, in an attempt to uphold standards of financial probity which are now only a subject for laughter to people like Deputy Lenihan, cancelled food subsidies, took other unpopular measures and found themselves put out very soon after.

I do not delude myself that the country is full of such spartan, Cincinnatus-like austerity and willingness for self-sacrifice that they are going to be cheering us on for this budget, which is certainly unpopular. I also do not deceive myself that blaming our predecessors is going to go more than a certain distance. It certainly will not need emphasis with the more intelligent of them, but I have no illusions about the difficulties we will have in putting across a budget like this and in taking the measures which will have to be taken, not just this year but probably next year too, although I genuinely and honestly have no idea of what dimensions they may then assume. It will depend on how we get on for the remainder of this year.

I have no doubt we are going to have difficulties in selling these and in recruiting popular support behind them. If we pay the political penalty, let it be so. I do not think there is anything necessarily dishonourable in being on the Opposition benches, although some gentlemen over there bear it with a very poor grace. There is nothing necessarily dishonourable about being in Opposition, even for most of one's time in politics. It is a function upon which democrats should look with more indulgence than they look on the other side of the House. I take all these political hazards in my stride.

We have to do this job. We asked the people for their votes. They put us in a situation which I would have wished to be a bit stronger. I would have liked to have a better grip of the Dáil; but we cannot choose now. The people made their choice, which seemed to be clearly against the outgoing administration. But, I freely admit, it is not as unambiguously in favour of the Coalition as I would have wished. We are going to have to work very hard to make them like it and want more of it. There is no point in being little boys about this, making vainglorious, blustering speeches about a budget of this kind, thrust upon us though it was, that, say, Deputy Flynn or Deputy Lenihan would make if they were still in Government.

I want to remind Deputy Lenihan and his friends that Germany is governed by a coalition in which the by miles preponderant element is a socialist party. They are not a buttoned-boot crowd at all; they do not go in for celluloid wing collars. I have never seen Chancellor Schmidt being accused of being a stick-in-the-mud. I have never heard him compared with Ernest Blythe or anything of that kind at all. Funnily enough, he cares about deficits, both on the trade side and on the budget side. You will not find him running anyone into the Bundestag — unless, of course, he has a joker in the pack like Deputy Lenihan, which he well may have — you will not find him sending in someone to try to make a virtue out of recklessness, trying to form a league which would praise the behaviour of drunken sailors and hold it up as being exemplary.

The Governments of Holland, Belgium and Denmark are, I think, all

Coalitions, the composition of which tends to vary from time to time. I think I am right in saying that they usually have a predominant socialist or similar element. Funnily enough, they do not share the Lenihan philosophy, either.

Milton Friedman is a name which I hear being made fun of by people over there. They seem to regard him as a joke figure, and Thatcherism as a joke word too; although I was under the impression, until a couple of months ago, that the British Prime Minister was top-cat with Deputy Haughey. I do not quite see how her name should now come to be used as a butt for instance abuse and belittlement.

If I may be permitted to do something which the Opposition have done without asking anyone's permission, to express a view about the way the English economy is run, the English economy is not the one on which to try such radical medicine. Too much of it is too old and too sick. They have an industrial structure and a population structure which are completely different from ours. Problems in every dimension are different. What is being tried there is possibly too tough a medicine. It is like taking a man with a raging temperature and putting him outside on a snowy day in the hope that that will bring down his temperature. It is too tough.

I do not think that the medicine which this Government are trying to apply — not by choice but because they have been forced into it — is too tough. Naturally we are taking a chance. We must take a chance. There is nothing for it but to take a chance. Anyone can think of any number of similes and metaphors from all sorts of desperate situations for comparison. When the ship is sinking, swim for it; when the house is burning, jump for it. That is our situation. It may be that we have misjudged the jump, or have not placed the air mattress properly under the window, or have overestimated our power to reach shore. It may be that we will flounder and be in difficulties, but we must make these efforts. I have not heard any other suggestion made from the opposite side of the House, let alone from an independent commentator.

The last time I saw Deputy Fitzgerald we were confronting one another, either in here or outside. I was so flippant then as to construct a figure of speech in which a comparison emerged between himself and the late Field Marshal Rommel, both of whom were strategists. I often enough get abusive letters — almost always unsigned — but I keep them, nonetheless, because I have an eye for handwriting and I always hope to get a letter in the same handwriting which will be signed by somebody who is looking for something.

Very shortly after this episode, I got a letter from a lady whose name was signed to it, in which she said "Dear Mr Kelly, I am disgusted at your comparing Deputy Gene Fitzgerald, Minister for Finance, with the late Field Marshall Rommel. I consider that comparison of yours insulting and offensive — to Rommel".

Finance Bill, Dáil, 4 November 1981

Where is the noblest Roman of them all, the Mussolini of the Irish economy, the man who only had to make the well-schooled imperial gesture with the hand and everything falls into place as thousands of officials scurry off to do his bidding? Where is Deputy Haughey? Why has he not spoken in this debate? Surely if there was anybody with an overall grasp of the scene, surely if the Professor Moriarty of the national economy was able to control the sense on the way back the most remote movements in the economy and in the operation of all its branches, he would be here to contribute. Surely Deputy Haughey would be here to show us where we were wrong in the Finance Bill, the things which have caused it and the things that are going to flow from it. How is it that all these Deputies have given this debate which is going to end in a few hours a wide berth?

I do not know about Deputy Haughey because it may be that he is going to conclude for his side this afternoon — I do not know which of them will conclude — but I will give the House my guess as to why certainly the first three I mentioned have stayed away, Deputies Colley, O'Malley and O'Donoghue. I will throw in the name of Deputy John Wilson. It is only a hunch of my own but I suspect he would be in the same category. They have stayed away because they know that what was done in July had to be done. Those Deputies, Colley, O'Malley and O'Donoghue, urged, as far as they were in a position to do so , on the last Government that they not go ahead with the kind of U-turn and reckless spending which Deputy Haughey initiated and brought the semi-State bodies along with him in putting into effect in the last part of his regime. I do not think Deputy O'Malley is a man of instant charm or anything like that but he has got a certain endearing capacity or, should I say, incapacity to control his feelings which is a good thing in a politician. I do not like the cold-blooded sort who judge every word in terms of how it is going to be received by the media. Deputy O'Malley, at about this time last year when we were fighting a by-election in Donegal, in the course of a speech, not in Donegal, compared the people of this country to the inhabitants of the Easter Islands, or some of those islands, in which there is a cult called the cargo cult. I believe the Duke of Edinburgh is one of its recently elected gods and I believe that Deputy O'Donoghue might well be another one. Certainly, he would be instantly put up for membership of that pantheon if they knew about his existence. Deputy O'Malley gave an interesting talk about the cargo cult in the Easter Islands which got a good deal of attention here. He said that these people think that wealth falls out of the sky, that they do not have to do anything except sit around and the wealth will fall into their laps. He said that we in this country were beginning to go on those lines. That speech was made in September or October, 1980. Naturally, a man who has that belief and saw the way the country was being brought in that year by the Government would find it hard to reconcile with his principles if he had to come into the House and attack a Finance Bill which is probably line by line identical with or, in principle, not very far away from the Bill which he would have sponsored had he been in charge of the economy in the middle of 1981. That is the reason why Deputies like him have stayed clear. They have left the attack on the Finance Bill entirely to Deputies — I do not wish to offend them in this description — who in economic matters are fairly small fry. I genuinely do not mean to be offensive and all Members know that , but I do not think that any of the Deputies who have spoken on the Fianna Fáil side, regard themselves as, or ever held themselves out to be economic experts or even people who took much of an interest in how an economy works. The Fianna Fáil people who have some experience of the nuts and bolts of an economy, who have some grasp of the fact that one cannot distribute wealth until one first creates it, have stayed clear of this debate. I am entitled to draw my own conclusions from that.

The only thing that has been forthcoming from the Opposition in this debate has been a certain amount of name-calling. Naturally, I do not complain about Deputies Flynn, Keegan, Power, Briscoe, Vincent Brady or Leyden calling names because it is probably the only recourse open to them. It is the easiest way of getting through a bit of a speech but one bit of name calling which has been common here in this debate, and in another which preceded it, have been "Thatcherite" or "monetarist". I am surprised late in 1981 to find the word "Thatcherite" used as a term of abuse by a party led by Deputy Haughey who was very great with Mrs Thatcher at a time when it suited his publicity purposes to appear so. "Charlie and Maggie will fix it all up. There will be no holding the country once Deputy Haughey got hold of Mrs Thatcher's ear and was able to tell her a few things and talk straight to her". Naturally, the aura of glory which this publicity threw off reflected in part on Mrs Thatcher and she was head cat with Fianna Fáil for quite a long while, but now, suddenly, because nothing very much seems to have emerged from the cufuffle with Mrs Thatcher on Deputy Haughey's side, it is quite all right to use her name as a term of abuse. The word "monetarist", which I believe is imperfectly understood and which I freely confess I would not wish to lecture a class about, is thrown around here as a killing epithet which should make us wilt like salted snails when it is thrown at us.

As long as the Government are able, by keeping on borrowing, to pay the interest, we have got a good credit rating. The idea that a good credit rating bears any relation to a judgement of how the economy is being run in terms of the benefits it provides for our people is not worth a damn. These things do not interest the Deputies on the other side and we have not had any comments on any of these subjects from any of them. All we have had is dejected argument. We have had a depressing exhibition of the poor mouth.

I do not want to single Deputy Leyden out as I do not consider he is any worse than the rest of them. I was waiting to get in and I had to sit through his speech yesterday. I find it a depressing experience. I am fed up listening to him telling us that he comes from the west of Ireland, from Roscommon. Half of us either come from there or our parents do. All my people come from the west. I believe I know more about Roscommon than he does about Dublin South. All this beal bochtery about the west is something we can do without. I will tell him something about the west. He made a meal here yesterday of a speech of mine which I made in Claremorris last August. I will tell him something about Claremorris. I remember that little town when I was a small boy in the war years. I remember it when there was not even a car in the place. I remember it even before the petrol went off the roads during the war, when the only form of transport was an ass and cart. I remember it when there were people buying second hand clothes from one another, I remember it when there was not any metal on the streets. I do not single that town out as all the towns down there were the same.

When I went back in August to make the speech I am talking about, the meeting to which the Deputy referred, it took place in an establishment which would blind one by its opulence. The Deputy gave the impression that the people in Dublin South have no worries. He should come and talk to a few of them. I do not believe the whole of Dublin South contains an establishment, a restaurant, bar and function complex, as opulent as the one in which that function took place. I was only a small boy in 1941 but I remember the situation very well. If the people who lived there in 1941 were able to see this place 40 years later — it is still in the lifetime of most of them — they would have thought they were in dreamland. There is no sign of the ass and cart and there is no sign of poverty there now.

Everybody knows that the west came far better out of the mid-seventies recession than any other part of Ireland because of qualities which the people of the west have and also because they were given — rightly so — very favourable treatment in the establishment of new industry, which was less vulnerable than the established industries in the east and south. Those industries tended to close down far less and suffer far less in the mid-seventies recession than industries anywhere else in the country. If I were one of the constituents of Deputy Leyden and others like him I would object to the béal bocht hanging open like a liobar in this House whenever an economic topic is under discussion. I would object to being represented as he represents them, as a lot of helpless mendicants. They are not that.

Deputy Leyden knows of Roscommon people who have made good in their own county and outside it, in their own country and outside it and people from all the other western counties who have made fortunes for themselves and for all belonging to them, who have established businesses which are second to none in this country. He knows they have as much enterprise and as much self reliance as the rest of us. Why then is there all that béal bochtery? I resent it as somebody of western descent and I believe I speak for all the people in Roscommon when I say I resent that kind of talk. The Deputy's entire speech yesterday was "wisha, would you grudge him a few pence to put on a horse, wisha, would you grudge him a few pence for a pint, wisha, are you going to take the £3,000 grant off this incredible man who could not make up his mind if he wanted to get married or only wanted the money". He was in some dilemma which must be unique. He could not get married because he had not got the £3,000 and he could not get the £3,000 without being married. Wisha, could the Coalition not take pity on this unfortunate man, if he actually exists, the friend of Deputy Leyden. Wisha, could we not do more for the people, stuff more money into this and more money into that. If I was a Roscommon voter I would resent being represented in the national parliament as a mere recipient of charity. The same goes for the rest of Ireland and the whole western seaboard and every other part of Ireland about which language like that is used.

I am tired of hearing Deputies on the far side of the House saying that they come from a constituency in the west. It is as if the people who voted for them were the only real votes that counted, that votes cast by people in this part of the country were not votes at all, that the people who live in my constituency do not count and their nationality is only provisional. Most of my constituency organisation consists of people who were born in the country. There is no deliberate pattern about it but it happens that one of the branches in my constituency consists almost entirely of people from Cavan and Monaghan, another consists almost entirely of people from Cork and another one has a very strong Mayo representation.

One border is enough in the country. There is no border between east and west. We have all got roots all around the country. Some of the people I am talking about have brothers, sisters, aunts, uncles and cousins whom they very frequently see either in Dublin or the part of the country they come from. The béal bocht perpetually shown on behalf of the west is something which I believe the west resents. I had better remind Deputy Leyden that he comes from a county which is a banner county in a very important respect. It is a county in which Count Plunkett stood for the first Sinn Féin by-election in 1917. I am sure Count Plunkett, who stood for Sinn Féin, was not showing the béal bocht on behalf of Roscommon or the other counties around there. I am sure the message Count Plunkett gave and which the people in Roscommon wanted him to give was the message implicit in his party, Sinn Féin: "We will stand on our own legs and we will not go begging". If Deputy Leyden and other Deputies on the other side of the House have nothing better to say than to ask the Government to give another few ha'pence here and there, they would be better off staying silent.

60th Anniversary of Civil War, Dublin, 21 June 1982

Sixty years ago this week the Civil War began. The issues which split the national movement in two did not seem then worth having a civil war to settle; in the retrospect of today they make the war seem a tragic disaster, as though there were really some mí-ádh or jinx on Irish affairs, such as drew from Michael Collins the despairing cry: "Is Ireland never to get a chance?"

It is conventional to lament the "bitterness" which the Civic War left behind it, as though that were its only evil legacy. In fact, considering the terrible deed of taking up arms against the first native Government — the dream of generations, and supported by a clear democratic majority — and considering the terrible things the Government did to put down the rebellion, the degree of enduring bitterness has been very small. What animus can be seen in politics today is more the product of ordinary partisan sentiment — like the enthusiasm for a football team which can drive people to act like hooligans — than a residue of spite left over since before most of us were born.

A far worse, more lasting consequence of the events of 1922 has been the effect on the economic management of the country. The civil war divided the movement in whose original programme economic independence and prosperity had been an important feature, and, having divided it, set the sundered halves in competition with one another for political support.

This did not do much economic damage for as long as old-fashioned financial prudence and rectitude in the State's behalf were practised fairly consistently by both sides. But then standards slipped. We had a 12% wage increase — huge by the measure of the day — in order to win two by-elections in 1964; and we have now been running a current budget deficit since 1971. The deficit was at first fairly insignificant; but it has since increased by huge annual leaps and bounds, reined back only twice in eleven years, by Richie Ryan in 1976, and by John Bruton this year, on both occasions by means of a set of tough budgetary measures.

The unpopularity of this discipline was of course fully exploited by Mr Haughey and Professor O'Donoghue, who told the people there was no need to be "hypnotised by figures", and that another little fix of foreign debt wouldn't do us any harm.

That reckless and wicked style of political competition goes far beyond anything that this party ever attempted. We lost the 1977 election partly, and the 1982 election entirely because we stopped well short of any such ruthless unscrupulousness, by which the people's future, and their children's — so far as the State's capacity to influence it goes — is hocked off, bit by bit, for party advantage.

But the addiction to the drug of cheap popularity is catching. It would be absurd to pretend that this party never took a decision in Government, or made a promise in Opposition, influenced by anything but sober considerations of the good of the economy. And as long as we are in competition with a large party supported by much the same kind of people as ourselves, aiming at the same floating vote, there will be the danger, in spite of good intentions, of our trying to match their bogus generosity at elections.

Where does this leave the country and this party? I said before that we would do better to decline in advance any coalition with Labour, for so long at least as that party's internal rules and its recent mode of conducting itself make them so difficult to do business with; and for so long as their terms for coalition would include a programme designed to expand the role of the State — the reverse of what the country needs at the present juncture.

We should face the next election alone, with no compromises made with, or hostages given to any other party. I believe the support for Fine Gael and its leader has been growing steadily since 1977, and never faster than in recent months. This spread of support could develop wildfire speed according as disillusionment with the present Taoiseach's regime begins to turn into panic; and a Fine Gael campaign aimed at an overall majority through winning an extra seat in about half the country's constituencies would succeed.

That belief may seem a naive piece of partisan enthusiasm, and it could of course happen that in spite of a successful campaign and the gain of many seats, we were still a few seats short of control. No one can be certain of victory, and I do not think we should practice the vain "We'll be there!" boastfulness of Fianna Fáil which they went in for before their 1981 defeat, and again before their defeat in Dublin West, which had no effect but to deepen their humiliation when they lost. What options would in this event be open to us, assuming a Labour alliance had been ruled out from the start, and assuming that we would also decline the responsibility of running a minority Government depending on day-to-day Labour support or forbearance?

The options would be two. We could, firstly, remain in Opposition, consolidate, and hope for final success the next time round: this option, implying a continuing FF minority Government, dependent entirely on keeping in with and conciliating small numbers of deputies, would leave the country still travelling, but with gathering speed, on the downward slide.

The other option, admittedly not ours to command, is one which up to now, because of civil-war-conditioned instincts, has been unthinkable: an accommodation, a cooperating truce, with the forces from whom forgotten issues 60 years ago divided us, and from whom, if Ireland had been luckier, we need never have been divided.

I have no idea to what extent, if any, the present membership of the Fianna Fáil party would be open to such an idea. On past form, they would most likely treat it with unanimous scorn. At the same time, many of them seem lately genuinely disposed to put the national interest before party considerations, and seem worried by the way the country is moving; these, at least, might look closer now at an option which formerly was not in view at all. They might also reflect that the option must in theory be as easily exercisable this side of a General Election as afterwards.

If their reaction is to damn such a thing out of hand, they ought to reflect that the electorate, in the dangerous conditions of 1982, could easily take a poor view of politicians' intransigence. The Pavlovian reaction of party activists — on either side — does not necessarily represent what ordinary people feel about the prospect of mending the damage caused in 1922; and of freeing the national government, whether led by us or by F.F., from dictation by a minuscule extreme Left.

There are of course deep differences of ethos, of group temperament between us and our opponents. They are perhaps no greater that would have developed over the years anyway between people who found themselves divided into two separate groups by a quite random distribution, but they are serious enough to provide each side with a set of very negative impression of the other, which obviously must be an obstacle to cooperation.

To us, the Fianna Fáil character seems shifty and irrational on national issues; begrudging and ungenerous to opponents; crudely arrogant and triumphalist when winning; easily satisfied with what Liam Cosgrave called "verbal patriotism"; constitutionally disinclined to give a straight answer to a straight question. Their caricature of us is equally unlovely: I think I could outline its main features, but hope I can be excused from doing so here.

Parties so long estranged, intellectually petrified into postures of mutual hostility, cannot easily be got to cooperate. The National interest might be best served by such an association; but it does not need to be a merger or fusion. No one now is interested in such a thing, and in this party there would be at least as much resistance to it as in Fianna Fáil. All that it need be is an arrangement — I do not care whether it is called a coalition, a front, a pact, or an alliance — to support a Government chosen from both parties, and determined to put party considerations aside at least until the country's economy is restored to full health, with unemployment and inflation beaten, and the State once more able to pay its way year by year.

Any such large alliance, dominating the Dáil with an initial crushing majority of 140 seats or so, would contain dangers of its own. It could become complacent, self-serving, out-of-touch, even corrupt, monopolising power for the benefit of club members. If it allowed itself to forget the claims of social justice, and to be too closely identified with private enterprise and property at the expense of the needs of less privileged people, it could provoke a polarisation of politics here on class lines, exactly what would suit extreme left-wing ideologues.

If these pitfalls could be avoided, the most probably long-term result would be a continuous rise in support for the democratic Labour Party, as providing the only plausible Opposition and ultimately the only plausible alternative. It is quite likely that within one or two General Elections the Labour Party would advance to 50 seats, and hold at least one seat in every constituency in the country. But as things are going at present, with political rewards being seen to go to the most exigent and strident parts of the Left, the Labour Party seems in real danger of being overtaken on that wing by forces of a somewhat different kind.

Another problem of association between the two large parties would be the construction of a rational Northern policy on which both parties could agree; this is a large question which might be left for another day. For the moment it would be enough if we could look with an open mind at the general idea of an option which, on the basis of the general social and economic outlook of the two parties, would seem obvious and painless in any other Western country, but which here, up to now, the dead hand of 1922 had kept off the table.

Confidence Motion, Dáil, 3 November 1982

The Minister who has just spoken was complaining eloquently about "character assassination". He must have meant that his party's leader has suffered from it and been a victim of it. He then moved on to make some attacks on the people of this side of the House, and included someone who is not even in the House any longer. That, of course, is a normal ploy.

I must admit to a certain sympathy with people when they are in a corner and every man's hand seems to be against them. To some degree that is the situation of the Minister's leader. I have to say this to him: I am not aware that in this party there is any animus towards that leader, other than the feeling of resentment and rejection generated by his own actions and his own style over the years he has been in public life. If I may put it in another way, metaphorically speaking, characters who get away with murder cannot be surprised if character assassination attempts are made back on them.

I will be saying something which I hope will be temperate — I will not lay myself open to the rebuke the Minister delivered to my party at large — I will be saying something later about the question of style. It is not entirely irrelevant, particularly when we are a small open country with the presence here of a press corps from a country like the neighbouring British State, which, as the leader of my party said this morning, contains within it a latent hostility towards this country and a latent willingness, and sometimes by no means so latent, to take advantage of our weaknesses, to play upon mistakes, to exploit things which we do wrongly, or which are done wrongly in our name by the Government of the day, or by a faction of the Government, and make us look ridiculous in the eyes of the world.

I concede — and Deputy FitzGerald was quite right to say this — that unhappily that disposition is present in the British press, and it tends to be the medium through which impressions of this country are passed on to the outer world beyond. Therefore, it is particularly important for the Government here to avoid all acts, all utterances, all kinds of behaviour, even in matters not directly concerned with the business of Government, which can attract that kind of notice which makes ordinary Irish people squirm with resentment and sometimes with shame.

I realise I am leaving myself open to the charge of not being specific enough. I do not want to be specific, because I will be accused by the Minister and others of carrying on a character assassination campaign. The Minister opposite does not need me to recite the various episodes, not just over the past eight months, but over the preceding period as well, which invited and duly got very hostile attention from a not over well disposed foreign press.

I believe I am speaking for every Member of the House when I say that personally I am fed up with this country being pilloried in the British press for every half-considered statement thrown out by somebody like the Minister opposite who thinks he can get out from under the implications of what he says by saying: "Of course I am no diplomat". I am fed up with the country being pilloried, misrepresented, done down, blackened, made look ridiculous by things said and done by the party opposite. We have not got a perfect record either. I recognise it is legitimate for the Minister to mention things in our own record which were equally unfortunate.

In the case of the instance he mentioned, that of Deputy Donegan, I have to say this. Whatever Deputy Donegan may have done or said, he did it in a white heat of zeal for this country. What he said was deplorable and inexcusable in many ways. He chose a deplorable time and place to say it, but there was nothing base in his heart, no self-seeking in his heart. He said nothing with which I profoundly disagreed. It came as a thunderbolt to me to find that a member of the government I worked for even entertained such an opinion about the presidential function which President Ó Dálaigh was absolutely entitled to exercise. It never crossed my mind that any one in the Government thought the less of him for doing so. It was a thunderbolt when I heard on the midnight news that Deputy Donegan had spoken as he did. But what he said, deplorable though it was and deplorable though the circumstances were, was said in a white heat of resentment against murderers and savages who the previous day had blown an unarmed garda to pieces.

I wish all the episodes attached with the other side of the House could have at least that much said in their favour. Strangely enough, not so much seems to be expected of them. After the Donegan episode the *Irish Times* — and I am speaking from memory; I may not be absolutely exact about this; I felt very strongly about it and I was probably fairly far out on a limb about it in some ways — ran ten editorials in a row demanding that the then Deputy Liam Cosgrave should dispose of the services of Deputy Donegan and/or himself lay down office and/or go to the country. They based ten in a row on that episode. I am still waiting to hearing a fraction of that amount of indignation being expressed by The Irish Times or any other organ of opinion — about the rank hooliganism seen in the precincts of this House less than three weeks ago when these precincts drunken fisticuffs were engaged in, and why.

These are questions of style, questions of one's associates, questions of the atmosphere and the climate in which one leads one's political existence. The atmosphere in which the Fianna Fáil leadership leads its existence is rank and poisoned. I do not know why it got like that. The Fianna Fáil party were crazy, in my judgment, to have not dropped but sabotaged Deputy Lynch in the way they did. I cannot understand why they panicked at two lost by-elections and gave a chance to a man whose supporters — whom he had diligently massaged and back-slapped, some of them the most obscure and unremarkable members of the party in the Dáil — to collaborate and dig a trench for Deputy Lynch, push him into it and fill in the trench. I thought they were crazy to do that. I still think so, even though Deputy Lynch is a man with whom I often had hard words and to whom I often said hard things.

That is part of the atmosphere which underlies the lack of confidence of which the intention of this party to put down a motion is only a symptom. It is part of the background. I missed the first few minutes of the speech of the Leader of this party this morning, but he dwelt far less on that than on the facts and figures of the economy which alone would be sufficient to warrant any Member of this House voting no confidence in the Government leadership. That picture is a somewhat two-dimensional line drawing and, in order to be filled out, the landscape behind it needs to be inserted in technicolour. That landscape, that climate, that atmosphere in which the Fianna Fáil leadership lives, and in which it seems to thrive, will explain the feeling in the country and in this party and I suppose in the Labour Party — I am not in their confidence — and perhaps to some extent in The Worker's Party.

I think I said a few minutes ago that I could not resist a certain sense of sympathy for a man, whatever his faults, who finds himself in a corner in the way the Taoiseach now does and has been for some long time. At the same time I cannot absolve those who have at last found enough courage to stand up and express disagreement with him in his own party. It may be — I do not rule it out; it would not be a crime anyway — that sheer, naked personal ambition is driving on Deputy Colley, Deputy O'Malley, Deputy McCreevy, Deputy O'Donoghue and all the rest of them. So far as one might have reason to suspect their position as being disingenuous, I suspect it very strongly because, as I think Deputy FitzGerald said earlier today, these people were four-square behind the 1977 election manifesto which was the source and beginning of all our troubles today. Not only were they four-square behind it, but they were the principal dynamoes in it. Senator Eoin Ryan, if I may mention him, was the Chairman and Deputy O'Donoghue was the principal adviser of the committee who spawned this manifesto. I do not recall Deputy Colley or Deputy O'Malley disclaiming it. I do not recall even now that they have said anything publicly about how it was mistaken. Quite the contrary. Only recently — I hope that I am not doing him wrong by saying this — I heard Deputy O'Malley saying on the radio that he had not known about the Gregory deal. He heard Deputy Gregory read that deal into a record of the House the evening Deputy Haughey was elected Taoiseach before he himself had been nominated to the Government. If he was so shocked and astonished by it then, was it not open to him to refuse to serve in that Government? I admit that in the elation and euphoria of seeing the leader of your party elected your judgment can be distorted, and it may be that that excuse could be made for him, but that he knew nothing about the deal before accepting office and serving in that Government is not true. I sat here, as he did, and listened to the details being read into the record of the House before Deputy Haughey announced his Government, from which presumably Deputy O'Malley was at that stage free to withdraw. The same can be said for Deputy O'Donoghue, and he felt like that. I am not impressed by these political penitents, these political Magdalens who are now wringing their hands about the state of the country and the state of their party under its present leadership. They are going around with, so to speak, their long hair down around their shoulders in despair and contrition _____.

Mrs Geoghegan-Quinn: Not mine, Deputy.

I take the Minister's point — for the part they may have played in bringing it to its present condition. I have very little sympathy with them on that score, but I want to say this about the Fianna Fáil dissidents. I left the Front Bench of my party in order to do what little I could to encourage people on both sides of the House, and outside, to think seriously of where we were going, to look up from the smoke, dust and powder of the political battlefield and the silly bragging and blackening which goes on, which passes here for the deliberations of the national Parliament, and which goes on even worse outside. I have not met with a great deal of sympathy from my own party for the point of view I have tried to express. Those of them who are friendly enough to talk to me for my own good, so to speak, tell me that I am making a big mistake about the Fianna Fáil Party if I think that they have the national interest at heart in the way that I suppose, or that a number of them, or even any of them have. They are there for thing only — I am told — namely to get in and to stay in and the devil take the hindmost. Perhaps I am making a big mistake and maybe I am politically naive. In years I am not a child. I am very far removed, I am sorry to say, from childhood; but perhaps I am merely being childish in supposing that in the Fianna Fáil Parliamentary Party, or the party at large, or their support throughout the country, there is some willingness to put the country first and the party second. I may be making a big mistake; but I am willing to stake something on my belief that they are not devils incarnate, and they are not all, or all of the time, selfishly committed to their own party interest and indifferent to the larger issues which the country has to face.

Economic situation, Dáil, 26 October 1983

Provocativeness is a very relative thing. Now that we are talking about people being provocative, it is only about three weeks, in the context of the New Ireland Forum's operations, since a little deputation from it went to tour the North of Ireland. When Deputy Lenihan, much to his credit, and Deputy Andrews, who were part of the deputation, were entering a hotel in Derry they were met by a group of demonstrators representing the Paisleyite interests. All Deputy Lenihan had to say to them was, "How are you, lads," and the placards began to fly. The Paisleyites said afterwards that they were treated provocatively by the people from the Republic. They regarded that as provocation. They have got awfully thin skins in the Paisleyite party. They cannot even take, "How are you, lads?" from Deputy Lenihan without feeling provoked.

I want to say this about the "hard heart" allegation. Deputy Haughey himself has the name of being soft-hearted. To be fair to him, I have no reason to think that, on a personal level, he is hard hearted or unfeeling. I have heard from his friends and foes alike that he is a man to whom one can go with a hard case. That is a human quality for which no one wants to take credit from him. But, when he is operating on the public level, when he is saying things, whether in Government or Opposition, which are intended to affect the course of the Government's steering of the economy, expressions like "hard heart" and "soft heart"are out of place.

I want to remind him that some of the most disastrous bullies in European history prided themselves on their soft hearts. Hitler loved to be photographed with little children giving him bunches of flowers. Mussolini had a special personal office staffed with over 100 people, which did nothing else than receive, open, deal with and respond generously to petitions from people who were down in their luck.

A man like the Duce could ruin his people's hopes for a generation or two; he could drive them into adventures for which they had neither competence, spirit nor heart; he could cost millions of them their lives — but he had a "soft heart". It could never have been said about the Duce that you could not go to him for a 500-lire note, or that if you were in trouble you could not write to him for help. He would pat you paternally on the head.

When listening to Deputy Haughey it is quite hard to be sure whether he is in his inflationist, deflationist or reflationist phase, because his revolutions, according to whether he is in or out of power, according as he perceives some necessity relating to his own career, change so rapidly that you could be just about focusing on Deputy Haughey's reflation stage when you notice that that is all off, that was last month, and we are now on to a different facet of his philosophy. Then it was something more responsible, more stringent. This time he has decided that it is the moment for "modest reflation".

The talk which we thought we had put an end to at the time of the election in 1982 about "self-financing subsidies" is on the deck again. This time he has not got Deputy Reynolds to float it for him — we wish him a speedy recovery — but Deputy Haughey is himself floating the "self-financing subsidies", the "self-remunerating tax cuts". I wish Deputy Haughey would let the ball out to the financial wizards of the rest of the world who have not been able to think up simultaneously satisfactory self-financing tax cuts and self-remunerating systems of borrowing. Let us not be selfish about this. We are always boasting about our spiritual empire, bringing the higher light to the barbarians in the outer undiscovered parts of the world. Let us let out the secret of the self-financing tax cuts to them, the self-supporting borrowings and subsidies. Let us not be greedy about it. Many things could be said about the Irish, but we are not an ungenerous people. We are not dogs in the manger. Therefore, let us hear about how to establish and run a self-financing tax cut or conduct self-remunerating borrowing.

Naturally, none of them is home grown, because the party of the rear guard do not believe in anything homegrown. Mr de Valera is gone. They sniggered about him behind his back when he was there, and they can laugh freely about him now, whatever they may say in public. His slightly homespun variety of economics is, of course, forgotten, as is that of Sean Lemass. Instead of using words coined by either gentleman, they import their vocabulary of political abuse. According to them, the people on this side are "monetarists", "Thatcherites".

I do not believe that there are three people on the Fianna Fáil benches who could give on the back of a postcard a coherent account of what monetarism is. But it does not matter, because it has a nasty complicated ring about it. It conjures up professors, well paid, battening on the taxpayers, who will never stand in a dole queue. It has a nice populist ring about it that can be slung from the top of a barrel or the back of a lorry at an election meeting and the simpler souls, who are probably in their pockets anyhow, will be impressed with it.

We are being accused of "Thatcherism". There was a time when Mrs Thatcher was top cat with Deputy Haughey. That was when she started out. She and Deputy Haughey were going to put the North of Ireland to rights. He suddenly discovered that Mrs Thatcher was made of the kind of stuff that is not very much in evidence in his party or perhaps even in wider circles. He began to realise that it would take more than a silver teapot to make her do what every instinct warned her against, namely, to trust him. And, of course, she became public enemy No. 1 and now she is so low in the stakes that her very name has become an acceptable term of abuse.

I will tell him something about Mrs Thatcher — although, if I were British, I do not think I would ever vote for her party because I regard the English Tories, from occasional glimpses of them on television, as a crew I have not much in common with. I will say this for Mrs Thatcher and the single-mindedness with which she has pursued a certain policy, namely, that of reducing inflation: the result of this policy can be seen in this republic. I will tell you how.

Deputy McGahon is behind me; and he will bear me out, and he will be able to speak more eloquently about it than I. Weekend after weekend busload upon busload of our people, with their pockets stuffed with our money, cross the Border to the North and buy goods there, not merely goods that are differentiated against by high excise rates of VAT here but even flitches of bacon, sides of ham, halves of sheep, to bring back here for their deep freezes. That is what Thatcherism is about in the UK economy. At a dreadful cost, undoubtedly, in terms of unemployment, she has managed that, because she has succeeded in reducing the prices of goods sold in the shops in the UK to a point when it pays the people in Dundalk to desert Deputy McGahon's constituency and travel over the Border. It pays not only them, but it pays people in Deputy Durkan's constituency. Publicans and shopkeepers in Mayo are wringing their hands at their public representatives and in appeals to a Government who failed to apply that kind of discipline in recent years.

If we had had that kind of discipline here since 1976 or so, if Richie Ryan, who is nearly approaching national hero status, had been allowed to continue in 1977, if he had not been put out by Dr. Bunsen and his tax-free cars, this situation would have been reversed.

If we had had a Government here since 1977 — we have one now which may get back to that situation — our affairs would not have taken a turn away from the direction begun by Richie Ryan and the Government he worked in, and which I worked for with pride. It would have meant bus trips over the Border — but they would have been in the opposite direction, as once upon a time they used to be. There would have been buses travelling over the Border in this direction, stuffed with people with pocketfuls of money buying in the towns represented by Deputy McGahon. That is what Thatcherism is, about which we hear in the whingeing and whining of people who are deserting those towns because they do not want to spend money in them. Deputy Haughey should remember that when he talks about monetarism and Thatcherism.

There is no secret about monetarism. I am not an economist and I could not give a coherent account of monetarism that would satisfy my son, for example, who is in the course of becoming an economist. But basically it means something that everybody does anyway in their own private housekeeping, namely, making sure that the amount of money they spend in a week or the amount of credit they take up does not exceed the amount they take in, or, if it exceeds it in one week, making sure they have a good chance they will be able to cover it within a reasonable time. I will give it a home grown name — it is Lemassian or de Valerian economics. When I hear people talking about this Government having a "hard heart", being "obsessed with figures" and being anxious to "run an economy while not having any time for the people", I have to say "show me any difference between that point of view and that which you were proud to support when it was being put into effect by Deputy Lemass and Deputy de Valera 30 and 40 years ago

There were hard times in the thirties. I have often said in this House that I

74

have a regard and a respect for many of the acts of the Fianna Fáil Government of those days, and I do not feel they were all devil-inspired, as some of my colleagues at that time used to think. They were hard times of poverty and deprivation. That did not all end in 1932 with the change of Government. The thirties were times of hardship, although I can sympathise with some of the reasons for the Economic War, Deputies opposite are too young to remember anything about it, but they know that they were times of hardship, as were the forties, except for the unusual war conditions which meant that there was a strong market for many Irish products and there was nothing to buy with the money, hence reserves were built up. There were also hard times during the fifties, but whether a Fianna Fáil Government were in office or an inter-party Government, no Taoiseach or Minister for Finance went in for the "soft heart". They would have thought it beneath them and despised that talk. Of course, they themselves had soft hearts; and I am certain that Deputy de Valera and Deputy Costello and their Ministers felt grieved at the condition of ordinary people. But they were not contemptible enough to accuse one another of having "hard hearts" because they did not borrow recklessly in order to alleviate conditions temporarily.

Deputy Haughey of all people is the most discredited when it comes to economic management. He has given a whole new meaning to the word "discredited". He begins where the rest of his party leave off, even Deputy Lenihan. There is no man in Ireland whose name is entitled to be listened to, on matters of economic management, with less attention than Deputy Haughey. To have that Deputy demand two days of economic debate is like Al Capone calling for a crackdown on gambling rackets.

In the years after 1977 almost every economic indicator, except for those temporarily influenced by simply throwing money at the economy, went downhill. Deputy Haughey made great play this morning of the dreadful unemployment figures which are likely to get worse before they get better. The events of 1977 are receding into history, and I can see at least one Deputy in the House who will not remember as an adult what was happening then. In that year we were promised by Deputy O'Donoghue, who at that time belonged to the despised tribe of academics, that we were going to break out of encirclement. He compared us to a party of settlers crossing some unsettled, uninhabited and dangerous part of the mid-West surrounded by a moving circle of whooping Indians. Were we to stay there crouched behind the wheels of the wagons and the powder barrels trying to pick off the occasional Indian and being gradually worn down ourselves, or were we to try to break out? His solution was that we were to break out. By that time the economy had already very largely broken out of the mid-seventies recession, and every important indicator was tending upwards, as he had the courage subsequently to admit. It came rather curiously from a man who was saying the exact opposite in 1977.

Haughey and President Reagan, Dublin, 1 June 1984

It is elementary courtesy that if you issue an invitation to someone, expecting him to put on a particular kind of performance for you, you inform him of this at the outset, so as to give him a chance of refusing. It is a breach of elementary courtesy to allow him to accept, and then ballyrag him in public, the day before he arrives, about how it will be a "grievous disappointment" if he does not do this or that, and about how his hosts "are not prepared to accept vague expressions of friendship and goodwill". Moreover, it is insulting to invite someone to address you, thus pretending that you are interested in hearing his opinions, when in fact what you want to hear is your own opinions coming out through your guest's mouth.

Mr Haughey committed both of those faults in his speech yesterday to the Cairde Fáil lunch; and, because he insists on keeping such a high international profile on Northern Ireland affairs, has to some extent involved the rest of us in his crude political manners.

The episode, however, has dimensions going beyond mere political etiquette. It shows the Fianna Fáil leader's complete ignorance of, or more likely his contempt for, the feelings of the Northern majority. The sight of his pulling at American coat- tails in an effort to get them to push the British into forcing the North of Ireland into this Republic is certain to infuriate even moderate unionists, let alone people like the primitive bigot on the Belfast City Council who wants to incinerate Catholics.

If he had deliberately set out to make them dig their heels in, if possible, a couple of inches deeper, he could not have succeeded better.

Surely, also, there is something shaming in the sight of an Irish party leader going in for this public whingeing with the object of getting a foreign power to initiate the arm-twisting of other Irish people? Surely ordinary members of Fianna Fáil — and not merely Des O'Malley and his supporters — must feel that the national pride, as well as the ultimate conversion of unionists, demands a more self-respecting approach?

It might seem a desperate choice, but I think I would rather see Fianna Fáil's Northern policies entrusted to the breezy recklessness of Brian Lenihan than to Mr Haughey's unerringly malignant touch.

The Electoral Message of the Europe Poll, Dublin, 25 June 1984

Mid-term electoral tests on small polls are untrustworthy but they are all we have to go on. This month's national election for the European Parliament suggests that, if a General Election were held, Fine Gael would win perhaps 64 seats, Fianna Fáil perhaps 72, and the remaining 30 would be split between Labour, the Workers Party, Sinn Féin and Independents.

Whether, even supposing a continuation of the Coalition agreement, Labour could provide 20 out of these 30 seats, so as to give a clear Coalition majority, must seem highly unlikely. Fianna Fáil would also be about a dozen seats short of power; so that we would see airports, free ports, self-financing tax cuts, and all manner of deals and strokes flying like snuff at a wake. Then when the resulting hamstrung Government of political cripples had collapsed after eight or nine months, the whole process would start all over again.

It is a prospect to make the Irish people feel like shutting up shop altogether; and there will be people waiting for that moment to exploit their despair, to wreck our free institutions, and to turn the running of the country over to East German "technicians" and Cuban "advisers".

It is intolerable that the broad mass of people, who want to work, to build up some substance for themselves while helping the needs of others, to pay a fair rate of tax but no more, should be defeated time after time in these legitimate wishes by the paralysis of the political system, in which the chronic malignant distribution of forces means that every initiative is checkmated or undermined by threatened loss of sectional support, and that political fear every day dominates the counsels of Government and Opposition alike.

An alternating succession of weak and apprehensive administrations can make no permanent impact on the large national problems which we scarcely seem nearer solving now than we were 15 years ago. Only a Government with support so broad and deep that it need not fear sectional unpopularity, or the erosion of occasional defections, can hope to achieve:

a) the land reform which will ensure that, whether by incentives or disincentives or more imperative means, the best use is made of what is a limited national resource, and that people willing to make that use are not denied access to a viable holding;

b) control and reduction of the swollen public service numbers, and the general extravagance of public expenditure, which clings with the deadly luxuriance of ivy to the wasted stem of wealth tax should figure as a measure of social equity;

c) a thorough reform of taxation, in which at least some moderate element of wealth tax should figure a measure of social equity;

d) the elimination of abuse in the social welfare system, which together with crushing taxation drives the industrious P.A.Y.E. earner or self-employed to infuriation;

e) a proper reform of local government organisation, in which instead of the present futile structure of nearly powerless councils, making news mostly through lamentable interventions in the planning process, extravagant delegations to useless "conferences" abroad, and mean party hogging of mayoralties and chairmanships, there would be a system which would oblige each district to accept responsibility for its own economic development and welfare as well as for the more traditional areas of local administration, barely changed since the days of the Irish R.M.;

f) the elimination of abuses and defects in industrial law and practice, such as the insane proliferation of unions and the resultant destructive competition for members.

This list could be supplemented with a recital of various social ulcers, like the problems of itinerant people, which seem equally beyond the nerveless grasp of the parties alternating in power. When we have solved problems like these, it will be time enough for us to lecture the world about our sacred neutrality, or bore the ears off them about the "unitary state" we "aspire" to.

A weak Government, with a fearful eye cast permanently over its shoulder, has little hope of beating even one of these problems; and this description must particularly include the kind of administration we would get from an under-strength Fianna Fáil, even now making sheep's eyes at the Labour Party in the hope that the latter might somehow be persuaded to make up the deficit in seats to which the former, by its ruinous recent record as well as its deeply suspect leadership, is doomed for the foreseeable future.

The only way to give the people the kind of government they want and are entitled to is for the two big parties to declare an indefinite truce; to pick up the frayed ends of the broken bonds which once united them in the same great national movement; to find, as they will easily find, enough common ground on which to build a programme of progress and reform immune from political disruption; and ruthlessly to discard any factional leader whose political life depends on mean and petty bickering and begrudging, on reckless stunts that are to be paid for God knows by who, and on keeping Civil War ghosts on a cynical life-support machine.

F.F. declining into senility,
Dublin, 19 November 1984

The hysterical reaction of Fianna Fáil to the liquidation of Irish Shipping is a perfect sample of the quality of Opposition over the past two years. Indifferent to the Company's disastrous recent past or its prospects, reckless as to how much money it might cost to rescue it or as to where that money was to come from, seeing only a chance to shout "national saboteurs" at a Government trying to save £200m of people's money, their performance once more cruelly exposed their bare intellectual cupboard.

In this episode Fianna Fáil can be seen to have retreated into a mindlessness that one of their great heroes, Sean Lemass, would never have displayed. Sean Lemass said once that while State companies were needed for carrying out tasks that private enterprise could not manage, there was always the danger that they could cease to serve the national interest, or begin to serve only themselves. The sane frankness of Sean Lemass seems however to be no longer in fashion in the party he left behind.

This was seen also in their reaction to the Government's economic plan "Building on Reality", discussed by the Dáil on its resumption last month. This plan is not perhaps of electrifying excitement. It shows some signs of compromise, and contains no fundamental innovation, no radical turning of the soil of the Irish economy and society of the kind we need. But it is a plain, sober statement of intent, concentrates on attacking obvious problems and avoids all cheap flummery. There is no brandishing of 1977-style phrases like "tens of thousands of jobs only waiting to be created". On the contrary, by the starkness of its admissions and by the very modesty of its targets, it compels respect.

The Opposition reaction to it, on the other hand, was as dull, as negative and uninspiring, as anything a bankrupt party ever spent five tedious days elaborating. Plenty of weary, predictable, uneatable rhetoric; but not one usable idea can be trawled from the speeches of Mr Haughey, Mr O'Kennedy, Mr Reynolds, Mr Flynn and the rest.

Their theme was "heart", and the Government's lack of it. To hear all their talk about "heartlessness", you would swear that Government expenditure, when Fianna Fáil were in office, all came out of Ministers' private pockets; and that Fine Gael economies on the other hand are attributable to Ministers' personal meanness. If the ruinous prodigality of the 1977-81 period showed "heart", we have had enough heart to last us the rest of our lives. A little more of Mr Haughey's "heart", and we would be trying to sell off a couple of counties to pay for it.

In the same debate Mr Haughey placed great rhetorical emphasis on "the spectre of emigration". I think it is absolutely wicked for an Irish politician to keep alive in 1984 the fetish against working outside Ireland, as though a well-paid, exciting, and — depending on the individual's wishes — not necessarily final job in the continental E.E.C., one hour's flight from Dublin, still carried the horrors of the Queenstown wakes.

To recognise the reality of our rapid population increase, and our inability in the past to provide jobs for everyone even when the increase was less rapid and conditions more favourable, is not defeatist but only prudent. If we shout down those who point the problem out, and point also to the opportunities on our European doorstep — where in Western Germany there will be 6 million fewer people of working age in 25 years' time than there are today — we are sacrificing young people's chances of fulfilment to a cheap politician's desire to have his vainglorious boasts taken as firm guarantees for the future. Now is the time to adapt our educational and placement services, and not leave those of the next generation who may wish to work abroad, with no better prospect of doing so than as tongue-tied hewers of wood and drawers of water.

Junk politics, Dublin, 24 June 1985

If the local elections results can be read — as a comparison of our canvass and tally returns suggests they can — as a demonstration of listlessness on the part of many Fine Gael supporters who did not bother to vote, together perhaps with an element of protest against the pace of "pluralism" which some of them do not like, there is no great cause to worry. No damage has been done that two years of sustained good government and effective communication with the people cannot put right.

On the other hand, if Fianna Fáil are correct in their reading of the result as a vote of censure on the Government's whole economic management,then the country is in very serious trouble indeed, and the long-term outlook for us as an independent and prosperous state is terrifying.

What the Fianna Fáil interpretation means is this: the people are entitled to fully-staffed schools and hospitals wherever they find it convenient to have them; to an endless supply of State-created jobs; and, where a lobby vocal enough can be assembled, even to airports paid for out of public funds. On the other hand, they ought not to pay land tax; they ought not to pay wealth tax; they ought not to pay water charges; their P.A.Y.E. burden ought to be lightened. They ought to be given more "power" in the shape of more funds for their local councils to dispense; but their councillors ought not to be asked to carry the responsibility and odium of raising those funds through any form of local charge or tax.

This is a dreaming child's vision of life; but this unfortunately is what Fianna Fáil of late have specialised in persuading the people to accept as reality. Their currency is the self-financing subsidy, the self-supporting concession, the

80

sums made to add up through "buoyancy" and "savings", the soft option, the cheap cheer.

It was not always so; and many people can remember Sean Lemass's constant theme, the need for people to understand that we could not give ourselves, in pay or services, more than we earned, and that the result of living beyond our means would be disaster in public affairs, just as it is in private life.

The present juncture illustrates clearly what I have tried to say for the last three years: in the philosophy of financial and economic management there is no difference between the two big parties; or rather, between ourselves and what *used* to be Fianna Fáil under de Valera or Lemass.

Nothing is being done by the Fine Gael-led Government that de Valera or Lemass would not have done if beset by the same central problem of gigantic public debt. Neither of them ever saw, or would for an instant have countenanced, a budget deficit filled by borrowing for current purposes. Neither of them would, if left in charge of a State owing *fifteen billion pounds*, think of offering to relieve taxation by increasing the debt still further.

There are thousands of influential people in and behind Fianna Fáil who know this perfectly well. Why then do they put up with the corruption of their party by the kind of junk politics which Mr Haughey has perfected? Do they really hate Fine Gael and Labour so much that anything, even the destruction of the economy and of the independent Irish State and people, is a fair price to pay for winning elections?

If so, we are in the grip of something like a modern analogue of the pressures on the late Roman emperors, who could secure the stability of their government only through the loyalty of their soldiers, and who were forced to buy that loyalty through bigger and bigger distributions of money, which their rivals were obliged to emulate and outbid.

I don't say the local elections point to the decline and fall of the Irish Republic. But I do say we are in the grip of a most malignant competition, in a political world gone mad. It is up to Fine Gael, and the responsible element of Fianna Fáil, to break a way out of it together.

Confidence Motion, Dáil, 20 February 1986

None of their contributions that I can judge, with very rare exceptions, contains a constructive suggestion. The moment one of them comes near saying anything new, challenging, interesting and true, he shies away from it because it may be a political hot potato. I marked with a red letter a date last October when Deputy Michael O'Kennedy said here that we should look to the EC as a place in which we might find a quantity of good permanent employment for the people who cannot find it here. When I applauded him he recoiled and said he was not saying that at all. It was the one interesting contribution he had to make but even that was not allowed to stand.

Last week we had the shouting and banging of tables about the book-keeping on the one hand and the cutbacks on the other. That is not a serious way to treat the people who elected us or the Opposition; we behaved like that in the past but never with the same degree of recklessness or monotony. I dealt at some length with Deputy Haughey's contribution on the budget last week. I carefully combed Deputy Haughey's contribution for a single constructive contribution which might lead to any sort of concrete economic development. The only one I can find, and even that is not so clear, is contained on column 1637 of the Official Report for 5 February. He said:

> Britain and France, though in the midst of an economic recession, are about to undertake one of the biggest construction problems ever. Should we not be thinking along the same lines with of course European resources being involved?

The reference, I have no need to tell the House, was to the Channel Tunnel agreement signed a couple of days previously between the British and French Prime Ministers. Are we to take it seriously that he is now considering a tunnel not crossing the English Channel but St. George's Channel, the Irish Sea?

It is not unfair to ask somebody who has a very high opinion of his own skills in economic management to say exactly what he meant by that reference. Does he want to see a tunnel across the Irish Sea? It may well be that one day technology will become so cheap and available that that will be a serious proposition; but is it a serious proposition at present to mention something like this in the context of a budget debate, when this is his only concrete suggestion, except for the old talk which has been there from the time of Arthur Griffith about forestry and fisheries?

The trade and passenger traffic between Britain and the Continent is roughly 15 or 20 times greater than the volume of trade and passenger traffic between this country and Britain. It has still taken the British and French Governments the best part of a century to come to an agreement in regard to building a tunnel, although the techniques of tunnel building, even submarine tunnel building, were available as long ago as the 1860's or 1870's. It has still taken that long for them to feel that the thing can be an economically viable proposition; and the tunnel they are talking about will run across the shortest of all the sea passages in these islands except for the North Channel — 14 miles. That is about a quarter of the distance from Dún Laoghaire to Holyhead or from Rosslare to Fishguard. I do not want to be regarded as a stick-in-the-mud or as throwing cold water on a project which may indeed one day be viable; but is it sensible for a man who thinks so much of himself in this area to speak like that now?

That is the only concrete suggestion I can find in his budget contribution, and it is so wildly ludicrous, so recklessly out of touch with any sort of reality, economic or for all I know even engineering — there may be problems about the Irish Sea that do not exist in the other channel — that one really questions his title to the rank of economic expert which he seems happy enough to have others bestow on him.

I look then at the other side of national policy, the electorally not very important but nationally important matter of Northern Ireland, and I have to look at how this substitute alternative Taoiseach conducted himself over the last two years and led his wretched party. Deputy Cooney said that he was head and shoulders above them intellectually, and that is so, because anybody comparable to him intellectually has got out of it or never joined it in the first place. He is able to reduce by bullying his footmen and lackeys to order and keep them there, and he was able to lay on during the Forum operation in 1983-84 a plot to sabotage what might come out at the far end.

He started that Forum operation off on a basis which was clearly unrealistic, and he took advantage of the Taoiseach's good nature and anxiety for success to load that Forum report with three impossible options which absolutely guaranteed that the Government and people of this country would endure the humiliation which Mrs Thatcher inflicted on us in November 1984 at Chequers; which is why I did not sign it.

I said before that I think the Taoiseach was mistaken to seen consensus with Fianna Fáil on a matter like this. A maiden lady might as well be seeking consensus with a highwayman as to seek consensus with Fianna Fáil under their existing leadership on a matter of this kind. It would have been far better if we had had a minority report, or two or three or ten reports, rather than leave this Government holding an absolutely unviable, unfloatable document. I felt terribly bitter and badly about that. I could see it coming from the day Deputy Haughey made his first speech at the opening of the Forum; I cannot tell the House how badly and bitter I felt about it. An immense quantity of Government time was wasted on the Forum culminating in that report, the first four chapters of which are harmless and pacific and with which I have no fault to find, but the rest of which could not possibly recommend itself to anybody in the world except an Irish Nationalist — and we are dealing with people one million of whom would fight rather than accept that label.

I do not need to tell the House of the misgivings I have had all along about a Coalition of my party with Labour, but I could not support a motion of this kind. How could I vote no confidence in a Government the only alternative to which is that?

When I come to the style of the alternative Taoiseach I do not need to dwell on the autocracy which he enforces on his own party. There have been some comical developments in the last few weeks. There was some talk of declarations of loyalty being exacted from local units, on the style of the Oath of Supremacy which Henry VIII exacted. I do not know if that process has gone very far, but I remember it being signalled. I do not want to be run by a Government led by a person with that sort of political instinct. I would far sooner by led by somebody who is tolerant, as the Taoiseach is, who is willing to accept dissent in his own party without feeling it is a personal effort to undermine himself and who is prepared to be civil and courteous to those who have a different view about his Government strategy. I believe the people prefer that too.

I want to draw the attention of the House to another feature of the Deputy's style which, for some reason, never seems to surface here in a general debate. This is his treatment of this House and specifically of yourself, Sir. I have been watching him here over the last year or so, as everyone else has, and I have been contrasting it with his original declarations of good intent to tidy up the Dáil. He was going to be the cool, clean hero riding in from the prairie to clear the ill-conducted elements out of this House. We were going to have a little order at last. Anybody who compares the Dáil reports of virtually any day nowadays with the way they were under Deputy Joe Brennan, under Deputy Seán Treacy, or Deputy Pádraig Faulkner will see what has happened. Day after day — I am sorry to say this to you, Sir, you know that I combine this with a strong regard for you — you are forced to submit to bullying from the Leader of the Opposition. I have leafed through the reports since the beginning of the session before Christmas and there are at least a dozen instances since late last autumn, when the House re-assembled, on which he was told on the Order of Business that he was out of order and on which he kept on talking. We are all out of order occasionally but this has been brought to a system and naturally his footmen imitate him and think they are going to get a good mark if they turn the Order of Business here day after day into a dog's dinner. We seldom start the real business here before 15 or 20 minutes have elapsed after the Taoiseach has announced the Order of Business. That is due to the example given by the Leader of the party who had put down a motion that he should step into the Taoiseach's shoes. Never.

He has an oh-so-well practised, urbane exterior but sometimes that exterior slips. Sometimes the front slips and then something not quite so pretty emerges.

I did not enjoy having to speak as I did in December 1979 when Deputy Haughey became Taoiseach. I genuinely dislike having to speak in this way about the person who is at the core of and behind this motion — because it was he who first announced that he intended to put such a motion to the House. If that Deputy was to leave public life, if he was in some other setting in life, I have no doubt that we would get on very well; but I regard it as essential, although I dislike having to do it, to draw attention to these characteristics which for me and for a huge majority of Irish people disqualify him from the leadership which he seeks.

The record of the years when he presided here for speaks for itself. A couple of Deputies from the Fianna Fáil side, either by way of interruption or in the course of a speech, claimed that in the era 1977 to 1981 — the Government ran for three years and ten months — 80,000 jobs were created. That is a very curious claim because the seasonally adjusted unemployment figures show that there were fewer people employed in June 1981, seasonally adjusted, than there were in December of 1979 when deputy Haughey first came in. When one goes down through the list of other economic indicators — inflation was left at 24 per cent, the trade deficit was out through the roof — one wonders at the nerve, as Deputy Cooney said, of a party who could seriously pretend to offer themselves, at any rate under their existing leadership and with their existing policies, to the people again.

I will keep repeating as long as I have a seat in this House, that the divisions between the two sides in here are unreal, that the true divisions are ones between — I say this without any hostility or animosity — people who think like Deputy MacGiolla and people who essentially think about the economy in the way Deputy O'Kennedy and myself do. It is because of the unreality of this that we are driven back on this awful political dog-fight that is intensely boring to the people. They hate it. I cannot understand why Deputies opposite, or those on this side, will not get that into their heads. They go to their own Ard Fheis, see their party leader on the platform being wildly applauded by 6,000 or 7,000 people, but do not understand that that is a tiny minority of the people in the country.

It may be that they have left three times that number at home who could not make the journey to Dublin or could not be bothered. it may be that there are 50,000 or 100,000 people who feel strongly about politics and would like to raise a cheer when they hear their opponents being lambasted. But the huge majority of people do not raise a cheer. They are sick and tired and browned off. If these two parties — I have the honour to represent one and Deputy O'Kennedy has the honour to represent the other — could face up to those facts and lay aside the style of contention which the Leader of that party seems anxious to perpetuate, I believe we would do a better job whichever of us was on this side of the House in the future than is now being delivered. The conceit of a party and of a leadership with that record behind them, especially their record of 1979-81 and of 1982, imagining that there is some national necessity for their recall to office is so monstrous that I will only say this about it; that it is, I suppose, compatible with sanity, but only just.

Standards in Election Debate, Dublin, 8 December 1986

About three weeks ago the independent Senator Shane Ross, addressing a professional gathering, attributed the decline in business morale not only to disappointment with this Government's record in controlling public expenditure, but also to lack of confidence in the ability of the only visible alternative

Government to do any better. If this interpretation of the mood of business is correct, then it will have received powerful confirmation in its pessimism from the weekend speech of the Fianna Fáil spokesperson on finance, Deputy Michael O'Kennedy.

Deputy O'Kennedy solemnly warns the Government against any too radical pruning of public expenditure, on account of the deflationary effect such an action would have. Instead, he urges a "significant redeployment" of expenditure from current to capital; and, under the heading of desirable extra capital expenditure, he lists increased investment in arterial roads, tourism development, and extension of the gas pipe-line.

Nobody wants to be bothered with Deputy O'Kennedy's personal or party priorities for enhanced spending on roads or anything else, unless he is willing also to point out where equivalent savings are to be made on the current side. Which items of expenditure would he prune, and by how much? Unfortunately this is the question which, according the Fianna Fáil penny catechism of cuteness, it is mortally sinful to answer.

It is important to get the whole question of reducing public expenditure into perspective. Of every £1 spent by the State, 21p has to go immediately in interest payments on the State's debts; no cuts here are possible without, in effect, defaulting on our creditors and destroying our credit for the future.

A further 33p, roughly, goes on public service salaries and pensions; and approximately 27p on social welfare payments. Unless Fianna Fáil intend actually to reduce these items, we are thus left with only 19p in the £ of the State's expenditure which is in any sense negotiable or available for discretionary reduction or redeployment.

Measures which are light-heartedly mooted, such as closing down half our embassies abroad, or abolishing the Senate, or reducing the size of the Dáil, would, even if taken all together, remove only a cupful from the barrel. Deputy O'Kennedy knows this quite well; and it must be truly frightening for observers outside politics to see us apparently heading for yet another general election in which the Opposition refused to deal in hard realities, and expects the people to buy, once again, a bundle of junk phrases and promises in the style of 1977.

All that is not to say that Fine Gael has a complete answer, either, to problems which are different only in scale from what most of Western Europe is experiencing. There, too, governments have to battle with growing unemployment and patterns of public expenditure which seem to be genetically programmed for almost un-stoppable expansion. But if ever we are to drag ourselves clear of this nightmare, it will certainly not be done by parties which cannot break the habit of competing with one another in flattering the voters with visions of easy options. In this competition Fianna Fáil, even if not the only offenders, have always been the most shameless.

The Irish media, both national and provincial, will carry a heavy burden of guilt if in next year's election campaign they do not insist on an accurately costed, properly defended financial plan for every party's programme, and if

86

they do not mercilessly hound any party that fails to deposit this minimal bond for its good faith and serious intent.

A failure by the media to throw their influence into the scale to secure, even at this late stage, a rational and responsible political debate, will bring us several steps nearer the day when Irish destinies will be determined no longer by ourselves but by foreigners. If those foreigners are merely the International Monetary Fund, we will be lucky. At our present rate of recklessness, of which Mr O'Kennedy's speech is only the latest symptom, it is more likely to be the Cubans.

Public Capital Programme, 27 October 1987

I confess I have no difficulty in identifying with people whom I know well on the opposite side, such as Deputies Lenihan and Collins, for example. I could see myself working happily with those two Ministers. However, all my experience tells me that they and the most of their party are conditioned always to refuse that simple consideration, always to oppose and wreck unless they can have the ball 100 per cent of the time to themselves. That way this country's destruction lies.

It we have a weather-window politically now, and if this Government have the ball at their feet and are not being hand-tripped, it is because this party are sinking the temptation, which I know plenty of my colleague Deputies have, to hand-trip them, to make difficulties for them, to make political capital on the ground in their constituencies out of the economies the Government are imposing. I beg Deputies opposite to ask themselves whether this must go on forever, whether when this weather-window ends we are going to get another mish-mash Government over on the far side, with the very same cycle of doubling the national debt in four and a half years all over again.

I hope that the consideration that a general election might not work out as I believe it would tomorrow morning will induce in Deputies opposite, and in everybody in this House, a consideration of the duty which this House, the original institution of this State, the Dáil, owes to the people to throw up and, having thrown up, to sustain a Government of people who are like-minded; and not because of petty jealousies, tribal rivalries, recollections of what fathers and grandfathers may have told about events 65 or 70 years ago to obstruct the agreement, consensus and the co-operation on which the prosperity of this State and its people depend.

SECTION 3

Northern Ireland, Britain and the British

Dr Hillery's speech to the United Nations, Dublin, 8 October 1971

Most of Dr Hillery's eloquent speech to the United Nations General Assembly is clearly the work of some first-class Iveagh House official whom — if the pattern of recent events in other Departments is a guide — we can expect to emerge from anonymity into the public view according as the incompetence of his political superiors becomes more and more unbearable. For the present, however, he has to take Dr Hillery's instructions, and clearly the main part of these instructions consisted of a direction to blame the British for what is going on in the North.

According to Dr Hillery, the British Army is being used as a one- sided coercive instrument to prop up the Stormont regime. This is true enough, but it is only half the truth. We all dislike the idea of British troops anywhere in Ireland, but Dr Hillery knows very well that, if the British soldiers in the North are now in an anti-Catholic, anti-Nationalist posture, it is largely because they have been deliberately manoeuvred into that posture by self-elected militants, whose activities South of the border have been tolerated for years by Dr Hillery and his friends for their own local political reasons. By getting his script-writer to avoid telling the truth about this, Dr Hillery has lowered this country in world esteem, and ranked us among those states, bombastic and snivelling by turn, whose dishonest pleas the rest of the world has learned to ignore.

Why has Dr Hillery done this? He has done it, not to impress the delegations of Ghana and Guatemala, who probably unplugged their earphones rather than listen to stuff so familiar and tiresome, but to establish his position with the unscrupulous crew of instant-whip Fianna Fáil hard-liners who see their way back to influence via this nice man, as appealing as Mr Lynch himself, though — as those who saw the Fianna Fáil Ard Fheis will remember — with a good deal less self-control.

No one in Fianna Fáil has the slightest right to affect indignation about the North; in the long years of peace before 1968 that party never gave the North an hour's thought and never converted a single Unionist. It is bad enough that the North is now giving this incompetent Government an opportunity to divert public attention from the rapidly deteriorating economic situation; but it is altogether intolerable that it should be used as a vaulting-horse to power by Dr Hillery and his sinister retinue.

Fine Gael says to these men: Do not leave us out of your grimy calculations. You do not own the Irish people, and so long as Fine Gael is there you will never win.

Mr Lynch and the Anglo-Irish problem, Dublin, 25 June 1972

On Wednesday last the daily papers published extracts from an article by the Taoiseach in the American magazine "Foreign Affairs" in which Mr Lynch set out his ideas about a final solution of the Irish, or rather Anglo-Irish question.

It is to his credit that the tone of the article is temperate — he quotes constitutional patriots like Parnell rather than those in the physical force tradition — but if it is to be regarded as the considered position of the Republic's political leader, it displays several serious defects, and strengthens my belief that very little genuine thought has been given by this Government to the realities of the North. Indeed, it is hard not to feel that these realities are deliberately ignored, and that euphoric optimism about Irish unity is deliberately cultivated here for domestic political reasons. This is certain to end in public disillusionment and cynicism, and seems to me very hard to forgive.

Mr Lynch's central theme is expressed in a sentence: "I consider that the only solution in an Ireland united by agreement in independence". Like nearly everyone else in the Republic, I would consider this a desirable solution; but it is, unfortunately, a very far cry from being the "only" one. The obstacle to Mr Lynch's "only solution", which he never once mentions, its the absolute determination of the Ulster Unionists to resist it; and in my view it only hardens that resolution, rather than undermining it, when Mr Lynch speaks as though it did not exist.

Just as with the expensive publicity operations which the Government has undertaken abroad, I cannot see the sense of trying to convert Americans, Australians and New Zealanders unless the Unionist inhabitants of Lurgan and Portadown are converted too; and, if I were one of the latter, I would dismiss Mr Lynch's article as just another piece of foolish, empty talk from a Southern politician, meant for home consumption by a people much given to wishful thinking.

First, there is a deep ambiguity concealed in the phrase too often heard and now used again by the Taoiseach: "unity by agreement". Does it mean that he and his Government are content to wait politely for unity until a majority in the North is agreeable to it?

If so, he should say so openly and in so many words: and he should say that he will accept the (foregone) conclusion of the promised Northern referenda for so long as they favour retention of the Border. This is naturally a bitter pill for any Nationalist to swallow, but evasion and equivocation on straight questions like this make the worst impression on those who are already sufficiently distrustful of us.

Remember that Mr Lynch and his Government are widely suspected, among Unionists, of having tried to give material assistance to the I.R.A. in

1969-70, and of being quite willing to ride into a united Ireland on the backs of the Provisionals if they had succeeded in beating the British forces in the North. With that load of suspicion lying on him, he has a special duty to be explicit and unambiguous. As the phrase stands, "unity by agreement" is open to the interpretation, from the Northern side, that Mr Lynch would do his best to squeeze "agreement" out of the North by getting the British to lean on the Unionists: a policy which seems to me crazy, if only for the reason that no Irish party, Nationalist or Unionist, would ever be likely to surrender to such treatment.

The reason why this interpretation is possible is that, almost in the next breath, Mr Lynch declares that " the more intransigent among the Unionist minority in Ireland are not entitled to a permanent veto on harmony in Anglo-Irish relations". This is only another way of saying, as Mr Kevin Boland does, that "no section of the Irish people is entitled to opt out of the nation". As a political proposition, this is fair enough; but if you advance it in the same breath as the doctrine of "unity only by agreement", you can reasonably be described as blowing hot and cold. You are affecting to be merely trying to coax someone out of a position which you say he has no right to take up in the first place.

I dislike Partition as much as Mr Lynch does, and I believe that it is rooted in injustice — but an injustice done chiefly in the 17th century. The world is full of boundaries founded on "injustice" in this sense; and while we may have strong feelings about the Border, it is pointless, in my opinion, to regard it merely as the product of a wrong committed by Lloyd George and thus fresh enough to be effectively challenged as illegitimate.

But even if readers think I am wrong about this, i.e. if they feel we ought never to acknowledge any legitimacy whatever in the Partition settlement, we still have to escape from the contradiction, enunciated now again by Mr Lynch, between on the one hand saying the Ulster Unionist interest has no rights to a separate constitutional existence, and on the other hand saying we want, and intend to get, unity by "agreement". If readers will put themselves mentally into the position of a Unionist they will see that this two-faced, "heads-I-win-tails-you-lose" approach is, of all possible approaches, the one most likely to keep suspicion and distrust of us on the boil. I cannot believe Mr Lynch has not enough wit to see this, and this is why I take him, as I have often said before, to be playing essentially to a 26-county gallery; to be less interested in winning hearts in the North than in holding on to votes in the South.

Another feature of his article which, if I were a Northern Unionist, would alienate me even further, in his announcement to the world that Northern opposition to a united Ireland is weakening. "Many of the Unionist community", he says " realise that Irish unity is inevitable and are increasingly willing to consider the idea". This is splendid news, if it is true. But where is the evidence for it? Where are the converts? Can Mr Lynch point to a single significant individual, let alone a single significant group on the Unionist side of whom this is true? How is it that even the New Ulster Movement would not recognise itself under this description?

This movement, in a pamphlet published only a few weeks ago, says inreference to the "Wolfe Tone argument" (adverted to obliquely by Mr Lynch) that this "puts too much weight on an unrepresentative sample of historical precedents. The United Irishmen were a long time ago. . . . Since that time there has been no evidence that at any stage more than a handful of Northern Protestants were prepared to accept a united Ireland outside the United Kingdom". To hear this from the most moderate group in Northern Ireland today is naturally bitter. But of all possible reactions to it, the worst is to pretend that it is simply untrue; to pretend that (as the New Ulster Movement put it in a more recent pamphlet still) "inside every Protestant there is a United Irishman crying out for liberation".

There is some good sense in other parts of Mr Lynch's article — in particular his pointing to the fatal results of the British allowing the Unionists to misgovern a large minority for 50 years — but the unreality of his view on the "only solution" is very culpable.

In my opinion there is only one way to get Irish unity: not by force, or propaganda, or constitutional window-dressing, or trying to get the English to apply economic pressures, but by winning the hearts of the Northern Protestants and making them feel wanted as people, and not merely as an outstanding score to be settled in favour of the Nationalist side.

This can only be done, if at all, by patient tedious work, very little of it on the political plane and very little of it like to pay off in Southern votes. Mr Lynch himself gave a creditable example of what is needed when he lately had an ex-Prime Minister of Northern Ireland appointed to the Board of the National Gallery in Dublin: a small gesture in itself, but nevertheless something in the right direction, just as the sending of the Dublin fire brigades to the help of Belfast in the air-raid of 1941 was in the right direction.

If we can have a generation or two of concrete good neighbourliness, with no political strings, yet provide a historic movement in which ordinary human good will towards us having taken the place of hatred, will be decisive in giving us the solution we all hope for. It is to the generating of this good will in our own island, not to cute diplomacy or expensive publicity abroad, that any Dublin Government's energy should be directed. If we are unwilling to face this long, hard grind, we might as well forget about the North and concentrate on the local problems of which God knows we have more than enough.

Taoiseach's meeting with Mrs Thatcher, Dáil, 29 May 1980

I must admit straight away what I have to say today will not be as statesmanlike as what has been said by other Deputies. I feel I have to say something about the more domestic and parochial political aspects of the situation which ultimately produced this debate, and the domestic genesis of the Fianna Fáil Government's present stance in regard to Northern Ireland and associated questions. Anyone who pretends that this can be divorced from recent developments in their own party has not his feet on the ground.

Its most recent history — the last chapter of it began in the autumn when Deputy Sile de Valera, who despite the mystique which surrounds her name and which she is willing to have attributed to herself at one remove very seldom attends this House and virtually never gives us the benefit of her views on any question except this one, went to Fermoy and made a speech. I would have said that as a young girl she should be sporting in some flowery political meadow, like conservation or children's rights, but she has chosen instead to inhabit the dripping vaults of old-cod republicanism. She made a speech, the timing of which I cannot believe was planned entirely unassisted. In that speech she advanced a point of view in regard to Irish unity and Irish destiny which she associated very strongly with her grandfather.

Since nobody on this side of the House brought her grandfather into the argument, since he was gratuitously made part of recent developments by herself, I feel I am entitled, without disrespect to his memory, to say that if one man more than another did his best — perhaps, without knowing it — to dig deeper the ditches which separate the two peoples of this country, it was that Deputy's grandfather. If there was any possible way of doing it, he would find it. It was with him as Taoiseach that the Criminal Law (Amendment) Bill was passed containing a section which the House has heard so much about. It was he who drafted, introduced and got the people to pass the Constitution which contains an assertion of the right of this Parliament to rule the Six Counties, which contained, until the people removed it in 1972, an assertion of the primacy of the Catholic Church, which contains the prohibitions on divorce. Not one of those provisions was in the Constitution of the Irish Free State. Those are the albatrosses we are all trying to unhang from around our necks placed on them by that Deputy's grandfather, who now thinks fit to extol him as an example to follow in regard to restoring Irish unity.

What was done in his time, or in the time of his successor for that matter, for Irish unity? Did he convert a single Unionist heart? Did he win back a single inch of the Six County territory? Not one, is the answer to both questions. I will take no lecturing from that branch of Irish nationalism, which has done its crazy damnedest to leave this country unhappy and divided for ever.

95

The intellectual quality of her arguments was devastating. We were one island; it was a geographical unity and so it must follow that it should be a political unity. The island next door is a geographical unity and I should like to know if that means that Deputy Sile de Valera would give the back of her hand to the Scottish Nationalists or the Welsh Nationalists? Are they traitors? Is their behaviour treasonable or are their aspirations treasonable? Would she advise them that since Britain is a geographical unit there was no sense, reason or right in anybody ever to dispute that it should be a political unit also? The Iberian Peninsula, the Scandinavian Peninsula, are geographical units, but after long wars and dissensions the rights of people other than the predominant people, were established in both peninsulas. Nobody thinks there is anything strange about that. The cowboys and the Indians shared the same territory. It could be said that the Middle-West was a geographical unit; but that did not stop one side trying to exterminate the other before being scalped themselves.

That is the devastating level of the intellectual argument on which the Deputy opposite me rode to power here. It nicely coincided with the discontent within the Fianna Fáil Party which rose to panic level after the Cork by-elections. It nicely coincided with the mystique, with the impression of tacit but volcanic commitment to the North of Ireland which has been allowed to grow up around him, and around his followers, over the last ten silent years. It was essentially in the wake of that wave of feeling in the Fianna Fáil Party that the change of last December took place. When the change was accomplished, of course we saw a development unfolding which was by no means un-precedented, because every leader of that party since it was founded has had to do the very same thing, trim in his arrogant sails that he floated so proudly in Opposition, haul them down and sing very dumb and low about the things which were non-negotiable before that. Not one word has been heard since then, or since 1977 when the Fianna Fáil Party returned to office, about the "unilateral commitment by the British to withdraw" which they wanted to obtain and which they identified as being the one way to national peace. We have not heard a word and like all his predecessors, he has scaled down his demands. There was no word of unilateral withdrawal. Instead, we got a demonstration from him, the second within one year, of what he understands by an Irish solution to an Irish problem.

The Irish solution to the Irish problem consists in words, in old guff, speak a few, write a few, even put a few in a law or constitution; and the job is right. The ignorant supporters — the more ignorant they will be the more numerous they will be in a context like this — will consider the person a hero if the words are correct.

It is the verbal patriotism on which Liam Cosgrave poured such justified contempt when Taoiseach, and the verbal patriotism for which this party still has nothing but contempt.

After the change in December there was a new Irish problem on the floor, the problem which Deputy Haughey had brought upon himself, the problem of how to satisfy the muddled heads in his own party, the muddled heads chief of them being that of Deputy Sile de Valera. The problem was how to make them feel that something was now happening which could not have happened under Deputy Lynch. He allowed his publicity machine to create the impression which his admirers in the media eagerly took up, that something was going to happen when he met Mrs Thatcher and that there was now going to be an initiative of a sort which had never been seen before.

It is, in fact, likely that there will be an initiative. I believe Mrs Thatcher, the Prime Minister before her, Mr Wilson and Mr Heath, are sick and tired of the North of Ireland. I do not think there is any such thing left in Britain as Unionism in the old sense, namely an emotional commitment to the political union of a part of this island with the other. I do not believe there is such a thing as a Unionist in that sense left in the island of Britain, in either party. I believe they would be thoroughly glad to be rid and shut of the whole problem. If Mrs Thatcher can think of some way of doing that while not betraying the SDLP — that is the vital part — I believe she will do it. I hope she succeeds in thinking up something like that, because the British should surely have learned by now that if one refuses to do business with reasonable people one will end up doing business with unreasonable people. The British should have learned by now that the elected representatives of the Northern minority have behaved for the last 12 years with unparalleled restraint and courage, very often personal courage. They must not be let down by this State, by either Government or Opposition here; but the British Government, even in their own selfish interest, have a duty to them. I believe they see that not so much as a duty but as a necessity to stand by them and that section of the minority which has not fallen into the arms of the gunmen.

I believe an initiative, sooner or later, will be forthcoming. However, I have just given the reason for it. It certainly will not be in consequence of any conviction or confidence that the present Fianna Fáil Government or leadership has succeeded in awakening. The emphasis, stressed here at great length and much more sober length, I admit — I say that in admiration — by Deputy FitzGerald this morning, placed by the Fianna Fáil Party and its leadership in this matter is on the wrong point. I may go further than Deputy FitzGerald in this regard but, as I said before, I regard the British as nearly irrelevant in this situation.

Of course, it is nice to have their goodwill, it is nice to have their assistance and it would be preferable if they were helpful rather than unhelpful. But there is only one real obstacle to Irish unity, and that is the absolute unwillingness of the Northern Unionist interest that such a thing should come about, or at least that it should come about under the aegis of this State or as part of that State.

That unwillingness, so long as it exists, will prevent Irish unity from coming about. I regard the talk about unity by peaceful means, unity only by consent and renouncing the use of force, as being disingenuous as well as being, if it is combined with talk about getting the British to withdraw guarantees, down-right dishonest and counter- productive. It is disingenuous because this State would not be capable physically, morally, or financially of taking over the North of Ireland any other way. I hope nobody will think it seditious of treasonable to say that. I should like Members on the far side, or on any side of the House, people in the press or elsewhere to ask themselves how many volunteers could be raised in this State to conduct an offensive operation against the North of Ireland with the aim of incorporating it in this State and keeping it incorporated in it? We are put to the pin of our collars to keep order in Sean MacDermott Street. What chance do we have of bullying by force one million Unionists into a State which they would fight rather than join. The answer is no chance. The answer is that we do not want to do it, even if we were capable, and we could not pay for such a thing. Why give ourselves credit for renouncing the use of force when everyone knows that it is not a possibility to start with? That is disingenuous and even the humblest Unionist with even the most modest education and with the deepest prejudices can see that. Still we talk about unity only by peaceful means. At the same time we produce the double-think and double-speak in regard to the second leg of what is supposed to be our State's policy as represented by the present administration.

Double-think was described by the man who invented the phrase, George Orwell, as holding two contradictory opinions simultaneously and accepting both of them. In this State, with the miádh that rests on it, it has another meaning. It means not only accepting these opinions but pretending that others ought to accept them too. It means attributing a certain blindness and under-privilege to the Unionist population if they cannot see we are right about it. It is dishonest and counter-productive to talk in one breath about unity by consent and in the next to say we deny the right of a minority to opt out of the Irish nation. In other words, we deny them the right to withhold their consent. What kind of consent is that? The word "consent" in any setting, not just a lawyer's one, implies a free consent.

An extorted consent in any legal system or constitutional system in the world means that what is consented to is a nullity. It must be a nullity in justice, because it is not a real consent. If I were a Unionist I could not find words to express the contempt, scorn and bitterness I would feel on hearing someone on the benches over there, himself and his faction already deeply suspect in my eyes for other reasons, mouthing about " unity only by consent and peaceful means" but being willing to blackguard me into giving that consent, talking to the English as though it were up to them to withdraw guarantees, to undermine me, to pull away the platform on which I stand and the plank to which I cling. I am far from being in love with the unionists. I make no secret to the House of my feeling that we do a lot of flowery talk about the inherent unity of Irish people but it is more than a lot of us feel. I do not have much in common with Dr Paisley or the Rev Martin Smith or any of their followers. It would take a lot to make me emotionally convinced I had. However, I am willing for the purposes of the debate to go along with the proposition.

If we are going to talk about these sundered brethren and these Irishmen who share a different tradition but love the same country, we must look at it from their point of view. What are they to think when they hear "unity by consent" in one breath and in the next that they have no right to withhold that consent? They are "not allowed to opt out of the Irish people." They are to join us only if they agree; but they are not free to disagree. What are they to think when they hear that the things to which they cling are in some way illicit or illegitimate and that the people who offer them those guarantees ought to withdraw them.

I know what I would do. I would dig my heels further and further in and I would say: "Be damned to you. Be damned to that kind of talk." I am not a unionist and have very little fellow feeling with them. I admit that, which Deputies do not often do. If I were, that is what my reaction would be, and I believe it is what the Government's reaction would be if someone proposed to dispose of their future behind their back over tea with an English woman. That is what their reaction would be. They would say "Over my dead body will that happen". As Deputy FitzGerald said even the most moderate, liberal and mildest of unionists have been switched off over the last ten years by a combination of the IRA and the double-think from Fianna Fáil. The IRA it was not possible to find a mention of in the presidential speech at the Fianna Fáil Ard-Fheis or in today's debate on the Fianna Fáil side. What is a unionist to think?

I have often said and I will say it again, that the unionists have only themselves to thank that a monster like the IRA has risen in their midst.

They neglected and ignored all warnings and advice whether loud or soft, issued by the British or by ourselves or by their own minority. They brushed aside all warnings. They treated the civil rights movement which was non-violent, with contempt. They walked on the Nationalist people and created a state out of which nothing but something like the IRA could come. I do not ignore or overlook the fact that they brought those disasters in the long term to a large extent on themselves. However, that does not free us from responsibility, when we find murderers flying our flag and pretending to have the right to fly it and speak for us, it does not diminish our responsibility to deny that they speak for us, and to keep on denying it. That will cost Fianna Fáil votes.

We did not have a bishop in the Coalition, we had Cruisers not croziers. The Cruiser denied it week in week out. Perhaps he overdid it and probably lost votes as a result, because volatile Irish opinion will only take a certain amount of hectoring along those lines. But in a presidential address at an Ard-Fheis of a Government party we would expect something about it.

I know why there is not a word: a large section of the Fianna Fáil Party attribute the defeat of the national Coalition to their having taken a firm, unyielding unvarying stand about the IRA and violence. The week after the national Coalition went out the Roscommon County Council sat in conclave. A Fianna Fáil Councillor, a colleague of Deputies Leyden and Doherty, said that the reason the Coalition had gone out was because they had "persecuted republicans". Did we persecute Deputy Haughey or Deputy Meaney? They are republicans. Deputy Leonard is a republican. Deputy Conaghan is a republican, Deputy Farrell is a republican, Deputy O'Hanlon is a republican. Did we persecute them? No, only the gun-republicans. It was the gun-republicans and not the guff-republicans we were out to get. But that was enough to put us out, in the view of a segment of the Fianna Fáil Party; and therefore their present leadership was very careful not to tread on those sensitive toes.

What is a unionist to think when he finds speeches from that leadership in which not one word is said about the things which he, misguided as he may be and selfish as he may have been, identifies as the root and main cause of the violence which is ruining his life and his children's future? Unionists have been a contemptible crew in the past and perhaps still are. They have yet to produce a leader who speaks the truth fearlessly to their own savage wild men in the way Liam Cosgrave and Deputy Lynch spoke to the wild men who purport to fly the tricolour. When such a leader shows a sign of surfacing he is trampled under foot at once, witness O'Neill and Faulkner.

I have no great regard for them, but I recognise that they look on the bit of this country that they occupy as their country. Where else are they to go?

It is no use saying they can go back to Scotland or England, as I hear some ignoramuses saying. They have as much roots there in spite of their distant origins in the place, as the Afrikaners in South Africa have in Holland. The settlements took place in the very same century, and the links are about as strong. If there were some kind of national calamity such as an earthquake which split the six Counties into bits the British and Scottish would presumably be willing to "take them back", but in no other context would they dream of it. It does not make sense to talk like that. I recognise the reason why they are there is one which is full of horror, shame and humiliation for the nationalist population, based on the history of the seventeenth century. But where else are they to go? They only have that bit of ground, and regard themselves as a people apart. They have a certain legitimacy there. I do not overlook their sins, crimes, neglect and selfishness. They probably have themselves largely to thank for the horrors that have come in their midst.

But the sensitivity which I would expect a Taoiseach in Ireland and his party to show to the feeling, instinct and rooted beliefs of the very people we must convince — if we are ever to achieve unity — is just not visible with the present Fianna Fáil Administration. It was visible when Deputy Liam Cosgrave was there; it was visible when Dr Garret FitzGerald was Minister for Foreign Affairs. Let me say it is visible in every word that Deputy Harte utters when he speaks on this subject.

There are two things only that we can usefully do. Both of them involve ignoring the English, or regarding them as being an unimportant part of this situation. One is to talk directly to Unionists. It may mean doing things never done before as I have said taking pages in the local and provincial press in the

North or in whatever fragments remain of the Belfast press, whole pages, and employing the advertising skills we use in persuading the Irish voter to vote for Fine Gael, Fianna Fáil or the Labour Party, and try and tell them so far as we can honestly the truth about this State. We will not free them of all apprehension — we will not free them of all — because we have a lot of blemishes, but at least try and disabuse them of the wrong ideas they have got about it. Secondly — and I must credit Deputy O'Hanlon with having said it — we must build our economy to the point that it is a source of envy and admiration to them.

Adjournment Debate, Dáil,
18 December 1980

We are supposed to assume or accept activity on the Northern Ireland front, culminating in a meeting ten days ago, much heralded and publicised, between the Taoiseach and Mrs Thatcher. We do not know what happened at that meeting. It is part of the Taoiseach's stock in trade to think and this adds to his style, that it confers some added dimension of mystique on him, and apparently for some people it does. I have never seen a press or a set of commentators so uncritical of what exactly is going on in regard to Northern Ireland policy.

I am sorry to say, and I hope it will not be misunderstood, that I detect in the way that visit was reported in the press a certain strain of that awful paddyism which has been our curse. There is a certain note of self-congratulation because as many as four Englishmen travelled over. The gentry had looked into the gate lodge, and not only the master of the house but his dowager mother-in-law as well, and had admired the stove.

I did not speak on the last occasion and I just want to get in my twopence worth. It does not matter what Deputy Haughey and Mrs Thatcher agreed. I agree it would be worth while to have British goodwill on that or any other front, in relation to the economy or something else, but it does not matter what we agree with the British because the British are not in a position to make any given solution stick in the teeth of the opposition of the Northern majority. I do not admire them, I do not respect them, I consider they very largely brought their own misfortunes on themselves by their grotesque selfishness towards the minority over whom they were allowed to rule for 40 years, but we have to live with those people on the same island and Mrs Thatcher is not in a position to make a solution stick with them that they will not have. Among the proofs I have of the mesmerisation among the media, who were vocal enough when we were in power, is the extraordinary uncritical way in which that fact has been forgotten. Take The Irish Times, a very fine paper, and everybody who works in it or for it or runs it deserves in a general way admiration and congratulations for what they do. But on this point an extraordinary uncritical attitude seems to have come over the people who dictate the editorial line.

They do not seem to read their own Northern editor, Mr McKittrick. He sends an endless stream of realistic stories from Belfast, which I believe, but they do not make any impact on the editorial office itself. Two or three people there, who make the Northern editorial line, were, ten years ago in the business of prophecy; they were heavily into the Moses line. There was not even going to be a federal solution according to them; we were going to have one Thirty-Two county republic. And they relied on cultural resemblances and affinities which they thought could be detected in peggy's leg and yellow man and Lammas Fair and RUC men playing the tin whistle to carry us over the reluctance, which they simply did not want to know about, of the million other people to have anything to do with a solution of that kind.

I can remember one thing that sticks in my mind because it was one of the first scripts I handed out after being elected to one of the Houses of the Oireachtas. It was in Dunleer in County Louth. This was in the Autumn of 1969 after the trouble got very bad in the North. I said that there was no reason why, in a federal Ireland, the people in the North should fret about our divorce laws or contraceptive laws, whatever my own feeling about them might be, because they could have their own, because any federal solution would make sense only if a certain range of things, of which these are very obvious examples, were remitted to the independent legislative expression of whatever authority functioned in the North under the federal arrangement. I was severely rapped on the knuckles by The Irish Times. That would not do at all; that was hibernianism. I was back to the old Irish Parliamentary Party or something even more feeble, something that, as Deputy Haughey said not long before he took over in Fianna Fáil, had so degraded and humiliated public life that no one of any sensitivity or intelligence could touch them. That is the way he spoke about men who either bled to death or gave their lives in other ways for Ireland. I was back to the stage of these old chaps with their buttoned boots and their stick-in-the mud ideas if I spoke about a federal solution. There could be no question even of that. It was the whole or nothing.

We are a long way from that now. The same paper and others were telling us that there was no such thing as a Unionist backlash, that we could press ahead, do what we liked in the North, twist the arms of the English and everybody else in sight. I must say I cannot blame them for that because the same kind of message was coming from the SDLP, that we need not worry about the Unionists, that they would lie down, that they were only a paper tiger. I am sorry to say that three or four hundred murdered Catholics since then proved them wrong. Three or four hundred absolutely innocent and uninvolved people, the victims of sectarian violence, proved them bitterly wrong.

It does not matter what Mrs Thatcher consents to and I have not the least doubt that she would be delighted to clear out of the North in the morning if she could and her party with her and the rest of the British public. They would be delighted to disengage themselves and I do not doubt they will do so as soon as they feel they decently can and perhaps even if they do not think they decently can they may well do it. But how are we going to make this stick? How are we going to make anything stick up there unless we are able to persuade the Northern majority that they can live in peace with us and that they can have their own traditions and they will not be priest ridden.

Michael Collins, somebody whose valour will not be questioned in this House from either side, openly said that there could be no question of coercing the North. I cannot help noticing — I do not want to be abrasive or inflame old wounds — that when the Civil War broke out here in 1922 and the summer of 1923 the anti-Treaty side were damned careful to restrict their activities to the Twenty-six Counties. They never fired a shot in the North or for the North, notwithstanding that presumably the State up their was just as illegitimate as the one functioning here in Dublin.

The only consequence is to show that in those days people here who had some show of popular support in this country for their activities keep clear of the North and the reason is clear. I am not going to hammer on it but I want to say something else about this.

Even if it were possible for us to make a particular settlement stick in the North against the will of the majority up there and even it were physically possible and financially possible to do it and I do not want to dwell too much on what it implies because anybody can imagine for themselves what it would imply — we must ask, is the will of the people in the Republic there for such an operation? I cannot see that it is. They have plenty of willingness to go in for boozy ballads about the rifle's crack and the Thompson's flash and the rattle of this and the rattle of that. They have plenty of time for that and verbal truculence and verbal patriotism, as Deputy Liam Cosgrave said. But I do not believe they have the will to undertake economically, financially, militarily or any other way, the kind of operation which we would have to undertake if it was left to us alone to make a settlement stick in the North which the Northern majority did not want to wear.

Therefore it is up to us or any Irish Government which is serious about this, which does not just feel that it can gain votes by having themselves photographed with the neighbours, to tackle the situation. I have said enough about the neighbours. It is important for any Irish Government which is serious about this to seek ways forward to the people in the North on all sides and never to lose sight of our duties towards the minority who have the claim on us that they have nowhere else to look to. They certainly have the claim on us; I recognise and acknowledge it and I would never, I hope, go back on it or disclaim it if I were in a position of authority. These people have nowhere else to look but to us. But we must look for ways forward to the other side too and that means disabusing them, enlightening them, contradicting them openly and publicly when things are said about us which are not true. It means doing things which perhaps have not been done before, and I have suggested this on other occasions too, things like buying pages of the Belfast Newsletter and covering those pages with a properly constructed advertising message demolishing myths about our laws, demolishing myths about our way of life in the Republic.

That of course is not going to convert anybody overnight, but so far we have done nothing along these lines. Deputy Wilson knows better than I do, because he lives nearer the Border, the degree of ignorance up there.

To some extent it is wilful ignorance. But the degree of ignorance up there is absolutely horrifying and, since we are the ones that are going to have to live with whatever settlement is reached, we should be doing something to reduce that ignorance. So far we have done nothing. I would begin to change my mind about Deputy Wilson's party and his Leader, if they accepted these realities and stopped merely posing for the cameraman with well dressed neighbours.

Haughey and Paisley,
Dublin, 12 February 1981

On the eve of Fianna Fáil's Ard-Fheis I can almost hear the agony of the script-cooks in the Department of the Taoiseach as they labour to run up some nourishing paragraphs on the North for the busloads of hungry republicans. Their raw materials are of the poorest; their master a most imperious type. What can they possibly concoct that will not taste like thin, recycled gruel, shreds of fly-blown communiques and gaudy obscurities like "institutional not con-stitutional" floating in it, a cheap packet minestrone that only Mr Lenihan would manage to serve with a flourish?

They need not worry. Their republican clientele are no political Wine and Food Society, no sticklers for the pure flavours of reason and logic. To the wholesome fare of plain language they have a positive allergy; even a spoonful of the truth brings them out in spots.

And the truth is that neither Mr Haughey nor any of his faction have ever made the smallest personal contribution towards lessening the historical antagonisms on which partition is based, nor seem to have any desire to attempt such a thing. Why should they bother, when their supporters evidently do not demand it, and are perfectly happy with a policy so low in self-respect that it consists only of perfunctory guff about the nationhood, and pestering the English to do for us the job we ought to be doing for ourselves.

There is more than merely a negative side to this humiliating caricature of what a national policy should be. There is the very serious dimension that the Haughey approach is meat and drink to the evil genius of Ian Paisley. We have not forgotten that back in 1967 Mr Paisley was raving about a "sell-out" just because of Terence O'Neill's very tentative moves to break the Ulster ice — a "sell-out", no less, by a man who saw his own success in terms of the Catholics he succeeded in converting into Unionist voters. Naturally this noisy bigot finds a new excuse for raving, and parading a new Carsonite militia, in Mr Haughey's intimations that big, though unspecified, changes are being hatched by himself and Mrs Thatcher, over the heads of the people whose future is thus an issue.

Of course, I know perfectly well that no such changes are in contemplation; but to allow the Fianna Fáil faithful to wink knowingly at one another, while at the same time not producing an account so plainly wrong that Mrs Thatcher would have to contradict it publicly, the Lenihanesque formula "institutional not constitutional" is brought into play. This insulting prevarication will pass muster in the R.D.S.; but Mr Paisley is able to build an Orange nightmare out of it.

This, each for his own purely local political purposes, Mr Haughey and Mr Paisley are feeding the prejudices of one another's followers. Each is keeping the other in business. And meanwhile the only possible context of a permanent Irish peace — mutual respect, restraint and trust — is kept as far out of sight as ever.

It can be said without much exaggeration that the only worthwhile initiatives from the Dublin side towards achieving that context through practical co-operation were made under the leadership of Fine Gael. The late and respected Sean Lemass is fairly given credit for his pioneering trip to Belfast. But fifteen years before that it was a commonplace for Dublin and Belfast Ministers to exchange visits in pursuit of concrete joint governmental projects. Dan Morrissey and Liam Cosgrave travelled North in the time of the first Inter-Party Government; the late Major Sinclair and others travelled South. Joint legislation and other action on the Foyle fisheries, the Great Northern Railway, the Erne hydro-electric and drainage schemes were the fruit of those efforts.

In the years 1973-4 far more dramatic — perhaps too dramatic — co-operation came in the shape of the Sunningdale meeting and agreement.

That bright dawn was soon clouded by the I.R.A., by loyalist intransigence, and by the weakness of the British. But I did not remember Mr Haughey or any of his faction straining themselves in praise or in defence of the settlement which might have been the beginning of a happy ending to the sorrowful history of this country. In the tradition of their party, they were too patriotic to support a concrete advance won by others. We, however, in this party will in Government once again attempt such an advance, with candour and plain language; and will not worry too much about the scruples of the patriots.

Nomination of Senator Dooge as Foreign Minister, Dáil, 21 October 1981

I want to say to Deputy Lenihan and Deputy Haughey in particular, who were out in front in this debate here yesterday, that it is not enough to be talking about our aspirations. God knows, I lean over backwards to try to find points in common between my party and the Fianna Fáil Party, as my essential belief is that the Civil War has damned this country for the last 60 years and it should be brought to a close. But no sooner have I leaned over backwards to find points in common than I find suddenly that I am being pushed away out to sea again by reasoning of this kind.

The attitude of the Fianna Fáil Party towards the Northern problem would seem wicked if it were not childish; but since it is the attitude of a child one cannot take it seriously enough to attach a severe adjective like "wicked" to it. They speak about their "aspirations" as a child would speak about a flock of balloons. When somebody comes uncomfortably near them you can almost hear them shouting. "Mind me aspirations!" They think it is enough to recite that aspiration and their national duty is done.

Deputy Lenihan, above all, is in a weak position although, as I once said, his endearing characteristic is that it is impossible to embarrass him. His shamelessness is an all-purpose, all-weather shamelessness. As I have said, Deputy Lenihan has been around for a long time. He has been a political force of sorts for nearly a generation. While in Scotland visiting a convention of Scottish nationalists about 1966 or 1967, not long after I joined this party, he said referring to our experience, that "independence was not all it was cracked up to be". That was Deputy Lenihan's advice to the Scots 14 or 15 years ago, and this is the man who cast doubts even on the degree of independence that we ourselves had then achieved.

I want to emphasise another thing about Deputy Lenihan who gave us all a lecture here yesterday about "aspirations". He was the man who himself, in the most humiliating possible way, was put over Mrs Thatcher's knee a year ago when he misrepresented for local purposes the nature of the talks which the British Government had been induced to have with our Government. Deputy Lenihan came back with the usual business about the whole think being raised to a new plane. It has a new kind of globality, it was a kind of global arrangement now, the old stuff was past history, we had a new relationship, globality a totality of relationships. He came back talking about that kind of thing. Naturally it caused panic in the North of Ireland among the people I was trying to describe a little while ago. Mrs Thatcher had to come out and disclaim him. Imagine the humiliation of that. The rest of us felt it, even those of us in Opposition at that time. I object to having a Foreign Minister, whichever party appoints him, who is publicly ticked off by a British Prime Minister and implicitly accused of misrepresenting what has gone on. Naturally, Deputy Lenihan who is as difficult to embarrass as it would be to sink a cork by throwing stones at it, came up with another one. He said the new globalities are all "institutional, not constitutional". With this formula he was allowed to skate through Christmas into the new year. A man who has been publicly forced by the British Prime Minister to admit that there was nothing in those talks which bore on the constitutional status of Northern Ireland is in a pretty weak position to lecture Senator Dooge about not having said anything to the United Nations about our "aspirations".

I regret to have to comment on a despicable reference in Deputy Haughey's speech yesterday, which only echoed an equally despicable moment at the Fianna Fáil conference in Cork last weekend when he berated Senator Dooge for not having thrown his weight against the scheme which I announced in the Seanad last Friday whereby four different kinds of arrangements among a variety of others, some of which were found to be impracticable, are going to be adopted here with the intention of facilitating the travel of Northern people to the Republic and making them feel welcome.

Within a week of becoming Minister I asked my Department to see whether, under the cover of my tourism hat, I could devise a package of schemes which would be clearly seen as a goodwill gesture towards the Northern community of whatever creed or class, and which we could live with financially. I want to commend here, as I did in the Seanad, the extraordinary enthusiasm and diligence with which officials in my Department and also in the other Department involved, reacted to that request. After some delay, part of which was due to my absence abroad, I was able to bring a set of four proposals to the Government.

One was to extend to residents of Northern Ireland the facility for free travel for the elderly which we have for our own citizens. The other was to make available in the same way for people conforming to the conditions free travel for disabled people from Northern Ireland on our buses and railways. A third was to make a token contribution by means of extending an existing Bord Fáilte voucher scheme towards the cost of accommodation for people from the North. I went out of my way to say it was only intended as a gesture of welcome that I could not pretend, when the scheme eventually surfaced, that it was going to make any substantial contribution to the cost of their holiday. It was merely a gesture of welcome, and to put it into that perspective and not appear to be claiming a dimension for it which it did not have, I said it was a gesture in the sense of a discount which might meet the cost of a meal or a couple of rounds of drinks. Finally, the Department of Education very enthusiastically agreed to extend the youth incentive scheme to Northern Ireland youth groups, thus offering some support towards their costs in coming here for sporting or cultural events.

I am proud of that scheme; but it does not really matter whether I am or not. The point is looked at objectively it is the first time in 60 years that a Dublin

Government have done something concrete towards making the people in the North feel wanted here. Even if the scheme does not work, if it is a failure, perhaps even counterproductive — I do not claim to have any foresight of wisdom about this — it will still remain the first effort in 60 years to do something of this kind. But what do I find with the Soldiers of Destiny, with their breathless aspirations to Irish unity? What is their reaction?

They got a tame SDLP man to come down to their platform and denounce it as being an exercise which will only excite resentment — I think he said contempt — in the North. That point of view was repeated here yesterday by Deputy Haughey. How dare he speak like that? He knows perfectly well that it is sincerely meant. He knows perfectly well there is not one ounce of local partisan feeling or input in that scheme. He knows perfectly well it is intended without reference of any kind at all to the local political scene, and if somebody has predicted that we could get that reaction from Fianna Fáil I would not have believed it. I would have said they may do low things on us but they are not that low, to try to discredit a scheme which has plainly and patently got only one purpose, to try to spread goodwill among people who hate us and to whom Fianna Fáil have given little enough reason to change their minds. I did not think they could be low enough to do it; but I was wrong. They were able to get their party leader to do it and also a man from the SDLP to do it. I consider that one of the most despicable things I have encountered since I entered politics 12 years ago, to undermine a scheme which has no other purpose than to reconcile the people of this island, because I do not expect that its concrete tourist spin off will be anything but marginal. It may even be non-existent.

In the Seanad last week I said that I would look at the scheme in a year's time and if parts of it were less productive than others we reserve the right to ourselves to close them down because there is a limit to the amount of money we can spend, even on this scheme, modest though it is, and I do not advance it as being more than modest. It will cost a significant sum of money which we can ill afford at this time, thanks to the bungling and the hoofling of the party opposite over the last four years. If we find some parts of that scheme are less productive than others we will close them down and switch the money from the less productive to the more productive areas. Perhaps someone will get a better idea and perhaps some further dimensions of the scheme will become possible. In that case, we will put the money into them. I do not want anyone to think, as long as I am in office, that we are committed to exactly the four points of the scheme. We are not, but it is the first such efforts ever made in this State, and that is the way it is greeted by the Legion of the Rearguard.

I consider that a shameful performance, especially when uttered in the context of trying to discredit the appointment of Senator Dooge whose words I quoted at the beginning of my contribution and whose approach to Northern Ireland is absolutely correct — let us go a little distance and try to persuade them to come a little distance and then look again. That criticism in the context of trying to discredit Senator Dooge is absolutely contemptible. I am sorry to have spoken heatedly about this but I feel very badly and very strongly about it. I cannot believe that decent people who support Fianna Fáil can have felt anything but shame when they saw what was said on the platform at the weekend by Mr Mallon and yesterday in the Dáil by Deputy Haughey.

The Key to Progress on the North, Dublin, 22 May 1984

British policy created the problem; British stupidity and neglect allowed it to suppurate into violence; and the British certainly owed a duty to the people they considered British citizens to try whatever goodwill and courage could do to create a decent, just and peaceful society in the North. This should have included a willingness to learn by their own mistakes, and to listen to sober and moderate advice; but as recently as the hunger strikes of 1981 the British unfortunately showed that the willingness was lacking. The election of an I.R.A. spokesman to the House of Commons is a symbol of the price which they, and we, are paying for this recent British folly. But the fact that someone has caused a problem or has aggravated it, does not prove his capacity to solve it. "The British presence in Northern Ireland", said one of the Northern people who made oral submissions to the Forum, "does not consist of the British army or the British administration. It consists of the million people there who regard themselves as British. They are the British presence". The truth of this seems to me too plain to need labouring; and for this reason all the clamour about British withdrawal completely misses the point.

The British could pull out their army and government structure in the morning, and pass what legislation they liked about extruding the six counties from the U.K; the result would simply be an Ulster version of Ian Smith's Rhodesia, but one not in the least danger of evolving into an Ulster Zimbabwe, because, unlike Rhodesia, the regime would be supported by a majority strong enough to impose their will on the rest. To pretend that the population of this State would even desire to use force to prevent such a development, let alone be willing to pay for and mount the kind of military operation capable of preventing it, would be a transparent and pitiable falsehood. As far the assertion sometimes heard, that if the British declared for a united Ireland and simply withdrew, it would "bring the Unionists to their senses" and "get them to the negotiating table", where their notorious loyalty to "The half-crown, not the Crown" would lead them to see that integration in this State would butter their bread for them better than staying outside it: this position seems to me so feeble, so diseased, so perverse, as to be beneath discussion.

It flies in the face of all our experience of unionists. It is contradicted by everything they say and do, as when they say they are ready to eat grass rather than be forced into a 32-county Republic.

It credits them with none of the spirit that we ourselves would show if others proposed to take over and absorb our State. It takes for granted the favourable balance of an economic calculation which is highly doubtful. To assert so zany a belief as a basis for Northern policy is not just lacking in self-respect, it positively invites the ridicule and contempt of the world, which must conclude that we actually prefer to inhabit a leprechaun dreamland rather than to grow up.

I would like to see this party, and the other democratic parties which flourish in this State, take up the Northern problem once more, and every other problem as well, in the original spirit of the State's early leaders; with the frankness, the dignity and the realism proper to a republic and republicans, before those words were usurped by whining balladeers and murderers' touts. And the first step in this process must be to strip away the Anglocentric slant which Northern policy has been developing over the last five or six years.

Mrs Thatcher has a role to play, in particular that of making sure nothing is done to make matters worse; but the main task is for the people who have to live on this island. Either Irish people of all traditions can find means of tolerating one another, and allowing breathing room for one another's hopes, and co-operating with one another in preventing the island from sinking into barbarism and tyranny; or we can look forward first to a Lebanon and then to a Cuba.

Irish Americans, Dublin, 6 September 1984

The Lord Mayor of Dublin, Councillor O'Halloran, deserves congratulaions for his firm and dignified behaviour in connection with the appearance of a New York police band at a commemoration organised by Provisional Sinn Féin.

Irish-Americans too often make the mistake of supposing, just because of the peculiar degree of affection which the United States enjoys in Ireland, that they have a licence to conduct hit-and-run interventions in this country's domestic affairs. The Lord Mayor's action will have a useful effect in correcting this impression. When these interventions are on the trombone and flageolet level they may not matter very much. When they take the form of collecting financial support for the I.R.A. they become intolerable; and it is time these misguided "exiles" were called to order by the elected and resident Government of the Irish Republic.

Irish-Americans are either Irish citizens or they are not. If they are not citizens, they have no more right to interfere casually in Irish affairs than Americans of German or Italian descent have in the affairs of Germany or Italy. Perhaps Noraid might ask themselves what kind of reception a German-

American committee would get in Bonn if they came over to promote the cause of the Baader-Meinhof gang, or how Italian-Americans would be received in Rome if they proposed to raise support for the Red Brigades.

If on the other hand we are dealing with American residents who still hold Irish citizenship, we are entitled firstly to comment that these are citizens who take very good care to avoid the burdens the rest of us have to carry. They take good care not to live here, not to pay Irish taxes, not to endure the hardships of an underdeveloped economy, not to risk living with the consequences of their actions. This alone deprives their interventions of any claim to respect.

But there is more to it than that. Article 10 of the Irish Constitution declares that fidelity to the nation and loyalty to the State are primary duties of the citizen. People who flagrantly do that which tends to undermine the State, and which conflicts with what all democratically elected Governments here have followed as national policy in regard to Northern Ireland and violence, are in breach of that primary duty.

Moreover, by Article 28 of the Constitution the Dáil which owed its original success in no small part to Irish-American support for Irish independence, is the only authority in the country entitled to declare war. Anyone who makes war on his own authority, or who helps those who do so, in flat defiance of the repeated declarations of the Dáil for Irish unity only by peaceful means, is in breach of the fundamental constitutional rule. Perhaps it is wrong to speak such hard words about people many of whom are misled by gross ignorance of the situation, which they seem to think much simpler than it is. Many of them do not seem to know that — disagreeable though it is for us to have to face these truths — a large majority of people in Northern Ireland regard themselves as British and want to stay British; that they look on the R.U.C. and the British Army not as an occupying force but as their lawful and only protectors and that that community has roots in Ireland which antedate the Mayflower settlement in America. Moreover their presence here, and their local predominance, rests on exactly the same kind of history as that which, at about the same period, cleared New York state of Red Indians so that Irish people, among others, might live there in comfort.

I deplore that history, and if I could turn it back I would. But we here have to live with it, come to terms with it, and build the best Ireland we can out of the materials which history has left us. That cannot be done by fire and slaughter, whatever may be the opinion of those who can Jumbo back to New York at their ease, out of harm's way. All this has been said before, and perhaps it is now time that the Irish Government considered whether, by showing our own naturally friendly feelings to America too eagerly, we have given the impression that we will take anything America sends us. Perhaps when the next St. Patrick's Day comes round, it would be wise to keep the Government in Dublin rather than send half of it to reviewing stands on the far side of the Atlantic. Perhaps then the misguided minority among our American cousins will begin to get the message.

In the wake of Mrs Thatcher's "Out, Out, Out", Dublin, 22 November 1984

Any true friend of the British Prime Minister might advise her today to conduct a thorough screening of her whole apparatus of cabinet office, aides, advisers, and even colleagues. The advice she seems to be getting on Northern Ireland and Irish affairs generally appears so malignant, and results in such world-class folly, that one has to suspect a deliberately destructive influence at work somewhere close to her. And as the British establishment has thrown up in this century such a luxuriant crop of traitors, the hypothesis of yet another mole does not seem so wild.

That the three options put forward in the Forum report were unrealistic or, at any rate, very premature is not the point. The point is that the British Government has managed to allow six months to go by during which hopes were visibly raised that some change, welcome to nationalist opinion, might be on the way; and then, by the cold and sudden manner of its discountenancing these hopes, left the whole of constitutional nationalist opinion not merely empty-handed but feeling positively slighted.

No doubt Mrs Thatcher and all the Western allies would be dismayed to see Ireland, or even part of it, in the grip of people compounded of elements of Gaddafi, Galtieri and Castro. Yet London's apparent policy of allowing the work of constitutional Irish nationalists to appear futile, and of inflaming the passions from which the I.R.A. draws strength — as happened during the 1981 hunger strike — looks like a brilliant attempt to bring that situation about.

That said, it can be admitted that it was never likely that Mrs Thatcher would have said Yes to any of the Forum options. The simple truth is that, although the British Government created the North of Ireland problem, allowed it to fester unheeded, and seems frequently to do is best to make it worse, it cannot cure it. The British cannot force a million people into a State they do not want to live in, except by methods that have not been seen in Europe since 1945, or in Ireland since 1650. This is why the whole thrust of Irish policy, since Mr Lynch as Taoiseach first started talking about "new political initiatives", seems to me misdirected.

I have no illusions whatever about Unionism of the baneful part it has played in bringing so much misery on this country. But the Unionists always have been, and remain, central to any settlement, and no diplomacy which even gives the appearance of going over their heads is wise.

They and their people compose one of the poles between which this country rotates; the republic's Government and people, and the Northern minority which looks to them for support, compose the other. The whole secret of pacifying this island, and making it safe against murder and tyranny, lies in reconciling these forces with each other, first in toleration, then in trust, then in friendship, ultimately perhaps in unity of whatever constitutional pattern.

The most the British can do is to try not to allow their congenital folly, where Ireland is concerned, to wreck this process; and they might, perhaps,in some secondary ways, help it on. The main burden of initiative, and of what will for many years be thankless toil, must lie with us.

On this reading of the scene, the role of the Fianna Fáil Opposition, in pushing the Forum — by taking advantage of the Taoiseach's anxiety for consensus — into making what are, at any rate at present, impossible proposals, was either malicious, or, if not malicious, was in a class of boneheadedness that could almost be called British. Mr Haughey recklessly insisted on setting up that which anyone could see Mrs Thatcher was certain recklessly to knock down. Anyone watching this process could only groan at the national humbling that was being stored up for us — of which Mr Haughey should be the last to complain, as he contributed more than anyone to bring it about.

He is, however, not any more sensitive than Mrs Thatcher to the effect of his actions on others. There were people in this country who felt even more humiliated by the events of the summit of December, 1980, when he as Taoiseach and Mr Lenihan as Foreign Minister gave a performance which had all the style of the front and hinder parts of a pantomime jackass. This was the summit after which they told us there had been a "historic breakthrough"; the "totality of relationships" in these islands had been "raised to a new plane"; everything was now "on the table"; there would be "institutional structures" which Mr Haughey did not mind insinuating could involve constitutional ones. There was instant uproar in the North, after which Mrs Thatcher publicly exploded this whole farrago of invention.

Moreover, if Mr Haughey is anxious that people might at last take him for the statesman which his promoters have been trying to sell him as for twenty years, he would have done far better, instead of attacking a Taoiseach whose unremitting and dedicated efforts had met a bitter disappointment, had he shown some sympathy and solidarity with him, some willingness to share the blow for which Fianna Fáil's policy had played the major part in setting him up.

By the total course he chose to adopt, however, he shows himself not just as having kicked a man when he was down, but as having taken advantage of his idealism, and his eagerness for national consensus, to lure him first on to ground on which he was certain to trip.

Adjournment Debate,
Dáil, 14 December 1984

I mentioned the United Kingdom a moment ago. I want to finish on this note in the time remaining to me. That United Kingdom — as I never tire of saying in here — represents for us an intellectual burden and an incubus which we must throw off, whether it be in the field of copying their industrial relations, their administrative systems or anything else. This is a good moment to reassess our approach to it, in the time after the Chequers Summit, which allows us an opportunity of taking a cool look at what passes for national policy in regard to the world outside our frontiers.

It is essential here to treat Northern Ireland in a special way, and not just as an ordinary item of diplomacy, to treat it separately from policy in regard to the rest of the world.

The Northern Ireland problem was confronted, in theory, by the New Ireland Forum but from the first day that New Ireland Forum was led astray by the Fianna Fáil Party, under its present leadership — I do not believe all of their members would have gone along with what they did — and by a small element in the SDLP. Deputy Haughey — who knew the Government's anxiety to achieve consensus, who knew the Taoiseach's passionate commitment to the object of the whole exercise insisted on dragging the whole operation on to ground which was, to use a military metaphor, indefensible. One can use what metaphor one likes. He lorried the Taoiseach with an absolutely unsaleable document, insisted on doing so; it was as though, Sir, he had pushed the Taoiseach out of an aircraft with a parachute designed so that it would not open.

One tends to exaggerate, put things in superlatives when, by next week, some other superlatives will have come to one's mind — but I do not think I have seen a more revolting spectacle in the time that I have been in politics than to see what then happened, that the Leader of Opposition, who had made certain that the Taoiseach was gong to London with an unsaleable package, turned and rent him, savaged him for not being able to sell the dud which his party has insisted on wishing on him. Naturally, he was seconded in it, by his own Forum team. I will not damn them all, because there were some honourable exceptions among them but, by and large, the Fianna Fáil New Ireland Forum team showed no interests in what the Forum was up to. That was seen by the public in their absolutely perfunctory examination of the bishops last February when the Hierarchy's representatives were at The Castle. They showed no interest in what anyone of the Unionist kidney had to say. Their ears were stopped up when anyone of the Unionist, or even Alliance persuasion came to the New Ireland Forum to talk. They behaved from the beginning, as they were designed to behave, like a busload of Bodenstown gasbags. They had nothing to contribute, no single idea.

Their whole approach to the thing is so wildly adrift from any form of reality that it is obvious their party leader never, in his heart, expects to have to deal with Northern Ireland people in any constitutional structure but the status quo. He knows that he himself is stitching himself and, to the extent that he influences its future, this whole country into the status quo, and that permits him all the Bodenstown talk.

We should conduct ourselves towards Northern Ireland like people who genuinely want to live in peace and harmony with all Northern people, work without offence, without causing them offence for the time when they will all share our vision of a mixed Republic, a mixed Republic which is proud, which is different, and which intends to be the best in the world. The Unionist people are at the core of the problem here. Unless we have their hand loyally and faithfully in ours, no unity that the British might be ballyragged into imposing would be worth having or would be worth living in.

Towards the British, and towards the rest of the world, we should conduct ourselves without complexes; without either the complex compounded of the grievance and resentment of recently emancipated people in our dealings with the rest of the world, such as we display when we talk about "our traditional policy of neutrality".

Where the British are concerned we should maintain a neighbourly, civil but firm distance, a reserve such as Mr de Valera would have understood and practised, but such as the teapot ballyhoo and idiotic overplay of, for example, the 1980 summit excludes.

The British are in many respects some of the most decent and best people in the world — as many Irish people, perhaps most Irish people who have lived there as I have, would, if they were honest, acknowledge: however, in regard to Ireland whether because of their oldest colonial adventure having brought more shame and hostility on them than any other, or possibly because they resent our rejection of what they consider the privilege of Britishness which they cannot understand our not claiming — because they think all the people of these islands are entitled to it — they have an unsure but unfailingly destructive touch in Irish affairs. They may not mean it like that, but that is how it comes out. Their combination of resentment and exasperation, and their distraction by other issues which, perhaps naturally, loom larger in their own minds lead them in Irish affairs into folly after folly and, occasionally into crimes.

We should, in trying to settle the island we have to live on, steer clear as far as we can of inviting their clumsy offices. We should have enough dignity and self-respect to treat them as we would treat our other European and Atlantic neighbours.

We should be big enough and men enough, and not slaves, to support them when they are in the right, as I believe they were in the right in the Falklands War. I do not defend all their actions then, but mainly they were in the right. They had been attacked; another civilised state had broken the first rule of civilised states by taking the law into its own hands and attacking them. I am not pre-judging the long term legality of the Falklands sovereignty, but, as far as the immediate issue was concerned in the war, they were clearly in the right and we should have been men enough to put behind us whatever resentment the Government of the day felt about other things and supported them.

Conversely, when they are in the wrong we should stand unbendingly up to them, in the way the Government in the fifties and sixties failed to do when they allowed the British to turn a blind eye on what was going on in their Stormont backyard. That was a failure on our part just as bad, indeed far worse. At all times, whether in supporting them or in standing up to them we should keep them at what I might call a diplomatic arm's length, and not be falling over ourselves to meet them and to be patronised by them, or putting ourselves in positions where we can be offended by them or setting ourselves up to get a black eye which was quite predictable from them. We should treat them at a neighbourly and civil but full arm's length.

Any closer contact we make in this part of the world should be reserved, as soon as they are willing to accept it, for the Protestant people in the North of Ireland. Those people have characteristics that may not appeal immediately to the emotions of somebody from this part of Ireland, and that is not necessarily their fault. They are, to some extent a different people even though we have a lot in common. But there are things about them which we do not acknowledge often enough, which we allow our resentment at their follies and their crimes to obscure. We owe the tradition which they stand for a great deal. When the Orangeman sings about the man who "forsook the old cause that give us our freedom, religion and laws", the freedom and laws he is talking about, whatever about the religion, are the freedom and laws of which the State is also the inheritor.

Although most of us were brought up in school by the ludicrous way history was taught in those days to regard ourselves as having lost the Battle of the Boyne, the fact is that most of the things that make life tolerable in a country like this which qualifies the State to rank as a Western democracy, the rule of law, the freedom of speech, the freedom of the press, the freedom to be in Opposition without endangering one's own life, are things that the Protestant people of the North defended on the side of King William and that we, on King James's side, because of an historical combination which was, as usual tragic, were led to oppose. Not one of those values was upheld by the Stuarts. Not one of them was admitted. Not one of those freedoms was conceded but the story of human rights, the rule of law and the freedoms we take for granted in the Western world contains within it as one of its chapters the victory of King Billy on the Boyne.

I share, because of my ethnic membership of the thing, in my blood and guts the feeling of disappointment about the Battle of the Boyne. I try to put it behind me naturally. I would not, I suppose, fight it all over again. What I would fight over again if I could, and win this time, would be an earlier battle at the beginning of the seventeenth century which destroyed what might have turned into a Celtic monarchy and ultimately into a distinctive modern Celtic state. We have to acknowledge, whatever the feelings that were bred into us by our race of our schooling, that the Protestant tradition which we appear to make little of is regarded by the people in the North of Ireland as their religion. Their civil and religious liberties are, in their eyes, intertwined. That explains the fact that they have clergymen in parliament and clergymen ranting and raving. I do not defend the ranting and raving of some of them. One of them has done more than any single man in Ireland to bring misery, bloodshed, hatred and misfortune on the country and I could never say anything else about him. The reason is, in spite of those excesses, that their impression of religious and civil liberties is intertwined. It is part of a history of which we have been and still are the beneficiaries. When they express apprehension about what is going to happen to them if they are absorbed into an Irish Republic we should occasionally say, "The liberties you are concerned about are ones we could not live without either, and we acknowledge your contribution in the history of civilisation in having asserted those liberties, and upholding them, at least for this part of the world and for the part of mankind which, broadly speaking, can be described as Western democracy".

They are the people we have to share this island with and conciliate. It cannot be done by fire and slaughter, and it cannot be done by Bodenstown gasbags either. It has to be done by a Government which does not bother about raising a cheer at an Ard-Fheis or raising a drunken howl at the end of a ballad session but works patiently to make some bridges and contacts with people with whom we must live in peace if those who come after us are to have an island they can be proud of.

Advice to Denis Healey,
Dublin, 5 March 1985

Mr Denis Healey, the British Labour Party's shadow Foreign Secretary and former Chancellor of the Exchequer, is reported today as having said in Dublin that Mrs Thatcher "realises she has a better chance of moving to some sort of improvement of the Northern situation with the present Irish Government than is likely to occur if it changes", and that he felt this to be so "for the same reason that most Irish people feel that".

It is perfectly true that the present Government, never having played domestic politics with the North and having always been more realistic about it than its opponents, has a better prospect of getting progress than Fianna Fáil. But the last thing any Irish party wants is an expression of approval from a

British politician, and it is amazing that a senior figure like Mr Healey should have so little sense as to talk like this.

The utterance, although obviously unplanned, is in the same category as something similar said by a Tory Minister during the November 1982 General Election here. Criticism of Mr Haughey and his party should be left to us. Coming from a British politician, its only effect is to stir sympathy for its target, even among people who have no notion of supporting Fianna Fáil.

The safest rule for British politicians to observe is to keep entirely clear of Irish politics. Even their most well- intentioned interventions — and I accept that Mr Healey meant well — risk, at best, appearing condescending, and, at worst, evoke the old calculation that anything which suits a British party is unlikely to be in Irish interests.

Moreover, even in contexts less delicate than Northern Ireland, it is improper for a public figure when abroad to let himself be drawn into comments on local political parties. Irish leaders on all sides have scrupulously respected this rule when in Britain or elsewhere, although very possibly they held views on the local political scene which would have interested the press; and one would imagine that the British, who are considered the world's greatest sticklers for propriety, would not need to be reminded of world etiquette on this point.

Fianna Fáil's Northern Policy, Dublin, 22 May 1985

Deputy Haughey's malignant hounding of the Taoiseach on his efforts in regard to the North is, of all manifestations of the present Fianna Fáil leadership, the hardest to take.

Apparently the Taoiseach and the Minister for Foreign Affairs are guilty of disgraceful backsliding if they countenance, even as a measure designed to relieve today's tensions, any Northern settlement failing short of the Forum options.

Leaving aside the question whether the Forum options are realistic — and I believe that at the present time they are not — and leaving aside the degree to which Fianna Fáil and Mr Haughey in particular are responsible for their unreality — and I believe they must carry most of the blame for it — any settlement, however far short of the national aspirations which brings peace, now to the ordinary people of the North will have the support of the mass of people here in the South.

I do not believe we are so inhuman as to prefer own "aspirations", for which very few of us have sacrificed a night's sleep or would assent to an extra five pounds taxation, to ordinary people's chances of living free of bloodshed and terror.

Perhaps this point can be put beyond doubt, the next time an IMS or MORI opinion poll is carried out, by including some question such as " Would you support the Government if it worked for an intermediate solution designed to restore peace in the North without prejudice to our longer-term aspirations on unity?"

The central flaw in Fianna Fáil doctrine on this matter goes back to a previous leader, Mr Lynch. Mr Lynch certainly did his best to cool Northern passions in 1971 and 1972; made all the right noises, at least, about grasping nettles and breaking old moulds; and not only broadly supported the Sunningdale formula but accepted credit for paving the way to it. But later when back in office himself, he began to talk about new political initiatives meaning British initiatives.

We should have learned then, and most certainly should have learned since then, that nothing is to be had from the British. If we wish to win the North, we must win the Northern people; and — concealed behind all the talk of Sinn Fein's "success" at the local elections in talking 10% of the vote — the Unionist determination, as evidenced by their nearly 60% of the poll, is as solid as it was 50 years ago.

All the Bodenstown blather down here has done nothing to weaken it; nor has the I.R.A.'s campaign; nor can Fianna Fáil, almost 60 years after the party's foundation, point to one single Unionist whom their words or their deeds have converted to the Nationalist creed.

It is time, and far past time, that we had the honesty to face those facts, and to give over the foolish talk — repeated last night by Mr Haughey — about an all-Ireland constitutional conference including the Unionists. Can Mr Haughey point to a single Unionist who would attend such a conference? Would Mr Haughey attend a constitutional conference called by Unionists with the aim of getting us back into the U.K.?

Mr Haughey's talk about "mobilising American opinion to get it made U.S. policy to press for Irish unity" is not only lacking in self-respect, it is lacking in sanity. What does he think the effect on Unionists will be if an Irish Government, having despaired of ever reaching the Northern Protestant heart or gaining its trust, tries to get foreigners to arm-twist what are supposed to be our neighbours and brothers?

The parallel with Germany which he suggested breaks down at the first and vital test. The Germans' territory was divided by the allies, but the German people remain one in blood and tradition; and if a free plebiscite were held tomorrow, no doubt they would vote overwhelmingly for unity on both sides of the border. None of these conditions holds true here.

Perhaps it is not literally true that there is nothing to be had from the British. Certainly they can regularise by their legislation something which political consensus has worked out; they can refrain from making things worse by the stupidity they often display here; they can provide reassurance and support for those who look to them. But if we are talking about getting a constitutional move under way, the British can only provide the choke; the starting motor and ignition must come from us.

Any policy based on seeing those roles reversed is, I believe, going to subject us to humiliation after humiliation — and we will be lucky if it stops at mere verbal humiliation.

It is of course in Mr Haughey's interest that, if these humiliations arrive, Dr FitzGerald should be seen as presiding over them. This is the cynical reason for the Opposition leader's ostensible impatience to see "dialogue" and "summits" between ourselves and the British. But the Government will scarcely need to be warned about the character of the urging coming from this quarter of the side-line.

Anglo-Irish Agreement, Dáil, 19 November 1985

The Taoiseach in his speech referred to the many messages which he has received from people in all parts of the country and representing all persuasions after the conclusion of the Hillsborough agreement. He spoke of these as being messages of congratulation. I think it would perhaps be more accurate, if I might correct him, by saying that they were messages of gratitude and of admiration for the immense effort which he personally has invested in the task of trying to end bloodshed and savagery in the North of Ireland and to reconcile Irish people, ever since the trouble there broke out 16 or 17 years ago.

All these messages are entirely understandable and correct; but, while I join in the gratitude and admiration which they convey, they are very easily confused, and perhaps, in the representation which the Press has given of people's feelings, they have become confused with what can very easily be mistaken for euphoria. There is a big difference between congratulating someone on a brave and lengthy effort and jubilating, perhaps prematurely, over its success, because the real reason for the appearance of euphoria being out of place is that it still remains to be seen whether or not this agreement will work. In addition to that, we have the lesson of Sunningdale, which is only 12 years old, to warn us that any demonstrations of satisfaction in Dublin awaken alarm and consternation in Belfast and that anything in this part of the country which gives the appearance that we are satisfied with our progress towards a national aspiration is likely to redouble the determination of people 100 miles from us or less never to let that day arrive. So that anything in the nature of euphoria or jubilation about this very important and courageous but very fragile step is totally misplaced now and will be for some time.

I had to admit that I had misgivings about the process which led to this agreement. My misgivings related to the basis from which the process began, namely the report of the New Ireland Forum of last summer 12 months. That report was the fruit of a very long and high-profile series of meetings in which, ultimately, the four Nationalist parties there represented agreed on a set of options. The report contained more than these options; and with the introductory chapters which set out the very admirable sentiments about respecting the traditions of other people I unreservedly agree, as I hope I do not need to tell anybody in the House. But the options, I am sorry to say — and I have said this in the House before — were taken on board, I think, secretly against the better judgment of many of the people there.

Since the Taoiseach has rightly appealed to us to keep the temperature of this debate low, I will not speak about that event as perhaps I would in another setting. But we did, some of us at least, take on board those options against our better judgment. They had to be against the better judgment of anybody who reflected on the matter, because all three of them were totally unacceptable to anybody except the Nationalists. And the one which we labelled as being our top preference was the one most wildly unlikely to be accepted by anyone in the country or outside the country except an Irish Nationalist.

We then looked exceedingly foolish when the British Prime Minister shot down these three options in as many tens of seconds at the Summit in England a year ago. Everybody in the country appeared to be hurt and surprised, although that fate for these three options was absolutely predictable from the day they appeared in print for the first time. The Government were then faced with the task, which I must say they manfully and courageously discharged, of putting their disappointment behind them, trying to take up the pieces, trying to salvage from the New Ireland Forum report whatever scattered pieces of material were still usable, by putting them together into a stage of a platform on which the contacts with the British about the future of Northern Ireland might be resumed.

In due course, the agreement which is today before the House emerged. That agreement does fall far short of providing for joint authority, which was the least drastic of the three Nationalist options. It falls for short of that; but it goes a long distance further than mere consultation. It does provide for an official Irish presence, even with a role which is hard to define exactly, in the governmental structure of the North. If it works, in fairness, that must be recognised as a very substantial advantage to the Northern minority who have no one else to speak for them on the surface of the globe, except the people in this State and the Government in charge of it. If it works it will be a very substantial advantage to them and I would like to hear any lady or gentleman on the far side of the House say otherwise. But, of course, it has built into it the intensely provocative feature of the very thing which the Unionists regard as the thin end of the wedge. It is there institutionalised for them to see and will, therefore, redouble their determination to prevent it from working. I am very sorry that the Leader of the Opposition, in a speech which was centred almost entirely on the legalities, as he sees them, of Article 2 and 3, did not condescend to consider this aspect of the matter, this aspect of this very fragile agreement which might confer very substantial benefits on the minority for whom I suppose everyone in the House would wish to be thought to speak, and would wish to be thought to have their interests at heart. This agreement is under the very severe danger that even though it goes a few inches only along the road Deputy Haughey says he would like to see us going, it goes far enough along that road almost to guarantee that we will have the best part of one million people trying to block its success.

Personally — and I have said this often — I would have preferred an internal solution, not because I do not want Irish unity in the long term but because I am not so arrogant as to prefer my aspirations, long term or short term, to what are the obvious crying needs of ordinary human beings today. If their lot can be bettered and their hopes for themselves and their children can be given a lift by some solution — even if it is one which does not leave me with a display of flags of the very colour I would like in front of me — I will go along with it. I will leave it to my children, or theirs, to take the thing a step further if they can and want to. Second, I would have preferred that an internal solution had been achieved, not by negotiation with the British but by negotiation with the other million Irish people with whom we have to share this island, and who would still be there if the British left in the morning; who would still be able to make life intolerable for everybody in this island and cause deaths by the tens of thousands, even if the British left in the morning. They are the ones we have to deal with and let us never lose sight of that fact. To give the Taoiseach the credit which he more than anyone in the House is entitled to, he has never lost sight of it even during the periods in which we have been entangled in this inter-governmental process.

Failing the possibility of involving the Northern majority in the achieving of an internal solution the next best thing might have been there imposition of a power-sharing executive. I think so, but I have to bow my judgment to that of people nearer the scene. I recognise also that the Unionists, by the incredible crassness of their leadership, have virtually disqualified themselves from consideration in this context. No leadership was ever more intransigent, and I say that in the strict sense of the word of being unwilling to compromise or settle. I understand their feelings and their fears but everybody has to settle something some time. Perhaps, as the vice-chairman of the Alliance Party said on radio this morning, it may be that there are, in some places — though certainly not in this House, I hope not in this House — people who are not sorry to see them momentarily discomfited.

I hope that feeling will not persist, but it did seem to be the case — and perhaps this is the reason we have an agreement in this particular shape — that nothing was to be achieved from them, that no movement was going to come from them. Then the British, in other words, their own sovereign government, ultimately lost patience with them. Therefore, while I feel sorry for their plight — in the sense that they have, I think, a fair point in saying that a settlement has been reached over their heads and without involving them in any consultation — to some extent they must, in fairness, bear the blame for that themselves.

In addition — again I have to bow to local knowledge; obviously I do not claim to have a knowledge of the thing at first hand myself — the Nationalist population would appear to be now so alienated that a merely internal solution would no longer have satisfied them, in particular would no longer have rescued them from the clutches of people who, although flying a green flag, would leave no life worth living for anyone on the island if they got their way. It would not suffice to keep them out of the clutches of such people. Accordingly, we have to make the best of this agreement. It is not the one I personally would wish to see. It is a brave effort, it is deserving of support, and everyone should give it a fair trial. We have to make the best of it, although I must say I have a very uneasy feeling in the pit of my stomach about having to depend on the British for anything in the context of Irish affairs. I would far prefer, if ever we could get that close to them, to establish a standing relationship with the people who differ from us in regard to the destiny of this island, the people who at present say violent and frightening things about the lengths they would go to to prevent the unity of the island from ever being achieved.

It is important that, in the course of this debate, some Deputies at least should express some understanding for the emotional repugnance which the Northern majority feel towards what is — even though they may have to some extent themselves to thank for it — a deeply unwelcome structure which has been wished on them by two Governments they do not trust, one of which perhaps they never trusted and the other of which they no longer trust.

I would ask Members of the House, in order to get them for a second to stand in Unionist shoes, to picture an arrangement — I am not saying that you can exactly swop the terms in this image of speech; of course you cannot — but I would ask the House roughly to picture an arrangement in which the Unionists and the British, between themselves and without consulting us, erected a system of structure under which British ministers would appear, in whatever capacity, in Merrion Street and British police officers in Garda Headquarters. That would be deeply unwelcome to us. I cannot suppose that their is any Deputy in the House so poor in imagination, so contemptuous of others, that he cannot give the Unionists the credit of assuming that their feelings would be at least as strong as his. That is the situation, more or less, with which they feel they are now confronted. We need not go into who is to blame for it. We need not go into the question of where the historical responsibility for it lies, or who will stand judgment for it on the last day. We need not go into who is right or who is wrong. That is their perception of their situation at present. We have to take it like that and try to bring sympathy to bear, so far as we can, on the people who have to share this island with us, many of whom have been here before the surnames of some Deputies in this House were ever heard in this country.

It is against the background of these Northern feelings that I have to ask the House — and I propose not to disobey or depart from the Taoiseach's injunction to be moderate in speech about this — to consider the Opposition amendment to the Taoiseach's motion. How are we to judge the attitude of the Opposition, an attitude which essentially condemns this agreement for not securing unity, or at any rate one of the expressed Forum options, and as Deputy Haughey said for having conceded, as he thinks, formally and legally a position which it is not constitutionally competent for our Government to concede in regard to British sovereignty?

This agreement, which provides for only a relatively mild dose of in-stitutionalised Irish influence in Northern affairs, has by all accounts — accounts which I believe — caused a frightening level of anger among Unionists who, as the Taoiseach said, have not perhaps had the time, the leisure of the atmosphere to consider the agreement deeply enough. I have had public and private reports of this frightening level of anger. What would the reaction be like if that dose were not a slight one but a double dose, an image we might apply to the joint authority option that was the least drastic of the lot? What would happen if it were multiplied by ten, as in the unitary state option which the Fianna Fáil input to the Forum resulted in our putting up front? What would the reaction be then?

I am aware there is an opinion that the Unionists are "bluffing" and that "their bluff has to be called". I cannot see anything in the Unionist record which suggests that they are only bluffing. I know that in the 1973-74 period about 400 uninvolved and innocent Catholics in Northern Ireland fell victim to sectarian murder, not to speak of the fact that 11 years ago 30 people were blown to bits in this city, some of them a few hundred yards from where we are speaking. Where is there anything to suggest bluff? Would we be bluffing if we threatened to fight rather than be reabsorbed into the United Kingdom? Would anybody be justified in thinking we were only bluffing? Why do we credit them with less spirit than we lay claim to? Is the proposer of a unitary state, who faults the Government for not producing it, or for discarding the possibility of achieving it, ready to face up to the consequences of that kind of situation? What forces would be deployed to keep order in six counties mad with rage, when we are barely able to keep order in some parts of the city of Dublin? Does anyone imagine that the Unionist reaction would stop at the Border? I despair when I hear this talk that we ought to have gone for this or that. Does anybody reckon the fallout from getting something and measure against that achievement the cost that would be borne, not by the people in well protected, upholstered offices, but by ordinary people blown to bits by indis-criminate bombs?

As for the Opposition's suggestion of a "constitutional conference representative of all the traditions in Ireland", what would Deputy Huaghey's proposal be if, as seems quite certain to me, the entire Unionist spectrum boycotted such a conference? Suppose the two sovereign Governments did call it and suppose we were told by the two Unionist parties to take a running jump at ourselves, what would the fall back position be then? Neither of the two Unionist parties would so much as come to the Forum. How likely then is it that they would come to a table on which they would be expected to lay down for good their present constitutional position? Are we living on the moon or is it that we think our constituents are living on the moon?

The Sinn Féin position has not yet been mentioned this afternoon. I see that Mr Adams is very displeased with the Government for what he calls "the tearing up of Articles 2 and 3 of the Constitution". Since when, we may ask, have Sinn Féin and the IRA developed such a tender regard for the Constitution? Have they not themselves repeatedly torn up Article 9, which prescribes loyalty to the state as one of the fundamental duties of the citizen? Have they not repeatedly torn up Article 15, which describes the Oireachtas as the only legitimate body in the country to maintain an armed force? Have they not torn up Article 28, which vests only in the Dáil the right to maintain a war? Have they not torn up Article 40, which contains the right to life? What about Article 41, which proclaims the right of the family, which these sanctimonious butchers have on hundreds of occasions destroyed by robbing wives of their husbands and children of their fathers, bringing grief and desolation into thousands of innocent homes? All this and we are supposed to take lectures on the constitutional proprietors of Articles 2 and 3 from Mr Adams. I will return to Article 2 and 3 if I have time, but the scope of this debate has to be much larger.

I want to appeal to Unionist people, if it is not ludicrous for someone in this House to do so, to accept the assurances which the Taoiseach and the Minister for Foreign Affairs have tried to offer them, which I know they sincerely mean, and to give this agreement even a year's chance to work. Surely the bruise to their self-esteem which I know the institutionalised Irish presence at Stormont will represent will be a small price to pay if in the end their Nationalist neighbours can be reconciled to them and if their province ceases to be a by-word for rancorous hatred, for destruction and for murder.

That is an appeal which many Deputies will make in some form or other during this debate. I beg Unionist people or their leaders, if they read what goes on here, to believe that we mean it sincerely and that we have the interests of ordinary people at heart.

For myself, I am prepared to put Irish unity on 20 back burners if it will save both Catholics and Protestants from the nightmare which they have gone through during the past 16 years. It does not mean I am not a Nationalist still. It does not mean I would not be over the moon if we could have Irish unity and I could think of some way of reaching it. I recall something for which the far side can claim credit when Mr de Valera made an inspired gesture during the Belfast blitz by sending the entire Dublin fire brigade to help. That was worth doing and it did more to break down hatred and promote understanding than a thousand speeches at Bodenstown.

I want to offer a few impromptu comments on Deputy Haughey's general proposition that the Government have behaved in a manner which is not properly constitutional in, as he put it, acknowledging the sovereignty of the British over Northern Ireland. I cannot read that acknowledgement into the article of the agreement to which Deputy Haughey was referring. It is true if I were polemicising on the other side during a budget debate or in some tuppeny half penny debate on a Bill I did not like the look of, I might rack my brains to try to twist that meaning out of it, but I am damned if I can see it. It is also true that in the whole sphere of constitutional arrangements in this country and in England, and in relations between the two, there is an area which necessarily must be one of subtlety where one does not pursue logic too far and it is best to leave certain questions unanswered. This is one of them.

The Constitution asserts in Article 3 the right of the Government and Parliament established by the Constitution to exercise jurisdiction over the North, but the owner of a right of the person who has to articulate it, which means the Government under our Constitution, is entitled to forebear its exercise or its assertion. The owner is not entitled to jettison or disown it, but is most certainly entitled to forebear according to his judgment on a particular occasion its exercise or assertion and to pipe down about it for a while. If the interests of humanity, peace and decency require that that be done in regard to the bit of paper which the Deputy opposite quoted from — because it does not weigh very heavily with me against people's rights — then it is the right thing to do.

It is incumbent on the Government to say as a matter of political policy that they propose to behave in a certain way, that they will not discuss legal rights now, but that they will act in a way which implies forebearing to assert those rights in a particular context, for a particular period, or in a particular setting. If that is the Government's intention, I see nothing unconstitutional about it and, were it otherwise, I would be in favour of freeing a Government from a constriction of that kind.

Before I leave the question of subtleties, let me remind the House that Mr de Valera, whom I mentioned with respect a few minutes ago, was a Republican. That is how he always advertised himself and I accept that the description fitted him before the phrase was hijacked by murderers. How is it that when he drafted the Constitution, from which Deputy Haughey has been quoting, he did not think fit to declare the state a Republic in that document? Why was he so shy of it? Why did he maintain a fragile link with the Crown with the King accrediting our diplomatic representatives up to 1949? I do not like to press the point. Others did not like to press the point then.

I recognise that he had some good intentions of perhaps even maintaining a fragile link with the North which I believe was his motive. That was an area which was perhaps best left unexplored, in which it would have been destructive to push words and logic too far. No more strident example of the point I am

126

trying to make exists in the constitutional history of the State than Mr de Valera's own performance.

In regard to acknowledging the legitimacy of the constitutional positionon the far side of the Border, I cannot see that Article 1 of this agreement does so, but we do it every day in the way we operate our laws. In regard to exchange control, we recognise that there is a different sovereignty on the far side of the Border. None of us in this House can open a bank account in Portadown or buy a house up there without getting the permission of the Central Bank because it is a different jurisdiction. If we are going to be that fundamentalist about the matter, surely exchange control is unconstitutional in so far as acquiring property or moving money around in Northern Ireland is concerned? What about customs offenses? Why do we have customs posts along the Border if it is not a different jurisdiction and if we have not formally recognised it as such? What about the area of criminal law in which a prosecution here would depend on the offence being committed within the jurisdiction? If the prosecution could not prove that the offence took place in Cavan rather than Fermanagh, the case would be dismissed. These are niggling legalities but I did not start them. I have been dragged into them by the Leader of the Opposition, as others will be during the next couple of days.

The only thing I see as having any kind of constitutional question mark over it in the agreement relates to the possibility of instituting mixed courts. That is a very tricky matter because mixed courts in this jurisdiction, even if we needed them, are not the same as those existing in Northern Ireland.

If such courts imply the sitting of a Northern judge administering justice or sharing in the administration of justice in the Twenty-six Counties, that will not be constitutionally possible unless that judge simultaneously accepts appointment as a judge under our Constitution. Otherwise we may find ourselves in a difficulty under Article 34.

It would be helpful to everybody if we did not run this three-day debate on legalities alone. I felt I had to say a word or two without having time to reflect on them in reply to Deputy Haughey's remarks but it is more important to stick to the large, political outlines of the problem which we are up against and which the Irish people as a whole are looking to us to solve. Despite the misgivings which I have expressed, I again express my admiration for the Government's efforts, and my plea to the Unionists to give the Agreement a chance to work.

Murder of UDR Officer,
Dublin, 3 December 1985

By contrast with the many predictable voices issuing from the unionist leadership in the last two weeks, that of the Presbyterian Moderator at the funeral of a murdered U.D.R. office in Kilkeel, County Down, strikes a note which genuinely invites the understanding and sympathy of everyone in the island who wants peace.

Many hearts among the Northern majority, he said, were sad, confused and anxious, and he spoke of the "fear and uncertainty" among the peace-loving and law-abiding Protestant people. These, he said, "felt betrayed and that they had no friends".

It does not matter that most of us in the Republic feel, as I do, that the people for whom he speaks have, by their toleration of a political leadership which understood only intransigence, made a lot of their trouble for themselves: an opinion which one can reasonably hold while with equal sincerity condemning and rejecting the I.R.A.'s barbaric campaign against them.

What matters now is that they feel, as Dr Dickinson said, that they have no friends; and as these are the people with whom we have to share this island, and who are crucial to its chances of remaining habitable by humans at all, this is the time to beg them, for once, and for a year or two, to try to see us southern Nationalists in that role.

A small fringe of people in the Republic have neither sympathy nor patience with Northern unionists, and would not be sorry to see their society ruined or submerged. The rest of us, I believe a huge majority, have no interest in oppressing or humiliating them, or in getting the British to do it; we hold far more values in common with them than they realise, including a love of the civil liberty which the Protestant victory at the Boyne played a part in achieving — late though Irish Catholics were in getting any benefit from it; and we recognise our common interest with them in holding the line against tyranny and murder.

For the holding of this line it is vital that the Northern minority be given a full place in the sun; and, even if this now involves measures which stick in the unionist throat, surely they are a small price to pay for the chance of a peace and normality that even adults in the North can no longer remember.

I wish the Presbyterian Moderator and his people would see in us the friends they look for now in vain elsewhere. I do not ask them to put away their caution towards us, but merely to give the Hillsborough agreement, in its entirety, time to prove itself more of a gain than a loss to them, and to give us time to prove that they can safely shelve for good their distrust of this Republic.

Fatuous Fianna Fáil guff, Dublin, 10 March 1986

As so often in the past, extreme unionism and fatuous Fianna Fáil guff are sustaining one another again today, at the expense of the ordinary people of Ireland, north and south.

The extreme unionist position can be expressed as follows: they are not willing to accept the consequences of being a minority in Ireland; and they are not willing to accept the consequences of being a minority in Britain. Such a stance points logically in only one direction, namely an Ulster U.D.I.; and, while probably the present British Government in present conditions would prevent this, the mood of exasperation with Northern Ireland in Britain is such that there could be no certainty that a future British Government would not let them get away with it.

If this happened, I have no doubt that the Loyalist junta — deprived, presumably, of the British subsidy and of British-financed security — would want to shed some of its economic and security burdens by shortening its frontiers, and would withdraw from several Border areas. This would leave us, probably, with the Bogside and Crossmaglen; while a weakened and intimidated minority would be left behind the Border, at the mercy of the rulers of the Ulster Transvaal.

Of all possible scenarios, this is the worst; and anything we can do to avert it must have our first priority. This means, above all, holding on to whatever shreds of moderate unionist opinion are still around, not alienating them, trying to increase their substance and influence, and not giving them the feeling that we are out to destroy what they believe in.

Measured against this necessity, one reads Mr Haughey's silly speeches in America with despair. At the very moment when the North is threatened with Loyalist disorder because of their opinion that the Hillsborough agreement goes too far, Mr Haughey is telling Irish-Americans — themselves well out of harm's way — that it does not go far enough, that the only recipe for the North is the total and final demolition of its link with Britain.

You do not have to be a very extreme Unionist to feel sickened and enraged by the fine words about "recognising the unionist tradition" coming from people who propose to annihilate the only thing which makes that tradition valuable to them, i.e. the union itself.

Mr Haughey, if asked about what he sees as the shape of a Northern solution, will talk airily about an "all-party, round-table conference". Why should unionists — who did not even come to the harmless talking-shop at the Forum — attend such a conference? Would any of us attend a conference which proposed to bury the Irish Republic and was meeting merely to discuss the funeral arrangements?

Such talk, even to a moderate unionist, is beneath laughter; and his reply to such an invitation would be to tell Mr Haughey and the rest of us to take a running jump at ourselves. With unionists of a different kidney, we would be very lucky if the response stopped just at talk.

British Foolishness, Courtmacsherry, 24 March 1986

The British comedian's depiction of an Irishman as someone who does not know his right foot from his left must seem a ludicrous inversion of the truth, if one can judge by recent events in relations between these two jurisdictions.

We had first of all the British Minister for Northern Ireland doing his foolish best to destabilise the Dublin Government's very delicate position under the Anglo-Irish Agreement, by imputing to the Taoiseach the abandonment at Hillsborough of Nationalist aspirations to unity. The fact that this was instantly disowned by the British Prime Minister did not undo all the damage; as lately as two weeks ago Mr Haughey felt able to cite Mr King to an American audience, naturally without mentioning Mrs Thatcher's repudiation of his words. There is no easier way of wrecking the fragile hopes which lie in this agreement than making it a domestic political liability for the Dublin Government; but it appears one can reach Cabinet rank in Britain without even the minimal gumption it takes to grasp so simple a point.

And now we have last Saturday's shambles over the Glenholmes extradition case. This, needless to say, has been presented by the British media in such a way as to somewhat fudge the fact that the cause was slapdash behaviour at the London end — the mixture of ignorance and neglect which he British like to think peculiarly Hibernian. Possibly the British Authorities feel that, where we are concerned, any old document will do; but one would have thought that, in seeking the extradition of someone wanted on such frightful charges, they would have left nothing to chance.

Of all people in the world, the last ones to complain about the strict and scrupulous application of law should be the British, from whom we in this country inherited the whole idea of the rule of law and legality, which we acknowledge as the basis of civilised existence, and do our humble best to preserve; and to represent an action of a court which refused to enforce an invalid warrant as "freeing a wanted person on a technicality" is to belittle the first principles of their own jurisprudence. Naturally there has been the usual raucous chorus from the North.

That Unionists should not care about scrupulous legality in particularly odd; since their own best known ballad, the "old orange flute", complains of a protestant who "forsook the old cause, that gave us our freedom, religion and laws". The legacy of King William and his victory — of which everyone in this island enjoys the benefit — was the establishment of legality the rule of law, rather than the arbitrary rule of the Stuarts. The only kind of court that might have overlooked a basic flaw in a warrant would have been a court subservient to the wishes of the executive; and I am sorry that any Unionist should wish to see such a thing again anywhere on Irish soil.

Mr Paisley and his friends, instead of their mindless jeering, would be better employed making sure that their own Northern Ireland police procedures are adequate. He ought to be reminded that twice within recent months wanted men have been captured here and extradited to the North, only to be acquitted by the court in Belfast for lack of evidence. Should Irish policemen be asked to risk their lives for such a result?

Loss of Citizenship for Terrorists, Dublin, 9 November 1987

When this state was established, and in the early years of its existence, one of its leading ideals was the aspiration to set the world a high example in ethical standards. This often came through in the pathetic persuasion that we were — as bishops until quite lately used to say — an "island of spiritual values in a sea of materialism". All the same, the aspiration did correspond to a high level of human decency in official and group attitudes and behaviour; even so ungenerous a critic as Winston Churchill was ready to pay a tribute to the Christian and civilised State that had arisen here.

All this is placed at risk, and our pretensions made to look like hypocrisy, by the horrors committed by terrorists in the name of an Irish cause. We do not want to be ruled by the I.R.A., the I.N.L.A., or any of their sneaking-regarders. We do not want Irish unity, if it is to be had only by their methods. But over and above that, we do not want to be contaminated by the guilt of their savagery.

How to mark the repugnance of ordinary citizens towards murder and mutilation is a problem. Terrorists do not ponder over newspaper editorials, and they despise the words of weary condemnation which churchmen and political leaders use about them. Despite the part which — like the Mafia — they force Catholic ritual to play for them when it suits them, they hold that Church in contempt; the Pope himself went on his knees in Drogheda in 1979 to beg them to give up killing, and got the same response as if he had been addressing a cruel gang of pagan bandits in the darkest of the Dark Ages.

There remains as a possibility the withdrawal of Irish citizenship, as an emphatic sign that the huge majority of us do not wish to share with them what should be an honourable status, but which their activities are turning into a mark of dishonour.

The law at present makes no provision for deprivation of civic rights (as in some other countries) as a consequence of conviction of terrorist offenses; but the Constitution expressly envisages in Article 9 that citizenship can be lost as well as acquired, and that ordinary law can regulate the conditions of such loss.

I think it would be an appropriate signal of the abhorrence felt by most Irish citizens if they authorised, through their elected representatives, the additional deprivation of citizenship by order of a court on conviction of a serious terrorist offence.

This would be not merely a token. Firstly, since our existing citizenship law has the effect of conferring citizenship on virtually the entire population of the island, North and South, and since "republican" terrorists from the North often use Irish passports, it would cut them off from at any rate legally obtained passports. Secondly, no person so deprived could be registered as a Dáil elector. Thirdly, a non-national marrying such a person could not acquire Irish nationality. Fourthly, the lack of citizenship would arguably deprive such a person of the standing to challenge the constitutionality of an Irish law. These do not add up to a major deterrent, least of all to a deranged mentality. They would, however, represent as strong a mark as were able to give of our determination that Irish citizenship and acts of barbarity will never be accepted by us as mutually compatible.

Anglo-Irish Relations, Dublin, 9 March 1988

Relations between this country and Britain are deteriorating at such a rate that is important to make sure no false judgment or over-reaction of our own contributes to the mess. On this standard, the behaviour of the Government, and of others, in recent weeks deserves criticism. Issues have become muddled, gestures of protest and distrust have been misplaced, with the result that when something happens which really does cause serious concern, our voice, devalued by having been raised too often and for insufficient reason, is likely to be ignored.

There is, firstly, the abusive tone which it has become common to use about British justice. Have we forgotten how enraged everyone here, rightly, becomes if the British media suggest that an Irish District Justice is maliciously and needlessly throwing difficulties in the way of an extradition process? What would we say if our own Court of Criminal Appeal were spoken of in Britain as though its proceedings were a symbol of prejudice and malignance? What would we say if a British Minister publicly said the Irish Attorney General was not fit for his job?

By this I do not mean to endorse whatever a British, or any other foreign court or prosecuting officer may do, and I do in fact think the Stalker episode in particular is a deplorable story. I only say it is unreasonable and childish to speak insultingly about people whose own periodical incivility about us we resent so deeply; and wrong of us not to be willing to make the same assumptions for their institutions as we expect them and others to make in favour of ours.

Then there is the Government's performance in publicly setting up a Garda enquiry into the Aughnacloy shooting which took place across the border from the Republic. I have the same suspicions as everyone else about this death; and consider that the British, in choosing this moment to release, and readmit to their army, a soldier convicted of murder in Northern Ireland, behaved with a recklessness barely compatible with sanity.

But does this justify a provocative gesture like asking an Assistant Commissioner to investigate the matter from this side of the Border?

Is it not a needless exasperation of even moderate Unionists, who naturally see it as an insulting signal of distrust towards the R.U.C.? Is it not creating an endless precedent? If the Garda Síochána investigate one incident which took place outside our jurisdiction, why not another? Need they remain in Monaghan? Might we not send a team of plain-clothes detectives to Belfast, or for that matter to Gibraltar? Is it not certain that someone will sooner or later demand something like this?

Then there is the current level of indignation about the British Prevention of Terrorism Act. Every sovereign government is entitled, within the limits imposed by general standards of human rights and natural justice, to take whatever measures it sees fit for the protection of its own people and its own security forces. If anyone denied the right of the Irish Government to do so, I can imagine the roars of indignation that would be heard. Why then may not the British do so too? Must their legislation on this subject be exactly the same as ours, if it is to escape censure? May they not be themselves the judges of what anti-terrorist measures suit their situation best? In the course of such measures, an excess of caution or of zeal may occur and innocent people may be interfered with.

But the maxim "better be sure than sorry" applies with particular force in the context of terrorism and its practitioners.

I am sorry to see a public representative usually so sensible, Mrs Eileen Lemass MEP, making a silly fuss about being asked to fill up a card under the Act. Why should she, as an Irish citizen, have to do so, she asks, while other EEC nationals are free from the requirement? The answer is that there is no Dutch or Danish terrorist organisation which commits outrages on British soil in the name of Dutch or Danish national aspirations; If there were, Mrs Lemass may be sure the Prevention of Terrorism Act would quickly be applied to Dutch or Danish nationals too.

The net result of all this is that when something extremely grave occurs, like the Gibraltar shooting, our protests sound to the British like just another in the series of predictable indignant Irish noises, on tap at the slightest or no excuse. The Government, in trying to have those three deaths properly investigated, will thus be carrying psychological handicaps partly of their own making.

Nevertheless, they must insist, as well as they can, that the public inquest have before it the British security personnel involved in the incident. They must also remind the British that the deliberate killing of someone, even a terrorist, who might have been arrested without clear risk to life is murder; and that the people who evolved this rule, in this part of the world, were the British themselves.

If the British are seen to treat this proposition with scorn, the net gainers will be the I.R.A. They have lost three of their gang; but they will have a propaganda victory which will seem, on their inhuman scale of values, cheap at the price.

British Justice and Irish Defendants, Dublin, 1 November 1988

Due to our unhappy history, the IRA and their touts have no easier job than stirring up sympathetic sentiment when Irish people appear to encounter the rough end of British Justice. This sentiment spreads beyond the circle of the "sneaking-regarders" and extends into the usually sober areas of editorial and episcopal offices. It is, therefore, all the more important to resist any public mood which gives comfort to cruel and sanctimonious gunmen who — along with the barbaric wing of unionism — are a shame to Ireland and a disgrace to civilisation.

Britain is a different country from this, inhabited by different people, operating a different legal system. This system in some ways is more favourable to the "republican" interest than our own; for instance, until now there has been no censorship of IRA interviews on the State broadcasting organs (and even now the censorship will be less total than here); and the fresh appeal procedure of which the Birmingham prisoners got the benefit, such as it was, does not exist in this country at all. If there are also less favourable dimensions to the system, like the shape of the conspiracy law, or the relative lack of concern about prejudicial utterances like Mr King's, these differences are of the sort that you can expect to find in any foreign system.

The British system, moreover, is operated by a very different people. They are a race congenitally less sympathetic to prisoners and accused people than the Irish are. Their attitude to crime is a great deal more ruthless. They were the last people in western Europe, except for the French, to give up the practice of capital punishment, and a powerful lobby there still wants it restored.

People convicted in Britain are sent to prison more readily, and for longer terms, than is the case here. The prison population of Britain, both absolute and relative to population, is the largest in Europe, and is relatively about twice as large as ours, with a crime rate roughly similar. They are as strict with their own people as with foreigners, as witness what happened to Lester Piggott. Who believes Irish Lester Piggott would have been sent to prison by an Irish court for a tax offence?

In other words, where crime is concerned the British are a tough, unsentimental crew. People who enter British territory in order to play rough games with them ought to remember this.

Secondly, the suggestion that innocent Irish people are systematically imprisoned in Britain, although it would rightly concern the rest of us, is a peculiarly unlovely plea in the mouths of Sinn Féin and the IRA. Since when has the IRA had so tender a regard for the rights of innocence? When was innocence ever a protection against their cruelties?

The last people who should be heard to complain about wrongs done to innocent people are those whose bland doctrine it is — to excuse even horrors like Enniskillen — that the death and maiming of innocents is imply a regrettable but unavoidable by-product of their horrible war.

It remains a tragedy that very young people, perhaps sucked into the IRA or its front organisation by factors which an outsider cannot understand, should have their lives ruined by long imprisonment. But if the IRA and Sinn Féin genuinely want prisoners released, the most decisive single action towards that end is in their own hands. Let them call off this foul campaign at once.

If this were done and the North allowed to return to peace, I think it would become possible within a year or two to talk realistically about amnesty measures. I think an Irish Government would seek an opportunity to propose them, and I think even a British Government — mindful of precedents all over the world— would be willing to listen. Until the cease-fire comes, however, the British will continue to take the IRA at their word when they talk about being at war; and casualties of that war — the luckier ones — will continue to sit in British jails.

Review of the Anglo-Irish Agreement, Dáil, 16 November 1988

Everyone watching Fianna Fáil over the last few years listened to the Taoiseach, Deputy Haughey, talking about Northern Ireland being a failed political entity. The cheek of him to say that in one breath and with another breath invite them to come to see him and have tea. How can he talk like that to people, illegitimising their institutions in our Constitution and then making fun of them in casual expressions of that sort, cheap, glib expressions which would enrage us if anyone used them about us? What prospect is there for a party with a leader who spoke like that and which bullied the New Ireland Forum — which I must admit was no difficult task — into putting a unitary State at the head of their list of preferences, making it absolutely certain that Mrs Thatcher would throw the lot out the window? Their intent was to humiliate the Government and leave them in a hole. What was the prospect that a party with that record would row in on a referendum to amend Article 3? Absolutely none. That was one foolish referendum the last Government did not embark on because had they done so naturally it would have been defeated and there would have been the same campaign against it, except this time it would be an overt campaign, mounted by the far side. I know Deputy Wilson would not willingly tell a lie to the House and I do not believe he would even contradict me, but they would have opposed that.

They are in a different position. They are dealing with a very different kind of opposition, as they know, on the economic front. We do not hand trip them. We are not in here every week with Private Members' motions calling for more and more expenditure, whingeing about this, whingeing about that, whingeing about people who think they are left short because of Government measures. We realise the Government have a disagreeable job to do and we are deliberately, even at the cost of votes to ourselves — and many of our grassroots do not like it — refraining from making difficulties for this Government. As I said, this Government are facing a very different kind of opposition.

This is a "weather window", as I have said in another connection, in which it will be possible to do these things because the Government will not get opposition from over here. I have not heard this subject being formally debated in the Fine Gael Party — I do not think it has been debated recently — but I know that Deputy FitzGerald, the former Taoiseach, thinks as I do about this. It is not right to involve other colleagues by naming them, but I am as certain as I can be that a proposal to go back to something like the 1967 formula in the report of the Committee on the Constitution would be supported by this party. This is the moment to do it. That might unfreeze relations. That might signal to the Unionists that we are doing something over and above our obligations under the Hillsborough Accord, that we are moving out to meet them at a cost of putting our pride, on many of the words we have spoken, in our pockets, forgetting about them for the moment.

It may be — and I am certain it is so — that there are people up there whose rooted objection to doing business with this State is so ingrained into their bones that nothing will make them think otherwise. If so, I am at the end of my resources. Who says our lives will be a failure? Who says we will all pass through the world without any achievement to our names if we do not see a united Ireland? Would not the achievement of peace and normality for 1.5 million unfortunate people be achievement enough? Are we so unhuman that we will postpone that to a childish desire to see a tricolour waving on City Hall in Belfast? If that is the collective feeling of this House, I will leave it but I do not believe that that is the case. We have had this idiotic, chauvinistic idea wished upon us and we are afraid to throw it off. I am sorry to say something disagreeable but if we said we would go back to the position of 1925 we would accept that you had a right to live with your own institutions and that, in order to normalise relations between us and to induce normality in the North, we ought to relinquish our claim. We would say that we would never revive it although we would always have the aspiration to unity and you could not kill that on us. We could say that we would not make a claim of right which would always lead you to suppose that even when we were holding a hand out on one side of our body, we would have a hatchet behind our backs.

I know that Deputy Wilson is a reflecting, thinking man. I also know that he has a short fuse and a large dose of Ulster blood — I suppose it is all Ulster blood — and that I am not, therefore, speaking to someone who is necessarily receptive emotionally to what I am saying. However, I know that intellectually he will listen to me and the House and I would be grateful if he would float this idea in his Government.

I should like to end by saying this to him in regard to the Government's general performance, by way of analogy and not by way of getting away from the subject. The moments in which the Government have got applause — perhaps muted — and approval from people who never voted for them and perhaps never will vote for them, but who recognise an honest day's work when they see it, is when the Government have gone back on things they said which they ought not to have said, when they have not persisted in politics or attitudes which were wrong. It may be rather sentimental and sloppy of them but Irish people are inclined to give a cheer to someone who recognises that he has made a mistake or taken up a wrong position saying sincerely that they are sorry. Irish people admire that and it is a great trait. They do not value a pedantic consistency; they value somebody admitting and acknowledging, even grudgingly, that he was wrong and doing something else. The Fianna Fáil Party would come out of it with nothing but credit if they were to initiate a referendum process of the kind I mentioned. I cannot believe they would not get the assistance of this party, I cannot speak for the Progressive Democrats but I expect the same would be true of them and of Labour. It would be a major contribution and something to which no amount of political rhetoric about the two great traditions in this country could compare in its long-term effect.

SECTION 4

Dublin, Local Government and the Environment

Local Government Vote, Dáil, 6 July 1977

I suggested that it may be illegal for the Government to refuse motor taxation for periods subsequent to 1st August. If I were connected with a motoring organisation I would not mind putting a few hundred or a few thousand pounds into taking a test case about this matter.

My main objection is that it is the sheerest of handouts. It is the greatest political gobstopper that I can recall in my years of observing politics. There was no audible public demand for it. It was quite separate from the rates. I know there was a universal demand to abolish rates. I met it on the doorstep sat this election campaign, as I did during the campaigns of 1969 and 1973. There was an audible public demand for the abolition of rates.

Although I do not think the ground rents problem can be constitutionally solved by the Government as simply as they think, at least that problem corresponds to an audible public demand. However, there was no audible public demand for the abolition of motor tax and that is why I call it a political gobstopper. It is rather like a granny or a great-aunt who has no responsibility for the upbringing of children but who seeks to ingratiate herself while she is in the house for a few hours by bringing along a bag of lollipops and sticking them into the children's mouths. By the time she leaves the house the damage will be done to the children's teeth. Effectively, that is what this car tax proposal represents.

It is commonplace in taxation that various indices of affluence — they may be only rough criteria of affluence or consumption; the two things go together usually — are taken as items to hit in taxation in order to keep the State afloat. Nearly everything we use is subject to taxation in some form. Even without the road tax motoring is subject to taxtion because of the tax on petrol, VAT on the car and so on. Everything is potentially subject to taxation and there is nothing scared about a motor car. It is arguable that the necessities of life such as food and medicine should be free of VAT. Fianna Fáil did not think so before the 1973 election; they derided our promise to get rid of VAT on food and medicine. We took off that tax as promptly as Fianna Fáil are now removing motor tax. There was something to be said for removing VAT from the necessities of life but that argument cannot be made in respect of the motor car. There is no reason logically why a car should not be taxed. This is the purest of handouts. It is as though each member of the electorate were offered a £50 note, as though his ballot paper came to him wrapped in that note. It is the purest of bribes.

I do not make that criticism of all items. I have not described the £1,000 house grant in that way because I agree there is something to be said for that but what has been done with regard to motor tax is total bribery. When we calculated that in order to replace the lost revenue it would take an amount of money which if raised in petrol tax would amount to another 19p per gallon, Fianna Fáil told us they were not going to do it that way. We have not been told

141

how they are going to do it.

I do not expect an Opposition party suddenly caught up in a general election to produce chapter and verse in every minor respect for their programme but it will have to be done here. The roads and the various facilities connected with them must be maintained and the money will have to be got from the people in some way. I want to warn the motoring public about this. I know that elderly widows driving 15-year old Morris Minors will not fit into the following rough definition but generally 90 per cent of the motoring public are people who are able to afford to put petrol into their cars, who are able to afford not only the necessities of life but even a few luxuries. These are the people who will be hit by whatever revenue raising device is resorted to by the Government in order to replace road tax. My solemn advice to every car owner whose vehicle is 16 h.p. or under is to calculate what the motor tax would have been and to put it into a Post Office savings account because as sure as eggs are eggs that amount and probably even more will be demanded from him in some way or other.

Intoxicating Liquor Bill, Dáil, 9 November 1983

The purpose of this Bill is to regularise what may seem to the Minister or the Government a quite subordinate part of the Concert Hall's operations. However, I think and I am sure many others would agree, that there are some kinds of entertainment — I do not mean to be facetious — which are enhanced by the fact that you can have a drink before or after them. That is something that Myles na gCopaleen, one of the greatest Irishmen ever born, poked fun at, but seriously, because he saw the point too when he wrote how extraordinary it was that no one seemed able to put up with an evening at the theatre completely sober, that when the interval arrived there was a "humiliating exodus for whiskey". Nonetheless, what he said in satiric form is true. There are a range of aesthetic experiences, of which the theatre is one and a concert is another, which are enhanced for the visitor and made into an evening out in the sense that an evening at the cinema or an evening at some other entertainment never could be, by the fact that one can have a social couple of drinks with friends — or by oneself if one is a solitary drinker — before, in the middle of or after the performance. The legal doubts about the legitimacy of serving drink in the NCH should now be put to rest.

From something in the Minister's speech for which she is in no way to blame I cannot help observing the extremely nannyish attitude of the Irish State towards the whole subject of buying and selling drink. Needless to say, it is not because the Irish themselves are in their nature nannyish about that subject.

You yourself, Sir — but perhaps it is not in order to make comments about the Chairman's personal abstinences — the Irish as a people are not nannyish but they have allowed nannyish manners to be wished on them in this as in so many other things, by our neighbours.

It is fantastic that the Minister should make a speech here referring to licences for the Dublin theatres and — note this for scrupulous nannyism — only for those Dublin theatres which have letters patent granted originally under the Dublin Stage Regulation Act 1786. Are we to issue a stamp in commemoration of the bi-centenary of that Act? Is that why you cannot get a drink in the Gate or Eblana Theatres? I do not know the reason. Perhaps I am wrong to mention these theatres by name; I cannot tell the press what to print, but I regret now having mentioned them, because for all I know I may have been doing an unwilling injury or causing annoyance to their proprietors and managers, and I do not want to do that. If only certain Dublin theatres which conform with regulations laid down in 1786 received special licensing consideration, the whole structure must be one of the most absurd of all our legislative structures.

Put that beside what the Minister went on to say especially about licences — I hope she does not mind me putting it in this way — she said proudly: "Special liquor licences have been given under various Intoxicating Liquor Acts to places such as the bus station in Aras Mhic Dhiarmada." You must go up two flights of stairs to get a drink if you are at the Eblana and you want a drink. The last time I was there, one had to walk up the main concourse and push through crowds waiting to go to Navan and Tullamore and go up another flight of stairs to get to the bar — by which time most of the interval was over — and then one had to force one's way through the thirsty throng. The bus station in Aras Mhic Dhiarmada has a bar as have airports, railway stations and greyhound tracks. Are we not a great little people? We have managed to licence greyhound tracks, but we cannot make sure that one can get a convenient drink in all theatres. Above all we have not succeeded in curing the greatest omission of all in this area, the absence of proper liquor licences in ordinary restaurants. We must be the only country in Europe in which that is so. The Minister made special mention of airports. I do not mind making a parenthetic prediction, that the best business done at Knock airport will be in the bar — providing some 18th or 19th century Act will entitle Monsignor Horan's company to apply for and get a liquor licence.

Local Government Bill,
Dáil, 21 March 1985

When I came into the House a few minutes ago I heard Deputy Carey talking about the situation in Clare County Council ever since the State was founded. There are other councils like Galway where the very same was true until recently. I have no doubt there are councils in which Fianna Fáil were kept out for as long as anyone was capable of doing so in the very same way. The more one fumes about that, the more devalued one's voice becomes and the less notice is taken of one. It is quite intolerable that the people's government, at whatever level, should be carried on as though it were not the people's government, but the government run for the benefit of the politicians who take part in the game. That is not what they are there for. It seems to be an index of how little the people care about local government, how little real importance it has for them, how little they really feel it affects their own lives, that there is not a public outcry about that system.

There must be people in County Clare who do not give a damn about politicians one way or the other, who do not care what crowd are in or out, but who object, on principle, to the staffing of a vocational educational committee or whatever else it may be on the political side by nominees from one party only, and who feel that it makes for a less efficient committee. If they felt these committees meant anything real in their lives, there would be an outcry about these things. It is quite intolerable. It is a disgrace to this House and a disgrace to Irish democracy and to the system which the people who went before us worked so hard to achieve and, in some cases, gave their lives to achieve.

That is not the only instance of dog-in-the-mangerism, though it is one of the worst. An even worse one is the long hogging of county council or borough council chairmanships with which, I am afraid, this Bill does not propose to deal. It is quite wrong that for 20 years there has not been a Fianna Fáil Lord Mayor of Dublin. That is not because I see any particular virtue in Fianna Fáil; I hope I do not need to make that plain. It is because I recognise that roughly 35 per cent, and sometimes more, of the people of this city tend to vote for that party. Why should they not occasionally have a Lord Mayor of their own political colour?

The same was true for many years in the opposite direction in the city of Cork. It is absolutely intolerable that we have to wait until a squabble develops between the two Coalition parties in Dublin corporation, in such a way that the Labour people rethink their local strategy, before Fianna Fáil can get a smell of the mayoralty. I am not saying that in order to disarm anybody on the far side. It is just as intolerable when the same thing happens to us. Could we not put all that Paddywhackery and Tammany Hallism behind us and drag ourselves into the kind of world in which the rest of the people have to live?

They regard this whole structure of dog-in-the-mangerism and poltroonery with contempt. They resent having to pay for it.

Why is it that journalists find that it makes a welcome headline and something which will pass a sub-editor's scrutiny when they are able to report that county councillors from a county that has nothing higher in it than a two storey building are off to an international conference in Delhi about high-rise housing? It is not because they begrudge a public representative, who is doing a serious job, the serious acquaintance with the outside world which he really ought to have. It is because they do not see them as doing a worthwhile job but as in there to try to hog whatever is going on the backs of the ratepayers that they resent it. Probably that is an unfair perception, and I do not say I entirely share it; but that is the reason why they resent it.

I said in this House before that when my brother was a member of Dublin Corporation, which he was for one term, he told me that having innocently travelled to Helsinki to a housing conference he found that the Irish contingent, gathered from the forty or so councils we have, outnumbered the rest of the world put together.

The fact that people resent that, but do not care very much about the political hogging of committees, is an index of the standing of local government and of the people who take part in it. It may be unfair. It may be a perception which is unjust to the people who do a good job. I have no doubt it is, and I am willing to be contradicted and put right about it by people who have first-hand experience of local government which I have not got.

That dog-in-the-mangerism extends in other directions as well. A good few years ago I had the experience of going to a civic reception in Dublin at which I could scarcely see any politician who was not of my own colour. There were about two Fianna Fáil councillors there, and they were like the ugly sisters at the ball. The room was filled with sparkling Coalition Cinderellas, if I may put it that way, and there were two or three ugly sisters over on the side lines. Perhaps they did not look at it that way, but out of charity I went over to talk to them because nobody else had a word to throw to them.

I hope it will be accepted that I am making that point against my own side. It is every bit as bad and as scandalous when it happens the other way around. Surely we could grow up and realise it is the people's money which is being spent for a purpose which is supposed to be in the people's interest and for their benefit instead of — as though any of us was short of the price of a drink or a holiday — in small ways trying to steal a march on one another and milk the old sow I spoke about a few years ago and which I have not been let forget.

On the day the report of the commission or whatever it was came out, I heard a former Fianna Fáil Minister saying in indignation to somebody else: "Do you know that 1,500 people are being taken out of the town of Oughterard and moved into Connemara?". It was almost as though you could hear the roar of the engines of the Wehrmacht lorries as unfortunate people were loaded up over the tail-gates with many a hearty prod from a field grey uniform and a rifle. All that was happening was that, instead of being given one crowd of politicians to vote for, these 1,500 people would get another crowd of politicians to choose between. That is what is meant by "shifting people". That is the preoccupation which is uppermost in the minds of the people involved in this business. I would have thought it was far more urgent for us to ask ourselves what is local government for and what is it all about. Ought we not get clear in our minds what the task of local government should be, and what we can afford to confide to people elected at local level, before we start to decide how many of them there should be, or where the boundaries of their electoral districts should be drawn?

I will not lecture the House about the history of local government, but local government was introduced by the British in 1898 more or less in its modern form as part of the move to "kill Home Rule with kindness". The local authorities set up around 1898 were one of the main targets for the humour — I never found it very funny; I do not like that kind of condescending humour — of Somerville and Ross. Their humour is near to the mark to this extent, that early local government representatives in this country were not infrequently corrupt and very frequently incompetent. So incompetent were they, in fact, that in 1940 Mr de Valera, who was no Fascist, stripped them of nearly all their powers. He left them their tricorn hats, their chains, their gowns and their coaches, but vested nearly all their powers in managers. They were left with a certain number of powers, the main one naturally of taxation, but even that has been removed, not because of incompetence but because of the political desire to remove rates from residential premises. What exactly is left of the whole local government structure which justifies its very expensive continuance?

Dublin Transport Authority, Dáil, 12 June 1985

Over the years I have come to look with horror at those big envelopes I get in the morning to see will there tumble out of them yet another Bill proposing another authority, board or commission. We have enough boards, commissions and authorities to sink a battleship and we do not need any new ones. If there were a case to be made for a new board, it would be a board with the specific draconian remit to close other boards down. I tcould be called An Bord um Threascairt Bord or An tUdaras um Dhúnadh síos Udarás, but we need that more than anything else. Any board being given birth to by a Minister accouched in this Chamber is entering the world on the defensive, required at every moment to justify its existence and by reference to standards more compelling than merely that it would provide posts for a certain number of public sector people.

This is a general observation about new boards. In recent years I am afraid I have detected a tendency to create boards and authorities with the purpose of relieving persons who have held themselves out as being anxious to exercise public authority of that responsibility. A couple of years ago — and it was not the first time it was mooted — our colleague, Deputy Noonan, Minister for Justice, floated the idea of a police authority. We do not need a police authority because the whole point of having a Minister for Justice, a Government and a Dáil to which he is responsible is that he must carry the wind. He must stand up to the whirlwind of criticism and take responsibility for the correct functioning of the police force and its proper command. He must make certain that the only thing a policeman has to fear is not doing his duty — if he does his duty he has nothing to fear, but has everything to fear if he abuses it. That is what a Minister is there for, not an authority. I am delighted that the Minister, Deputy Noonan, heard me say this at a meeting. He has gone off the theme and we have heard no more about the police authority.

I am talking about the question of this latest proposal of the Government in regard to Dublin. I am not trying to flatter the Minister. I know that in his heart he will be as conscious of this as I am. Although the Bill necessarily has to concentrate on one theme only, namely transport, I have to say this about the casting of the Bill and the drafting of the explanatory memorandum and, indeed, the Minister's speech, that none of these seemed to reflect a consciousness of any dimensions of what I might call the life of a capital city. You cannot look at transport, particularly that in a capital city, in an isolated way. We are not now dealing with all urban transport in this Bill, but with the transport situation in the capital city of our Republic.

A capital city is in a special category, a special position. It is, or should be, a showpiece and a source of pride, not merely to those who by accident, choice or whatever reason become, or have been always, its inhabitants, but to everybody in the country. There were a couple of Deputies from the country in the House this morning and I am hoping that they will contribute on this Bill, because the conditions of the capital city should be as close to their hearts as they are to those of Deputies like ourselves on this side who happen to live here. A man from Letterkenny or Gortahork, or Belmullet or Two-Mile-Borris ought to be as interested and as proud of the capital city of his Republic as those who live here. Most of us are "Cuid-a-Dós" one or two generations back. I was born here, but neither of my parents was. The same is probably true of many Deputies who represent Dublin constituencies. There are some representing Dublin constituencies who were born in Cork and some do not seem to have arrived from Cork too long ago.

We should all be interested in the capital city and a piecemeal treatment of it as though it were just some other town is wrong. During Deputy Richard Bruton's very factual contribution, the Chair did not have to pull him in the whole of his excellent speech. That Deputy thought that there was more to planning than simply drawing a red line on a map or designating a zone and hoping that all would then go well. One had to make sure that something happened. One had to make provision for the necessities which arise from people living in the place, as citizens of a capital city and also as the human front of the national showpiece.

I do not want to be making needless jibes at this Bill. One does not expect to find too much in a Bill like this about anything except what it sets out or purports to do. I would have wished, at least, some passing reference to expressly environmental considerations. However, one does not expect to find that. This Bill seems to envisage the city as potentially an easily moving spaghetti of roads in the inter-slices of which ordinary people, businesses and public administration must exist as best they can, no doubt a dimension of their lives facilitated by freer moving transport but not necessarily any other dimension of their lives enhanced and the general picture of the city not necessarily improved.

I am not saying that a city that is a world by-word for traffic jams — perhaps like Lagos or some other place — should be indifferent if we head in that direction. Of course we should not. The overall planning and government of a capital city is something that requires a united treatment that does not simply co-ordinate or go some distance towards co-ordinating the police, the nationalised transport company and the planning authorities, but which absorbs the other dimensions of government.

I am not of the opinion that merely to call somebody a Minister will make any serious difference to what he is supposed to administer but I have always thought that in a country like this, because of our peculiar history and the fact that for so long Dublin was merely a provincial or colonial outpost capital, we should have a Minister for the capital. We should have a Department for the capital with the budget covering all dimensions of government. They should not merely make recommendations and give advice but should have the spending of money for hospitals, schools, roads and for the policing we need. I do not see it as necessarily essential to have a national police force. I can see the political reasons for it and I support it in a general sense. However, the policing of a capital city of this size, particularly when it is so far out of scale with other towns, is a problem all of its own. There would be a case for a centralised governmental authority herewith a budget to do everything so far as this city was concerned

We want Dublin to be a city of which all of us can be proud. Although traffic congestion is bad enough in my opinion it is one of the least of our problems. At the moment this city can only make one weep. Yesterday my colleague, Deputy Coveney, got coverage for some hard truths he spoke about Cork. He was right to speak his mind because in the long run we do not do ourselves any good by deceiving ourselves about the things around us. For what my opinion is worth, Cork is about the only good looking city in Ireland and I say that with apologies to people in Limerick and Galway. Cork presents an infinitely more smiling, more interesting and more human face than does Dublin, even if it is on a smaller scale. Perhaps the Leas-Cheann Comhairle does not notice it as he goes hurriedly with his bag to the station on a Thursday evening, but Dublin has become an absolute dog's breakfast. If I were a member of the Dublin Corporation I would hang my head in shame — if I did not hang myself — at the shame of being part of the alleged or supposed government of a city like this which can decline so far and so fast. When I was a student in the fifties there was still some faint charm about the admittedly ramshackle quays, the old bookshops and so on. Perhaps they would have fallen by now anyway.

There is more to a city than simply facilitating traffic flow and that if you facilitate traffic flow you may destroy several of the reasons that led to the city being there in the first place. It may be turned into a wilderness from which people want to escape. That has been the experience of cities that have got an overdose of fly-overs, double junctions and so on, where people want to get away from the 24 hours a day noise, filth and dust. Such cities are no longer places where people want to live or to do business. The history of inner city decay in American cities is a problem so great for them as to have serious political diminsions. It has a history of fly-overs, freeways, 16-lane highways of all kinds and the traffic flow facilitated but the people are no longer able to lead a decent existence.

The Irish title of this Bill is An Bille um Iompras Bhaile Átha Cliath. That is a good one. I often think of the weary heroes in Rannóg an Aistriúcháin in this House slaving for a lifetime — I have to say with amazing skill and perseverance — to turn the inventions of politicians into plausible Irish. Occasionally I think that perhaps one of them may say, "We'll try this word. It was never used since the world began and never will be used until the world ends, but we'll see if we can wish it on those óinseachs in there and see if they will swallow it".

I wish to draw attention to the amazing feature whereby the Authority are to be allowed specifically to direct their attention towards the erection of bollards and ramps. Where have we arrived in this ancient city when the only idea in the Bill that has any teeth would seem to be the erection of bollards and ramps? It is surprising that Rannóg an Aistriúcháin did not think to call the Authority Bord na gCuaillí Concréide. Are the board or Bord an nIomairí Concréide to concentrate on the provision of concrete bollards and ramps which are not used by any civilised city in the world except perhaps, Belfast which has its own problems to deal with. Are we to admit that the place has become ungovernable and unlivable in to that extent and, if so, why can we not produce in the Bill some provision that would give some hope to the people that they might finish up with a city of which they could all be proud instead of having a situation in which visitors have to be brought from the airport at night or by some circuitous route in order to avoid their seeing what is going on?

Urban Renewal Bill, Dáil, 24 April 1986

About a year ago we had a chance to discuss this matter in the House, I cannot remember on what Bill or Estimate, and I described the city in similar terms then. I said that it was the scruffiest capital in Europe. I repeat that now; and let me add that it is the scruffiest capital not by a nose or a head but by several lengths.

I was taken to task by a Deputy, a member of my party, outside the House, who either went spontaneously to one of the evening newspapers or was willing to discuss critically something one of his colleagues had said in reply to a telephone call. Because of the strictures I had employed in regard to Dublin he accused me of having and deploying in my criticisms an elitist attitude towards what a city should look like. He mentioned a couple of ancient universities that I had the privilege of attending and he said "Deputy Kelly seems to think that everything should run according to the architectural standards of these European gems" or something like that. I think I am not substantially misquoting him.

I say to this Deputy — whom I will not name because I do not want to cause more trouble; I have not referred to it in the meantime and I never even remembered it until we started to discuss this Bill this morning — that he or any Deputy who feels that criticism of that kind or expressions of anguish uttered here or elsewhere about the dereliction, dirt and decay all around us in this city reflect an elitist point of view should ask himself whether he has ever walked from Butt Bridge to Kingsbridge along the south quays and from Kingsbridge back to Butt Bridge on the north quays. If not, let him spend some hour and a half — which is what it would take — doing so and instruct himself about what this city looks like at its heart and core. That is one of the areas designated — not under the Bill in front of us but under the Finance Bill — which the Minister proposes, if I understood his speech correctly, to bring under the umbrella of the Urban Renewal Bill which is before us.

I ask the same Deputy whether he has ever gone by train between Amiens Street Station and Westland Row — as they used to be called before we celebrated I have forgotten which anniversary of 1916 since we seem to be celebrating them at the drop of a hat these days — and looked at the backs of the houses, the streets and the buildings all around them. Let me start his journey a bit further out in Drumcondra and go as far as Lansdowne Road. He should then ask himself whether anything similar is to be seen in the heart of a capital city.

I recognise that you seldom see the most flattering aspect of any city from a raised railway line but I am not simply talking about the fact that the back of a house does not look as attractive as the front; it has to accommodate pipes, services and so on. I am just asking whether there is any other capital city in traversing the centre of which you see so many broken down, dilapidated buildings, so many roofs like colanders, so many houses, the demolition of which was begun but never finished or the construction of which was begun but never finished. There is so much rot and decay and any Deputy who thinks I am applying elitist standards by talking like that really ought to ask himself, particularly when he is a member of Dublin Corporation, if he is taking a serious and responsible view of his own duties.

We are much given in this country — I sometimes think so much given to it that probably in an inverted way it conceals an inferiority complex — to saying that this or that Irish item is "second to none" in the world. Irish food is "second to none" Irish music is "second to none". Everything Irish, like everything French, Finnish or Japanese, has a character and value of its own, and there are some dimensions of it which may indeed be world beating, but I object to the automatic assumption — which is not sincerely held but affected, to apply an anaesthetic plaster to a deeply felt inferiority complex — that one is being an elitist, or a West Briton or, as Kevin Boland said, a belted earl or one of the gin and tonic brigade if one says we are not in the same league as other capital cities in western Europe. I do not want to go on about the differences between myself and a colleague as I am sure he was saying no more than many other members of Dublin Corporation would say, all of whom should hang their heads in shame, if they do not hang themselves, over the condition of the city which in a sense they are paid to preside over, not with a salary but with perquisites of all kinds.

I wonder how a Deputy or a councillor who feels that way about "elitist" critiques would be received in Florence or Amsterdam. Admittedly those two cities are world famous for their visual impact. In the case of Amsterdam it is not because of the immense array of magnificent individual public buildings, as its array in that regard is very small, but because of its very carefully maintained streets. It is the totality of Amsterdam which creates the impression, not because it has palaces, it is rather short on these things. The Dutch are frugal, simple and modest, at least that has been their traditional character, but they are also careful and clean and respect things, including themselves. They do not feel that anybody among them who says that something is dirty, broken or needs to be maintained, repaired or preserved is an elitist.

I wonder how certain Deputies and councillors would get on not just in Florence or Amsterdam but in the humblest Dutch towns or Italian towns for that matter. How much of the unsightliness which is not only presided over by Dublin Corporation, county council or any other local authority but actually promoted by Section 4 directions, would be tolerated by anybody, even by the Communist Party who, to do them justice, are very much to thefore in these countries in trying to maintain the appearance and symbols of the past? You would not get by in Leningrad if you were to propose clearing away the sybmols of the Russian imperial past on the grounds that you did not want to be reminded of them.

That point of view has been expressed about many institutions in this city.

A Deputy here — he had left the House long before I was heard of — belonging to Clann na Poblachta thought that Trinity College should be turned into a car park because it stood for all he hated. I have no connection with Trinity good, bad or indifferent and I do not hold any brief for it and, even if I shared his feelings about the college, which I do not, I certainly would not take that line about it. It does not matter what its history is. It is part of our history too. We cannot escape or avoid it and we should be civilised enough to respect the environment which has been left to us in order, as Deputy Brady said in a fine speech earlier, to pass it on to those who come after us.

I cannot claim the same acquaintanceship with areas in Cork, Galway, Waterford or Limerick, but I do not think any of their areas would have been let go as far downhill as those in Dublin. The quays area, the north inner city area, the Gardiner Street and Mountjoy Square complex and Henrietta Street would not have been neglected in other cities. Henrietta Street was built around 1750 and it has been allowed to deteriorate to the point that it is nearly dangerous to walk along it for fear that some of the buildings might fall on you. In so far as the Minister is concerned we are starting this urban renewal scheme in the humble and not very exciting context of rates remission which will be no good to purely residential areas. We are starting that renewal from a very low point. We have a long way to come from the distance we have gone back and the lesson for us there is not that we may carp about the measures contained in the Bill but to avoid mistakes in the future.

The time to look at urban renewal in the case of districts which are only just beginning the journey downhill is now. They should be renewed now and not when they are like the south side of Mountjoy Square, when they are like an old man's jaw with about two or three teeth left in it and those that are left scruffy enough themselves. That is not what I understand by urban renewal. It may be cheaper and better all round just to bulldoze what is left and start from scratch.

Urban renewal should start from the very moment decay begins to appear in a widespread patterned form all over a district. There are huge areas in Dublin not envisaged in the Finance Bill, or the Bill before us, which are quite outside the Minister's present intentions. I am well aware of the financial dimensions of any sort of scheme for helping people, whether by tax remission, direct grants or anything else, on an enormously large scale, but I should like to draw attention to the alternative. The alternative is that we are going to allow other huge areas of Dublin, mostly residential, to keep running downhill until they are in the same state as Henrietta Street and the other districts which are designated or in mind.

One of the members of the category of buildings which should be renewed now are Government occupied offices throughout the city. That applies not merely to the Civil Service but to local authority or State occupied old — fashioned houses which are being used as offices. There is a phrase in a novel by John Le Carre — it does not matter where it comes from because it stands on its own — in which he describes the espionage or counter-espionage outfit in some distant dismal surburb of London as being housed in an old mansion which "showed that air of controlled dilapidation characteristic of Government buildings everywhere". In other words, they do not quite let the roof fall in or the gutters fall off, the down pipes fall out, or the floors fall through.

The thing is to maintain them at a point below which it is not possible to maintain the building. Then, naturally, the cry goes up that new offices must be obtained, that the old ones are uncomfortable for the staff — I can see that. The building is abandoned and left derelict. Nobody wants to occupy it in that condition and very often it is not suitable any longer for anything except offices. Horrible partitions are put up, the tracks of strip-lighting remain and reconstructions of an interior-type which would be excessively costly to reverse are carried out.

Government offices are prime candidates for a review in this connection. They must represent a very large slice of housing in the inner part of this city between the canals — I am not speaking about the brand new ones — and in general they are only in a state of controlled dilapidation as far as a casual glance can show.

If one took a wide angle green filtered Sunday supplement photographer's picture of the village of Ranelagh no doubt it could be presented photographically, with a bit of October mist hanging around, so as to appear quite attractive. It would awaken in me nostalgia for my early childhood which I spent living near it. However, if one walks up to the place, around it and on the roads near it one will find what I am talking about. Above all one will find the infallible signal of houses on the way down, the ten or 12 electric door bells which spell multiple occupancy in a house never intended for that purpose. I can recall canvassing two storey houses — I am sure Deputy O'Brien is still canvassing them — intended for a middle-class people in 1860 or so which now carry eight or ten doorbells.

One cannot treat an old house like that without signing its death warrant. Very often those houses produce huge rents on which, I have no doubt, frequently no tax is paid. The owners may not be well-off and the house may represent their only investment. The owners may not have the capital to renovate the house properly or be able to afford to reduce the number of occupants to keep it at a certain standard with the results that roads are beginning to sink quietly down. However, they are sinking at a faster rate than Venice is sinking under water. They sink at such a rate that there is quite a perceptible difference between the condition they were in when I was a student in the fifties and that which they are in now.

A lot of people in Rathmines are living in houses which were not designed for the type of occupancy they have to endure. That whole suburb is sinking downhill. I consider that an early or mid-Victorian suburb is something that will in our children's or grandchildren's time be quite as much a rarity deserving preservation as a Georgian street is today. Even if I am wrong about the aesthetic

153

perceptions of two generations hence, I do not think we have any right to be making the assumption that they will not give a damn if we turn it into something that one would see in Iowa, with fast food joints, a couple of petrol stations and a desert of dusty concrete in between. We do not have any right to make that assumption about our grandchildren.

Environment Estimate, Dáil, 9 May 1986

What we see left of local government is very often what I can only call misbehaviour. I do not hesitate to describe it as such when a council refuses to strike a rate simply because it is popular to appear to buck a system which imposes charges on people. It is a misbehaviour when they decline to charge for services although both main parties of this House at various times have expressed support for the principle of charging for services. Nobody likes having to pay for things. I do not want to be out in front of everybody else in recommending water charges or other charges, but, once the domestic rates were abolished and the Central Exchequer faced the colossal burden of sustaining most of local government, these had to come. Fianna Fáil when in Government, and our party, were committed to them; and that democratic approach or decision of the House, under whichever Government, has been in some cases frustrated by local authorities taking it on themselves to cease imposing water charges.

Local government in its present form is in many respects a negation of democracy. It means the wielding of power, in some cases the disgraceful wielding of power as in the shower of Section 4 motions of which the business of some councils seems to consist nearly exclusively; the bestowal of rate collectorships many of which are sinecures, or near sinecures, because the number of rates collected has dropped substantially although the number of collectors on the ground has remained the same; the enjoyment of perquisites, expenses which are collected very often at a rate which guarantees an income rather than mere reimbursement; skites, of the sort that Deputy Burke presides over as chairman of Dublin County Council, have reached a level where they are a public scandal. I have said that often in this House before and the public know it. I have had free trips many times and enjoyed them, but I must say that the thing as represented by the Irish local government structure goes beyond all bounds.

The power is being wielded and the perquisites are being enjoyed; but the local authorities refuse — and this is the crunch in democracy — to carry the odium of imposing the revenue necessary for these things. They want central funds to carry it. That is not democracy. I will not apply an epithet to it which will be offensive to the many decent people who are members of local authorities, as I believe they nearly all are; but whatever it is, it is not democracy. Democracy means taking responsibility, taking the rough with the smooth, making the unpopular decisions as well as getting the high profile, the perquisites and public approval. It means all of these, not one but all.

I want to say that the corporation have done, within the limits open to them, a lot of of very fine work, some of it not very well advertised and a delight when you stumble on it, for example, the little park which has suddenly sprung up behind the village of Ranelagh on the site of an old convent and, for example, a thing which amazed me to see, the perfect rehabilitation of a set of Edwardian lamps and the parapet on the bridge over the Dodder at Ballsbridge. I wish that it was possible for the corporation and for every other local authority to follow up efforts such as that, and to declare war on the kind of developments which the Minister, not I, has officially condemned.

He might also have added what would be improvements to buildings. I refer here particularly to a thing which I especially hate, which is the haphazard nailing of creosoted timber battens onto perfectly decent Irish gables and fronts in a pathetic effort to give an impression that it is half-timbered. You can see that ghastly crazy diamond shaped, rubbishy, tatty would-be improvement applied to shops all over Ireland. It is a disgrace to us. People who come here must say to themselves, if they have any eye for such things, "where do these people come from, what kind of training have they or above all what kind of local government system have they got that would permit such a thing." Try half-timbering a house even in a slum in Florence. Try putting a fascia of plastic even on a slum in Amsterdam, and see how you get on. These countries are not run by fascists. They are not dictatorships. They are democracies as proud as ours; and their Governments are as a rule usually a good deal further to the left than ours, particularly their local governments. They are not afraid and ashamed to stand up for standards which render their cities places that people travel across the world to see.

I want to say a word or two about the Chernobyl disaster and its effects here. To make a literary reference, there is a Sherlock Holmes story called "Silver Blaze" in which the local plodding police officer, in a case where a race horse had been stolen said to Sherlock Holmes, "Is there anything else to which you would wish to draw my attention?" Sherlock Holmes says "Yes, to the curious incident of the dog in the night-time". The local inspector says: "But the dog did nothing in the night-time". "That" says Sherlock Holmes, "was the curious incident." The analogy I draw here is the total silence from the benches of the Workers' Party, from Deputy Gregory and from a host of outside bodies whom I will not name because they are not here to defend themselves but these are all usually very vocal when it comes to the British, to Sellafield or to the Americans. Had it been a West German power plant that exploded and looked like poisoning half of Europe to a greater or lesser degree, they would not have been behind the door in raising a row. In the Sherlock Holmes story it was the trainer who had stolen his own horse, and the dog did nothing in the night-time, did not bark at or attack him, because he was familiar with the trainer. He felt among friends. I suspect that my analogy, without pumping it to death, can be extended to the uttermost limit of that parallel.

Finally, I wish to refer to Sellafield. Deputy Reynolds was shrieking here the night before last that it was not good enough for the Government to "express concern" about Sellafield, they should "demand" that it be closed down. What would happen if the English ignored this demand? When President Hillery was Minister for Foreign Affairs he was challenged by Deputy Mark Clinton as to whether he was satisfied with some disadvantageous situation which had arisen out of the Anglo-Irish free trade area. Deputy Clinton asked if the Minister was satisfied with the position and if he was going to put up with it. Deputy Hillery replied, and I had to hand it to him for one of the best parliamentary ripostes I ever heard: "I am not satisfied, but I can do nothing about it. What would you do, beat them with your cap?"

Metropolitan Streets Commission, Dáil, 29 October 1986

I have listened to the Minister's speech with interest and agreement for the most part, though I could not help a wry smile when I heard him refer to the O'Connell Street area as a national asset. It must be the only physical national asset in a capital city that I would drive two miles out of my way to avoid if bringing a visitor from the airport. It is the centre of a crumbling, decaying revolting dog's breakfast of a capital city that would make you weep on your return to it from even the humblest town on the European continent — I will not say in Britain because British standards are not a great deal different from ours in that regard although I think not even the British have anything to show comparable to this capital city.

I do not want to be unfair to anyone in the corporation. Any dealings I have ever had with corporation officials have been marked on their side always with courtesy and goodwill, but who is the average citizen to blame when he looks around and sees the desolation which this capital city contains? I suppose you can blame the Irish people themselves for being insufficiently sensitive to the fact that they are ankle deep in their own litter or to the decay of buildings or to bushes and trees, the seacha growing out of the top of 18th century buildings. They do not mind these things or are willing to live with them. In a broad sense one can say we are all to blame because we are willing to put up with this. We do not like to speak the hard word, we do not like to tell somebody not to smoke in a non-smoking area or not to drop litter when we see somebody emptying an ashtray out of a car. None of us likes to do that. There is a general disinclination to adhere to standards, a general cowardice about insisting on their maintenance. To that extent we are all to blame. Focusing it to a somewhat narrower lens it could be said that successive Governments are to blame.

The Stalinist monotone that is Deputy Burke's usual method of declamation — quite different, let me say before I make an enemy of him, from his very agreeable persona to meet and talk to outside the House — of his blaming the other side and patting his own side on the back was seldom seen to be less appropriate than this morning. He squarely blamed the Coalition for the decay of Dublin city. So we have been complaining about this city ever since I was a student, and probably long before, except I was not conscious of it. Many of the things which are the most shocking and strident examples of official vandalism, and not merely carelessness or litter dropping, are directly attributable to official decisions taken during periods of Fianna Fáil Government.

I do not want to answer Deputy Burke back in his own coin, but let me remind him that that — as I think I formerly called it in here — capsized egg box in Fitzwilliam Street which contains the ESB headquarters was put up in the teeth of the peaceful advice and campaigning — no one held a pistol to the Government's head — of every conservationist group, of every association of architects and people in the county who might be expected to know something about these things, and they were simply walked on.

When the thing finally went up, remorse began to set in. The softer hearts on the Fianna Fáil benches began to relent. Deputy Lenihan, when he was Minister for Power, or whatever the thing was then called — one has to grasp at the title of the Department quickly these days before it is changed — paid an official visit to the building. Even he stood appalled by it and, humble though his contribution in aesthetic terms may have been in trying to ameliorate the situation, at least he made it. He said: "Would you think of putting a lick of whitewash on it? Would you think of taking a bucket of whitewash and see could you brighten it up that way?"

When I hear Deputy Burke going on about the sins of the Coalition in this regard, that is only the tip of the iceberg. I am not going to answer him back in his own coin. I could spend the rest of the morning here doing so. I could go through the list of buildings and of planning permissions dating back to the grim days of former Deputy Kevin Boland and I suppose beyond, right up to and including the new Dublin municipal offices, which have contributed, each in its own small way, to destroying this city, robbing it of the character that it still had when I was a child or even later, and making it something which other people pity us for living in.

In a general sense the Irish people can be blamed. In a less general sense successive Governments can be blamed, Fine Gael just as much as any other. But the people who are really in charge of the appearance of a city are their elected representatives and the officials who undoubtedly in some respects have a wide ranging independence of them, but not in every respect. Although I do not want to be unfair to individuals, I cannot blame anyone really for the condition of Dublin city if it is not the corporation. If the Minister has now decided to put his own weight and considerable brains behind this official vote of no confidence in Dublin Corporation, I am solidly behind him.

Deputy Burke seemed to think it was terribly undemocratic of us to be taking this line to be carving out a bit of the city and putting it under a special commission instead of leaving it with the Corporation. I want to remind Deputy Burke of a little bit of the history of local government in this country. It was started off by the British in 1898 in much like its present form as part of their then campaign to kill home rule by kindness. They got a shower of gombeens and little hacks into the councils throughout the country which made the local government system at the turn of the century into a laughing stock which is richly parodied and satirised in the books of Somerville and Ross. The combined incompetence and corruption of local government in this country and the misuse of local government functions in order to debate matters which were not within their competence at all, were such that Mr. de Valera, in 1940, stripped the local authorities of nearly all their formal powers and handed them over to managements, to the faceless dictators Deputy Burke was foaming at the mouth about half an hour ago.

That was Mr. de Valera's contribution, and I cannot bring myself to say that he was wrong. He left behind a certain number of functions, including the striking of a rate and including also, at that time, functions which have otherwise since been whittled away from them, but the large end of local government was taken away from elected representatives in 1940 because they had proved incapable of discharging them properly. That is what Mr. de Valera thought. That is what the whole Fianna Fáil Party that trooped into the lobbies behind him then thought. I cannot dissent from it.

National Museum, Dáil, 28 May 1987

The National Museum, as long as I can remember in my adult existence anyway, has been housed in very difficult conditions. One of the first debates in which I took part on being elected to the Oireachtas 18 years ago was one on a report of the Visitors of the National Museum which took four years even to get into print so despised was that institution by the Government of the time. Although I hope matters have changed with the various changes of Governments in the meantime, the museum still is very much an institution which, even a casual glance, will show has been treated in a stepmotherly fashion. It is the Cinderella of the State institutions. I compare it even with the way it was when I was a child and used to be taken round it by my father. I am appalled, not just at the lack of development of its facilities, but at the degree to which neglect, clutter and inertia have overtaken it and, to some extent, demoralised the very devoted staff who work there.

I can remember for some purpose visiting the labyrinth of rooms which underline this building and the adjacent Government Buildings, when I saw there in a state of decay items I remembered seeing on display in the National Museum when I was a small boy more than 40 years ago. The research, restoration, repair, study facilities, all of the facilities which in any normal museum in western Europe are taken for granted are present in the National Museum at shoestring level only unless things have changed very radically in the few years since I last had a look at the insides of it. Not only that but the space allotted to it is wildly insufficient for its needs. I am speaking both about the Antiquities Museum and the Natural History Museum. On the first occasion when I was taken through the back parts of both of these parts of the National Museum I saw exhibits which mean nothing to me — because I am too ignorant on that plain — geological exhibits stacked in corridors in boxes which were bursting, they were falling out into the corridors having been unceremoniously extruded from the original position they had occupied in the museum premises. One might well ask why and the answer is that the Houses of the Oireachtas had moved in on them and taken up the space on which they had formerly relied. That was when the extensions here were carried out about 20 years ago. The condition of the main geological collection was a national scandal, with large lumps of rock which mean nothing to me but of course are important to those who understand them. If they would not fit in packing cases they were simply beaten with sledge hammers until they did fit. That sort of conduct I mention only because it symbolises the State's attitude towards the National Museum down the years. There are not many votes in antiquities. There are not many votes in geological samples from comets, meteors, from this or that disused quarry. Accordingly the museum was very much in the condition of the weakest of the farrow of bonhams and was very lucky if the sow did not roll over and kill it.

Kildare Place is one of the saddest and most disreputable chapters in the architectural history of this city and in the history of official taste, both governmental and corporational. It is a backwater as far as streets are concerned because it is only a recess in Kildare Street but it used to be an architectural gem. There were three or four early 18th century houses on that street which, even as an uninstructed schoolboy, I remember admiring and which people who knew about these things very strongly admired. Those houses were pulled down ruthlessly in the sixties or perhaps the late fifties to make room for an extension to the Government buildings complex. It was the era of the rising tide which lifted all the boats and it was the same era in which the ESB were allowed to pull down a whole range of buildings in Lower Fitzwilliam Street. It was an act of official vandalism not markedly worse than any other at the time or any other which we have seen since but we should try to prevent the same happening again. I do not want to see prefabricated buildings on Kildare Place, apart from the functional and the security difficulties which any system of entrance and exit would cause there.

The staff of the National Museum have a very difficult and important job to do which is too often the object of a perfunctory salute. They have been as one can see by inspecting their conditions of work, the victims of official indifference over generations. In the most primitive emerging country in the world there would scarcely be as much collective indifference shown to the sort of things we like to pretend we are interested in as we have shown towards the National Museum. We are great at inviting American Presidents and showing them the Book of Kells, the Tara Brooch or the Ardagh Chalice, having a quick photo call of some dimly understood, glamorous item from our past and then we put the museum out of our minds for the next five or ten years until some other dignatory arrives and Pat is again asked to tip his forelock and be photographed with him. I always notice when photographs are taken that the Irish Minister looks up admiringly at the foreign man who looks straight ahead. At those times we take an interest in the museum but at other times it is neglected and forgotten.

The Smurfit Fountain, Dublin, 10 February 1988

There is really no limit to the impudence of Dublin Corporation. Not content with presiding over what they have allowed to become the tattiest capital in Europe, not ashamed of allowing a party whip to be applied from Leinster House so as to have a road scheme blocked at one moment and pushed through the next, some of them reportedly thinking it only their due that streets should be named after them, they now propose to allow a private firm to erect, in the main thoroughfare of the city, a hideous illuminated fountain, fit to recall the era of the Bowl of Light, and the Tomb of the Unknown Gurrier on O'Connell Bridge which public opinion, after 20 years, succeeded in having removed.

The most outrageous aspect of this proposal is that it reveals the Corporation as thinking the city belongs to them. This is because, by "adopting" this offer of a fountain from a private firm, they can apparently exempt the project entirely from planning control. In other words, whereas if Smurfits proposed to erect this monument on their own property the neighbours would have a chance to object, these Councillors, by allowing them to put it up on the premier public location in Ireland, can close off all objections, and prevent any of us from having our reasons against it fully considered. No doubt there are a lot of people who think a fountain in O'Connell Street would be an addition to the place and who have no objection to the kind of design proposed (although this, according to reports, has evidently been commissioned without any form of public competition or consultation). It seems to me that any kind of illuminated fountain built in a modern idiom will do violence to a street which, tawdry though it has become, still retains classical proportions and a fine classical building as a centrepiece. But even if I am wrong about what I admit is a matter of taste, the general appearance of the city centre in recent years must tell us that a basin of water will need the constant attention of a couple of men with nets, poles and hooks if it is not to become an unsightly sink full of crisp packets, ice-cream wrappers, beer cans and supermarket trolleys.

Let the Corporation show enough public spirit, enough humility, enough real concern for the city's appearance, not to inflict on us — after months of traffic disruption and inconvenience during construction — a monument for which I have never heard any public demand, without giving us a chance to object and to consider alternative schemes. At the very least let them allow the project to remain subject to the usual planning procedures, rather than abuse their powers by removing it from even this very feeble measure of control.

As for Smurfits, if they are really willing to spend a couple of hundred thousand pounds on a public project, any of us could easily suggest a dozen other schemes which would do them honour, rather than associate their name with a classic piece of civil misgovernment.

SECTION 5

Socialism, Labour and the Trade Unions

FG/Labour alliance proposed, 1968

The East Limerick by-election is a delusive victory for the Government, a moral victory for the Labour Party, and a moral disaster for Fine Gael.

The Government held the seat, and that is all that matters on the surface. In fact, the conversion of an overall majority of 2,500 into a minority of 4,700 — and a a constituency where the emotional sympathy factor was all in its favour — is another in the series of clear indications, dating back to 1966, that Fianna Fáil is heading for a defeat in the next general election. Assuming no change in the electoral system, it looks as though it will be lucky to keep 65 seats in a House of 144.

The Labour Party, on the other hand, did astonishingly well (though it was always fairly strong in Limerick) and seems set towards an advance. But its showing in last year's local elections suggests that any advance will be confined to urban areas; and this would leave it, at the most favourable computation, with about 28 seats. The party, in the words of its chairman, is "reaching for the stars", but it ought to reflect on the massive difficulty of progressing from a base of this size to a condition of overall majority. Fine Gael, after all, had 28 deputies twenty years ago, and, although it has slowly and painfully pulled its strength up to 46 today, even a Fine Gael optimist would scarcely say that an overall majority was just around the corner. Labour, therefore, would be well advised to temper its hopes with a little pragmatism.

Fine Gael fully deserves the chagrin it is now experiencing. Its candidate did not do at all badly, considering how many factors, particular to the time and place, were working against him: that he was relatively unknown and inexperienced, that his nomination was not all harmony and concord, that the party leader had chosen the previous week to make a statement of agricultural policy which Fianna Fáil were quick to convert into devastating ammunition among the small farms of Limerick. A Fine Gael candidate without these handicaps would almost certainly have repeated the party's success in Wicklow. But Fine Gael's failure to drive forward strongly has deeper causes. The party leadership is not aggressive enough and does not work hard enough; even when it takes up a promising issue, Fine Gael never seems to have the energy to pursue its quarry to the kill; Fianna Fáil is allowed to put the national mystique in its pocket and run off with it, and Fine Gael never challenges its miserable performance in regard to the Irish language and the North; Fianna Fáil, backed by unlimited party money and the whole resources of government, is able to offer a picture of material progress and prosperity, while Fine Gael does not seem able to produce the burning visionary and sacrificial ardour which alone could halt the Fianna Fáil machine. An opposition party out to destroy a cynical but successful establishment needs a heroic profile. Fianna Fáil once had such a profile in the years of its rise, and Fine Gael would do well to study it.

In the meanwhile, what can the Irish people look for by way of an alternative Government? One valuable result of the events in Limerick was the disclosure of the Fine Gael second preference votes. Of O'Higgins's 10,039 supporters, the regrettably high number of 1,956, or nearly one in five, did not express a second preference. But of the rest, over 80 per cent. gave Labour their vote. This is the first clear evidence in a long while that Fine Gael voters are not hostile to the Labour Party; and the Labour voters demonstrated the converse in Wicklow. There is a broad common opposite to Fianna Fáil government, as well as large areas of agreement on policy; and, while the party leaders do not seem to be doing any deals at the top, the behaviour of the party workers and voters in Wicklow and Limerick ought to make them think again. This is where the Labour leadership needs to temper its ideals with realism. As for Fine Gael it ought to think in terms of joining the Labour Party as formal partners in a loosely organised Social Democratic Alliance. This political mixture might generate once again the dash and fire of the old Sinn Fein; and God knows we need it, in a country where every day it is becoming more difficult to see that the national struggle was really worth while.

Left-influenced policies no help, Dublin, 29 March 1982

The achievement of the Coalition Government was not only to bring the people towards a realistic understanding of their situation, but also its valiant effort to break the influence of party politics on economic management.

Some would say that that effort was a rash one, and amounted to simply disregarding the political effects of budgetary measures. But it very nearly succeeded; and it is a sad sight to see our successors — having themselves created the conditions which made radical remedies necessary — now in the process of re-establishing the malignant connection we tried so hard to destroy.

The brute fact about the Irish economy is that it is, in European terms, underdeveloped and geographically disadvantaged; while having to support a population growing much faster than the rate at which productive employment can be expanded, yet having the same material expectations and aspirations as our far better-placed European neighbours.

This complex of handicaps can be outweighed only by continuous massive reinvestment of the national product in the development of wealth-creating enterprise, and by constant restraint in pay rises which, in the private sector, threaten jobs by making Irish goods uncompetitive and so ultimately unsaleable; and, in the public sector, constrict the State's capacity to use its revenues to underpin, subsidise and shape that development.

The simple analysis is not a specifically capitalist one. A socialist economy in Irish conditions would have to recognise the very same facts of life. The only difference is that a Marxist government here would impose by force rather than persuasion the policies which those facts of life suggested; with the added dimension that it would combat population growth by building flats for its people in which no more than one or two children could be brought up.

In a free country, on the other hand, the people must depend on the calm and objective guidance of an elected government, doing every day what it judges best for the economy, and not just what in the short term may seem most electorally popular.

Pleasing the ideologues of the Left is the last thing the economy needs, if it is to survive and prosper. No one doubts their serious purpose and their sincerity, or the justice of the social claims which they have been elected to articulate; but the fact is that their policies relate more to spending wealth than to creating it, and it is the latter function, not the former, that we need to concentrate on first.

What we need, in plain terms, is about ten years of fairly old- fashioned house-keeping, giving a high priority to old-fashioned concepts like thrift, getting value for money, ploughing back profits into further development, avoiding the wicked waste of reckless, useless projects and of "jobs for jobs' sake".

No doubt after ten years whatever Government had delivered all this would itself have become complacent, tired, excessively conservative; and it would be time to replace it with a more socialist alternative. But if we do not get first a good spell of businesslike government — which at the moment only this party seems willing to provide — a socialist Government, when we get one, will preside only over wreckage and despair.

FG's role in forming the next government, Dublin, 31 May 1982

Several considerations convince me that, at any rate in present conditions, a coalition arrangement with the Labour Party would not be in the country's interest or in that of Fine Gael.

I say that not in any spirit of estrangement from former coalition partners, and least of all wishing to offend them at a time when they have experienced a disappointment in Dublin West, for which all of us are sorry. It is rather the result of a calculation based on the way the party has lately been running its affairs, and on the dubious contribution which certain aspects of socialist thinking are likely to make to solving our problems in the conditions of 1982.

During the term of office of the recent Coalition, the Fine Gael party became wearily inured to something which did not happen in the previous period of Coalition government between 1973 and 1977: the constant public sniping from members of the Labour Party, including its parliamentary party, either at the very concept of coalition with us, or at one or other aspect of the economic management which that Government was struggling to apply in conditions which, thanks to earlier misrule, were very nearly out of hand.

Even office-holding members of the Labour Party — colleagues with whom we had always had a very good relationship — felt able to take up public stances critical of the Government to which they owed their jobs. For example, one Minister of State, in the period before the Government decided to halt work on Knock airport, publicly opposed the project and thus created the impression of conflict within the administration of which he was a member. I personally agreed with him, as did others; but the constraints which the Fine Gael Ministers felt applied to them, as regards voicing individual doubts about what was still an officially approved project, were not recognised by all of our colleagues.

We even got to the stage, in the interval between the ambiguous election and the Dáil reassembly, where the Labour Party as such was making public demands, in relation to modifying the January budget, on the Government of which it itself was a component.

On top of this, finally, there is the permanent element of doubt represented by the Labour Party's structural arrangements, which have the effect that the Fine Gael never knows where it stands, or where it may stand twelve months from now, in regard to Labour's willingness to enter, or to remain in, a coalition pact. This is an impossible handicap to us, as it inhibits the planning of both our own day-to-day tactics and our longer term strategy; and it is unfair to the electorate. Apart from these features of the present political scene, which debilitate our party's effectiveness both in Government and in Opposition, there is the whole area of policy, in which I honestly believe Labour solutions are not what the country needs in its present difficulties.

There are times in the history of every democracy when a government becomes fat, complacent, arrogant, perhaps even corrupt, tending to serve the interests of its own supporters to the exclusion of social justice and social advance: Fianna Fáil in the mid-1960s, the era of Taca and the repeated attempt to abolish P.R., was like this. At such times a corrective from the Left is needed: such as Fine Gael supplied with its inspirational Just Society programme, and such as the Labour Party also then offered in not very dissimilar form.

(It was a historic tragedy that this was the very moment, that the Labour Party chose to repudiate all coalition agreements, thus allowing Fianna Fáil to win the 1969 General election, which a coalition pact with consequent high vote-transfers would have easily prevented. What a difference it could have made to the country's subsequent history, North and South, had the Government been led, when the North first exploded, by Liam Cosgrave and Brendan Corish.)

There are, however, other times, such as those in which we now live, in which our problems are to a great extent the result of easy-option, soft-soap, populist government. At such times the application of socialist remedies — to the extent that these are based on expanding the State's role in the economy, and abridging that of private enterprise and capital — are exactly the opposite of what is needed. Such remedies can only aggravate the infection which Fianna Fáil's vote-buying on borrowed money has generated, by reducing still further the people's sense of individual responsibility and of the need to pay for what is consumed; by increasing their growing instinct to look to the State for everything, without caring whether the State can pay its bills; and by inflating the apparatus of the public service which is already a near-insupportable burden on the back of the struggling productive private sector.

I know that the intentions behind the Labour Party's State investment doctrine are excellent; but Fine Gael may make the mistake of accepting these intentions as a substitute for rational proof that such solutions are what we need. The "National Development Corporation" is a recent example to hand. This was originally a Labour Party idea, first articulated I think by Brendan Halligan around 1975. It found its way into the 1981 Mansion House document which was the basis of the recent Coalition; and Fianna Fáil have now got the Dáil to vote five million pounds for a "National Enterprise Agency" which is their political response to what was first a Labour idea.

I have no objection in the world to a State agency or corporation engaging in some activity beyond the capacity of private enterprise; but which activity is in mind in this instance? We are still waiting to hear; and the Minister who introduced the relevant Estimate in the Dáil two weeks ago was unable — though I questioned him persistently — to give the faintest clue as to what kind of productive activity his Agency was going to engage in return for the £5m. we were voting for it. As to the ability of his Agency, however — once installed in expensive headquarters and having recruited an expensive staff of executives — simply to get through that large sum of money, I have no doubt at all.

This is the kind of thing that Fine Gael must resist: but resistance to which is weakened for so long as we feel obliged to look over our shoulders at our former Coalition partners. It goes without saying that all these misgivings would apply with much greater force to any attempt to conciliate, for transient parliamentary purposes or otherwise, forces even more doctrinaire. The spectacle we had after the February election, of the two major groupings in Irish politics each hoping to get the Dáil support of the SFWP and Independent deputies was a sad one; luckily, the Fine Gael Taoiseach drew the line at any notion of trying to bid up the promises extracted from his less particular opponent. But for a time, it looked like turning into an act unique in the annals of the Irish political circus: a tail wagging two dogs.

The result of all this is that I think the time has come to face up to the next General Election, and to conduct ourselves in the meantime in forming policy and tactics, entirely on our own feet, free of association with Labour; and to tell the people clearly that no Labour coalition will be formed after the election either.

Finance estimate, Dáil, 17 June 1983

I hope I will live to see the day — I mean this sincerely and not in any way sarcastically — that there will be a Labour Government here, that Deputy Bermingham and Deputy Ryan will be Ministers in that Government and all the other office holders and their successors. I am not in the least apprehensive about that day when it comes because in order to form a Government in a democracy they will have to get the votes of half the people. In order to get that percentage of votes in a country like this they will have to change their tune very considerably from the tune now being sung by many of their Members. I am sure they would be a valuable corrective to a Government who might have become fat, complacent or perhaps corrupt. A corrective of that kind would have been no harm in the mid-1960s but, unhappily, that was the very time when the Labour Party decided they did not want Government at any price and when they turned their face against Coalition Government. I know the Government have an item on their programme to the genesis of which is to be found in the Labour Party programme for 1977, namely, the National Development Corporation. To counter the national development consortium Fianna Fáil in the election of that year proposed an industrial development consortium. When they won the election they proceeded to set up that consortium. Very wisely, however, Deputy Lynch as Taoiseach, confined that consortium to Deputy O'Malley who took damn good care to make sure that not a halfpenny of public money was ever spent on such a hare-brained enterprise. Although I dined long and richly on the industrial development consortium in the period 1977 to 1981, let me say now, since I have grown more sober and worried about the country than I was a few years ago, that I think Deputy O'Malley was quite right to keep that consortium as a kind of spook — I used to call it the spook of Schoolhouse Lane. It had no palpable existence that could be seen — it had no office, no address, no telephone, no staff, no budget, no functions. It did not even have a desk. It did not figure anywhere in the Estimates. It was only a reason why, for a few months, a certain number of civil servants had to abandon the work they were paid to do and go through the motions of trekking over to Kildare Street to meet other civil servants who had done the same thing that morning. Even that pretence was dropped after a short while and rightly. The reason I say rightly is because it was an excuse for pretending by means of setting up an organisation and funding it — although in this case Deputy O'Malley took damn good care to make sure it never was funded — that something was being done by way of flattering ideologists who

170

never did what I might call a wealth producing day's work in their lives and would not know how to go abut it if they were required to do it.

I am still waiting to hear — I know my friend Deputy Bermingham too well to suppose he will do anything except take this in good humour — from Deputy Mervyn Taylor, Deputy Ruairi Quinn or other Deputies what wealth producing function a national development consortium or industrial development corporation will perform. If there is such a function I want answers to two questions. First, why have the private sector fought shy of it? Second, if there are good reasons, is it not a function of a kind for which an existing agency already caters? In other words, if it is something to do with the sea, do we not have An Bord Iascaigh Mhara? If it is to do with bogs, do we not have Bord na Móna? If it is to do with taking alcohol out of potatoes, do we not have Céiminí Teoranta? There is an endless zareba of semi-State bodies. They are so numerous that some of them have not been looked at for years to see what they are up to or how they justify their place in the Estimates.

TCD Debate: "Socialism is an outmoded philosophy", Dublin, 19 October 1983

Whether socialism, or any other political creed, is outmoded or not must depend on circumstances of time and place. In this country, ever since independence, there has always been a strong element of what could be called pragmatic socialism, with the early establishment of State-owned enterprise in areas once the preserve of private interests: electricity generation with the ESB, banking with the Agricultural Credit Corporation (both founded in the 1920's), then, later, sugar production, turf development, nationalised rail, air and road transport and so on. On the good sense of many, if not all, of those nationalised undertakings there has been a fair amount of general agreement. But in the further dimensions of socialism, different answers would have to be given, depending on the conditions of the time, as to whether they represented a sensible or useful course for us to follow.

The State's first Government, for all its many virtues, is generally admitted to have been socially too conservative understandably so, perhaps, as those young men tried to rein in the forces which the national revolution had unleashed. Mr de Valera's election victory in 1932 was brought about not so much by the support of those who shared his hostility to the Treaty as by that of the people dissatisfied, in the middle of a world slump, with a Government insufficiently progressive socially, and insufficiently sensitive to the needs of the poor and deprived. That there was room in the early 1930s for the kind of programme which Mr de Valera, initially with Labour support, pursued, is undoubtedly true; and the failure of Mr Cosgrave's party to see the needs of the moment certainly started the party on a 15-year decline, only halted and reversed by its leadership of the Inter-Party Government formed in 1948.

There is no knowing how many things would have been different, and better, for the country, and even for socialist politics, had our only socialist party been able to make its dreams fit what was in practice attainable. In all probability the convulsions of Government following the arms crisis of May 1970 would not have happened — though, as I have admitted before, we too would have been at risk — and therefore in all probability we would have been spared the sinister rivalries, and the public hatreds, which arose in that year and which still corrode the Fianna Fáil party and poison the atmosphere all around. In the latter 1970s, and indeed in part related to Fianna Fáil's own internal problems, politics here developed an even more malignant dimension — that of buying votes by means of quite reckless acceptance of extra burdens on the shoulders of the State, according as tax reliefs were promised, and quite unjustifiable State projects, inaugurated for the sake of winning General Elections and even by-elections. This overall approach of some political interests brought the people on a mad Monopoly-like board game, in which three successive throws laded them on squares reading "Pay no rates or car tax", "Collect an airport", and "Pay a billion pounds in interest on State debts".

This is far from socialism, and it would be insulting to a party which, when it finds itself in office has always behaved with great responsibility, to suggest otherwise. But the atmosphere generated in the last six or seven years, constantly replenished by drug-pusher hints from some political quarters that another little fix will do us no harm, is very hostile to any attempt to re-establish the sort of prudent State housekeeping that the political leaders of both sides once upon a time took for granted. It is therefore not the moment for doing what socialism, in its current Irish form, advocates; not the moment for enhanced State expenditure of borrowed money, and the acceptance by the State of new burdens; and not the moment for further involvements of the State in areas of economic enterprise where the State's efforts up to now have been far from uniformly impressive. To that extent — although its time will probably come again — socialism in this country must be treated for the time being as outmoded.

Ideology and the NDC, Dublin, 24 January 1985

This State was damned for the first 60 years of its existence by divisions arising from the Civil War; and is now in danger of being damned for the next 60 years by ideology, unless we get a bit of sense. This can be seen from the present fuss about the National Development Corporation.

The genesis of the National Development Corporation is as follows. The Labour Party and Brendan Halligan thought it up before the 1977 election. The Fianna Fáil party planned to capture whatever facile allure the phrase had, by including in their own 1977 manifesto of evil memory a "Sean Lemass-type Industrial Development Consortium, chaired by the Minister for Industry and Commerce".

After their 1977 victory, that Minister — who was Des O'Malley, now politically emarginated and sleeping under bridges — took great care to ensure that not one penny of public money was spent on this "Consortium", which never existed except as a poor spook, like the "Employment Action Team" and the "Land Development Authority", about whose functioning it seemed after a while cruel to ask too many Dáil questions.

I believe no one in Fine Gael is opposed to public ownership of any project where this seems the most appropriate format, i.e. the one most likely to result in a flourishing enterprise. What some members of the Labour Party seem to think is capitalist or right-wing resistance to public ownership is no more than a reserve, or a distrust, in regard to its objective efficiency; and God knows there are enough examples in the Irish boutique of semi-State creations to well justify that reserve.

Fine Gael people simply do not want to add to the number of ruinously expensive models for which the Irish taxpayer has to foot the bill; but if the Labour Party or anyone else can suggest, in the concrete terms which might lead a businessman to risk his money, some demonstrably good and promising ideas which can only be realised by publicity-sponsored enterprise, there will be no ideological opposition from anyone.

The unions, the economy and society, Dublin, 29 January 1985

Mr Tom Garry, President of the F.W.U.I., when speaking yesterday at a Jim Larkin commemoration, raised an interesting series of questions when he deplored the absence of political unity in the trade union movement. Some of them, however, are questions which it is up to the trade union movement itself to answer.

For instance, if the entire trade union movement were politically united behind some existing party, or were to form one of its own, how exactly would it deal with any one of the problems for the existence of which Mr Garry seems to blame society at large and in particular the private sector?

As far as unemployment is concerned, we have a clue — and not a very encouraging one — in the recent I.C.T.U. document "Confronting the Jobs Crisis". If this is the best that the trade union movement can do, they have even more problems than Mr Garry imagines, chief among them an appalling lack of originality or realism.

There is the usual demand that "the State should have a more active, interventionist role in initiating and directing developments in the economy" and "involvement in the high-growth areas of manufacturing industry and natural-resource based industry". We are entitled to ask, once again, just which enterprises are in mind here; and why the private sector has been blind to what the I.C.T.U. obviously thinks are lucrative possibilities. Until we get some hint of the answer to this question, we are entitled to suspect that what is being demanded is public enterprise for its own sake, whether or not it turns into a collection of giant financial millstones round the necks of the taxpayers — including the large numbers of taxpayers who are also trade unionists.

The I.C.T.U. document also tells us that public sector employment must play a major role in the process of job generation. In fact this is the very thing which, by being more rapidly expanded in the 1970s than the wealth-producing part of the economy could bear, has been the principal cause of our crushing burden of public debt and of taxation to pay for it.

In the education field, although what we most urgently need is more emphasis on subjects tending to predispose young people towards industrial, agricultural and marketing careers, the Congress does not stress this at all, but speaks of "developing social skills necessary for the participation of people in democratic decision-making", the "elimination of sexism in education" and "courses in citizenship and politics". These are fine; but their connection with the proclaimed theme of the document — "Confronting the Jobs Crisis" is not too clear.

On the other hand, this document says not a word about any of the problems in industrial relations which have in fact contributed to the disappearance of thousands of jobs — nothing about unofficial industrial action, nothing about absenteeism, nothing about inter-union rivalry, nothing about inflexible practices, nothing about uncompetitive levels of productivity.

The public are often said by the media to be fed up with the party political process as it operates in Ireland, and to be disillusioned with their politicians. If this is true, it is very disappointing that, at any rate on recent evidence, the trade union movement shows no sign of delivering any higher level of inspiration or of critical self-examination than politicians have done. The vacuum which the President of the F.W.U.I deplores arises not so much from the movement's lack of political consensus, but from its lack of ideas on which such a consensus might be usefully mobilised.

Ideology and the public sector, Dublin, 18 March 1986

Mr Tomas Mac Giolla gave us last week a glimpse of the kind of world we could expect from the Workers' Party when he accused the Government of an "ideological hostility" to public ownerships after it published a Bill to split CIE into three separate enterprise.

In fact this Bill does not propose to remove from these new enterprises the near-monopoly of public transport which CIE enjoys, merely to see whether better value for money can be got from a reorganisation along those lines. We may conclude therefore that Mr Mac Giolla's real objection to the Bill relates not to any element of privatisation — since it contains no such provision — but to its tacit implication that a State- owned enterprise is not sacrosanct, and can be broken up if it ceases to justify the public money spent on it.

Surely even a Socialist must have some regard for the proper use of public money — for as long, at least, as he remains answerable in a free electoral system to the people who have to provide it. And surely even a Socialist might ask himself whether it is not time to try a little reorganisation on a body so voracious of public money as CIE.

Last year the Government had to provide £115m. to plug the gap between CIE's earnings and its expenditure; in plain language, to cover its losses. This means that, on average, every man, woman and child in the country contributed £34 just to keep the State transport monopoly on its feet for a single year. In the last ten years, 1977-86 inclusive, the cumulative subsidy provided by the taxpayer to CIE, expressed in 1986 money values, exceeds one billion pounds, or about £320 for every man, woman and child in the country — on top of fares no lower than the European average and in some areas exceeding it.

Instead of carping about the Government's very modest attempt to see it

175

this intolerable situation can be improved by reorganisation, Mr Mac Giolla should give us his view on the 25 years it has taken CIE to get agreement on the one-man buses which are standard over most of Europe; of the unofficial stoppages which are a feature of our public transport; and of how easy it must be for CIE's management to deal with industrial relations in a concern where the workforce of about 16,000 is represented by something like 27 different unions.

There is no option for the State, if we are to remain a viable democracy, but to disengage quickly from the excessive burdens of semi-State subsidy, and of public-sector numbers, under which it is staggering. The Mac Giolla solution — to do the opposite, and extend State involvement on principle — will leave us where it has left Socialist countries in eastern Europe: with crippled economies whose inefficiency is tempered only be corruption, and with populations free neither to change their system of government, nor to escape from it.

Marxist theory, property and the Irish legal system, Lisdoonvara, 22 July 1986

The task of quantifying the State's wealth is one before which the mind reels. The list of lands buildings and harbours in the care of the Office of Public Works alone fills 57 sheets of a computer print-out, with 53 entries to each page, a total of about 3,000 properties. Add all the installations of the Defence Forces, of the Health Boards, all the libraries and the fire stations and waterworks of the local authorities, al the buildings and equipment of the university colleges and the N.I.H.E., the trackless infinity of offices, equipment, plant of all kinds throughout the national and local administration; then move to the State-owned bodies and compute the value of the E.S.B. stations and transmission system, of the telecommunications network, of the railways, depots, stations offices, hotels, and vehicles of C.I.E., the airports and aircraft of Aer Rianta and Aer Lingus, the natural resources belonging to Bord Gais and Bord na Mona: the total — all, in intention, the patrimony of our three and a half million citizens — seems beyond all computation.

The valuation of a single national resource and its per capita distribution will perhaps give some faint hint of the point. The State owns about 320,000 hectares, or 800,000 acres, of growing timber. Assuming very roughly 2,000 per acre as the value of half-grown softwood, this asset works out at equivalent to £1.6 billion, in other words, about £500 for every man, woman and child in the country, or over £2,500 for every family of average size.

Summing up these various points, it seems to me, firstly, that the legal system imposes limitations on private property rights so far-reaching as to be quite inconsistent with its being the mere tool of an exploitative minority; that its accommodation of State monopolies is equally inconsistent with it; and that the patterns of both land and home ownership suggest that, if property ownership is an index of belonging to a dominant class, this class is so large in Ireland as not remotely to conform to the Marxist model of and exploitative clique. Secondly, the massive expansion in State investment and in the volume of state- owned property, since it represents the permanent withdrawal of an immense quantum of wealth from the market and the reach of capitalist ambition and its permanent freezing in areas of public utility, equally suggests that the legal system, the mould in which this policy is given effective shape, is not the tool of any dominant class.

I may conclude by drawing attention to the phenomenon from the other side of the argument, namely, that well-distributed though wealth may be in this country, a very large number of people have not benefited, except through State services, from this dispersal. This seems to me to be suggested by a comparison of the contemporary figures for annual mortality with the figures for admission of wills to probate, or the grant of letters of administration of the estates of people dying intestate. In 1985 the total mortality in the State was about 32,000; a small fraction were young or youngish people whom one would not expect to have accumulated any great substance; but in over-45 age group there died about 31,000 people, and this figure does not change much from year to year in the short term. On the other hand, the average number of wills probated each year in the last four years, added to the average yearly grants of administration, amounts to only about 15,500, i.e. exactly half the approximate annual mortality. Unless I am overlooking something, this seems to show that only about half the population leave behind them on death enough property to justify the trouble and expense of formally distributing it to those entitled to succeed to it; and even where a grant is taken out, the deceased's estate may be very small. This suggests that, while the ownership of substantial property is very widespread, we still have a long way to go before everyone has the personal stake in the country which is the best guarantee of its stability and progress.

The policies which might lead us in that direction lie far outside the scope of this talk. I will only say that they seem to me to lie, not in the forced or artificial further redistribution of material resources, but in education, and in the abolition of our worst forms of underprivileged: chronic poverty of knowledge, of skills, and of understanding of the greater world outside us.

Government, the employers, the unions and ideology, Dublin, 5 November 1986

Twenty, even ten years ago — as recently as the National Coalition Government led by Liam Cosgrave and Brendan Corish — the differences which arose between Government, employers and unions, particularly in the context of national wage agreements, were played out simply in terms of what one partner or another could afford to pay or could afford to accept: a simple, subjective interchange on which objective values or ideas seldom intruded except in the shape of general appeals to "justice" or the "national interest". But then Mrs Thatcher won a British general election in 1979; and with her coming to power a few miles away from us, the vocabulary and ideology of her dominant wing of the Conservative party became audible over here, and quickly found a receptive following anxious to promote them on the Irish scene. Words like "privatisation" — which I doubt was ever heard at the F.U.E. conference in say 1975 or 1976 — and phrases like "cutting public expenditure" became part of the currency of political industrial and economic discussion.

On the other side of the industrial relations divide the sharpening of Conservative ideology seemed to provoke a sharpening of doctrine on the Labour and union side as well; and naturally, anything current in England is always, sooner or later, slavishly imitated here, it was not time at all until the Irish Labour Party and Irish Congress of Trade Unions began to use ideological language of a kind never heard from Brendan Corish, to say nothing of William Norton, or of union leaders of an earlier generation. There were, indeed, a few stray Labour ideologists who in this respect were ahead of the trend; I remember Brendan Halligan in 1976 floating the idea of a National Development Corporation, on which a certain amount of ideological bunting could be seen to flutter; but I think it was not until the 1980s, and the era of the second or third National Coalition Governments, that Labour and I.C.T.U. voices began to openly evangelise in the name of state expenditure and state-owned enterprise for its own sake — the more of it, the better.

It seems to me that both capital and labour — and the Government that has to make them both happy, and even, as at present, run the country while containing both their representatives within its own cabinet — are wrong to get themselves mutually polarised by adopting competing ideologies both of which are fairly recent imports.

In a small country like this, without a huge industrial population, with no history of class antagonisms at all as sharp as Britain has had, with educational structures which, although far from perfect, offer quite good routes of social mobility. I think we would do better to stick to the less pretentious vocabulary with which politics and industrial relations used to make do in the relatively recent past, and to cut the hypertensive ideology out of political and economic debate.

I cannot see that these considerations smack of conservative or right-wing philosophy. Indeed in recent years they seem to have become orthodox thinking in countries which have been socialist in the totalitarian sense for more than a generation, such as Hungary and China. They arise from simple observations of human psychology, which is as much common to both sides of the world ideological divide as oxygen in the air.

Personally, I believe the possibilities for legitimate state initiative are even now not exhausted; the massive expansion in forestry which the European timber shortage and our own uniquely suitable climate call for seems still quite beyond the organising capacity of private enterprise; and something similar may be true of fishery development and some forms of land use alternative to traditional patterns.

Equally, I would not like to see the notion of cutting public expenditure harden into an ideology or fetish. Obviously wasteful or extravagant expenditure, or expenditure which is not achieving the policy purpose at which it is aimed, is wrong and should be stopped. But I would expect even a socialist to agree about this; even he would not wish to perpetuate some of the practices unearthed in the last couple of years by the Dáil Committee on Public Expenditure, or by the Comptroller and Auditor General and the Public Accounts Committee between them. On the other hand, a lot of innocent people depend, through no fault of their own, on the maintenance of a certain level and certain direction of state expenditure, and anything in the nature of a crusade raised against it on principle, leaving out of account the human consequences of radical cuts, is likely to prove socially divisive and perhaps in the end to do more damage than the savings will justify. I have often advocated cutting expenditure, but this objective should be pursued with prudence, and not raised to the level of an ideology in its own right. To make this concrete: it is one thing to reduce excessive public service numbers by applying an embargo on replacing natural wastage of personnel; it would be quite another simply to disemploy large numbers of people (as has been happening in Britain, with bitterly disruptive social consequences).

Here there are some extraordinary view to be heard. For instance, there is the doctrine that the private sector has "failed" to provide enough jobs, and that the State in consequence has the duty to do so, apparently without regard to where extra State salaries, or extra State investment in areas from which the private sector has abstained, are to come from. This doctrine overlooks the fact that it is not the function of business to provide jobs, but to do business; the jobs are a natural by-product of business's success, and loss of jobs a natural consequence of business's failure. No one has any illusions about the altruism of private enterprise, any more than one might have such an illusion about a swarm of bees; they produce jobs and honey respectively not as their main objective but as its concomitant.

But oddly enough, hand in hand with this dismissal of private enterprise for its "failure" to do what it never set out to do, there is the doctrine that it is wrong even to try to get private enterprise going, to start one's own business or create one's own job. Last May, according to Maev-Ann Wren in the Irish Times of 13 May, a concert was organised in support of a self-help job-creation campaign called Self Aid. this "annoyed" the I.C.T.U., because, as their assistant secretary is quoted as saying, "we would be totally opposed to the ideological connotation that it is up to people to create their own jobs", though the Congress "still saw the concert as a useful mechanism for focusing attention on unemployment which could make people start asking questions about what the Government and political parties are doing". To try to shame private individuals out of the human instinct to do something for themselves seems to me a grotesque misapplication even of socialist philosophy, and is doubly out of place in a country like this, where any form of serious enterprise needs all the encouragement it can get.

It seems to me that all groups in this country have a strong interest in draining ideology out of our system. Our problems are so obvious and so easily analyzed, and our population even still so homogeneous, that something like consensus on broad principles should be possible: a consensus which, while leaving room for differing political parties and methods, would at least exclude the needless sharpened tensions which foreign-grown ideologies and slogans add to the scene, tending to destabilise the equilibrium which should exist between government, business and labour.

FG free of Labour, Dublin, 23 January 1987

The ending of our association with Labour must act like a lungful of oxygen on Fine Gael, locked for the last six years into a room thick with ideological fog. It is no offence to respected friends in Labour — who loyally bore their share of Government burdens, and in Brendan Corish's time did not impede the Government unduly with ideology — to say that their beliefs on the respective roles of State and of private enterprise are the reverse of what the country needs, and of what it must now be Fine Gael's undivided task to deliver.

The first step on this road has been taken with the publication of Fine Gael's budget proposals and associated projects, notably the admission of private enterprise to some of the existing State monopolies. This idea, by no means new, has caused alarm among the ideologues of the Irish Congress of Trade Unions, fearful of seeing the standards of financial efficiency, to which private business must conform, applied to the immobile semi-State mammoths now at the mercy of their unions.

It may be noted that the I.C.T.U.'s own contribution to the debate on unemployment, made in a document issued in 1985, listed among other recipes

180

for job-creating "the elimination of sexism in the class-room". This sort of bosh ought to disqualify its authors from having any notice taken of their views on economic development; but these are the very people to whom Mr Haughey immediately wrote, after the publication of the Fine Gael proposals, reassuring them that he shared their opposition to any such programme of privatisation, and that their unique mix of backward conservatism and trendy loopiness would be safe in a world run by Fianna Fáil.

Mr Haughey — as his former colleague Mr O'Malley noted the other day, with the Pauline austerity of the late convert — has spent the last four years making promises: from the abolition of D.I.R.T. and the Residential Property Tax to the provision of ferry facilities for Aran. But he now expects credit for forswearing all pre-election undertakings. Which position are we to believe? Or has his party so insulting an opinion of the public intelligence that it thinks Deputy Jekyll will get away with a show of responsible restraint before the Dublin business community, while Deputy Hyde is scattering I.O.U.'s for £400 million over the provinces?

We have had too much junk politics of this sort, and it must be Fine Gael's task to downface and discredit this junk politics for ever. This party's courage in publishing a very tough financial programme at the start of an election campaign will, I think, be a turning-point in the State's history. It is up to us not to disappoint the very many people from whom this sobering move will represent the first hopeful sign they have seen from Leinster House for many years.

Public utilities and the right to strike, Cork, 8 May 1987

It is disingenuous to pretend that, so far as the right to dispose freely of one's labour is concerned, no distinction should be made between an employee of the E.S.B. and an employee of a privately owned bank or hotel or supermarket. yet our existing laws fail to reflect the real difference that exists between the situations of the two kinds of employee; and, in this failure, the laws offend by omission against the precept of equality contained both in natural justice and in Article 40 of the Constitution itself. To treat as equal things that are naturally unequal is not equality but inequality, and plain bad government.

In a certain limited range of public-utility monopolies, most certainly including the E.S.B. at the head of the list, I think the function of the utility should be seen as being just vital as the functions of police and the army, and the right of its employees to cease their normal work in order to bring pressure in an industrial dispute should be curtailed by law.

I know the howls of rage that any such opinion is likely to provoke. The issue however is not only the rights of labour or the rights of unions. The issue is also the rights of the people, too often regarded as located on an altogether lower plane of values when the sacred practices of industrial action are involved.

In 1966 Mr Lemass's Government, faced with a situation like the recent one, secured the passage of the Electricity (Special Provisions) Act, which, during the periods when it might be brought into operation by Government order, made strikes in the E.S.B. unlawful and provided penalties for taking part in them. The Act was brought briefly into operation, but was not a success; strikers imprisoned for refusing to pay fines had to be released when, according to folklore, their fines were paid for them by the Government, which also sent them home in taxis.

There are however significant differences between the conditions of today and those of 21 years ago. In 1966 the country was on the crest of a world boom. Unemployment in the month when that Act was passed stood at one-fifth of today's figure. Current budget deficits were unknown; huge State debt, the oil crises and the world recessions lay in the future. Mr Lemass could count only on the support of his own party in the Dáil.

Today, with the economy in crisis, amid a mood of public despair and with a large majority in both Dáil and public in no humour to let a battered economy suffer still more at the hands of a relatively small group in pursuit of their own claims, the scene is quite different.

The 1966 Act was repealed in 1969; but a similar measure, strengthened and supplemented if necessary, should be again enacted and applied the moment another strike in the E.S.B. is threatened.

Industry and Commerce estimate, Dáil, 28 May 1987

I suggested here a couple of years ago that we should have a new agency, a board whose only function would be to wind up agencies. It would be An Bord um Threascairt Bhord whose only criterion of success would be the number of agencies it succeeded in closing down.

The Minister spoke in general terms about this matter in a way I could only approve of and I am disappointed to find that a little later he spoke about the National Development Corporation in terms which suggest that they have his warmest approval. I hope I am not being unjust to him or to anyone in his Department or to anyone working under the umbrella of the NDC, but I suspect that we have here under our noses in the Minister's speech an example of the tenacious will to exist which is breathed into any State institution as soon as pen is put to paper to give it birth. I remember as a father going to nursing homes when my family were increasing in number and I was struck by a phrase that nurses used about how a baby had a stronger grip on life on that day than he had on the previous day and this at the age of two and three days and so forth. They did not mean the baby had been ailing on the previous day; they just felt that the baby had got a sniff of the air of the world and was that much more determined 24 hours later to hold on to it. That is what happens with institutions and when I read the bland statements in the Minister's speech about the NDC I ask myself whether his will to cut down these agencies can be trusted and whether we can really make an act of faith in it.

We now have the National Development Corporation. I see that their first full year's report has not yet been produced. Their activities seem to have been thin enough. I do not quite see what can be the delay in producing their report. The Minister has taken the corporation under his wing. He is like the hen on the old penny with all the chickens flocking around it. He has happily adopted this Labour Party chicken under his wing and is providing it with warmth, support and protection. Is there anything which the National Development Corporation is doing that Fóir Teoranta, the IDA, the Industrial Credit Company or one of the banks cannot do and, if so, what is it? If there is some interstice, some tiny space, between the meshes of the existing State agencies through which perhaps the odd firm falls, unable, for one small print reason to get money out of the IDA, or unable, for some other reason, to get it from Foir Teoranta or from the Industrial Credit Company, would it not be an easier matter to extend the remit of one of the existing institutions in order to close that interstice between the meshes than to set up an entirely new organisation? I argued this point, I suppose, a dozen times in this House. Naturally it cuts no ice with my friend Deputy Desmond and his colleagues. I would have expected it to cut some ice with my own party. I was disappointed in that, as in other things. I would have expected it to cut some ice with Fianna Fáil, but no, the Minister for Industry and Commerce has quite happily enfolded this little day old chick into the warmth of his dusty wing. It will survive and thrive and tomorrow its hold on life will stronger than it is today.

Regarding the National Development Corporation — NADCORP; it even has a little acronym now and I suppose even at this moment some natty little architect with a tweed tie is designing a stainless steel plate with a little logo with the word "NADCORP" neatly fitted beside it — the Minister said: "NADCORP has an important role to play in industrial and job creation strategy".

God be with the strategists. I remember the time with Deputy Gene Fitzgerald was always telling us abut the Fianna Fáil Party strategy. It was all nostalgia for the world war which he could dimly remember his people talking about — everybody on those benches used to talk like that then — they could remember their parents talking about it at the time. They were like little

Rommels — the word fell easily from their lips — they had a strategy for industrial development. The Minister continued:

As the State's venture capital agency it can complement the grant, loan and advisory functions of the other State industrial development agencies. . . .

Why cannot one of the others have its remit extended? Why must we have a complete new stainless steel plate logo and acronym in order to provide this complementary aspect? The Minister went on: either on its own account — (here is a new arrival on the semi-official jargon scene) — or by leveraging in other investors can act as a catalyst in the initiation of new projects that might not otherwise get off the ground.

I know roughly what a catalyst is and I know what a lever is but I am damned if I know where in the world of chemistry or in the world of a metaphor outside chemistry one can use a lever to produce a catalyst. That confusion of metaphors is not really the point I am trying to make. Nonetheless it is important because, when one finds language like that, it is masking a confusion of thought. How does one leverage in other investors? An investor is somebody with spare money. He is somebody with money surplus to his day-to-day requirements which he wants to invest and make a profit on. If he sees something which will yield him a return he will put the money in without any leverage from anyone. If he does not foresee a return he will not put the money in.

I do not know what return NADCORP envisages because I see, in the very next paragraph of the Minister's speech that he says it will be a more patient investor than most private venture capital companies, that it will be prepared to wait somewhat longer for a return on its investment. Of course nobody in NADCORP — as he takes down his hat and coat from the Office of Public Works hat rack in the evening, puts them on and goes off to the DART or to his car in the carpark to go home — will lie awake at night worrying about whether it is perhaps taking a bit too long for a return to show on its capital. It is not coming out of his pocket. I say that in no sense critically — and I hope it will not be understood in that way — of public servants and officials who loyally, faithfully, sincerely and honestly do a lifetime job — my own father was one of them.

I am not setting up as a critic of the Civil Service or public service mentality at all but I am saying that necessarily someone in public employment does not have the stimulus of risk on the one hand and profit on the other which an ordinary investor has. When I read that NADCORP, with one hand, will be leveraging in investors my reaction is that I am damned if I am gong to be leveraged in by NADCORP if I am going to have to wait for a return until NADCORP's patience runs out. They will be doing that with one hand and with the other more or less twirling a daisy waiting for a time to pass. What is the point in talking about cutting down the plethora of institutional supports to industry while at the same time keeping alive this perfectly redundant socialist chick?

184

Dick Spring's Caring Society, Dublin, 8 September 1987

The vigour which Dick Spring is showing in criticising current Government economies is a healthy sign. It means there is the nucleus of a proper Opposition of the Left, which will not let itself be taken over by forces to whom free elections, and political freedoms generally, are tiresome obstacles to be dispensed with as soon as possible. Some day, no doubt, there will be a straight socialist Government in this country; but when that day comes we would certainly like the democratic Labour Party of Mr Spring to be on top of the heap, and not the sinister prowlers who would make sure that that change of Government would be the last.

Mr Spring, however, has a long way to go if his party is relying on democratic methods, as of course it is. In order to command a Government here by the free choice of the people, he must win a large part of the middle of the road as well as the natural permanent residents of the Left constituency. If he ever hopes to be Taoiseach, he will have to win the support of hundreds of thousands of modest property-owners, small businessmen, even farmers, the sort of people who, even if with a grumbling reluctance, today are accepting the necessity for the sort of financial stringency now being applied.

Just how far Mr Spring is from that achievement can be judged from one or two of his recent speeches. The note struck is always the same: the Government's ruthless economies are spelling the end of "the caring society".

That smug slogan "the caring society" is the hardest of all to stomach in this context. The Left's idea of "the caring society" is to insist on having what is desirable today, and leave the bill for the children of tomorrow. That is not "caring", but stealing.

Mr Spring of course does not omit to make the — fair enough — point that the taxation system here is unjust and that property gets off too lightly. But his own party's contribution to solving this problem — the Residential Property Tax, one of their 1982 coalition conditions — was grotesque. Firstly, this tax is erratic: if you own a streetful of property and live yourself in a luxury apartment belonging to someone else, you pay no R.P.T., nor does your landlord. Secondly, its yield in money is low, while the public annoyance caused by its whiff of ideology is considerable. Thirdly, despite its chewy socialist flavour, it actually costs most of those who pay it far less than they would now be paying under the old-fashioned system of rates.

Mr Spring's vision of the country as divided into "those deprived of any access to the wealth of the nation and those well positioned to skim that wealth off the top" is also more simple than the reality. Many well-paid people in this country, in business or professions or the public service, find the burden of direct and indirect taxation taken in conjunction with the cost of living so intolerable that it is they, no less than the unskilled and jobless people at the bottom of the barrel, who think about emigration; or, if they are beyond the age of that much personal mobility, their well-educated children are thinking about it. The degree to which this situation has been brought about by the State itself, in the demands it must make to service the debts of the "caring society", is very considerable.

Financial resolutions, Dáil, 9 February 1988

It galls me not to be able to contradict what the Leader of Fianna Fáil has said since I have spent 20 years in politics trying to do them down but I have to agree with the Leader of that the party that what he has said is correct. Once 1983 came and went we were goosed as a Government which could hope to revive the economy and to inject some sense into the public finances. I have to bear the chagrin of that personally, and I mean personally, because I pay a certain price for sitting on the back benches. I went to the back benches because I could see that coming. I have to bear the chagrin of that and had to wait to see in power a Government who did their best to destroy the economy of the country with the mood they built up among the people. I had to wait to see them take the first apparently solid step towards regaining the position which they for reasons of political partisanship and greed threw away.

It may be said that they are penitents, they are political Magdalens. A Renaissance painter would depict them with their long hair down over a bare shoulder, politically speaking. I am willing to accept that their penitence is genuine and I am going to take it at its face value but I have not forgotten the old days. I have not forgotten the rhetoric which was launched at the unfortunate Dr FitzGerald shackled to a party he never ought to have touched with a barge pole politically, nice though they are as individuals. It is easy to have a pint with them but politically they are poison in the eighties. It was pathetic to see him having to deal with colleagues like that and being confronted on the far side of the House not by sympathy, not by solidarity, not by support and not by a party that might have had the generosity to say, "let us close down the Civil War; come over here and work with us or let us cross the floor and work with you and not mind those fellows whose ideology comes from 2,000 miles to the East". I do mean the Parliamentary Labour Party when I say that.

The first illusion that a Government is under an obligation to repress intellectually — there will be people, of whom Deputy Higgins is a mild and gentle enough representative, who might be anxious to see a sign of the jackboot in the use of the word "repress" — is the idea that we can take a short cut out

186

of our difficulties by what is called rescheduling our debts, by doing what I believe I hear a junior Fianna Fáil Minister recommend not long before Christmas, that is telling the international bankers to go and take a running jump at themselves. That kind of talk is baby take. If this country enjoys the topmost grade of international credit rating, it is precisely because no Government here of any colour has ever done that. If a Government here were to say that we are terribly sorry, that we cannot afford the instalment due on 10 March nor the one due on 1 June and that we are unilaterally demanding a rescheduling of our debt portfolio, under the threat of non payment, this country would be dragged overnight from its topmost position in the credit rating down near the bottom.

I seem to remember some junior Minister saying that some countries are supposed to have tried that and got away with it, but their experience shows no such thing. I will read from a recent bulletin, issued from a temple of capitalism which Deputy Higgins would not touch with a tongs. It is the bulletin of the Morgan Guaranty Trust Company of New York and deals with the subject of world financial markets. The issue of July 1987 dealing with Peru, states as follows:

One approach to limiting financial transfers is seen in Peru's unilaterally decreed limit on debt-service payments, in effect since 1985. Emphatically, this is not the right approach. Peru's debt-service limit has ensured practically no new money inflows from banks. It is virtually cut off from credit.

I do not know why anyone imagines this country's fate would be any different if we were suddenly to say we could not pay the interest or were unwilling to do so and that if our creditors wished to get any money at all they would have to accept lesser instalments and take them later. It passes my comprehension that anyone could imagine that an international bank would be any more understanding about that position than a private bank manager. Let us suppose that any of us carrying a loan or mortgage were to go and say, "Look here, I have decided I am not going to pay the March instalment of your interest and you need not bother putting it on my bank statement because I will not pay it. I cannot afford to pay it and I consider that you are making a lot of money for your shareholders. I do not see why I should make them rich and you will have to wait a great deal longer for your money". What would be the reception any of us would get in our local banks if we were to display that kind of lunacy to the man whom we had politely asked for a loan some time previously? What would his reaction be if we came in again to ask for an extension of credit or a new loan to underwrite a new enterprise? As they used to do in the 19th century, I should apologise to the House for arguing a point so absolutely clear.

Foreign Affairs and Neutrality

Politics, Taxation and the Third World, Cork, 24 November 1975

In case it is objected that a system of paying "optional tax" is unheard of, it may be of interest to note that in Western Germany a very similar system operates for the benefit of the churches: every taxpayer, unless he specifically opts out of liability, by declaring non-membership of a church, is surcharged 10% on his income tax for the benefit of the church to which he belongs. This system would hardly be constitutionally possible here just for the benefit of churches; but there could be no objection to the principle being applied to other objects.

As for the likely yield of such taxation, it would arguably produce far more for the benefit of its chosen objectives than they now get after competing with other, politically more powerful objectives.

The total amount collected in 1974 in income tax was about £252million. If we suppose, just for the sake of argument, a Development Aid Surcharge of only 1% and suppose that one out of every two taxpayers had opted out of the surcharge — though in fact I doubt if the opting-out proportion would be so high, if the system were accompanied by all-party exhortation to "stay in" — the amount collected for helping the backward nations of the Third World would have been £1.26 million — or roughly twice what the Government actually devoted to this object in that year over and above what EEC and UN membership obliged us to contribute. The system would also tend to ensure that voluntary development aid by the state at least kept pace with inflation.

A surcharge of 1% for development aid would scarcely hurt most people — it would be only £5 per year for a man or woman paying £500 in tax, and only £30 for the person paying £3,000. Conversely, under the present system whereby Development Aid has to fight for its share with more powerful interests, it could be said that of every pound of tax paid by Irish people last year, only a fraction of a penny went to countries suffering from chronic poverty, illness and destitution.

Of course it is perfectly true that the Irish taxpayer does generously contribute, voluntarily, to the welfare of underdeveloped countries by supporting Gorta, Concern, Trocaire, Irish missionary orders, and so on. I do not believe however that this instinctive charity would find an excuse for drying up merely because a state-channelled contribution was also being made on an optional basis.

Irish isolation, Cobh, 13 June 1980

There was a time, in the 1940s and 1950s, when Irish bishops would occasionally refer in their pastoral addresses to "the advantages which our geographical isolation conferred on us" by keeping us out of reach of foreign godlessness and corruption. Undoubtedly it did contribute to the survival here of a simple and admirable conception of family life, and of fairly austere standards of morality in certain areas, when these had been abandoned elsewhere. Today however the disadvantages, rather than the advantages of isolation are apparent, and the Church has played a full part in trying to remedy them, above all by trying to make Irish people realise the material destitution and misery in which hundreds of millions of distant people live.

But even in relation to countries which lie only a couple of flying hours away, fellow members of the E.E.C., our isolation is responsible for a serious ignorance of the way life is lived there. From the English, our nearest neighbours, we take all too many of our patterns of thought, taste, life-style and attitudes, which are all too easily mediated by the English language and widespread personal acquaintance with England itself. But most of us have as little clue about how Germans or Italians exist as we have about Mexico or Ceylon.

In relation to developing real links both with mainland Europe and with the Third World this party can fairly claim to have played a pioneer lead, both through the personal commitment of its leader, demonstrated over at least twenty years, and through the work of the National Coalition Government. It was Garret FitzGerald who first made the Common Market really known in this country, who ceaselessly evangelised for our membership of it, who was able in 1968 to point to a Fianna Fáil Foreign Minister who in a year's speeches had devoted to the European Communities only fifty-five words, who as Foreign Minister himself inaugurated our membership of those Communities and set a high standard of quality and responsibility for our participation. Equally it was the National Coalition which was the first Irish Government to introduce a programme of direct aid to poverty-stricken peoples, a programme which Fianna Fáil have been ashamed to wind up, but not ashamed this year to cut back.

It is a natural task for this party, then, to try to lead the people outwards in both directions. On the one hand we can see that many Irish people have no clue about what a German or a Dutchman or an Italian means by "work"; no clue about the standards of quality, of service, of value, which he takes for granted in industrial production, in food, in hotel and restaurant catering; no clue about what he regards as reasonable in industrial relations, and what he regards as totally unreasonable; no clue about the topics he thinks worthy of debate on the political level, and those which he leaves to bigots, idlers and children. It is not that I wish us to adopt continental norms in such matters, but

I think we ought to be familiar with better norms than the English can provide.

This being so, I do not think it would be absurd for this party to actively develop, as a matter of policy, much more adventurous schemes of study trips, industrial and agricultural scholarships, cheap group travel, language learning, cultural exchange of various kinds, and town and community twinning between this country and our mainland European partners. Our isolation makes this a special need for us; what is wrong with recognising this need and making it a political objective to meet it?

On the other hand, in common with the rest of the better-off part of mankind, we have a duty to those now living in hopeless indigence, with barely any life-expectancy let alone expectancy of any quality of life, as we glibly call it here. Even if that duty did not exist on the plane of justice and of charity, it would exist on the plane of prudence; for these wretched millions, whether spontaneously or under the incitement of others, will sooner or later rise in anger and in determination to claim their fair share of the earth's inheritance.

Even if it were not a matter of charity, therefore, it would be a matter of wisdom for us when that day comes to be numbered among their friends and champions, even in the small way that our means restrict us to; and I think the very same Irish community that tries to give itself a new view of what it can do for itself by studying the model of its European neighbours should commit itself also to transmitting hope and prosperity to some starving part of the Third World. Village for village, town for town, county for county, we can gain enormously from contact with the Western Europe grown old in civilisation and prosperity; and help to lift up young States in distant regions on whose good will even our own security may one day depend.

Neutrality, Galway, 2 March 1985

There may be good reasons for what is called "our traditional policy of neutrality". But if they exist, they have not yet been properly examined in a serious national or even parliamentary debate. It is no wonder that most people, never having heard the thing fully discussed or challenged, automatically assent to what they are told is "traditional" when they are asked about it in occasional opinion polls.

The "traditional policy of neutrality" is just one part of the wall of cant behind which this State has been living for most of its existence. It is just one more area in which we have preferred to turn our backs on the problems that the rest of the world has to confront and overcome. If only as a contribution towards the growing-up process which we have delayed so long, it is worth putting this "traditional policy" up on the table, examining its credentials, and debating whether it really is worthy of a Republic which has such a high official opinion of itself.

It scarcely makes sense to talk of a policy of neutrality as being "traditional" when in fact, in 63 years of independence, there has been only one juncture at which anyone needed our help and at which we thought it right to refuse it. This was during the Second World War; and while, in hindsight, it is no credit to us to have stood aside from civilisation's efforts to put down the Nazi regime, we can admit that the Government of the time — supported by the Opposition — had what then seemed adequate reasons for neutrality.

The war which broke out in 1939 probably seemed no more than a re-play of the First World War, which undoubtedly should have been no concern of an independent Ireland; memories of British rule here and of the struggle to throw it off were very recent; and the extent of genocidal barbarity which the unhappy Germans had been misled into supporting was unsuspected in 1940 and 1941. Neutrality therefore was a defensible posture, judged by the lights of the men of the time.

But when the post-war world emerged, and when nearly all the free democracies of Europe — including those which in 1939 had also been neutral, but were subsequently overrun, such as the Low Countries, Norway, Denmark and Greece — drew the lesson from their former isolation and unpreparedness and joined the N.A.T.O. defensive alliance, we found ourselves immersed, for local political reasons, in an anti-Partition campaign, and gave Partition as the reason preventing us from joining this alliance.

It did not perhaps seem a sufficient excuse, coming from a nation which esteemed itself highly for its unique Christian heritage no less than for its soldierly qualities. There was all too much reason, moreover, to suspect its sincerity, as coinciding conveniently with an unwillingness to spend money on an Army whose equipment, in the year 1948 or so, would have produced few surprises had it appeared on either side of the Marne or the Somme, or for that matter at Spion Kop or the Colenso River.

In the 1960s, with the fading out of official anti-Partitionism — references to the Border in the Dáil being for years on end pretty well confined to the context of the smuggling of eggs and pigs — and with the approaching likelihood of E.E.C. membership, different tones were sometimes heard; though the actual words used by Government and Opposition spokesmen tended to be very general rather than specific, the possibility of active co-operation in mutual defence with other free peoples began to emerge.

But in recent years, and particularly with an increase in the strength and articulateness of the Left in politics and the media, even those tentative tones have faded, and we now have a new exhibit in our unmatched national collection of self-delusive cliches. "Our traditional policy of neutrality" has joined our "priceless cultural heritage", our "world-wide spiritual empire" and our "twin national objectives".

A few aspects of this "traditional policy" and the usual considerations advanced to support it may be mentioned.

First of all, it is no good pretending that Irish people are in fact "neutral" in their preference as between living in a free electoral democracy with a mixed economy, and living in a Socialist dictatorship with a State-run economy. Perhaps it is a selfish and reprehensible resistance to an inevitable historical process, and a morbid blindness to the many evils in Western society, but it seems to me a fact that only a very rare and very unfortunate Irishman would willingly change places with a Pole.

Our "neutrality" therefore has nothing to do with indifference to the outcome of a military contest between East and West. If that outcome was the defeat of the West, this country's surviving people would sink into the poverty of the 1840s and the political servitude of the 1740s. The fact that this poverty and servitude would, unlike those times, be evenly spread between all classes — except of course Party functionaries — would I think be small consolation for the change. Why then is it our "policy" not to lift a finger to strengthen the defensive alliance which in fact is all that stands between us and that danger?

We flatter ourselves that if we remain "unaligned" our moral influence on the world will be all the stronger. This is an assertion in the same realm of baseless absurdity as the notion that if the British pulled out of Northern Ireland and the Unionists would "come to their senses" and "sit round a table".What has been the weight of our moral influence on events in the Middle East? in Afghanistan? in Cyprus? in Central America? If,as I admit, you can point to the effective exertion of some moral influence in some of those areas, how do you prove it is the result of our "neutrality"?

Surely it would be more rational to see that in Central America, for example, we would be far more likely to succeed in bringing pressure on the United States if we were that country's partner in a defensive alliance for western democracy generally? How do we delude ourselves that a Reagan Government will be less impressed by our representations as a worried ally, than as an uncommitted outsider? Or are we worried that our influence on the U.S.S.R., at present weighing as heavily on them as a feather on a bullock, might lose a little of its substance?

There is perhaps the idea that our trade relations with the non-Western world might suffer if we were associated by even the lightest form of cooperative understanding and shared contingency plans, with N.A.T.O. — and nothing more than this might be needed. Of all arguments in favour of neutrality this is the least reasonable as well as the least respectable.

If the states of the Socialist camp are really slow to trade with those who form a defensive alliance out of suspicion of them, how is it that the Soviets are glad to buy U.S. grain and E.E.C. butter? How is it that the Poles and Hungarians fall over themselves for Western finance and Western investment? How is it that the ninth largest trading partner of West Germany, the most formidable European member of N.A.T.O., is the Soviet Union, whose trade with West Germany in 1983 was worth 40 billion Deutschmarks? How is it that Hungary, Poland and Czechoslovakia — all Warsaw Pact countries — do more business with Germany than Ireland does?

195

It seems to me that these various arguments for neutrality — if by neutrality is meant abstaining from the shared defence of the West — come nowhere near establishing a case for it; and moreover, that even if there were some substance in any of them, they do not outweigh the duty which our self respect should lay upon us: namely, to be willing to help those from whose sacrifices we ourselves cannot help benefiting. To shirk this moral duty to our neighbours, while at the same time persuading ourselves that we enjoy a moral influence with the world at large, is unworthy of this Republic.

To persist in this posture will not amount to having us, as was once the conventional national ambition, "taking our place among the nations of the world". It will leave us simply taking our place among the hurlers on the ditch.

Irish Foreign Policy, Dublin, 22 April 1986

The whole question of passing judgement on conflicts between foreign states, or on internal conditions in foreign regimes, is something we badly need to get our minds clear about. What with our erratic and selective posturing about our "traditional" policy of neutrality", on the one hand, our anxiety not to give offence to customers, on the other, our whole foreign affairs stance often seems to lack both reason and self respect.

The current conflict between the United States and Libya is a case in point. When the Falklands war was on in 1982 the Fianna Fáil government invoked our supposed traditional policy of neutrality in order to evade participation in E.E.C. economic sanctions against Argentina, which, whatever the strength of her legal claim to the Falklands, had clearly and flagrantly broken the first rule of international law by resorting to aggression. But at that Party's Ard Fheis last weekend their foreign affairs spokesman, Gerry Collins, called for a much stronger stance against U.S. action in Libya, a country which he described as being merely "accused" of supporting terrorism, although its involvement in supporting terrorism in our own country — to go no further — is notorious. The Minister's careful treatment of the issue he thought pathetically weak.

Where now is that largely Fianna Fáil-fed myth of our traditional policy of neutrality? Can it be that we only get a fit of neutrality when we have a chance of being neutral against the British? Anything more slave-like could not be imagined.

From this episode it might be thought that this country was in the chronic grip of Left-led anti-Americanism. But this is far from the case. On the contrary, we reach undignified extremes of sentimental fondness in our official relations with the United States. If there are 20 million Americans of Irish origin, there are comparable if not greater numbers of Italian, German, Polish origin — not to speak of the most powerful but seldom-mentioned ethnic group of them all, those of British origin. Do any of these nations send up to ten of their Ministers across the Atlantic to help their "exiles" to celebrate the national day, with embarrassing displays of whatever corresponds in their scheme of things to Paddywhackery? — if anything does, which I doubt.

When it comes to the internal affairs of foreign states it is equally hard to be proud of our approach. We are willing to go along with condemnation of and trade sanctions against South Africa because of apartheid, which is unquestionably a wicked system. But are we equally high-minded in our policies towards other countries in which similarly large numbers of people are oppressed, or who pursue brutal and aggressive policies towards their neighbours?

Where is the rational tariff of evil, where are the fine callipers that allow us to read off an inhumanity-score for South Africa which puts it outside the pale, while leaving many other states within it — for example Libya, which has pioneered the gratuitous export of terrorism and thus confronted the civilised world — and international law — with entirely new problems? Or Iran, whose unhappy people were no sooner free from the Shah than they acquired a regime which is estimated by Amnesty International to have killed in its prisons not fewer than 6,000 people, and probably far more than that?

Or East German, which employs machine-guns and minefields to prevent emigration? Or the Soviet Union itself, whose violent presence in Afghanistan is a reminder of its acts in Hungary in 1956 and in Czechoslovakia in 1968?

There is, of course, a good and rational case to be made for keeping on speaking terms with all kinds of regimes, in the hope that we may exercise some small influence on them in the direction of peace and humanity. But this case has never been properly and fully discussed here; and, if ever it is, it will be interesting to see what principle, over and above fear of the media, is behind our selective ostracism of South Africa; or whether any principle, over and above protection of our beef and butter exports, is behind our friendly relations with other questionable regimes.

Our whole foreign policy in areas like these needs a close review, conducted with consistency and with what should be the self-respect of an adult republic.

Single European Act, Dublin, 19 May 1987

The Single European Act has an odd, confusing name, and its contents are not immediately clear to the layman's casual inspection. This is no excuse for the reckless alarms which its opponents have raised, nor for their attempt to drag every sensitive issue in Ireland into the debate. So far, I have not heard any of them suggest that the Act endangers Knock Airport, but this is about the only scare they have not thought of inventing.

In its impact on the national welfare, their attempt to stampede the people into a mood of blind rejection is comparable with the mischievious cry of "fire!" in a crowded theatre. Many of the No-activists have always been against E.E.C. membership and despise its advantages. To them, these are less important than the ground strategy of leaving this country isolated, impoverished and friendless, and the triumphs of a leftist ideology the practical application of which they are lucky enough never themselves to have personally experienced.

Their claim that the Single European Act will "endanger our neutrality" is particularly disreputable. Personally, I think our "neutrality" is a shameful piece of sanctimonious posturing, and I only wish the Single European Act did in fact mark its abandonment. Not only, however, is there not a word in it committing us to military alliances, but it contains a clause specifically and deliberately inserted to accommodate the Irish position, confining enhanced defence co-operation to those member States already in NATO or the WEU, and therefore excluding us. How are we to explain to our European partners that the protective sheet erected to save Pat from the sight of reality is being twisted into the shape of a pooka to frighten the wits out of him?

It is equally hard to know how to deal with claims that the Act will threaten Irish positions on such matters as divorce or abortion, or calls for "guarantees" that it will not do so. It is quite true that one of the routes to European integration will be harmonisation of laws. But no-one imagines that this can or ought be total; the Single European Act specifically allows a member state to ignore harmonisation measures which would conflict with its Constitution in areas of public morality, as any conceivable such measure on such subjects would do here.

Moreoever, there is nothing whatever either in the Single European Act or in the original Treaties specifically bearing on these subjects or anything connected with them; but apparently the silence of the text is itself suspicious and sinister. Do the alarmists really think the other nations of western Europe are conspiring to pull a fast one on poor Pat?

The arguments for a Yes vote are so overwhelming that it is hard to have patience even with the I.C.T.U., whose operations in the No lobby, if successful, would have the effect of putting at risk thousands of Irish jobs and thus the strength of their own membership. It is even harder to bear interventions in our referendum from abroad. It is true the people may have got cynical about native politicians. Is this a reason to make an act of faith in the words of foreign blow-ins and the overnight-mushroom groups who hire halls for them?

Neutrality, Dublin, 13 March 1988

Of all the moral and logical weaknesses in our so called "traditional policy of neutrality" I think the worst is its pretence that we really have no preference as between the states which share our values and those that do not; or at any rate, that even if we do have such a preference, we ought not to lift a finger in order to acknowledge it in any practical way.

Ireland has always been an integral, and for about 200 years in the early middle ages was a cardinal, part of western Europe. Its values — though both we and our neighbours may periodically disgrace them — are our values too; and the historical routes by which we come to share them, having helped originally to establish them, make up a pattern of rich and complicated texture. It is not a question of any implied hostility towards more distant peoples or towards unfamiliar systems. It is a question simply of recognising ourselves as part of a family, of living in the shelter of our near relations, and of our duty to contribute to family solidarity and to share the burdens of family security.

Who, among the rest of the world, admires our posture of neutrality? Mr Gorbachev, the Soviet Leader, was kind enough to send us a message as he flew overhead a few months ago, congratulating us upon it. But have we ever received congratulations on the point from the President of France, the Chancellor of West Germany, the prime ministers of the smaller European Community states such as Belgium, the Netherlands, or Denmark? Do our nearest neighbours to the east and west, the British and the Americans, commend us on it? It is left, uniquely, to Mr Gorbachev to do so; small wonder, since, nice man though he appears to be, it is the Soviet system which is the gainer from our leaving this gap in the defences of the west.

Who, on the other hand, gives us practical assistance with our own security problems, our democracy constantly threatened by cruel gunmen and their touts who deploy the bomb and the ballot paper with cynical impartiality as the tactics of the moment dictate? Who was responsible for stopping the "Eksund" and for giving the information leading to the current and successful round of arms searches? It was the French who did so, acting on American information.

Mr Gorbachev's bloc, by contrast, is where most of this machinery of death originates, in the Soviet Union itself or in factories in Czechoslovakia where Kalashnikovs are manufactured under licence; and it is, apparently, delivered through the Soviets' Libyan proteges. Has Mr Gorbachev intervened with the Libyans to get them to stop their connivance at arms shipments? Has he, or have his Czech Warsaw Pact allies, tightened their arms sales controls so that weapons do not fall into the hands of people who intend — apart from their activities in the North — to wreck the Irish State if they can?

We would cheerfully exchange all Mr Gorbachev's friendly in-flight radiograms for a bit of action from him on these fronts. And in the meanwhile we ought to take a look at the unsightly figure we cut among our own near neighbours and friends: absolutely dependent on the goodwill which they ungrudgingly show us, but selfish, and sanctimonious into the bargain, when there is any question of pulling our own weight, little though it maybe, in the common defence of European and western civilisation.

Foreigns Affairs estimate, Dáil, 17 June 1988

If I may appeal to the gentlemen opposite, Mr de Valera understood this and did not call for debates on this or that. He was scarcely willing, by all accounts, to tolerate debates even in his own Cabinet but he most certainly delivered leadership whether it was for the better or the worst, particularly in the conduct of foreign affairs when he thought it was proper to do so. He did not set up committees to discuss this or that.

Deputy Higgins cited former Senator Johnson who was a very respected Irish politician and statesman who gave this State very important assistance in the twenties in getting its democracy off the ground and keeping it there. My God, he is being cited 60 years on by Deputy Higgins as having articulated on behalf of the Labour Party a policy of neutrality. There were people in the Fine Gael Party who also did so, not least General Mulcahy and nobody will accuse him of being a pacific man and keeping to his own fireside. The reason Irish voices back in the twenties advocated neutrality was that they had the recent example under their eyes of the First World War when millions and millions of people were fed like cannon-fodder into the trenches and died in seas of mud for no discernible ideological reason on either side.

Many thousands of Irish people of both colours, orange and green, left their bones in Flanders and in northern France and the Labour Party's military wing in those days, the Citizen Army, paraded under a banner saying "We fight for neither King nor Kaiser". I believe had I been around, I would have cheerfully stood beneath such a banner because from the point of view of the Irish there was nothing to choose between King and Kaiser but that does not mean that there is never going to be anything to choose between two sides confronting each other.

On the last occasion on which I spoke here I had the great privilege of not only having Deputy Higgins listening to me but also Deputy MacGiolla and I asked them the following question: "Are you or are you not in favour of our having been neutral in the conflict of 1939 to 1945?" That seems to be an unanswerable dilimma in which to place people who prate about our traditional policy of neutrality. If they support, retrospectively, the policy of neutrality in 1939-45, if they are willing to say the State was right to stay out of the Second World War, then the ladies and gentlemen over on the left have no business to be going on about fascism because what they amounts to this — if they had been in a position to influence events 40 years ago they would not have lifted one finger to push down fascism. Yet they prate about it now when the world has been made safe for them to do so by the sacrifice of others.

If, on the other hand, they were honest enough to admit they would have been willing to join that particular conflict and that fascism was something unique, it would seem to be a very handy scapegoat for everybody. It is a sort of agreed point of reference, it is the parading of wickedness, no question of its unexampled wickedness but it is not the only wicked thing in the world. If they had been willing to say "Very well, we would have made an exception in favour of fighting against fascism and we would have lifted a finger against that as many people in their tradition fought against Franco in Spain" then they would be saying — and this, of course, is the truth — the issue of neutrality is not one you can permanently decide as a matter of standing State policy. It requires to be decided like any other question on which a man or a group of people have to decide, namely in the conditions of the time and in response to the challenges of the time.

When I put up that dilemma to them, I am sorry to say that Deputy MacGiolla and Deputy Higgins departed from the courtesy which the House had shown them when they were speaking and they both attempted to shout me down. They turned scarlet with indignation, the two of them were like a pair of turkeys gobbling at me with fury that I had put them in this unanswerable dilemma. They did not want to say they would have fought fascism and they could not say they would not have fought it. That is the plain fact of the matter. Somebody who is in favour of and advocates what they call a traditional policy of neutrality must take up a position about that episode, the only time since the foundation of this State when it mattered a damn to anybody what this State did and whether we fought or stayed on the sideline.

I want to refer to Anglo-Irish relations. They have been very much in the headlines during the past few days and I do not want to say anything in my small role here which would make things any worse. Having, in a couple of different media tried to defend this State against the indignation which the British always exhibit when anything goes wrong here or whenever anything here works in any way different from the way it worked in the days when there was a British Executive sitting in Dublin Castle, I said it is a separate State, it runs things in its own way and there probably is a different ethos and a different manner of doing things, even in the courts, from what the English are used to in their country. But it is not fair — and I must say this in order to redress the balance — to look on the British as being in the grip of some quite out-of-place post-colonial feeling of exasperation towards us.

It is not altogether the case that they feel this country should jump to their bidding or do what they expect of it simply because they do not recognise this as an independent country. There is also another element in it, and in fairness to the British I think I have to say this. They are not willing, no matter how many tricolours we fly or how we parade our independence, to entirely regard us as foreigners. That can be an amiable feeling in them and is not in any way sinister, even though it causes irritation here. Let me say again, to try to do them justice and to lower the temperature in so far as a speech from a backbencher can do so, that they show in their practice, not just in words, that they do not regard us entirely as foreigners. Their diplomatic missions in the many countries in the world in which we have no representation are automatically and regularly, as a matter of course, at the disposal of Irish citizens who are not within reach of one of our missions.

They have always permitted citizens of the Irish Republic, uniquely among foreign nationals to exercise the vote in their parliamentary elections. This ought to be mentioned because whenever a unit of the British airforce flies over Hackballscross or somewhere like that hoping to spot some terrorist activity, there are wild cries from the guff Republicans over there in the House about infringements of our air space and our national sovereignty. These people forget that our air sea rescue service, at any rate to the extent that it is not possible to provide such a service with the limited resources of the Irish Air Corps, are effectively provided by the British for nothing. I asked a question about this a few months ago and quite accidentally — I had no collusion with him of any kind — my friend, Deputy Enda Kenny, also asked a question on this. It emerged from the answer to these questions that in the past five years — I am giving the House very rough figures — British helicopters and other forms of aircraft flew rescue missions over Irish territory no fewer than 300 times for nothing. No charge was accepted for that humanitarian assistance.

I do not grovel with bogus gratitude towards another state which does for me what I certainly would do for it if the conditions were reversed, but I think these are practical forms of neighbourliness that it is unseemly for us to lose sight of. It would be well for us to keep them in our minds in trying to understand the British attitude towards this country, which exasperates me fully as much as it does other ladies and gentlemen in this House. I know that country quite well and, annoying though it may be to say it, they regard us as something special and not in the way they regard other foreigners. I believe many of them genuinely feel hurt and offended when they get from this country treatment which to them is incomprehensible. I say that merely to try to redress the balance because we frequently say too much about one another in the opposite sense.

I want to refer to human rights elsewhere. I know the first thing I am going to say will not please my friends on the far Left. I do not understand why South Africa should be a unique pariah in the world. I say that although it is obviously a regime that is detestable. I would not wish to live there and I would solemnly warn anyone belonging to me who lived there to get out of it. If I did live there I would try to make sure that at least my children left and lived somewhere else. I do not think they are going to be running that kind of a state in ten or twenty years time — one cannot put a date on it but it cannot go on the way it is as present. I accept all that but I do not understand why that makes it a unique pariah among the nations of the world.

The world is full of detestable regimes, with some of whom we have diplomatic relations. So far as I can see Iraq and Iran are murdering each others young men by the hundreds for nothing. Both of these countries have detestable autocracies. They do not know what the rule of law is all about. One can disappear into a prison there and never be heard of again just because of one's faith. I do not see any difference between one's faith and one's colour. It is true that one cannot change one's colour but ought I change my faith or opinions in order to be acceptable to the Government? If we are going to treat countries as pariahs, then let us have a single rule for them all. I suspect — and I am sorry to have to say this because I do not want to upset friends on the other benches — the reason South Africa has been souped up into a unique pariah in the world is because of its wealth and strategic position.

If it was an agricultural country in the middle of Central Africa with no Simonstown naval base, with no command over the waters between the African continent and Antarctica there would not behalf the fuss about it. It is because of its strategic necessity — and I am not saying people over there believe it, and it may not even have occurred to them — that some forces in the world want South Africa to be destabilised and that this unique campaign against that country, detestable though its regime is is mounted and maintained.

The last thing I want to say — and this will, I hope, make peace with my friends over here because it seems far nearer to what they like to hear — is that the improvements, or apparent improvements, in human rights conditions which appear to be on the way or to be in sight in the Soviet Union, while they still fall a very far distance short of satisfying a western European, but we are very privileged here, must be welcomed by fair minded people. I was not happy at the sight of President Reagan lecturing Mr Gorbachev so continually on the subject. He has to recognise that people must make a start somewhere and that there is a deadweight of 70 years — not 70, but 700 years — of brutal autocracy to be overcome. That cannot be done overnight. I am willing to assume that Mr Gorbachev does mean well and will do his best to improve matters.

Also, the Americans ought not to be let go without our gently telling them that there are aspects in their own policy which we here, and certainly I, would regard as intolerable. One that I shall mention is the regime which the various American States are allowed to maintain, almost all of them, in regard to the infliction of the death penalty. I consider that to sentence a man to death in 1979 or 1980 — it may be that he has been convicted beyond doubt of some appalling brutal mutiple murder — and allow him to sit for six or seven years in a death

cell when appeal after appeal is going on and perhaps even the law may have
changed in the meantime and then to drag him out and put him to death with a
gas capsule, or the electric chair, or invite in a corps of volunteer snipers to
shoot him to death behind a curtain, is an inhuman and disgusting display. When
the United States — and I mean the states individually because they are all
individually competent in this matter, not the union — put that particular part
of their house in order, I shall listen with more patience to their appeals with
regard to human rights in the rest of the world.

Dick Spring and Neutrality,
Dublin, 20 February 1989

The Labour Party leader, Mr Spring, ought not to be let away with the waffle
he gave the European Socialist parties lately on the subject of Irish neutrality.

"Our neutrality", he said, "does not imply indifference to the great issues
of peace and war which face us all". This is a fat lot of good to our neighbours
in Europe — including the many millions of them who support democratic
socialist parties — if our involvement in these issues stops short of lifting a
finger to help in the common defence.

I am sorry to see the Irish Labour Party, which down the years has been
guilty of far less old cod than the larger parties, going in for this sanctimonious
cant. It would be more honest to say straight out, as a Communist party might
say, that we refuse to fight for the capitalist West and against systems which
are closer to our heart.

Minimum reasons of self-respect require that we should be willing to
protect, to the best of our ability, those from whom we ourselves expect
protection. And who are they? Are they not, in the first instance, people like the
French, who certainly saved Irish lives by intercepting the Eksund?, the
Americans, who save Irish lives by arresting I.R.A. gun-runners?, the British,
whose air force has flown about 300 missions over the last five years to rescue
people in danger in Irish waters, and who send us no bill for this service which
we have not enough pride to provide for ourselves?

Or would it be more natural to see as our protectors the states whose
Kalashnikov rifles and whose Semtex explosives wind up in the hands of people
dedicated to our destruction? How often have we seen the Czech or East German
or Soviet police intervene to stop their activities?

Mr Spring thinks our foreign duties are done if we "play a full part in
dialogue for detente" and "in the work of peacekeeping and treaty-monitoring
around the world". What is to stop us doing both these things, while also

accepting the adult responsibilities of mutual solidarity in defence which all our E.E.C. neighbours accept?

France, Italy, Holland, Belgium, Norway, Denmark and Greece are all interested in promoting detente; and all of them, also, have provided contingents for U.N. peacekeeping. But all of them, at the same time, are members of the western defensive alliance. What extra portion of wisdom does Mr Spring think we have, that justifies us in sitting on the world fence like a row of holy leprechauns and considering our duties fulfilled by boring our neighbours with pious lectures?

If Mr Spring is keen on our playing an active part in detente, he would do far better, instead of praising our inglorious "neutrality", to call public attention to what is happening today across the socialist world. All over eastern Europe there is a crisis of confidence in the socialist model, as regards its suitability for a modern economy and as a basis for authoritarian government and a framework for human existence.

Possibly Mr Gorbachev is no more than the most sophisticated public relations package the Soviet Union has ever put together. Possibly he is in reality a greater danger to the West than anything since Stalin. Possibly the planners of expansionist Marxism are laughing up their sleeves at how easy it is to knock over the West by promoting a leader much as they might promote a giant panda.

But for the present, I am willing to believe that he and his supporters really intend an opener, easier, freer society for the Soviet peoples and for Europe's east, and I think we should give him all the help that human friendship can deliver. There is no reason, since we think so much of ourselves as independent peace-makers, for not inviting him to Ireland and letting him see the spontaneous interest and approval that any friend of freedom can count on here even if he is no more than a recent and tentative convert.

Similarly I think we ought to take a more active interest in other ancient European nations, such as Hungary and Poland, struggling more openly and humanly with their problems than would have seemed possible as little as 20 years ago. We already have nominal diplomatic relations with those states, and we might signal our solidarity with their peoples by seeking now to upgrade those relations by the exchange of full resident embassies and cultural missions.

The historical Europe we belong to does not stop along the line of the 1945 cease-fire; and the establishment of a vast community of the same human values and the same just and humane institutions from Connemara to the Urals is an objective worthy of any generation.

European Defence, Dublin, 10 May 1989

With the steady approach of European integration, Ireland is embarked upon her greatest constitutional adventure since 1922. The need for leadership is urgent; in preparing public opinion and improving public understanding; in maximising the advantages which the new Europe will offer us; and in dealing with the problems and disadvantages which we also cannot avoid.

In this respect Fianna Fáil's record has been lamentable: partly from inertia, but more particularly from political cowardice. It will be recalled that during the divorce referendum in 1986 that party was ostensibly neither for nor against the proposed change in Article 41 (though of course, on the ground, they did their best to have it defeated merely to embarrass the then Government). That sleeveen's performance is being repeated, under our eyes, in the context of European integration.

Firstly, the Government appears afraid, because of the ancient fetish about emigration, to point to the job opportunities which continental Europe, with its declining population, will offer us. They wait until massive emigration across the Atlantic has already taken place, very often to low-skill and low-paid employment, and then, wringing their hands as though this multiple disruption of family ties were none of their responsibility, expect credit when they officially beg for a few hundred extra visas. At the same time, for fear of being accused of encouraging what is going to happen anyway, they do absolutely nothing to point young job-seekers towards the nearby continent of Europe where we are entitled to live and work without a visa at all.

When did anyone see an officially published forecast of likely areas of skill shortage in the continental E.E.C.? When did anyone see an officially published directory of employment opportunities which may already exist there in some regions? Has our educational system been re-geared towards providing the technical training in professions for which our close neighbours in Europe can provide a market? Where is the crash programme to raise Irish proficiency in European languages, which now stands at the lowest level of all 12 member states?

Irish people, once they adapt themselves linguistically and otherwise to life on the European continent, get on extremely well there. Their good humour, spontaneity, and frank enjoyment of life are popular, particularly among the fairly serious people of the northern countries. Europe therefore offers us a gigantic opportunity which we should be grasping with both hands, a huge world which we could peacefully conquer, in which we could become the leaders of society, of the professions, even one day of politics. But so far as our present Government is concerned, Europe's main function is to pay for the Mullingar by-pass, while our bored and jobless youth can go and make their careers dishing up hamburgers in the Bronx.

Another political nettle which the Government have not the courage to

206

grasp is the whole question of European security and defence. They are mesmerised by the baseless notion that we have a "traditional policy of neutrality", and by the equally false belief that the Irish people are unwilling to pull their weight to help their neighbours. This latter perception is downright insulting. I do not believe we are so base that we could not be got to accept a system of joint defence.

Such a system would imply mere common prudence, not hostility to any other nation, as the very friendly relations between all the other E.E.C. countries and the U.S.S.R. prove. Indeed we ought to look a bit more closely at the "special position" which our neutrality is supposed to give us in the world, in the light of the humiliating Shannon "summit" when, alone of all European premiers, the Taoiseach had to travel 140 miles to get photographed with Mr Gorbachev on the tarmac.

If we continue to hang back from contributing our share, however nominal it may be, to European defence, we will not really be part of Europe, any more than Donegal would be really part of this State if its people refused to contribute in their taxes to the State's common security services or to accept their presence within that county. But again, change requires courage, and this commodity is always in short supply in Government here whenever Fianna fáil occupy the table.

The other side of the integrated Europe bargain — the problems it will unavoidably bring with it — are also not getting the proper kind of attention from the Government. Let me take a single example: the disappearance of frontier controls of the traditional kind, when passengers entering a country through a port, airport or road or railway crossing might expect to be checked by customs and immigration or passport officials. This, it is now proposed by the European Commission, will all be swept away in the context of achieving free movement of people within the Community. This would not perhaps matter very much it if were possible to maintain watertight checks around the Community's outer frontiers with the rest of the world. But it is freely admitted that this is simply not practicable. At the moment, there are virtually no border controls between Western Germany and Austria, which is not a Community member; and controls, in turn, between Austria and Hungary are now becoming very relaxed.

The implications of all this for the Irish State, and its power to police entry of non-E.E.C. nationals — not to speak of routine frontier controls as a check on terrorism, drug traffic, and other crimes — are enormous. Has there been one public word about it from the Government? What is the official Irish position on the scene which will open up here when border controls are abolished?

Many continental countries already have, and are well used to, other modes of control which will reduce the impact of this change; for example, compulsory identity cards, residence registration even for their own nationals, and hotel registration requirements more exacting than the "Visitors Book" which is a sort of music-hall joke in this part of the world. Are we ready for such things in Ireland? Has public opinion been prepared, or have new administrative structures been planned to deal with the new situation?

And I have not even mentioned the most important problem of all, namely, how far and how fast do we see European integration going on the constitutional level. What powers will ultimately be still left with our own Irish Parliament, Government and Courts? And what powers will ultimately be surrendered, or rather pooled, in common European institutions? Are we sure public opinion will accept, or can it be led to accept, some of the formats which may be proposed, and which Mrs. Thatcher was thought very unmannerly for pouring cold water on at Bruges last September?

In all these areas Fianna fáil's indifference to the problems, neglect of possible solutions, and failure to give a lead in public enlightenment, are likely to produce the worst possible result, namely, disenchantment with the whole European idea, which Fine Gael believes holds out huge possibilities for all coming generations of Irish people.

Ireland and Lithuania, Brussels, 4 May 1990

There is a painful contrast between Ireland's official self-perception as a champion of freedom, binder-up of wounds, peace-keeper welcome on all doorsteps; and our actual record when it comes to taking a serious initiative in a concrete case.

Of all possible situations that cry out for a helpful Irish hand and voice, the present juncture in the Baltic states must top the list, in particular the predicament of Lithuania. Here is an ancient European people, in numbers and in the complexion of their culture comparable to ourselves, who in modern times achieved independence, as we did, after the first World War. Lithuania's incorporation in the Soviet Union in 1940 — which the Soviet government has now itself admitted to have been wrong — was never recognised as lawful by the Irish state; the Minister for External Affairs made this clear as early as 1942, in a statement submitted to the courts, and the Irish position has not changed since, as that Minister's successor recently stated in the Dáil.

There may be people who think that the lapse of 50 years must cure what originally might have been wrongful. But we Irish must be, of all peoples, the least entitled to take up this attitude. Was such a thing admitted in our own case, in favour of Britain's status here, in the 1916-21 period? What would Irish politicians say if such an argument were put up today in defence of the legitimacy of partition?

The Lithuanian parliament, by its precipitate declaration of independence, has certainly done something unhelpful to interests far transcending those of

Lithuania herself. Anything which could unsettle the reforming efforts of Mr Gorbachev, who is probably the most admired leader in the world, would be a disaster for everyone. If he is seen to allow the Soviet Union to crumble away at its ethnic edges, it will weaken his position and strengthen those who want to revive the earlier tyranny. To this extent, the Lithuanians resemble a mountain-climber who insists on attempting the Matterhorn in a blizzard, thus endangering not only his own life but also those of the people who will now have to try to rescue him.

However, they have taken this step; perhaps rashly, but to an Irish mind understandably. They are seeking support in the world; and, so far as Ireland is concerned, all they have seen of us is the tip of our nose peeping out from behind the aprons of the EEC. Not one official word has been uttered by the Irish Government on behalf of this small nation, not one gesture of solidarity made to them; not even an offer to make our good offices available, if the Soviet government, with which we now have very friendly relations, should be willing to listen to us.

Many of the problems which complicate the situation and which give the Soviet government a sense of grievance over Lithuania's behaviour existed here, too, at the time of the 1921 Treaty negotiations. The British were anxious about their own military security; hence the agreement to their continued occupation of three naval bases here after independence. They were concerned — absurdly, no doubt, in view of centuries of misgovernment — about Ireland's share of the U.K. national debt, and the livelihood of Britain's former employees here; these matters were also regulated by the Treaty. Above all, they were concerned for the British element of the population, which amounted to about 30% of the people of the whole island; hence not only the partition of 1920, but the clauses in the Treaty designed to protect the interests of the remaining small minority in the South.

These were genuine and legitimate concerns, even if the solutions adopted were not perfect; and the Soviet Union's concerns in Lithuania, just as genuine, must equally be capable of accommodation. Here the Irish experience, and the Irish similarity to the Lithuanian case, are unique among the countries of the EC, as we are the only state which emerged in consequence of a pioneer secession from a huge empire, such as the Lithuanians are aiming at. This, independent of our natural feeling for another small European nation, should give us the standing to raise an independent and helpful voice at this time.

No sane person would wish to impede what Mr Gorbachev is trying to make happen in the world. But equally, no one can be willing to see the Lithuanians humiliated. The Irish Government should worry less about contriving photo-opportunities for itself during its EC Presidency, which has only a few weeks to run anyway, and more about exerting for Lithuania the moral authority which we like to think we possess. We will never have a better moment than this for putting it to the test; and we will I believe live to feel ashamed of ourselves if we do not make the effort.

We should be dissatisfied also with our general approach to the events unfolding under our eyes in all of eastern Europe. Here are scores of millions of people trying to claw their way out of the servitude and the poverty which has blighted forty or fifty years of their lives. Has the Irish Government got any policy of its own in regard to making friends of these people, and to helping them in whatever ways our limited resources make possible? So far, apart from the charitable action last winter on behalf of the half-starved Romanians, I have noticed nothing except admonitions to businessmen to prepare for the day when the better organised of these states will be able to pay for Irish goods in real money. This is not good enough.

We cannot construct a serious programme of material aid for this huge half-continent. But an Irish Government should give leadership and encouragement to private efforts to establish contacts, human and cultural and professional, with eastern Europe. Actions like town-twinning are familiar, though they have not yet caught on in Ireland to the same extent as elsewhere in western Europe. Over and above this, every institution in the country should be encouraged to build a link with a similar institution in the east. The moral, and perhaps ultimately the material effect of a mass of such contacts would be enormous.

Educational institutions are peculiarly well suited to this. In the Law Faculty of U.C.D. we have already made contact with the law faculty in one of the Baltic states; its warm response to our initiative was moving. We are still considering how best to give this contact a workable basis and a useful content, but are very hopeful that it will result in exchanges of academic visits, books, and ultimately students. Contacts of this kind must be possible not only for university faculties, but for secondary and even primary schools as well.

Even if we do not think beyond contacts which will produce long-term good will measurable in money, we could take a lesson from the Italian seaside resort of Caorle, near Venice. Here the local hotel industry has recently offered a completely free two weeks holiday to 1,000 East Germans. The scale of this generosity may be too much to expect from an Irish hotel industry plagued with the problem of our short season. But who could deny the moral impact of this gesture? Surely there are ways in which Irish business could replicate it, even if on a more modest scale. Now is the time to look for ways of doing so. He who gives at once, says the ancient proverb, gives twice over.

SECTION 7

The Constitution, The Law

The Hidden Constitution, 1967 or 1968

By the inner Constitution I mean the real patterns of power and responsibility in this State, without an understanding of which this little blue book is no more than a collection of lifeless forms. If you think this is an exaggeration, just remember that the Constitution nowhere mentions political parties; nowhere mentions the Opposition as such; nowhere mentions the tasks on which deputies spend nine-tenths hours of their time; nowhere mentions the civil service or its vital place in the State: nowhere mentions that the High Court, although in theory supposed to be the judge of all disputes whatsoever, is in fact carefully kept away from some of the most vital disputes that can arise; and nowhere mentions the almost complete inaccessibility of ministerial processes to scrutiny by the ordinary public. I admit freely that these are all matters which it might be impossible to deal with satisfactorily in what is not intended to be any more than a concise legal document. But none the less all the things I have listed are crucial components of our inner Constitution, and anyone imagining that this little blue book will tell him what the Irish State is really like is very far astray.

This is a good time, now that we are supposed to be engaged in revising our written Constitution, to have a look also at our unwritten one, and to see how well it conforms with the ideals clustered round the cental jewel of national independence. In suggesting what seem to me to be useful perspectives, I am going to be deliberately selective, and will deal with fairly well-worn topics. My excuse is that these very topics can serve to point up the gulf between the written and the hidden Constitutions, and can implicitly show the direction that reform must take.

Just like an underground river changing course, or a fundamental change beneath the earth's crust, which may eventually have terrific effects on the surface, there has been, over the last forty or fifty years, but more particularly over the last twenty, a very crucial shift in a constitutional area of the greatest importance, namely the area in which the State takes it upon itself, in the public interest, to regulate certain forms of activity. Any regulation necessarily involves granting something to X while refusing something to Y; and so, although the whole operation is meant to be for the general good of the public, its end result can be expressed as the State's power to enrich individuals. I am putting it crudely for the sake of simplicity and in order to cover as many cases as possible.

Now here is the shift I want to call your attention to. Once upon a time, in the bad old days of foreign government here, and in the early years of our own government, it was thought that, wherever the State took on itself a function which was going to mean that some people would be better off, and others not, it confided that function as a matter of course to a body whose impartiality was above suspicion; usually the judges (as in the case of granting, renewing or

213

refusing liquor licences), but sometimes also bodies which were at least semi-judicial, like the Land Commissioners. This is now all changed, and the change has been so gradual and insidious as to escape most people's attention. Nowadays, the judges are the last people to whom any function of this kind is confided.

During the last few weeks the Dáil has been debating an Opposition Bill designed to bring planning appeals out of the hands of the Minister for Local Government and before an independent Board presided over by a judge. The arguments used by the Government in attacking this Bill are most illuminating with regard to what I call our "hidden Constitution". One Deputy objected on the ground that the existing judges were already busy enough, and could not take on this burden as well — as though it would be impossible to appoint one or two extra judges for the purpose. Another Deputy had the impudence to say that since it was said that every man had his price, the judges would be equally liable to corruption. Three Deputies including the Minister and a Parliamentary Secretary, said that the Bill was designed to create a lawyer's paradise, in which litigation would fill the wallets of the Bar; a crude and stupid charge, particularly when it is remembered that a lawyer can work all his life and his whole life's earnings may not total what can be effortlessly earned by a developer on a single transaction involving planning permission. That a seriously intended Bill should be met in this way is bad enough. What is worse is that the Government which the Irish people elected should be so indifferent to the principle of clear and open justice and so indifferent to the reputation of government itself; that they should not care how demoralised and cynical the people themselves become if the Government willingly leaves them with the sneaking feeling that government is exercised without a complete and constant regard to the public interest and to the public interest only.

This then is a prominent feature of the hidden Constitution, of which the written Constitution with its fine phrases gives no hint. The power of the State to enrich or not to enrich its citizens is deliberately confided, not to the organ whose special function is justice and whose personnel sit in the open, but to the organ which is inextricably political as well as executive, and whose proceedings are mostly conducted behind closed doors with access to the public in by way of back stairs. It is no good saying, as the Minister for Local Government said last month, that the same kind of procedure was operated by the Coalition Government in 1957. This country has changed at a great pace since 1957. There is a public opinion in this country today, educated to expect new and better standards in everything, which demands and will be satisfied with nothing less than clear and open justice everywhere in government; and sooner or later that public opinion will get its way.

The Department of Justice has provided, over the last year, two excellent examples of how candour in this sense, like justice, is not a quality to which the Government attaches much importance. One example is recent; namely the refusal of the Department and its Minister to allow access to certain files to the

Comptroller and Auditor General, an officer whose position is actually regulated in the Constitution itself, who holds office on conditions not unlike those applying to a High Court Judge, and who consequently must be a person of the highest probity and discretion. Despite this, the Department thought it unsafe to allow him to see files which are, presumably, seen and worked on by unknown and unnamed officials within the Department. It may be that the Department honestly thought that all this was in the best interests of the public. I believe the public, on the other hand, would say it was secretiveness run mad.

Finally, a further important fact of the hidden Constitution is the slight regard which the government seems disposed to show for the spirit of the laws which it has itself "processed" through the parliament. One example, that of the Planning and Development Act, is notorious; a statute expressly intended to preserve amenities is being interpreted so as to destroy them. Another example is provided by the Broadcasting Authority Act of 1960, under which R.T.E. was set up. Section 31 of that Act empowers the Minister for Posts & Telegraphs to require the Authority in writing either to allocate broadcasting time for certain announcements, or to refrain from broadcasting certain material. It may come as a surprise to learn that neither of these powers under S.31 has ever yet been availed of; on the other hand, Ministerial announcements have been made, and, as is well known, unwelcome material has been dropped at Ministerial insistence. What can be said in defence of Ministers who by-pass the only provisions of the Act which give them the right to interfere at all? Is it any wonder that no one believes that the present dispute within R.T.E. has not been ultimately caused by interference, no doubt subtle and discreet interference, from the Government side? The Taoiseach has expressly denied that the Government demanded an end to "Seven Days", and of course, this solemn assurance has to be accepted. But are we also required to believe that every Minister, and every Minister's henchman, behaved with the same scrupulous restraint. If the Government wants such an act of faith from us, it will have to earn it; and it might make a start by rigidly sticking to the letter and the spirit of the law.

Sixth Amendment of the Constitution, Dáil, 14 February 1979

That is all I want to say except for a few brief observations in regard to the text of the proposed amendment. Why was it decided to write the Irish text of the new section according to spelling conventions which have been obsolete for 50 years? Rannóg an Aistriúcháin in this House, which I have praised before for their work in regard to the standardisation of Irish spelling, were set up at the same time as the Oireachtas came into existence and they immediately got down to the business of simplifying and standardising spelling. They did not finally standardise until 1947, but attempts were made in that direction, as one can see when one opens the statutes of 1922 and 1923. In 1947, Mr de Valera, intending to show that he was a more antique Irishman, more primeval than anybody else, went back to a spelling system which had not been used officially since the State had been founded and the Constitution was not only put in draft in the so-called Gaelic script but in accordance with spelling conventions which had long since gone — though from which I still suffered as a schoolboy — which officially had been dropped since 1922.

At some stage in the fifties, I think, a text of the Constitution was published in which a revision of the Irish text, according to the spelling standardised by Rannog an Aistriuchain was printed. I have heard a Supreme Court judge express the view that it is not within the power of the Taoiseach's Office — the Taoiseach is in charge of putting out these texts — to carry out any change at all, even the most minute spelling change, in the Irish text of the Constitution which must stay in the form in which the people adopted it.

I will not pronounce on this now. The changes, which were made arbitrarily in the Taoiseach's Office consist not merely of spelling changes, there are some slight grammar changes too, all done without any referendum. My point is that we should keep an eye at what we are at. Here we have a proposal to insert in the Constitution — the thing has been done in Roman script — a clause in which I see the words "sainraidhte", dhlighthe", "d'achtuigh", "sonruighthe" and "bunuigheadh". They have been all spelled according to conventions which were officially declared in 1947 to be obsolete, and which have in fact been obsolete since 1922 or 1923.

Is the Minister serious in putting into the Constitution a version of Irish Spelling which is not used in the schools and which has not been used in this House since its foundation? In the existing Article 37 I find that the word "dlí" is spelled "dlí" but I find that the Minister's amendment the word is spelled "dlighidh". Nothing can surprise me any longer in regard to the brazen and contemptuous indifference of the Irish State towards something it is supposed to love, cherish and revive, but is it not the frozen limit, assuming that this Bill will be enacted, that we are to have section 1 of article 37 according to the 1947 standards and section 2 of Article 37 in the orthography of 50 years ago? In other words, we will have a section in which, within a half-an-inch of each other, the same word will be spelled differently. Surely enough insults have been perpetrated, and by Fianna Fáil in particular, to the Irish language without having this one.

Is it the Minister's intention to display a degree of romantic antiquarianism in tribute to the memory of the late Mr de Valera? If, say, the Americans were to amend to day their Constitution which was enacted in the 1780s, in the days when admittedly spelling did not differ very much to what as then conventional English spelling but in which words such as "music" were spelled with a "k", can the Minister visualise the Americans passing an amendment involving the word music and spelling it with a "k"? Were they to do so the American Congress would be laughed at, but what the Minister is doing is the equivalent of that. I trust that in that small respect at least he will think again before going ahead with the Bill.

Health (Family Planning), Bill, Dáil, 29 March 1979

We really are a strange people, that five or six ageing men are willing to sit in this Parliament and solemnly discuss urine dipsticks in order to decide whether we are going to legislate along the fine tightrope of morality that the people expect of us. When did we ever apply that exquisite care to deciding over moral issues, to the justification of violence in any part of this country or outside it present or past, to the justification of things that were done 60, 100 or even 300 years ago? When did we devote this exquisite finicking care to deciding issues of morality such as dishonesty towards the State, such as failing to make correct income tax returns or claiming social benefits to which we are not entitled? These are moral issues also. My own view is that they are more important than what we are talking about. In a way I am ashamed to be part of this debate except for the purpose of pointing that out. I do not mean any offence to Deputy O'Hanlon, but I think it fantastic, and something that one would find only in a country inhabited by leprechauns whom life had spared from most of the major decisions the rest of the world has to face, that a handful of ageing men could sit around here talking about moral decisions that would be right or wrong depending on whether something was right or wrong with a urine dipstick. That is the first thing I want to say but it bears strongly on my belief about this Bill and about the Bill introduced by Senator Cooney previously.

This Bill is before the House on the initiative not of the Minister for Justice, to whose area of jurisdiction one might have thought it more appropriate, but on the initiative of the Minister for Health. If one looks up the statutory functions of the Minister for Health in the creation of his office and of his Department one will find very little in detail about it, but the Ministers and Secretaries Act, 1924, speaks about "public health" and that is almost all it says in regard to health in the section which created the original Department of Local Government and Public Health.

In those days public health was almost exhausted once one had enumerated functions such as making sure that poisonous shellfish were kept off strands so that people could not pick them, that blankets in a fever-ridden district were fumigated and that contagious diseases were controlled at the ports. Those were the kinds of things involved in "public health" in those days. I know that the functions of the State in relation to the preservation of health have increased, and rightly so, and I do not complain about it.

However, I do complain about the sham being exercised in this House and the pretence that the matter before us today is primarily a health matter. It is not. It is accidentally a health matter, in that it has a health dimension, but it is not primarily a health matter. I cannot understand a man such as the Minister for Health, to whom sophistication is imputed, solemnly coming into this House and pretending that a Bill about condoms, pills and loops is primarily a health matter. It is nothing of the kind. It is no more a health matter than it would be if the Minister opposite were to pretend that the licensing of motor vehicles of the licensing of premises for the sale of liquor was primarily a health matter. They, too, have health aspects. A person can get scoliosis or curvature of the spine if he sits in a badly-fitting car seat. A person can become an alcoholic if he spends too much time in a licensed premises. But does that make these items health matters? Of course it does not.

I think I know the Minister's problem, but he and his party have faced it in a cowardly way. There is everything to be said for being prudent, for not letting one's valour overtake one's prudence when dealing, as we were dealing and as I, as Whip, had to deal, with a knife-thin majority, and in the case of this matter when we had a minority of 16 votes. There is a lot to be said for a compromise then, if you want to make any headway. But there is nothing to be said for it when you have 84 rearguard legionaries, members of a radical party compared with whom we are a crowd of musty old grannies on these benches and the people on the Labour Party benches are living on the moon. On the Government benches are the party of radical reality; but this is the best they can produce on a topic that does not belong in the House at all.

Would it have been such a dreadful thing, would it have made the national heroes turn in their graves had a few of the legionaries revolted, had a few them walked through the "No" lobby, had a few of them gone along with a more radical Bill to clear this matter out of the legal criminal code? I do not wish to single out Deputy O'Hanlon — it is only that I heard him speak — but would it have mattered if he and his colleagues had said that they would not support the Bill? Would the veil of the temple have been rent, would the sky have fallen if the legion of the rearguard had walked in two directions through the lobbies?

At more radical Bill would not have been depending for its passage merely on the legionaries of the rearguard. I believe the Labour Party and Deputy Browne would have voted for it and I would have voted for it had I been l...

I believe many others in my party would have done the same. Would it have been such an abdication of responsibility, that we might get proper legislation on this subject. namely, legislation to remove this matter from the criminal code, if that legislation had to be passed by reliance on three parties instead of one party?

The correct thing to do would be to repeal section 17 of the 1935 Act and leave the country as it was before 1935. Nobody will pretend that this country was a vassalage of the devil until this section was passed. Of course it was not, nor would it be if that section were repealed. I would have expected from a radical Republican party, that pretends everybody else is still wearing button boots, a radical and courageous approach, and, if necessary, enough generosity not to impute the small-mindedness which they displayed here in 1974 to today's Opposition.

I do not believe for a second that it would have crossed the minds of the Labour Party to vote against them just for the sake of voting against them. It would not have occurred to the Labour Party or to most of my party to try and embarrass the Government by voting against the Bill, even though many people did not have any objection to it. It is a poor case when we talk in high and pompous terms about the Dáil, the Irish people's assembly, yet the Irish people are not able to get the legislation more than half of them want. Why? Because when we had a majority it was so thin that it could not cover half a dozen defections; and because this Government, even though they have an enormous majority, do not have the guts to expose even a minority of their Deputies to an imputation from a minority of the community that they are permissive. Permissive my eye. Are they never worried that anyone is going to think them permissive in regard to their ambivalence on violence, on people being shredded limb from limb?

Permissiveness in regard to this matter, which for many people is an outcrop of love — maybe not always but for many people it is — must be stamped down even by the party of radical reality. That could not be allowed. It could not be said that Deputy X or Y could be allowed to go back to the peninsula he lives on and have people pointing the finger at him that he was permissive about love-making, but he can hold his head high if he is permissive about murder. If that party consisted of a crowd of little altar boys who never pretended to be anything else, one might have taken another view.

Mr N. Andrews: There is no ambivalence in Fianna Fáil

Mr Kelly, I do not see any Deputy on the opposite side from Roscommon. One of the members of the Minister's party, a councillor in Roscommon, attributed, within a week of the last election, the defeat of the Coalition to the fact that we were too hard on the men of violence.

An Leas-Cheann Comhairle: That has nothing at all to do with the Bill.

Mr Kelly: But perish the thought that anyone might think that Councillor would be permissive about a condom.

Mr N. Andrews: Do not attribute wrong motives to Fianna Fáil.

Mr Kelly: Are we not a miserable people when we are represented by a crowd like this:

An Leas-Cheann Comhairle: Order.Deputy Kelly on the Bill.

Mr Haughey: Everything the Deputy is saying can be attributed to the man he supported during the Coalition, Deputy Cosgrave.

Mr Kelly, In the area I am talking about, there is no Member on the opposite side fit to polish Deputy Cosgrave's boots and the Minister knows that.

As Deputy Andrews knows, because he is in the same constituency as I am, I would be suiting a lot of people if I voted against the Bill, but for different reasons, some because the Bill do not go far enough and some because they do not want any change made in the law. The latter are a respectable minority of people and do not want the law liberalised in any shape or form. Their point of view was well summarised in a long letter which I got, not long after the McGee decision, from a well-known theologian. It is not necessary to name him. His argument boiled down to the fact that the Supreme Court had based their decision in regard to Mrs. McGee's rights on their view of marital privacy being something which the natural law guaranteed. He was paraphrasing the Supreme Court's view that marital privacy was a feature of natural law but, wrote the theologian, how can it be consonant with the natural law to permit something which is against natural law, namely the artificial prevention of conception resulting from sexual intercourse? My answer to that as a layman would be, let it be so. Perhaps it is against the natural law to prevent artificially conception resulting from intercourse but the point is, is it the State's job to be enforcing by means of criminal sanctions the prescriptions of the natural law?

We could easily admit that it is against the natural law to use contraceptive devices but I find it hard to be sure about that because I see theologians disagreeing about it. That is a long way from anwering the question: is it the State's job to be enforcing the natural law by means of a man in a blue uniform with a whistle. My answer is, and it is an instinctive answer, that it is not. I cannot argue this rationally, but to my mind it is not within the proper scope of the State to be enforcing any code of conduct in this highly intimate area of life. The arguments in regard to the natural law and the law of God are missing the point. We are not setting ourselves up in opposition to the law of God or to the natural law. If I was in control of the legislation I would be trying to draw the line between the area in which the State has a justifiable and defensible role and the are in which it has not.

The State is within its rights in forbidding abortion and I would oppose any attempt to shove the State out of that area. I am saying, in response to exactly the same instinct, that trying to legislate in the private, intimate, notoriously volatile and mercurial area of life in the way we have been doing since 1935 is something which should be outside the sphere of the State. They legislation should be withdrawn except section 13. Repeal section 17 of the 1935 Act and see what happens. If abuses develop we can sit down quietly and discuss how best to regulate them.

In regard to abuses — I know I am treading on a mine field — I am not sure what an abuse would be. I do not mean that facetiously but I am not sure that the public good is served by trying to impose excessive difficulties in the sale of, or dealing in, contraceptives. I will not explore that theme. There can be two different honest views in regard to this whole area. Whatever degree of control might be imposed if abuses develop or what a majority felt represented an abuse, it does not alter the fact that we ought to repeal a law which should never have been enacted.

I want to draw attention to the fact that the Bill contains a number of conceptions, phrases and ideas which it purports to deal with but which are not defined and which any attempt to define either by the House or by the people who will be called on to enforce it will result in absurdity. For example, let me cite the section which I will refer to as the laughing stock section, section 5 (1)(a):

> 5(1) A person shall not import contraceptives into the States unless—
> (a) They are part of his personal luggage accompanying him when he is entering the State and their quantity is not such as to indicate that they are not solely for his own use, or. . . .

I will not make the House or the Minister look more ridiculous by exploring that paragraph. It is not a question of what will the neighbours think. I do not think the neighbours would believe that we could be seriously enacting a paragraph like that. Who is going to decide this; who is going to police it? Can you imagine the dirty jokes this paragraph will give rise to? Of course, the truth is there is not the remotest intention to enforce this on the part of the Minister or anyone in the public service from top to bottom. It will be a dead letter from the day the President puts his hand to it.

Let us assume that the Minister intends to enforce it. Will he tell me who will make the judgment on whether the material being imported is likely to be intended only for the use of the person importing it? It is to be some beardless 19-year-old custom officer at Dublin Airport? Will the Minister solemnly sit in judgment on it? Are we likely to send it to the courts. The same section contains a provision that contraceptives are to be included in the table of prohibited goods inwards contained in section 42 of the 1876 Customs Consolidation Act. That list contains things like uncustomed tea, sugar, coffee, liquor and so on. The next section deals with gunpowder, explosives. The only cognate thing in the table is obscene articles. Is the Minister seriously thinking of using an 1876 statute for the purpose of outlawing the importation of contraceptives?

Section 4 of the Bill has this phrase, "bona fide for family planning purposes". Sir, it will surprise you to know perhaps that the Bill is entitled the

——————

the phrase "family planning" is not defined throughout the Bill? What is family planning? It is used euphemistically to cover a whole lot of operations, but what is it? And what is bona fide family planning"?

I should like to be told about these things. I would have to be told these things if I were an independent Deputy before I could make up my mind on how to vote. I have often heard it said by preachers, or I have read it, that in the Christian ethic family planning must be responsible — I am not thinking about the method, I am thinking about the object that it cannot be purely selfish. Who is going to draw the line here? Suppose a couple get married and they decide they cannot afford a child at the moment. Such a decision might be made by a couple on £60 a week or on £600 a week. It would depend entirely on their life style. Are we to have a doctor adjudicating on this? Who will say whether it is a selfish refusal to have children? Who is to decide whether they are in good faith. Who is going to draw up the catechism by examination on which anyone can come to a conclusion in regard to this matter.

That is another straw in the wind which tells me as plainly as if it were printed in black and white that there is not the slightest intention to enforce this law. It is not enforceable. Both sections 5 and 6 contain references to licences. I would draw attention to section 5(2)(b):

> The Minister may refuse to grant a licence under this section to a person who has been convicted of an offence under this Act or of another offence of such a character that, in the opinion of the Minister, it would be inappropriate that he should hold such a licence.

A master has to run a school in a fairly arbitrary way. He cannot draw up a comprehensive criminal code for dealing with the school boys. He has not got it written anywhere that it is criminal to set fire to a classroom, or something like that, but an instinct tells him it is, and the same instinct tells the school boy it is a serious offence and he cannot complain if he is punished for it. It is quite a different matter when we are dealing with law which we are supposed to apply to adults. What will guide the Minister's opinion in regard to somebody's criminal record which would render it inappropriate that such a person should hold a licence? If the Minister means that he has been convicted of an offence under this Bill, let him say so. If he does not, let him say so. Supposing a man has some ordinary smuggling convictions against him, will that disqualify him? Will prosecutions for brothel-keeping disqualify him? Will convictions for unlicensed practice as a chemist or a doctor disqualify him?

Not only is the thing uncertain, but there is the possibility of the thing being constitutionally objectional because on the face of it it gives the Minister power to impose a bar on somebody for something which is not related to the objects of the statute. It could be a bar intended purely to punish somebody, to get them out of business. The courts recently found that all laws enacted here have to be interpreted with the presumption in favour not only for the Oireachtas but also of the people who carry them out — it has to be presumed they will be carried out according to constitutional criteria. However, there are no criteria obtainable from these provisions which will show where the bounds of the Minister's opinion are in a matter like this. There is nothing which will clearly indicate when the point has been reached when the Minister will take into account a person's criminal record which has no bearing whatever on the fitness of a person to import contraceptives. That is another part of this laughing stock section.

I have no doubt that the delay in bringing this Bill on and in debating it

222

here in the House is related to a secret hope in the back of the Minister's mind that he will be got off the hook by the courts who are even now hearing or considering a case brought by one of these clinics which this Bill, if it is enforced, will have the effect of closing down. Undoubtedly if the courts were to give a pronouncement in favour of these parties the Minister could with a perfectly good conscience come in here to suspend going further with the Bill until the Supreme Court has ruled, and the Supreme Court might very easily let him off the hook by effectively destroying whatever is left of section 17 of the 1935 Act. This matter should not be the Minister's job, because it is not primarily a health matter; but if he is really going to take this side of his job seriously what he should do is scrap the rest of the Bill and simply ask the Dáil to enact section 13. The Minister is absolutely on the right lines in regard to the main part of his job, but when I find that he is saddled with this Bill I must ask whether the Minister for Fisheries was so far out of reach that he could not be given this job because it is a real Lenihan job.

The Bill has all the comical flagrancy of a Lenihan measure. It would be more in keeping with the style of the Government to have asked the Minister for Fisheries to sponsor the Bill rather than to leave it to the Minister for Health, who in regard to the rest of his functions is doing a serious job. I deprecate the way in which the Minister's efforts in the field of health in regard to exercise and smoking are so often sneered at by references to personal remarks about himself, but I trust that he will not be deflected by these remarks. However, in terms of this Bill the Minister is doing a bad day's work for himself, and is making himself look ridiculous in the eyes of people whose opinion, I am sure, he would value. This is a half-baked hot and cold piece of sham legislation.

Seventh Amendment of the Constitution (University Seats), Dáil, 22 May 1979

Constitution which we are proposing to amend in its historical perspective. I did not hear the contributions of the Minister and Deputy Collins and I missed most of Deputy Horgan's contribution and therefore, I do not know whether anybody has yet told the House in so many words that, as is so lamentably often the case here, we are dealing with something which was left behind by the English and which they themselves have long since scrapped. University representation existed in the British Parliament until 1945. The late A.P. Herbert was the most distinguished among an otherwise rather undistinguished lot of persons and he represented the University of Oxford for a long time. That situation did not survive the Second World War; in 1945, with a lot of other things, it was swept away. It was put into the 1922 Constitution here, characteristically without any flummery, a great deal more simply and more effectively from the drafting point of view than it was in the 1937 Constitution. The 1922 Constitution did not name any particular university; it simply spoke of the universities which existed in the State at that time. Of course, that boiled down to the same thing, but it was an altogether preferable drafting mechanism.

That Article which conferred a separate franchise on the universities which was exercisable through seats in the Dáil and not in the Seanad, was struck out of the Constitution in 1936; but when the new Constitution surfaced the following year, lo and behold, the Paddys were still attached to the university seats, they could not be done away with. As far as I know that did not exist anywhere else in Europe except in the country to be free from which we had, according to the received orthodoxy, struggled unremittingly for 700 years. However, like the smallest and most trivial bits of gold braid which the British had stuck on to institutions here, like the title of Alderman in borough councils, the chains, the cocked hats and the coaches, we naturally, being Paddys and being led by a party and an orthodoxy which was convinced that was the right description for us, had to hold on to special representations for the universities.

I do not think there is much point in arguing this nowadays in the sense that I have the authority of the Taoiseach for saying that if no one gives a dog a bone it is quite hard to get it away from him, as he is discovering as he examines his bleeding fingers over the last six months or so. It is hard to get a dog off a bone, and the bigger the dog gets the more powerful will the struggle become. The total university electorate in this State, or outside the State, is extremely large. I think the university voters value their votes. I do not want at all to belittle mine — I am glad to have it — but I recognise it for what it is, namely, an anachronistic privilege. I sat in the Seanad for four and a half years. I did not get in there through the university vote; quite likely I would never have made it through the university vote in the way that Deputy Horgan did, by a blitz campaign of unparalleled assiduity and, let me add, brilliance. But I would not have despised a seat in the Seanad even had it come through the universities. Had I sat in the Seanad as a university Senator, I still would not have been so craven as to deny that the existence of such a representation was an anachronism defensible only by Paddys to Paddys in terms of which only Paddys understand, namely, that the English left it behind them and anything they could do or did is more than good enough for us. I protest for the hundredth time in the House against that attitude of mind which is second nature to the party opposite, absolutely second nature to them. It is outrageous that this matter could be solemnly brought up again in 1979 without the Government — particularly when it is the Government of the Legion of the Rearguard, the Soldiers of Destiny — sitting down and asking themselves what is it about universities which gives them the right to six seats in the National Parliament.

This is not the first occasion on which we have seen instances of trotting lamely along behind the English; I would not mind, only wearing cast-off clothes of the English, the fashion of which they themselves changed over 30 years ago.

This matter comes before us in the context of the Minister's proposed amendment without any consideration about whether the Seanad fulfils a serious function at all or not. How often do we get a chance to discuss the other House? If a Deputy so much as mentions a Senator in this House in the ordinary way, he is sat on by the Chair — mind you, another old English convention — on the grounds that it is breach of privilege, if you please, if you are not offended. We would have the Speaker thundering on the door with his mace in a moment; Gold Stick-in-Waiting would be up on your back if one were to persist in referring , while speaking in one House, to the members of the other. Naturally all these ceremonies are more than good enough for us. We should be honoured to be allowed to ape these conventions.

Very seldom do we get the chance to discuss the Seanad and when we do, we should ask ourselves, what is that House there for at all? Does it fulfil any serious function? Could it perhaps be got to fulfil a serious function? I know it is easy for me to say that, having managed to get out of the Seanad and into the Dáil; and I do not want to close off too many options, although I must confess I would regret it if I ever found myself on the Seanad trail again. But since we get so few opportunities to discuss the matter, we might spend a minute or two asking ourselves if anything could be made of the Seanad, perhaps specifically in the context of the changing of representation, the shifting of the basis of representation which this amendment is designed to achieve. The Seanad has no serious power. At most it has an embarrassment value. Even the embarrassment value is slight because of the distribution of political strength in the Seanad. I think the last occasion on which the Seanad made a nuisance of itself to any Government was in 1959, at the time of the first of Fianna Fáil's two efforts to give us the English election system. I forget who was the Minister for Local Government then. Perhaps it was Deputy Boland who will go down in history for two futile efforts, trying to gaelicise the Army and to anglicise the voting system. At any rate Fianna Fáil's first effort to anglicise the voting system was defeated by the people in 1959 in an extraordinary display of political maturity because, on the same day they voted that down, they put the Fianna Fáil Leader into the Phoenix Park as President.

On that occasion the Seanad voted down, on the first occasion, the proposed constitutional amendment by a narrow margin; I have forgotten exactly how it happened — perhaps people were missing; it does not matter how it happened but they did vote down the amendment. Of course that was a very important feather in the cap of those who were opposed to having here the English voting system, having once succeeded in getting rid of it.

The Seanad on that occasion threw out the Constitution Amendment Bill which was a severe embarrassment. But that was 20 years ago and it has not happened since. The Seanad has the useful function of giving a Government breathing space and of hearing Senators' suggestions which, provided the debate takes place early enough in the year and amendments are politically non-contentious, may possibly be incorporated, and I suppose frequently do get incorporated, in the legislation. But is it useful enough? Would the same function not be fulfilled by adapting Dáil procedures so as to include a further stage of a Bill, a kind of extern stage of a Bill on which committees or outsiders might sit and give evidence? That would be an equally possible alternative and would save the expense of having a second House. But if we are going to have a second House at all, we owe it to the dignity of that House to furnish it with some element in its structures or functions which would make it more useful than it is at present. At present its function — and I do not at all despise this — is to ease beginners into serious politics and ease others out of it. That is an extremely useful function; it is a kind of political AnCo at the beginning of political life; it is a kind of social service, I suppose, in a sense, at the other end.

While I appreciate that, let me say that an indirectly elected House cannot in a democracy hold a veto over a directly elected House. I do not suggest and would resent any suggestion that the Seanad ought to have any extra power in the sense of being able to block legislation or override the will of the Dáil. Nonetheless if the Seanad could be improved as a feature of the Legislature by alterations in the methods of its elections and in the recruitment to it of different kinds of people — let me give credit if it is deserved; it probably is the intention of the present amendment to bring some new blood or new sources into the Seanad via the institutions of higher education other than the universities. But it seems to me to be a terribly marginal thing. It really is another feature of the perpetual fiddling that goes on in this country while Rome is burning. I do not want to stray away from this subject, but it is analogous to a Minister being on the far side of the world while there is an oil crisis here, with other Ministers worrying about the "national objectives" to which they themselves have made no personal contribution in 50 or 60 years of life, not one, and going on about national aspirations when the economy is falling into ruins around us. This is what I call fiddling while Rome burns. We have a serious chance of looking at the Seanad and doing something about its composition. Although I accept the necessity for the change being made here within the very narrow boundaries of those six seats, this change is a minimal one, and is pitifully small compared with what could be done and what needs to be done in regard to Seanad representation.

With regard to university representation, if I were constructing a Seanad from scratch I do not believe that I would be led by anything the English did in their own country or here. I would start from scratch and do it from what seems to me to be first principles. I would expect Deputy Collins, Deputy Horgan and everybody else to do it from first principles too, and to debate it with me on that level also. Since we have got this relic which the English left behind them, this oxidising statue with birds perched on its shoulders, in our political institutions, let us try and make something useful of it.

One of the greatest problems we have here, apart from that of unemployment and emigration, which apparently are always with us, is the problem of social tensions and the industrial tensions, which are only a symptom of those. I would ask myself whether this second House, even if it cannot override the Dáil, could not be given some role in the easing of those industrial and social tensions. I find that this was an expressed part of the purpose of having the House organised in the way it is and having it divided into vocational panels. I find there is a labour panel, an agricultural panel, an industrial panel, a cultural panel and an administrative panel. These are all intended to represent broad spheres of vocational and social interests. I do not quarrel with that way of doing it. Who do we find fills those seats? These seats are filled — and cannot be otherwise filled, because of the electorate — by politicos. I do not despise politicos, I am one myself and I value my years in the Seanad. I do not want to say anything which might lead one to think that I disparaged either it or the senatorship. I am deeply grateful for that.

I wonder now, while looking around me, and finding that farmers are snarling at the trade unions, the trade unions are snarling at the farmers and both of them are snarling at the Government — everybody seems to be snarling at the Government except the IRA, which is giving them very little bother at the moment — now that the social and the industrial tensions are so conspicuous in society and since they are also so powerful I ask myself whether or not all these interests and groups are the ones who are calling the shots here. Everybody is calling the shots except the Government. Since that seems to be the case why not acknowledge their power, their influence and their status in society, bring them in under this roof and allow them to sit down in an institutional setting which recognises their function as part of the law-making and ruling organisation of the country. It would not be a function which would override the functions of this House. It could not be that; but it would be one likely to be more fruitful than the function which they are at present discharging, which is simply that of extremely high-powered, very articulate, increasingly angry pressure groups, in all cases, no doubt, sincerely representing the best interests of their members. As the Ministers opposite are constantly lecturing us — once elections are over — in pressing those interests forward they tend

I cannot see why we should not organise the Seanad, particularly since the Constitution tells us to do so on truly vocational lines. I cannot see, when we are making this extremely marginal change, which will only have the effect of giving the vote to graduates of the NIHE, colleges of technology and so forth, and allowing them to elect people to the Seanad who may already be qualified for election by reason of being simultaneously graduates of NUI or Trinity College, why we cannot look more deeply at what goes on in the Seanad and ask ourselves if the Seanad might help in some way to ease the social and industrial tensions we suffer from by reorganising the way in which the Seanad membership is elected.

Let me say to the Dáil that unlike the provisions in regard to Dáil Eireann,

227

which are laid down in Article 16, which provides about constituencies, constituencies not having fewer than three seats, the way in which the constituencies must be evenly spread in regard to population, and so on, there are virtually no provisions in regard to the Seanad election. The drafters of the Constitution left it open to the Oireachtas to prescribe by law what should be the composition of the Seanad. Nothing is prescribed in the Constitution except the provision of the five interest groups, but how those groups are to be elected, who is to elect them, is not in the Constitution. There is no rigidity about the matter in the Constitution. It is not in the Constitution that the electorate must be the outgoing Seanad, the incoming Dáil plus all county councillors and county boroughs. That is not in the Constitution. That is an ordinary Act of Parliament which can be repealed overnight without the necessity for a referendum.

Garda Síochána, Dáil, 21 November 1979

I had intended only to make one point when speaking in this debate and I will make it in a relatively short time. These Estimates bear on the Garda and the prison service. They bring together neatly the two services which I want to speak about in a particular connection, namely, the connection of public transparency. When we were in office, from 1973 to 1977 we went through, as I hope everyone on all sides of the House would recognise, a paroxysm of political violence which spilled into this part of the country, starting in the North, but spilling over into the side of the country. We had dozens of deaths, most of them caused by bomb outrages originating with the Loyalist extremists. Not only did we have that, but we had a non-stop succession of demonstrations, some of them a very dangerous kind, all of them of a very emotive kind. Because it is a free country demonstrations take place as a matter of course, freely, and as of right, and that is as it should be.

I want to remind the House, because these things are easily forgotten, that there was hardly a month when the National Coalition were in office and Senator Cooney was Minister for Justice that there was not a hunger strike, that there were not demonstrations of one kind or another, that there were not chaps with sour faces and black berets marching around the country terrifying children, that there were not sieges of one sort or another, that the general atmosphere was not one of absolute head-on confrontation. Admittedly politicians, if they get into Government, are paid to put up with such things. I remember posters around the place attacking Deputy Cooney and Deputy Donegan, then Ministers for Justice and Defence, on the grounds that they were trying to collect money in order to increase the police force and the Army. For what purpose? They were increasing the police force and the Army in order to protect the people who elected them. I do not quarrel with the point of view that that is a thing which they should not have done.

I am trying to draw the attention of the House to the fact that all that element of protest has faded out. It is as though it had been turned down on a wireless set ever since the change of Government. When was there last a serious picket outside a Government Department? When did anyone last see a black beret and a sour puss and dark glasses striding around the streets. When was there last a hunger strike? When was a Minister's house last surrounded by angry people? When last were there placards or public marches? When were there last epithets applied to Minister like "Cockroach Cooney"? Has any one checked on the cockroaches recently in Portlaoise? No. I believe the Minister for Justice is making as good a job of it as he can, just as Senator Cooney did, but the point I am trying to make is that for some very obscure and strange little reasons that I wish I knew — I fear to think I can guess it — there is not the same atmosphere of confrontation.

It may be that the I.R.A. and their supporters recognised in the National Coalition a Government every single member of which was absolutely committed to putting them down so far as it could be done. It may be, therefore, that they see in the present Government a somewhat less committed enemy. I do not intend any reflection on the Minister or any one of his colleagues, but it may be in that party generally and the penumbra of support, or quasi support, or half support, or qualified support which that party enjoy, they see a kind of atmosphere in which it would be easier for them to breathe than it was under our Government. Accordingly, the confrontation has been scaled down to nothing.

It is very hard for people who have to watch the news day by day — for politicians who are interested in what journalists write: and in journalists who make their minds up about what politicians say and do to get a perspective over a few years. I should like anyone listening to these words, or who may subsequently read them, to throw his mind back to any of the years when the Coalition were in Office. There were no laws in operation then that are not in operation now, with the single exception of the Emergency Powers Act which

We were told from the other side of the House on that occasion that we were making the emergency up, that there was no emergency, but I do not want to reargue that matter now. We were represented as being the enemies of liberty. Why? Because we were substituting for a two day arrest which had been there for the past 40 years a seven day arrest, and no longer. Deputy Blaney and the former Deputy Boland sat as Ministers in government and sat, as Deputy Liam Cosgrave said, quiet as mice, at a time when so-called republicans were locked up not for seven days but indefinitely, and at a time when there was a Special Criminal Court not constituted of Mr Justice Hamilton swopping polite pleasantries with the Bar and Mr Justice X and Mr Justice Y, but constituted of Army officers who handed our sentences three times the length of what the

Special Criminal Court have been handing down. That was done under a Government which contained Deputy Blaney and Deputy Boland who sat there quiet as mice, but the Coalition were the enemy of liberty 15 years later. The Coalition were incipient tyrants because, on their tip toes and with apologies all round, they introduced a seven day arrest to enable the commission of crimes to be more fully investigated.

That is the kind of atmosphere the then Government had to face. I hope deputy Dr Browne would be generous enough to admit that even Senator Cooney, who is flesh and blood, with a strong streak of iron in him too which I salute, perhaps showed a sense of being beleaguered, as all the Government I worked for did in those years. Apart from ritual expressions of general abhorrence of violence how much support did we get from the far side of the House in those years?

If an English soldier or policeman so much as put his nose across the Border even by accident, Deputy Andrews, whom I saw over there a moment ago, was on his feet wanting to know why. Yet now we are supposed to buy an air corridor of a kind evidently which goes beyond anything the Coalition had, and we are supposed to say nothing about it and, for reasons of national responsibility on which perhaps my party will one day choke politically, we are saying very little about it. That was the wind of atmosphere we had to face. That was the kind of atmosphere in which we had to run a police force and a prison service. It was the kind of atmosphere in which there was nothing too low, too untrue, too savage, to say about our Government and about the people who worked for them, including the police.

There were accusations of police brutality from the moment we entered office until we left. I have not heard any recently. It may be — it is a logical possibility and since I know very little about how the police function and never sought secrets in the Coalition Government which did not concern me and, therefore, knew very little about the internal workings of the security side only except what I might accidentally hear at Government meetings — that people were brutalised in our time and that does not happen now. It may be so. I have absolutely no knowledge that it is so, but I admit, the theoretical possibility is there. Equally it may be the representations of Senator Cooney and Deputy Donegan as a pair of ogres who would eat the people if they were so allowed whereas they were men who were suffering, if anything, from an excess of zeal. That is the kind of thing we had to face, and we had to face it very much on the defensive so far as the police and the prison service were concerned. I hope that I am not letting any cat out of the bag when I tell the House that at that time without tripping them up or getting in their way or trying to make their difficult jobs more difficult I did quietly urge on a couple of my colleagues that we ought to have an independent police authority which would receive and impartially examine complaints about the police and complaints about the prison service. I would go this distance gladly and freely with people who make complaints about the police whether they are justified or unjustified, and that is that it is not satisfactory that the complaints should be investigated in the first instance by the very force against which the complaints are made.

I know that the situation was defended by the then Minister when we were in office, and we stuck together loyally as every government must, but I suppose I am not obliged to repress opinion on it indefinitely. I thought then, and quietly said so without making a nuisance of myself to men who were overworked and trying to keep the State from falling to bits, that there should be an impartial authority with the job of determining complaints against the police, and we might as well put the prison service into the same jurisdiction while we are at it. I agree that complaints about the prison service are much less frequent but they occasionally do surface — very occasionally — and there should be no reason for not subjecting the prison service to the same kind of jurisdiction. It should be an independent jurisdiction, and it should be one which has the necessary powers and facilities for making its own inquiries and its own investigations and which is not bound by the discipline of the police themselves and does not necessarily have to follow police procedures. That is not a revolutionary suggestion, but it is a particularly appropriate time to raise this point because of the tendency of the imminence of a Bill to set up the office of ombudsman. There is a lot to be said for a transparent police force, one in which the people can have confidence. I believe the people have confidence in the Irish police force and in the prison service, and I agree with Deputy Dr Browne that in this debate, in so far as I have heard it, people have if anything been trying to express that confidence and to express their gratitude to these two services for the ugly and difficult job they do. I would like to associate myself with that sentiment as well. But it is a mistake, a factual mistake, a mistake of policy on the part of any police force anywhere, to resist a system which will expose it to a conspicuously impartial system of investigation. It is in the interest of a force like that, that it should be and should remain beyond suspicion and beyond complaint. We can be proud that our police force is evidently free of the rampant corruption which appears to have overtaken the police in Britain. It seems to be the case every other month that a row erupts over there which shows that some unfortunate police officer or, perhaps, a series of them have given way to the temptation to accept bribes or to do things which are flagrantly inconsistent with their duty, so that scandal after scandal is the rule of the day in Britain. So if that is not the case here, I think, we can be extremely proud of it and grateful for it. In this increasingly difficult age, when more police are needed but when they are most difficult to recruit — and I wish there were more strains imposed on them — to keep the situation in such a way that we can hold our heads high nationally in regard to our police and prison service we should have an impartial system of investigation of complaints which may be made against them. I hope these will always be few and so far as possible without justification but if they exist at all it is in the interest of the police themselves that they should be seen to be acquitted, so to speak, by an impartial investigator of any charge made against them.

Let me remind the House about an incident in 1967 or thereabouts which had no political connection whatever. This was before the recent wave of the I.R.A. was ever heard of. A man who was in police custody in Cork died in his cell. The post mortem showed that he had suffered a large number of rib fractures and severe internal injuries including a ruptured spleen which is normally fatal. At the inquest the solicitor for his relatives appeared to suggest by the questioning in which he engaged that the man had been ill treated in the cell in the Cork Bridewell and that this was the cause of his death. That inquest lasted three days and the coroner's jury brought in a verdict of accidental death. The man was said to have fallen at a time before he was arrested and injured himself in this way and the coroner's jury, as it were, made light of these complaints. But the row went on. It gained in volume and the Minister for Justice at the time was Deputy Lenihan. There is nobody who can be compared with Deputy Lenihan except, I think Fouche who was a Chief of Police both under the ancien regime and also after the French Revolution and who seemed to pop up at all times and in all seasons with one kind of job or other but never too far from the action. I do not know if there is any Cabinet post that Deputy Lenihan has not held except for that of Taoiseach but he certainly has made a fair run at holding most of the others.

Anyway let us flash back and pick up one of the many files with his name on it. In this case it read, Minister for Justice, B. Lenihan and the file discloses that he was asked here repeatedly whether he would hold the proper judicial inquiry into the death of this unfortunate man in Cork and he said no. He did not, of course, say it in one syllable. He probably said yes but then proceeded in such a way as to make it clear that what he meant was no. He was pursued by the Press, by the Irish Association of Civil Liberties, by a lot of other mushroom organisations which came and when, by editorials in the papers, by Deputies here, by deputations from Cork and so on but he stonewalled until he literally had the whole country shouting at him. Everybody wanted a public inquiry into the death of this man for fear that there was anything in the charge that he had been ill-treated by the police in such a way as to cause these physical injuries.

In the end the Minister had to give in and he did set up a judicial inquiry which consisted of Judge Murnaghan and a couple of other judges — a Circuit Court judge, Judge Conroy I think, and a District Court Justice. They sat not for three days, which was the duration of the inquest, but for three weeks and heard a very great deal of evidence which had not come out at all at the inquest. A report was produced and published. I presume it is in the Dáil Library but it was plain and the death in question had, in fact, been accidental. There was a very rare injury involved, a kind of accident-in-a-thousand, but the judicial commission were satisfied that the death had been accidental and that the man had not been kicked or pushed or bullied in any way at all by the police.

From that good day to this no more was heard about it. That was absolutely the end of the matter, and the Garda came far, far better out of that than if the matter had rested after the coroner's inquest. Both the coroner's inquest and the subsequent inquiry acquitted them. After the proper inquiry, which was geared to investigate such a thing, there was never a whisper about that case. It is blotted from the public memory, and rightly so.

The result of that whole episode, now 12 years old or thereabouts, should bring home to everybody that the police are the principal beneficiaries of a transparent system of investigation. If we are going to have an ombudsman — and I cannot guess what will be the terms of their Bill — I would urge them expressly to include in that Bill a provision which subjects the doings of the police and the prison service to the jurisdiction of the ombudsman. I am saying that because it is in the interest of the police and in the interest of the public confidence in the police that there should be an impartial official, a person who is not answerable to any Minister, who cannot be fired by a Minister or by the Government, but who presumably will have a tenure comparable with that of a judge and who will have adequate staff or assistants and adequate machinery at his disposal for investigating everything. I urge that the Minister who is in charge of the ombudsman proposal should incorporate an express provision to that effect in the Bill. If it is not in the Bill when it arrives, I am going to try and get my party to put down an amendment to that effect.

Criminal Justice (Community Service), Bill, Dáil, 3 May 1983

I am sorry to strike a fairly neutral note in dealing with a Bill promoted by the Government I support. The Bill was well-meaning in its original form, which was a British form. It first surfaced in substantial form in the powers of the Criminal Courts Act, 1973, the sixty-second Act in the twentieth year of the reign of Elizabeth ll. There was the usual decorous interval of ten years during which alternative methods of penal treatment were mulled over by our domestic authorities of all political complexions.

Now we have our own little Bill, the Criminal Justice (Community Service) Bill 1983, the guts of which have been lifted straight out of the British Act. I cannot count the number of times I have complained about that in this House, nor can I count the number of occasions on which I had to criticise patterns of Government and administration here, not necessarily all statutory, in which we seem to have no ideas of our own and wait until the British have taken any kind of step before we take one for ourselves.

The conditions of criminality and criminal administration which led the British to introduce this experiment ten years ago were equally visible to us. 1973 was the year in which our jails were already bursting with offenders, may of them very violent and troublesome people. The kind of problems which led the British to make this experiment were just as obvious, if not more obvious, here as they were across the water. I am not going to labour this point because I have laboured it since I was elected to this House over ten years ago, and I do not want to weary Deputies or anybody else on the subject, but this is simply one more example in the ignominious parade of legislation masquerading under an Irish title "An Bille um Cheartas Coiriuil (Seirbhis Pobail), 1983" which is a British legislative idea taken over here and given a green outfit with silver buttons to make it look native. I protest against that.

The spirit of 1916 was invoked unctuously by Deputy Tunney 20 minutes ago. I believe and share the sentiments about 1916 which underlie what he was saying, but by a bizarre twist of his mind which no X-ray or stethoscope would show were it the case that politicians were ever subjected to the annual medical check which he so anxiously recommends for the Judiciary, he seemed to think that the difference which 1916 should have won for us is that we could sleep in our beds at night with properly patrolled streets and relative freedom from fear of marauders and Ribbonmen. The DMP provided at least that standard of tranquillity and security to the people of this city 70 or 80 years ago, but that is not what freedom was about, as I do not need to tell Deputy Tunney because I know his heart is in the right place on this theme. That is not what freedom is all about. It is about running our own affairs in a way which seems most appropriate to our own problem.

I must stigmatise this Bill, knowing I do not offend the Minister of State sitting in front of me, Deputy O'Keeffe, who has both a mind and a skin tough enough to withstand stuff like this from me, particularly since he knows that this Bill represents an area of consensus among both side of the House. Whatever Deputy Tunney may say about it, it is exactly the thing that 1916 was not all about. It was not all about tamely copying British legislation 10 years after.

In case, Sir, you do not believe me, it is true that the Bill does not literally, word for word, reproduce the British Sections, although there are examples in our legislation, may of them, in which English sections are reproduced word for word, the only difference being what the despised legal profession would call the operation of the mutatis mutandis principle. We were careful enough to take out some references that are no longer or never were applicable, in Ireland, like "county courts" and substitute "circuit courts". We took that much trouble with it. We change "London" to "Dublin", things like that. We are well able to make such changes, it is well within our competence, we are not stretched or worried to do that; but anything more substantial like recognising or analysing a problem which is under our own noses and doing it now and not wanting for the English to do it for us, seems to be beyond us. Whatever about the men of 1916, in the first years of the State under the late W.T. Cosgrave and ensuing years under the late Eamon de Valera, we had innovation and we used independent thinking. That has now become lost and submerged.

The Bill in front of us does not follow the 1973 English Act literally word for word, but in every important respect it does. It defines in the same way the conditions in which these community orders may be made. It defines "community service" in the same way. It defines conditions for revoking orders in the same way. It defines even the numbers of hours per week and per year which may maximally be spent on community service with the very same number of hours.

I do not think there is any ethnic or climatic reason to go out of one's way to differentiate between the number of hours of community service appropriate for an offender in Inverness and those appropriate for an offender in Tullamore, which Deputy Connolly was talking about a moment ago. However, I consider it uncanny, not in the nature of a free people, that time and again in our legislation, down to the number of hours we define, we decide that because the British did it it is more than good enough for us.

I have nothing against a 40-hour week of community service, or against 240-hour year, but the likelihood that we would have decided on these figures had we been approaching the matter ourselves without any knowledge of what the British had done, is infinitesimally small. It clearly is cogged, like so much of our own legislation, straight out of the English Act 10 years on, and as far as I can see, without any visible reflection of any lessons that the British may have learned themselves in the meantime.

The people who were behind this Bill, in whatever party and in whatever Department, did not look further than across the channel. Apparently they gave no thought to the possibility that community service orders might be appropriate in some contexts for that kind of offender. They restricted it to the kind of offender for whom imprisonment is commonly doled out. That is exactly the kind of offender, because of the kinds of offence to which it is usually attacked, the average Irish citizen will not want to have hanging around his premises, will not want to have weeding paths or clipping hedges outside his house, will not want to have next or near him. He will complain if he finds that a number of offenders of this kind are being employed in his vicinity, and employed not under constant police supervision, but in such a way that they can fill in the work in their own time, in any free hours they have.

What will be the cost of supervising adequately the kind of offender for whom this Bill is tailored? I do not know what the cost will be. Perhaps it will not be very much. The Minister made an allusion to the likelihood that he would have to recruit staff. We may be perfectly certain that is exactly what he will have to do. He said it may be necessary for the probation and welfare service to employ people either on a paid or a voluntary basis. How many is he likely to get on a voluntary basis if they can be paid for it, and if a case can be made to pay them? What kind of industrial problems does he think he will have if he imagines he will be able to run one part of the service for nothing while paying the rest? He said it may be necessary to employ people either on a paid or a voluntary basis to supervise the actual performance of the work. I am damn sure it will be necessary.

I should like to know whether any cost analysis has been done on the likely product of this system in comparison with expanding prison accommodation.

The Bill envisages the making of regulations for the refunding of travelling expenses, the offender's travelling expenses and presumably somebody to keep an eye on him while he travels down to Mountmellick, or wherever it may be, to do some community service there.

I am asking these questions only because, regrettably, the Minister's speech contains nothing on this point. I should also like to have known whether the Garda have any opinion about this Bill and, if so, what it is. The Minister was silent on that as well. The Minister in front of me will know I am not saying that in my carping sense. I would ask that of any Minister. That element is missing from the Minister's speech.

I should like to know whether the Garda look on this Bill as being one more headache, one more piece of cosmetic legislation which will increase the burdens on them, or whether they are willing to give it a chance. Are they indifferent to it? Are they cynical about it? Are they bitterly opposed to it? The garda have collective opinions on these things. Since they are the people who provide the cutting edge of the State in dealing with a criminality which most of us are lucky enough not to come in contact with. I would have thought their opinion was valuable.

If the Garda view was that this would put a lot of rogues back on the streets and put them back even quicker than they are now being put back, I would have been slow to go ahead with a Bill of this kind. I emphasise that in saying that I do not want to insinuate that that is the opinion of the Garda. I do not know what their opinion is. For all I know it may be that they are anxious to give a thing like this a change. That may well be the case. Very much to their credit, the Garda have done a great deal in trying to keep offenders, and particularly young offenders, out of prison. It may be that they agree entirely with the spirit of this Bill. At least the House should be told.

Malicious Injuries Bill, Dáil, 12 June 1986

The entire malicious injuries code in Ireland was an engine for keeping the Peep-o'-Day Boys, the Whiteboys and other perpetrators of local outrages in their places. It was a primitive engine of government, of remote Anglo-Saxon origin, which the British in more modern times never applied in their own country but which they applied here, with the idea that if they could stick the inhabitants of localities with liability for malicious injuries caused in their districts it would make them, as it were, police themselves, enforce on them the

236

necessity for a certain self-policing, "neighbourhood watch" system, as it is called today.

Therefore, the neighbourhood watch is not a new idea. It goes back to the times of Queen Anne, and before that Charles ll and Edward IV or thereabouts. That system of malicious injury compensation was intended to force on people a kind of neighbourhood watch: they were forced to carry a vicarious liability, an imputed responsibility for crime committed in their own districts, and they were made to pay for that crime if they did not make damn sure that whoever was likely to commit it was kept in his place or got rid of in some other way.

That system, in the time when I was in practice and until more recently, caused many anomalies which the legislation of 1981 got rid of and which this legislation, wisely, is continuing to get rid of. For example, because of the criminal nature of these offenses and their origin in criminal law, all the ordinary ideas of criminal law inhered in it, so that, for example, in order to achieve an award for malicious injury one had to prove beyond a reasonable doubt, and not merely on the "balance of probabilities" which is the standard of proof in civil cases, that the damage of the injury was malicious. That meant that children did not come into the scope of the thing because they were not capable of malice. It meant as well that the local authority could not compromise or settle a malicious injury application, in the same way that a criminal prosecution cannot be compromised.

These archaisms and anomalies have been got rid of. They burdened localities with the paying of compensation. That, to a large extent, has been got rid of by the assumption by the State of the liability in the form of reimbursing local authorities.

The old system had ludicrous anomalies built into it. I remember being in a case in Kildare — I forget which side I was appearing for, the county council or the applicant — which the C.I.E. were suing Kildare County Council in a malicious injury application for vandalism which C.I.E. said had been committed in a train as it passed through County Kildare. It was a non-stop express train carrying football supporters to Cork from Dublin., or vice versa; but, merely because the inspector on the train thought he was able to show that it was in the neighbourhood of Sallins or Newbridge that the damage had been caused, the ratepayers of County Kildare were expected to make good the loss to C.I.E.

These anomalies have been done away with, but there remains at the heart of the system the idea that the people at large must be made to pay for crimes committed in their midst. The anomalies are mostly gone, there is no longer the local charge or levy, but there remains at the heart of the system the idea that everybody else has to carry the can financially for a malicious act. Were it not for that system, rooted in a British mechanism for keeping us down, or, at any rate, the more unruly of us, the very same rule would apply to malicious damage as to accidents — that the loss lies where it falls. That is one of the ills that flesh is heir to; as a general rule in life, misfortune, accident or a malicious act committed against you, if it causes you loss or illness or anything else, the loss lies where it falls, and it is difficult to shift it.

I got a couple of letters last month from constituents of mine about a certain matter. By no means am I trying to belittle them or to make fun of them: I sympathise with them because they have suffered a misfortune. Their letters stated that they had booked holidays in Yugoslavia, and the weeks following the accident at Chernobyl they thought it would be safer not to go to Yugoslavia. I agree completely with them: I would not have gone there myself, and I would not have advised my family or friends to do so. Unfortunately, they had irrevocably booked their holiday that had gone by the board, and they wanted the Minister for Finance to compensate them. They did not ask for compensation from the Soviet Minister for Finance, or that this State might sponsor a claim against the Soviet Union for disappointed expectations on the part of holidaymakers. They wanted our Minister for Finance to compensate them for the loss. I have every sympathy with the people concerned and I do not mention their case in order to criticise them; I do so merely to illustrate how widespread is the public expectation that the State will carry the can for everyone. In my experience that has been the outside limit; but perhaps other Deputies have even more outlandish examples to give.

The Minister began frankly by saying that the reason for the legislation was to curtail public expenditure, to save public money. What is so shameful about that? Why should he be expected by Deputy Woods to apologise for that? That is what Deputy Woods called "naked Thatcherism". Have we lost touch with reality altogether, that a Minister or Government are to be faulted for trying to see where the people's money can be saved? It is not Deputy Dukes's money or Deputy Fennell's money. It is not the money of anyone on the Government side; it is the people's money. The absolute limit that can be saved this year is 20 million, because obviously some claims will still have to be met by the State. However, that money seems like peanuts to Deputy Woods, peanuts so far as saving to that State is concerned, but it appears to be fraught with disaster to far as industry commerce and schools are concerned.

The absolute limit that can be saved this year is 20 million; but to call what the Government are proposing "naked Thatcherism" is so babyish and irresponsible that it makes one despair of what will happen if this side do not win the next election. God knows, I have plenty of fault to find with the kind of schemes we are driven into by our comrades over here on the left, and I do not stand over everything this Government have felt obliged to do. However, there is a least some level of sense and responsibility in the Government somewhere. Wher will the country be if we are run by a Government who think it is "naked Thatercherism" to save £20 million, most of which can be funded from insurance sources?

I will tell you where those cries of naked Thatcherism will lead to. They are going to lead this country into naked Castroism. This State will simply collapse under the weight of the burdens which are thrust on it by politicians

238

so hungry to spend their declining years in power — most of them are not in their first youth, indeed are far from it — that they would promise anything. This Government which I am glad to support — to put it no higher than that if only when I look across at the alternative, and no offence to the two gentlemen opposite — started out with a programme of economy.

Before I leave the subject of Deputy Woods and naked Thatcherism, since he is Fianna Fáil's Front Bench spokesman on this subject, would he come back into the House to tell us if he will undertake the repeal of this measure if he is in Government in a year's time or in five years' time? Could we have from the Fianna Fáil Party, who are so bitter and determined in their opposition to this reasonable measure, a firm, clear undertaking that they will repeal this measure if they are in Government? I do not mean an undertaking which would be comparable in clarity and unequivocal character with their attitude to the divorce referendum: I mean something an honest man can understand. Will they or will they not repeal this measure when they get in? Deputy Woods did not tell us, but perhaps some other authorised spokesman will tell us before the debate ends. If we pass this Bill and if Fianna Fáil get in at the next election, will they definitely undertake to repeal this legislation? If they do we will then be back to the old British system of keeping down the Whiteboys and the Peep-o'-Day Boys, and we will be back to this system which this Bill seeks to abolish.

The Presidency in the 1937 Constitution, Donegal, 19 August 1987

This new Constitution contained some innovations, on which the Fine Gael opposition — represented mainly by their lawyers, Cecil Lavery, John A. Costello, Patrick McGilligan, and James Fitzgerald-Kenny — concentrated a heavy fire. Foremost among these innovations was the proposed new office of President, which was in certain formal respects to replace the office of Representative of the Crown, or "Governor-General", which had been abolished the previous year, but was given in addition some novel functions; moreover, under the draft Article 13.10 further, still unspecified, functions could be assigned to the President by means of an ordinary Act. Speaker after speaker on the Fine Gael side assailed this proposed constitutional personage, seeing in his office the seeds of a dictatorship, and not taking much trouble to conceal their conjecture as to the probable identity of the first dictator. It was in vain for Mr de Valera to point out that any such additional Presidential functions could not transcend the limits placed upon the President by the Constitution, effectively restricting his functions to that of a rubber stamp and only in two or three very special contexts entitling him to act in his own discretion; some minor confusion in Mr de Valera'a interventions only heightened Opposition suspicion of this sinister novelty.

This being so, the question arises whether the office of President, so far from bestriding the State like a colossus, is so insubstantial in reality as to justify its continuance, at any rate as an elective office requiring the expense and commotion of a national poll. This very point was foreshadowed by Mr de Valera himself in the Constitution debate when he suggested that, unless the office were assigned really substantial functions, it would not be worth putting the State to the trouble and expense of a national popular election to fill it. When one reflects that, in addition to having, most of the time, no serious independent functions to exercise, the President is inhibited even from making formal speeches to the people without the Government's approval, and in general has purely formal functions to which his own personal qualities can lend neither direction, nor force, nor even colour, then the question really does seem to call for a new appraisal, especially since — at any rate, if popular belief may be trusted — the very marginality, not to say the aimlessness, of most of a presidential existence must make the office unbearably boring for a hitherto active man (or woman) to discharge. There must, of course, be a ceremonial head of state, even if only to discharge purely formal functions and to receive goodwill visits from other heads of state; but for such an office I think we might contemplate, first of all, a shorter turn of duty — say three years — and secondly, appointment by some respectable body, such as the Council of State, who could be trusted not to give us a President unfit to discharge the duties of the office with dignity.

The same goes for the "special position" of the Catholic Church which the new Article 44 "recognised", but which had not been mentioned in any way in the old Constitution. Discussion of the new draft Article takes up about six columns in the official report, which means about 15 minutes of Dáil time; and the only protest about the "special position" of the Catholic Church came from one of the Deputies from Dublin University, Dr. Rowlette. Other Protestant deputies, including two from Border counties who could be regarded as "ex-Unionists" did not speak on the matter at all. Again, there is absolutely no sign of consciousness of the impact of the recognition clause in the North; even Dr. Rowlette's protest was one of principle, and not related to Ulster Protestantism and the State's hopes of conciliating it. As for the -equally new — prohibition of divorce legislation, again only Dr. Rowlette expressed reservations, and these of the mildest kind, about this clause; no other Deputy, Catholic or Protestant, so much as mentioned it, except for a purely technical legal difficulty adverted to by John A. Costello as arising on the sub-section following the prohibition; and no one adverted to this newly institutionalised gap between our law and that of the North, where a divorce jurisdiction had been instituted some years previously.

As against these amazing silence in the debate — as it must seem to us —

it is worth drawing attention to an element which id did contain but which is now, sadly, long since vanished from ordinary Dáil discourse; namely the painful consciousness of a recently shattered national unity of purpose. It would be untrue to say that this comes through regularly in the debate and it must be admitted that on the Fine Gael side it does not come through at all; but surprisingly, the contribution of the then Minister for Finance, Deputy Sean McEntee, who was in some moods the most bitter and combative of politicians, strikes this note very clearly. He appealed to the Opposition, in a tone which certainly reads as though it were perfectly sincere, not to raise bogus objections to the draft Constitution, and asked those "who do feel and who still carry in their hearts some remnant of the spirit that inspired them in 1916-21" to admit that the draft was, in fact, very like what they had hoped they might have got when they signed the Treaty. He even went to the length of saying, in connection with the Presidency, that he hoped the President would be able to get "united and concerted action in times of crisis, to try to smooth away the differences which have divided us in the past 15 years". These divisions were then extremely recent; the span of 15 years which separated the Constitution debate from the outbreak of the Civil War in 1922 is only the same as the span which separates us today from the referendum on joining the E.E.C.; even the span which separated the Constitution debate from the Easter Rising of 1916 is only the same as that which separates us today from the date when Sean Lemass was succeed as Taoiseach by Jack Lynch. Political divisions in this country, perhaps everywhere, tend to develop vested interests in their own perpetuation; and of all the contrasts with the mood of today which the Constitution debate of 1937 discloses, the disappearance of the sense of loss and bereavement caused by the Civil War split seems to me the saddest.

Extradition Bill, Dáil, 1 December 1987

I do not in any way want — as Sherlock Holmes used to say — to stake whatever little reputation I have on the prediction that the Supreme Court is not going to shoot down this Bill — or Act if it becomes law — at some future stage. It may do so. As former Deputy Jack Lynch said when he was Taoiseach: "The courts have become so adventurous nowadays that it is a brave man who will predict what they will do in the constitutional area". I do not want to appear any braver than Jack Lynch when he was asked whether he was sure he was doing something constitutional when he was introducing some measure here. It is possible that I am wrong about this, but for what my opinion is worth I do not think the function which it is here proposed to give the Attorney General is judicial in character.

241

Deputy Andrews is right in pointing out that the purpose of the Bill — on the face of it — is not as an extra oppression of the person wanted for extradition but as a safeguard for him, and I have no objection to there being as many safeguards as we can decently put in, consistent with our obligations under the European Convention. It is only fair to colleagues to remind the House that when Deputy Dukes was putting the Bill to give effect to that Convention through the House last year and was being asked then about a prima facie requirement he said, and I think he was quite right, that he could not insert such a thing without effectively attaching a new condition of our own to the European Convention. We have signed this Convention and we have go to give effect to it. We cannot import a completely new condition into it. That is a reasonable argument, and from that point of view one could perhaps say that the present Bill is objectionable. One could say that the Irish alone among the signatory nations are giving their own Attorney General the right to consider whether there is a reasonable spread of evidence sufficient to support a prosecution. I do not know whether this point has surfaced much during the debate; but that certainly would be something in which there might be some substance. Deputy Dukes quite rightly made that point last year. Apart from that point, the Bill is intended as an additional safeguard and not as an engine of oppression.

I want to try to remove another misapprehension. It is not correct to say that the office of the Attorney General is a political office; at least it is not correct to say it in the sense in which the expression has been employed in this debate. He is, of course, a political, appointee and he must be, if a Government are to be happy with him, somebody with much the same political opinions and background as the Government. Otherwise, he cannot sit at Government meetings and be more or less au fait with what a Government are doing or what problems they have. To that extent, of course, he is political. He is appointed by a Taoiseach who is not going to appoint one of his bitterest opponents and he will leave office, as I did, when the Taoiseach goes out of office. The Taoiseach can fire him or request his resignation in the meantime. But during his tenure of office he is not a political creature in the sense in which he is now said to be; and I do not believe that any Attorney General since the State was founded behaved in that way. He is supposed to be independent and he has always considered himself as independent and I do not believe that any Attorney General would ever allow his professional or official judgment to be bent or twisted in response to a political exigency expressed to him by his Taoiseach. He would have said "look, Taoiseach, I am here to give you advice and to advise the Government on the legality or illegality of what you are doing. My advice is as follows and I am not going to certify otherwise. "That certainly is how I would have behaved if I had been there long enough for such a matter to present itself. I have never heard the suggestion from any side that an Attorney General of any political persuasion behaved otherwise.

I want to finish on that note by citing to the House what three judges of the Supreme Court said in the one case in which the function of the Attorney

General was discussed at great length. It is a case which had avoided classification in many indexes because the head note to the case does not mention this aspect of it. Nevertheless, it is the leading case on the Attorney General's functions.

The court was divided but not on the point I am talking about here. The Chief Justice of the time, Conor Maguire said that the Attorney General "exercise executive power under the authority of the Government while he retains in the day to day decisions he has to make the independence which he has always enjoyed". Mr. Justice Kingsmill Moore said: "It is quite clear that the Attorney General is in no way the servant of the Government but is put into an independent position". Mr. Justice Cearbhall O'Dalaigh said; "Whatever room for debate there may be as to the position of the Attorney General prior to 1937 it can, in my opinion, no longer admit of argument since the enactment of the Constitution of Ireland that the Attorney General is not, in the discharge of his functions as public prosecutor, subject to the directions of the Taoiseach but is an independent constitutional officer."

I realise that Deputies who make the opposite case are not operating from malice or deliberately distorting a position but that corresponds with my understanding of the office and I do not believe that the present incumbent of the office would or could possibly have the faintest intention to allow that independence to be reduced. So far as that aspect of the matter goes I must declare myself as not sharing the apprehensions I have heard expressed. I apologise if I have given displeasure to colleagues. I would find it harder to forgive myself if I had either not spoken on this matter or had spoken in a sense which I did not believe.

Courts Bill, Dáil, 4 May 1988

I will not strike a disagreeable or disobliging note by saying that I could not help noticing two strictly political dimensions to the debate this afternoon, one provided by Deputy Woods, the Minister, and the other by Deputy McCartan. I know that Deputy Woods made a speech 180 degrees contrary to what he has been saying here today when the substance of this measure was before the House in the last Dáil. Of course every Fianna Fáil Deputy has to win his spurs — I am mixing my metaphors — as a brass neck and Deputy Woods, by his performance here today, has shown himself to be well up in the Lenihan class where that is concerned.

So would I, not perhaps for that characteristic but for other such as his lack of bitterness and his good humour, most of all but, certainly, his brass neck is of a 22 carat grade. The Minister here today must be assaying well over the 20 carat grade at least to judge by his performance. If the Whip had said to a more sensitive man: "Somebody has to move the Bill because other Ministers are out of the way; the Minister for Foreign Affairs cannot meet Tom King and therefore we have to send the two stock political plug uglies that they use for that purpose to substitute for him and we would like you to deal with this Bill" he might have said "There are after all 15 members of the Government and I am only one of then. I differ from the other 14 members in that I went out in front in opposing the measure you want me to promote in the House today". He might have expected from a sensitive Whip the response. "I had forgotten that; naturally we will find someone else, we would not wish to embarrass you by obliging you to say today that something is black which you said two years ago was white.

There has been much talk here this afternoon about the judicial and the legal world. I will say this for he judicial arm of the State. It is the one which has sunk least low in public esteem. I do not believe it has sunk in public esteem at all. It is easy to say, when a case appears on the front page, high on the headlines, that a judge has made a fool of himself, that he has not sentenced somebody to a term long enough, that he has let somebody off that should not have been let off or that he has on the other hand been too severe or has misconducted himself through foolishness or misunderstanding in some way or other. That is easily said but by and large I do not think incompetence or lack of conscience has even been imputed to the Irish Judiciary. I believe that when you make a man independent there is a very good chance that he is going to behave independently.

What I have to say about the Judiciary I say with total sincerity and I wish to make it clear that that goes for people appointed by all Governments. The Judiciary have come out of the last 60 or 65 years of this State with more credit and with less criticism than either this House or the various Governments that it has supported. I know that at moments when one feels like throwing an easy punch at something which cannot defend itself and which is not in the business of defending itself, it is easy to sneer at the benches, the gowns and the wigs, but when all these petty objections and resentments are disposed of, that branch of our State has delivered a service over the last 65 years, with all the failings that may be admitted to it, which ranks in the public esteem far above the service provided by this House or by the Governments, in other words, the Executive which it supports, let alone the various arms of the Executive. I am speaking about their political dimensions and not their official dimensions.

There is some sort of resentment of the legal profession in the judicial dimensions and the dimension of those who practise in the courts, which centres on things like the wigs and the gowns, the formalities, the outmoded forms of address, the language used in addressing a judge and so on. I sometimes hear people ask why cannot they all dress in suits like the rest of us, and not be intimidating plaintiffs, defendants and witnesses. I would be willing to defend the system to the last detail, not so much because it is as it is but because it is formal. There is a lot to be said for formality in court proceedings. It is not intended to, and it ought not to, intimidate people but if it does over-awe them, if it induces in them a certain reverence and a certain disposition to think twice before telling a lie, that is all to the good.

It is a matter of history that our judges and barristers wear a particular kind of outfit. I do not attach any special importance to that — but that there should be some kind of formality, most easily induced by dress and forms of speech, is entirely right. I know that point of view would be greeted with derision by virtually every audience in this country and probably would be by my colleagues and friends in this House were it not for the rules of decorum — but I believe that is a very important reason why justice here has been will administered.

I practised for some years in the courts. I have no doubt it is no worse here than any other country, but many people but not all litigants or witnesses are inclined to tell lies even on oath. Everyone who has practised, even for a very short period and I was there for five or six years — knows people are inclined, not perhaps wittingly, to tell lies. The side they are on somewhat distorts their recollections of an event or their appraisal of a situation. Any dimension of formality, even of over-awing, in a court procedure which tends to induce caution, a realisation in people that they are in something more serious than a conversation in a private house or in a public house, is to the good.

It is said that legal profession is a closed shop — whatever that means. To me it appears the profession is as open as any profession can be that applies minimal rules in regard to competence and which is geared and run for the benefit of its members at the public's expense. I am not in practice now nor have I been for a number of years, and I do not know if I ever shall be again, but I never felt like that about the legal profession. I have no axe to grind now and I do not expect, in the foreseeable future to be in practice, but in my years at the Bar I was never conscious that it was a conspiracy against the public. On the contrary, I always felt the public got a very good service. In particular they got from the Bar, the branch of the profession I feel best qualified to speak about, what I might call partisan emotion which never could be got from an engineer or an architect, and I say that not out of disrespect to those professions. It was common at the Bar — and I felt it myself — to become involved in a client's case. In fact, it was very important to try to maintain a certain perspective, to keep a certain distance from becoming involved.

I remember being disproportionately downcast if I lost a case. It might not have been my fault, but sometimes it was. Depression would fall on me for days at the thought of having allowed somebody to out of the court with no compensation because of a mistake I had made. What other profession is there in which this is so? Equally, I remember being perhaps unduly elated with I won a case. It did not matter that my fee in those days might be 14 or 15 guineas for having stood around for two days, but I felt a sense of satisfaction which infinitely exceeded the money involved. I am not holding myself out as an example, because I believe that was true of the profession in general. I know from my friends who are still at the Bar that they have a dog's life in many respects. They are not able to plan holidays, weekends or spend time with their families in the evening because they are tied to a grindstone and if they detach themselves from it, their practice can be gone in a very short time.

When I was at the Bar the incidence of T.B. was lessening but there were people who were laid up for four, six or eight months. When they came back to work their practice had virtually disappeared, not because anybody was trying to do them down but because the solicitors on whom they depended had to get their client's work done by somebody and they necessarily made new connections. They started to brief other barristers and when the unfortunate invalid finally resumed work, pale and convalescent, he might find that three-quarters of the solicitors on whom he had previously relied were no longer giving him the same volume of work. There is no pension, no insurance, nothing to fall back on if a barrister falls victim to the ordinary ills of the flesh. No one will cover up for him if he becomes an alcoholic. There are things which the public, who are apt to sneer at what they perceive as the privileges and selfishness of the legal profession, forget. Much of what I have said, I have no doubt, could apply also to the solicitors profession, although I have no personal experience of it.

I have strayed somewhat from the political point I wanted to begin with. I say this without meaning to offend him because I have never had any trouble with him and I do not want to get his back up or to make an enemy of him, but I think it was a graceless performance of this Minister, whose Bill this is not, to have acquiesced in coming here and putting a face on something which he argued 180 degrees against not many months ago. Having dealt as well as I can with the Fianna Fáil, now let me move to the other side of the rainbow.

Let me move from one leprechaun to another. I have listened with a lot of interest to Deputy McCartan's contribution and learned a good deal from it — I say that without sarcasm — but I could not but be amused by the praise which he heaped on the efforts which has successfully got a particular insurance company out of their difficulties, even though there is still a jury system in place. He was talking about the P.M.P.A. and how they had managed to haul themselves out of a deficit of more than £50 million. How had they done that, asked the representative of The Worker's Party with warm admiration in his voice? By dint of improved efficiency and competition. How much efficiency and competition would there be in the State Assurance Company in Dubrovnik if The Workers' Party were in power? It would be a State authority with no incentive, high or low, for efficiency or competition. Sauce for the goose must be sauce for the gander. I hopped off the Minister, Deputy Woods, for having been willing to say today something is black which he said not too long ago was white.

Although I have no personal quarrel nor have I had any trouble with Deputy McCartan, I feel he has made an extraordinary exhibition or himself this afternoon by appearing — and I do not think I am putting too unfair a gloss on

246

his words — to endorse not just a policy but a philosophy which his party were founded in order to destroy. If he really believes efficiency and competition are the secret of success he belongs in some other party, not with Deputy Taylor I agree, but somewhere else in the House, and not perhaps with the Napper Tandys we do not see too often unless we are discussing one of the pet subjects, but certainly not in the Workers' Party.

I would like to repeat the question other speakers have raised. What is the motive for this measure? I am sorry that I ask myself that question. It is a bit like the method of diagnosis which Conan Doyle learned as a young doctor which he thereafter grafted onto his creation, Sherlock Holmes: when you have excluded the impossible, whatever else remains, however improbable, must be the truth. I have run through the other possible motives for this measure, most of which have been dealt with very effectively by speakers here today, including Deputy Andrews. I have had to exclude all of those as impossible. I am left with the one which might seem in a republican Parliament to be highly improbable, though I am afraid long experience of that Parliament has taught me that it is by no means improbable, namely, that we are doing this because it was done in Britain. As usual, we are doing it about 40 years later than them. Not only do we catch their penny but it takes 40 years for it to drop. That is shaming.

I contend that one of the reasons the Bill before us is being promoted by the Government, as it was by the last, is the agitation which has gone on about high insurance premiums. I know very little about the working of insurance companies. Deputy S. Barrett in front of me would know a hundred times more. I believe the principle of the workings of an insurance company is that it operates on the basis of pooling the risk and that it varies its premiums in terms of the sort of pool that will be necessary in order to meet what it expects in the way of claims from certain categories of risk — fire, life, accident and so on. I believe that even within those categories assessments for the level of risk will vary, depending on the people involved.

If it has been the experience of insurance companies that 18 and 19 year old drivers constitute a higher risk than drivers of my age, why should they not charge premiums proportionately? I am damned if I can see the reason for not doing that — all this whingeing and whining about young drivers being penalised. I was 30 year of age before I could afford a car let alone pay the insurance premium on it. Granted, the exercise is troublesome. Let us look at it in this way: my own car is a four-year old Fiat and I am not in the two car category. For comprehensive insurance cover on the vehicle I pay in the region of £800 a year whereas, had I third party cover only, I am sure it would amount to very much less. Even supposing the premium amounted to £800 for third party cover, which is far in excess of what it would be, I would still be paying only £2 a day for that insurance cover. Is that a fortune? Consider that for those £2, I can drive while drunk, I can cripple someone for life, leave a family fatherless; I can write off a line of parked cars by side-swiping ten or twelve of them as I drive along the street. I can do all of these things with total impunity, at least civil impunity, for a mere £2 a day. Naturally it does not relieve me of my criminal liability for such behaviour. But, so far as compensating the victims of my behaviour, is concerned, £2 a day will let me out. Where is the excessiveness in that? Mind you, it is not really £2 a day because if I had merely third party cover the premium would be very much less and it is not very long since it was £1 a day.

What is the reason for politicians, with their tails between their legs, running away from young drivers? Are we never going to stand up to anybody and say "You must carry your own weight in the world and face the consequences of your own situation. Do you not have the compensation of being young, without mearling and whining about having to pay insurance on a car in a risk category which is particularly high? I have nothing but contempt for politicians who run with the herd like that. It is not very long since an 18-years-old person could not dream of having a car. When I was a student the families of most 18 year old students did not have a car, let alone the students themselves. Let us not run, driven by a stampede, shouting and roaring about premiums that has brought this Bill into the House.

Somehow we have been given the idea and sold the idea, the premiums will magically come down if we get rid of the juries. If I really could see a necessary connection between the abolition of civil jury trials in accident cases and the size of premiums I would probably have a different opinion. I practised in the courts for five or six years and I appeared several times before a jury in the High Court and addressed juries in accident cases. I have a little experience of this, though not, I suppose, as much as Deputy Andrews has, I also accept that my experience of it is now a bit rusty, but I cannot see the connection between these two matters. For example, I cannot see that the existence of a jury prolongs a case in duration substantially beyond what it would be before a single judge. Cases can also run for a very long periods of time before a single judge.

I should also like to know to what extent the prevalence of uninsured drivers on our roads contributes to the height of premiums and what relative impact compared to what we are promised now — and we are not really promised anything very concrete — catching up with these uninsured drivers would make. I do not think the public understand that the cost of uninsured drivers and the accidents they cause fall essentially on those people who are insured for reasons I am sure everyone in the House understands. It ultimately falls on them and it has the effect of pushing up the premiums because the insurance companies essentially have to carry the loss of people who drive uninsured. Naturally, if one could be sure that no uninsured drivers existed any longer, that ought to have an effect on the levels of premiums.

When I see the word "clampdown" or "crackdown" in the papers I always think it is like a picture when I said to myself "This is where I came in" and looked for my hat and coat to go home. I have been reading for years about

248

ministerial crackdowns on uninsured driving. Where is the sign of this crackdown? About six months ago I was in a line of traffic on which a spot check was being conducted by the Garda to see whether drivers had tax and insurance. This is very good idea. No doubt that kind of spot check will net a good many uninsured drivers. Equally, if the Minister and his crack-down team walked around the streets and spot checked parked cars which have no insurance disc — and in that regard I must commend the idea of insurance discs which I tried in vain to promote during the seven or eight months I was in the Department of Trade — that no doubt would net a good deal more.

I have not been told that the general level of uninsured driving has substantially fallen. I would expect a Government to crack down and keep on cracking down until such time as this country, instead of having 10 per cent of its drivers uninsured, would have less than 1 per cent, which would be the Continental European level. When that is done we can start looking at our system of judicature and ask whether it is perfectly adaptable to the task which it has on hand.

Rod Licence Dispute, Dublin, 19 May 1988

The formula agreed between the Government and the Archbishop of Tuam for the temporary settlement of the rod licence dispute, as reportedly noted by the Archbishop and as understood by those engaged in the fishing boycott, has very serious implications which transcend the original issue.

If the Archbishop was given to understand that angling activities could now proceed "uninhibited", i.e. without any enforcement of the licence requirement, then the Government have done something absolutely illegal and un-constitutional by purporting to dispense people from the application of a law of the Oireachtas, or to suspend that law's operation.

No authority in the country has the power to suspend a law's enforcement except the Oireachtas itself, and this attempt to by-pass the Oireachtas amounts to the assertion of a royal prerogative power which has not been exercised in this country since the Battle of the Boyne. It is bad enough that this Government has now capitulated for the second time in six months to a pressure group — thus reinforcing the public impression that disobedience will get you anywhere — but it is far worse if the precedent is established that a Taoiseach can put an Act of the Oireachtas in abeyance by an imperial wave of his hand.

SECTION 8

Miscellaneous

'John Boyle', Matters of Honour, Chapter I, 1964

I read a poem somewhere which used the whistling railway train as an image of loneliness, and often afterwards when felt lonely I used to take sad pleasure in moping about a railway line and waiting for a train to whistle, so that I could wallow in the high windy wail of it. Then I found there were other things about trains that melancholy could feed on: the lighted windows rattling by, excluding the solitary watcher, the red rear lantern disappearing round the bend in the track, then the vacant impersonal rails gleaming dully away to the horizon under the night sky.

After two week in the Pufendorfstrasse I was so sunk in a stupor of melancholy and homesickness that I took automatically to going out in the evenings and walking the few hundred yards to the big level crossing in the Romerstrasse, where an iron footbridge stood over a dozen tracks converging on the old sandstone railway station a quarter of a mile to the east. It was a busy junction, and the traffic had become so great that a new glass and concrete station was nearing completion on the west of the town; when that was ready the old station would be pulled down and all these rails and the iron footbridge would be taken away. But for the moment you could still stand on this rusting bridge and look down at the trains. Sometimes international expressed would run past, eighteen dull green carriages long : Copenhagen-Rome, Hook of Holland-Belgrade-Athens could be read on their destination boards under the garish red lights fixed to iron stalks here and there through the station yards. Now and then a small local train would chuff in slowly from Wiesloch or Mannheim, old-fashioned short coaches with stove popes and many doors; its ancient engine would cover me with smoke and steam as it creaked cautiously under the bridge. A minute later I would hear a muffled loud-speaker announcing through the night air its arrival at platform six or seven.

I used to compare all this with the only other railway station I ever knew well, a small junction in the West of Ireland where two main lines crossed and a single-track branch line ran twelve miles to a little market town on the shores of Lough Mask. I spend hundreds of happy hours playing there as a child, climbing in and out of derelict guards' vans, following rusting shunt lines till they ended in rotting wooden buffers, hopping from sleeper to sleeper along the Ballinrobe branch line as it curved a hundred years from the station around a little reedy bog-lake with a smell of turf-smoke in the air and a sound of curlews crying in the sky.

The Irish Language, Dublin, 14 May 1968

One might imagine, from the frequency with which the subject figures in newspaper correspondence columns, that the Irish language was still a very live issue. It is true that there are many self-sacrificing enthusiasts — mostly in Dublin — always willing to do battle with those who differ from them. But the majority of the people are indifferent or even vaguely hostile I believe. The main reason is that, not being fools, they see the conduct of their political leaders in the matter as a cynical farce, and therefore they refuse to take seriously what their leaders obviously do not take seriously. Their children are required to learn Irish and often to learn through Irish in school, but hardly any proper Irish school text-books exist. They are required to have an Irish qualification for State or semi-State positions, while only a minority of Ministers ever speak an Irish sentence, or would be able to do so, or would stop to listen to you if you did so. They know that the Gaeltacht, officially regarded as the very tabernacle of the national soul, is falling to pieces; and that this disaster is met by the brazen absurdity of putting "Baile Phib" and "X Araild" on the destination boards of the Dublin buses. The result is a weary disgust; and, worse still, that it will now be extremely difficult to get Irish people to cooperate in a serious rescue effort for the language which is threatened with extinction. I say "rescue", not "restoration"; because I believe that the first aim should be to save the Gaeltacht; if we succeed in doing this, we can then discuss further objectives but to talk about general "restoration" while the very Gaeltacht itself is at death's door seems to me to be insane.

But the recent Fianna Fáil generation has no belief. Office for the sake of office is their heathen creed; and if a token genuflection every now and then towards the once-glorious ideals will satisfy a few thousand uncritical supporters who still hold to the old faith, then the smooth operators who run the Fianna Fáil machine are quite willing to go through the motions.

The Donegan/O'Dálaigh affair 1975

We have been witnessing in the last week the worst outbreak of hysterical humbug that I can remember.

Both the matter and the manner of the Minister for Defence's outburst at Columb Barracks were deplorable. But the hysteria has not been confined to condemning him for this. He is accused by the Opposition and by much of the press of having, by his assault on the President, undermined the President's office — quite a different thing. It is a confusion of a type more at home in the solemn dictatorships of Eastern Europe than in a free Western republic, and has no possible justification in our Constitution.

This is a democracy — the Constitution says so in Article 5 — and central to our conception of a democracy is the right to criticise, including criticise wrong-headedly, those in public authority. This together with the right to answer criticism, is essential for the formation of public opinion. The public are as much entitled to form an opinion, based on listening to criticism and replies to it, on how any holder of public office has discharged the duties of this office. There is not one word in the Constitution about the President being an exception to this rule or having any immunity from critical tongues; and no reason why there should be.

A President of Ireland has functions both formal and informal. His informal functions — entertaining distinguished foreign guests, for example — are of some national importance. If a President were to shirk this tedious job, or if he behaved discourteously to this guests, or if he were mean and tight-fisted in entertaining them, may we not say so? He represents the People in such a setting and is paid by the People to do so, and may the People or their public representatives not complain if they think he neglects this task?

In the case of his formal functions, where these allow him an independent decision in his own discretion about matters of major national importance, this point seems to me even cleared.

For instance, under Article 13.2.2. the President "may in his absolute discretion refuse to dissolve Dáil Éireann". Suppose a Taoiseach found himself in that situation and requested a dissolution (i.e. a General Election) and was refused and told to carry on as best he could. Is the Opposition to remain obsequiously silent, forbidden to criticise a decision robs them of a chance to gain office, on pain of being charged with "undermining the institutions of State"? They might swallow such a proposition in Prague or Budapest, but I for one refuse to do so here.

The position under Article 26 is comparable — the Article which empowers the President to make up his own mind on whether to submit a Bill to the Supreme Court to have it tested for constitutionality , thus necessarily involving a delay in the Bill's coming into force as an Act. If the President's decision annoys someone, may that annoyance not be expressed? In the present instance the annoyance seems to me irrational and its expression could not have been more unfortunate, but the idea that criticism, as such, of the President's action is a blow to the Constitution is a piece of pious bunk which I believe those guilty of it will come to look back on with embarrassment.

Where did we get this absurd notion about the President? One or two voices during the past week accounted for it with the argument that "the President cannot answer back" and so should be immune from criticism. Why can he not answer back? Who is stopping him from explaining his point of view, in a press or radio or television interview or otherwise? It is not prohibited by the Constitution and in fact President O'Dálaigh did answer back, in detail, in a letter to Mr Donegan which no law forbade him to give simultaneously to the papers.

I think I know where to look for the origin of this totem-pole conception of the Presidency. It lies in our malignant paddyism, our instinct to look over our shoulder at what the English do, or did; and out abject acceptance that a convention good enough for the Queen of England is more than good enough for us. And indeed anyone listening to Deputy Lynch and Deputy Haughey in the Dáil last Thursday in their sycophantic references to the President's Office could almost have thought themselves listening to a pair of Hibernian Crawfies.

In the conventions of the Presidency several straight importations from Britain have established themselves, such as the occasional efforts to make the President a gift of a sturgeon, and requiring him to send £50 tips to centenarians. I suppose we should only be thankful that we are not expected to celebrate a bogus birthday for him as well.

The parallels with Britain go further in this present row. Many people will remember the hysteria that was set up there in the 1950's when Lord Altrincham criticised aspects of the Queen's personality and behaviour; he was unmercifully pilloried, one national newspaper going so far as to print on its front page a picture of him as he appeared on television at a moment of gross distortion. All the current old guff about Mr Donegan supposedly "undermining our institutions" is from the same mould.

Surely a more appropriate model for our Presidency would be those of the other Republics with which we have historic links — the U.S. and France — where, needless to say, the Presidents take and answer criticism as a matter of course and must be amazed that such a ninny's conception of the Presidency should exist in the Irish Republic. I do not overlook the difference in scale between the power of those Presidents and that of our own, nor their much stronger party political involvement. But the principle is the same whenever the Irish President exercises independent powers which inevitably have a political resonance, however impartial he may try to be.

There is one particularly unlovely feature of the present hysteria. It is that those who defend Mr Donegan, or try to put what happened in some kind of rational constitutional or human perspective, are themselves attacked — again reflecting a frame of mind similar to the official attitude in countries where lawyers are afraid to appear for political defendants. Mr Lynch, in opening last Thursday's debate, chided the *Irish Independent* for not being in line with the other dailies on this issue, the Editor of the *Irish Times* criticised me in a leading article and on "7 Days" for having defended a friend and colleague in the Dáil, and called it "shameful" that I should have done the Whip's job I am paid to do.

I wish Paddy Donegan had quietly chipped at the screen of un-Irish humbug that surrounds the Presidency, instead of putting his boot through it. But I believe that one way or another his gaffe will make people think about the Presidency in terms of the hard realities of political life.

Arts Council Vote, Dáil, 14 June 1979

As I said a moment ago, we have so much to apologies for. We have committed so many atrocities in the field of urban conservation, or in our failure to conserve. We have committed so many massacres of things which were handed down to us by the generation which saw independence here in 1922. Much that was worth seeing and preserving and keeping up and still living in, and which was here in our parents' time has now been swept away, and not swept away in order to make room for what still seem to be only car parks or derelict sites growing nettles.

Our record in this respect is so abominable that we need not apologies for suggesting that there should be set up a Department with specific responsibility for maintaining what there remains to be maintained in public architecture. The existing authorities in that regard have only a half responsibility, because a planning authority such as a county council or even the appeals authority must have regard to very many different factors such as traffic congestion, the lack of provision of public services in the place in what the application is made and the likely impact on the population in terms of a further 1,000 office workers coming into the street every day. In addition, the authority must have regard to the aesthetic considerations — they must decide, for example, whether an old street should disappear — but we should have an authority concentrated absolutely on this area, one which has no other function but to ensure that not another brick is removed from a brick in a building in this State which, on the basis of aesthetic considerations , should not be removed.

It would make one sick to hear the guff from Ministers and sometimes indeed from Opposition Deputies about our priceless cultural heritage. What is left of our priceless cultural heritage? One need only walk around this city to have that question answered. Consider what is happening to Lower Mount Street, to Holles Street or to Ely Place. One need only walk 100 yards from here to find a row of six 18th-Century houses at the corner of Ely Place which have been derelict since I was a student 25 years ago. In the doorway of one of those houses the city council have been allowed to place a large type of container which perhaps controls traffic lights. This is a large functional object which is inconsistent with the continued use of the door as a door. It is an eyesore, but the people have become use to looking at something like that in the same way as one becomes accustomed to not having a lampshade, or to having a crack in a wall, in some part of one's house. Yet we talk about or priceless cultural heritage. People who live in such conditions should not talk about such matters until they succeed in providing some structure for defending our cultural heritage.

Irish Film Board Bill, Dáil, 15 October 1980

We find a great trumpet of rubbish in the Minister's speech when he says "providing a potent means of presenting this country, its heritage and its people to the world and of keeping Irish people in touch with their distinctive environment". I am afraid there was a time when Irish people used to lament that wherever they went in Europe or anywhere else in the world nobody had ever heard of them. They, with that awful little village sense of smallness of themselves, used to lament the fact that if they walked into a hotel in France, Greece or anywhere else and said they were from Ireland people thought they were saying they were from Holland. They thought this was a sign of our great backwardness, that some unlettered or halflettered innkeeper in one of those places had never heard of Ireland. That situation has changed since about 1969. Everybody has now heard of Ireland, but for the wrong reasons. It is my experience that, if one goes into one of the most remote parts of Europe and one is foolish enough to say where one is from, one can immediately kiss goodbye to half an hour of one's holiday because, while people do not make noises imitating a machine gun or a bomb, they will sit down and ask one to explain what is going on in our country or why we are murdering each other.

It has often seemed to me a sign of the degree to which not so much the country but Irish society and a lot of Irish people — and I suppose that must include the Minister and myself because I am not going to make exceptions — have failed to become completely adult in the way that the world outside understands, that so much of our dramatic art is introspective and self-absorbed and really so childish in a way. The people's idea of a play about Ireland is not just a play which is set in Ireland in which human beings, men and women, with the same feelings and troubles and preoccupations that men and women have everywhere else just happen to be present on this bit of land; it is a play in which the awful old agonies of the Irish historical heritage, or supposed historical heritage or myths about the Irish heritage are dragged out and are made the scene of individual anguish and are made the subject of individual anguish. I know there has been plenty of anguish in the country and I just cannot believe that people have not got every other passion here as well. I cannot believe that the passions, which the other film makers or writers or authors write about quite independently of their nationality and without dragging in France or Poland by the scruff of the neck, do not exist here and do not flourish here and proliferate exuberantly in this country as well as feelings which are tied up with mother Ireland. I just do not believe it. I am made to think it; a collective establishment effort has been made to make me suppose that ever since I was a school child, but I simply do not believe it and I am glad to see that in the theatre in recent years Irish playwrights have emerged who are capable of feeling strongly about a dramatic situation and putting it into a well-written, well-constructed and extremely fine play which is only accidentally sited in

Ireland in which perhaps the only moment in which the green pillar box shows its head is when a telephone call it made to the local exchange of when a policeman enters or something of that kind but in which otherwise the action is irrelevant to the nationality. That is a sign of approaching adulthood, thanks be to God. That is a sign that we are growing up at last. It is a sign that we are growing up at last when a playwright like Brian Friel or Hugh Leonard is able to succeed not only here but across the Atlantic and anywhere else English is understood.

Eighth Amendment of the Constitution, Dáil, 9 February 1983

I regard the way in which a delicate moral issue has been politicised as disgusting. I regard it as disgusting that the Leaders of the two biggest parties should have felt compelled — I will not say by any ill-intentioned threats; it would be quite unfair to any group to say they were compelled — in the heat of an approaching election to give undertakings about a matter so serious as amending our Constitution.

I regard it as disgusting that the Leader of the party opposite, at the outset of the November 1982 general election, should have sought to fight the election on that issue. At one of his opening press conferences he said he intended to make this an issue, and it was only when he discovered that neither the press, the people or his political opponents were interested in making it an issue , that he dropped it. He was willing to make it an issue — and let me say this — not because I believe he is particularly, or peculiarly, or uniquely interested in this matter, but purely because he thought it might be a means of embarrassing political opponents.

To make a political issue of a legislative proposal in regard to land ownership, or free school transport, or something of that kind, is fair game I suppose. To make a political issue of something like this is a disgusting operation. It would have been beneath our political leaders in the twenties, the thirties, the forties, the fifties and the sixties. In the day when John Costello on one side of the House and Eamon de Valera on the other side were in confrontation on a wide range of issues, I do not believe for a moment that either of those gentlemen would have stooped to indulging at political level in a debate on a matter of this kind.

It is a dreadful reflection on the degeneracy of the way in which politics is now conducted that, with all the other things we might have done with the Constitution, we now find ourselves debating this Bill today for no other reason than that a well-meaning — and I concede that 100 per cent — concerned and anguished lobby came forward within the visible octave of an election in 1981, and again in 1982, and extracted from party leaders what ultimately amounted to a commitment on an ultimatum to which there was a date attached, if you do not mind.

I have said — and I hope I do not need to say it again — that the right to speak the truth and not be misrepresented is, in its own humble way, as absolute as the right to life. I hope that truth in its own important way is as sacred as the right to life. The right to speak the truth as one sees it is entitled to respect ever from those who do not agree with your vision of it.

I have said — and I do not want to go on saying it — that I abominate the idea of abortion. I never would support the repeal of any legislation which forbids it. I deplore it, and anything useful I could do to prevent people from resorting to it I would do. I say that in one breath but, in another breath with which the first is perfectly consistent, I protest against the political mechanisms and the methods by which this legislation has reached us here today.

I could not but be nauseated as every decent person in the country was, no matter what their view on this amendment, at the sight of some Deputies whom I will not name because I do not particularly want to wound them, who went out of their way in the recent election campaigns to try to pretend that a vote given to Fine Gael was a vote for people who were unsound on an issue of this kind. I remember one western Deputy in particular, a man I never knew to make a speech inside or outside this House, except perhaps at his own church gate, who went public on this issue. He is a nice man to meet, and I have no personal quarrel with him. He never gave me any cause for offence; but it is a sad reflection on politics that a representative of the Irish people should put himself before the notice of the public for the purpose only of suggesting what he must have known as an untruth about his opponents in another party.

I realise it is pathetic I should be even talking like this. We are all supposed to be adult men and women and have a bit of backbone and strength of character. We should not require rules and conventions to protect us from ourselves but, apparently, we do; and there should be a convention that lobbies are not entertained, except to tea, after a given time from the moment an election comes into view. There is plenty of time between elections to make points of view known and plenty of time for a party or parties to consider those matters maturely and decide what is the right thing to do. It is regrettable that parties should be pressurised or forced, by fear of the unscrupulousness of their opponents or fear perhaps of the simple-mindedness of people who will misconstrue outside even without one's opponents encouraging them to do so, to take steps which they otherwise would not have done. If they had the backbone they had in the twenties, thirties and forties it would not be necessary to say all this but the backbone of political parties has been whittled away, softened by the way we organise our politics that I am protesting about this last while. Until we decide what this whole game is about, what our objectives are and organise ourselves accordingly we are going to get worse and worse and go further and faster downhill.

This whole discussion is rooted in concern for the unborn child. What I have finally to say bears with particular force on the behaviour of the people opposite during the past five years, though I am addressing my remarks to all sides of the House: I should like our concern for the unborn to surface in a more concrete and more palpable way than merely changing an Article in the Constitution. I should like us to show concern for the unborn by way of not asking them to pay debts we incur in order to make life easier for ourselves, which is what we have been doing with increasing irresponsibility and recklessness since 1972. Perhaps the oil crisis made our behaviour defensible to some extent until 1975 or 1976 but since 1977 the situation has gone beyond all control. The "current budget deficit" is not simply an economist's stick with which to beat politicians, or to argue about across the House. It is something which in clear brutal language means that we are enjoying today what the unborn will be deprived of tomorrow. that is a valid and graphic way of looking at what we have been doing in this State in the past five or six years.

Again, the blame for that must be attributed to cowardice and to the insane way in which politics here are structured whereby one on this side is reluctant to advocate taxation in case Deputies opposite will try to make one unpopular for that reason and whereby many of them are slow to advocate taxation because of their being afraid of our telling lies about them. Although what we are doing today is a pious exercise by way of protecting the unborn against abortion, we are not protecting them against poverty, joblessness and misery of all kinds in the course of their lives. That is also an aspect that deserves thought on both sides of the House.

Appointment of Ombudsman, Dáil, 25 October 1983

An Ombudsman seems to have come into the public consciousness as being to the administration what Santa Claus is to a child's weekly pocket money: he is something over and above the usual pocket money, someone who showers benefits regularly, even though one has not had to budget for them. In the public perception, an Ombudsman is a person who will produce results from the administration which the administration itself has been powerless to do and which even the intervention of Deputies and Senators going around the country have not been able to do.

I want to strike a note of compassion for Mr Mills, and I do not want him to become dejected early in his career, but I am afraid he will be unavoidably the necessary source of a good deal of disappointment in the months ahead. I do not know when it is planned to equip him with the apparatus of office, the familiar wall-to-wall carpeting, the stainless steel plate and the graphic artist designed annual report — I do not know when all these things will being to happen — but the very moment he will take up office he will get the standard stationery office baskets which will groan with post. In the post I get from my constituency — a lot of it comes from throughout the country as well — I have yet to be able to recognise the handwriting on many of the letters. There are chronic grievances from people and I do not mean that they are all nut cases, though that category is well represented among them, but there are people are simply cannot be persuaded that the law applying to their cases is a proper law. Of course it may not be a proper law and Mr Mills will have the heartbreaking experience of writing to people who genuinely feel that the world had done them down, to tell them there is nothing he can do to help them because he is not empowered to change the law — he cannot tear up the law in the way Santa Claus can make confetti of a child's budget in Christmas week. He will have to stay within the four corners of what the law makes possible in regard to social benefits or grants or amenities and so on. He will have to steel himself — I do not think any speaker has said this today — to being the conveyor of a lot of what will come across to the people as bad news. People are inclined to turn ungrateful quite quickly and Mr Mills may find his name being bandied in the correspondence columns in the next six months of 12 months as a by-word, a somebody who can do nothing.

I have said all that because it would have been cruel to allow Mr Mills, who is flesh and blood like the rest of us, to read the reports of today's proceedings here and then travel on the wave of euphoria that I would feel if I had so many ladies and gentlemen speak well of me for nearly three hours. I am just warning him that he is bound to cause a great deal of disappointment. He will have a great deal of drudgery and many angry telephone calls and abusive letters from people who will be saying, "Have we added you to the list of well-paid State servants who can do nothing about my grievance?"

To some extent Mr Mills is being asked to duplicate, by a quasi-administrative process, namely that of his own office for which no strict guidelines have so far emerged, what is already being done in the courts. It is true that one might have to start in the High Court, which is an expensive business, and I do not suggest that the widow who cannot understand why should not qualify for free fuel should be sent to the High Court to prove herself right. I have suggested before that we might have a simplified, very cheap administrative process of a judicial kind within the familiar dimensions of the legal system to apply to all kinds of humble administrative decisions like the refusal of the welfare officer to put someone on the free fuel list. That may be too humble a thing to take to the High Court but it may be the only grievance that an old lady has. We ought to have an ordinary legal process, without any bowing and scraping and wigs and gowns, built into the legal system which will get to the bottom of these things quickly and with the minimum building up of files.

What will Mr Mills be doing? He will be administering criteria which are essentially legal criteria which the courts already apply but he will not have quite the same preemptory engine which the court represents. People are inclined to complain about the old fashioned panoply and intimidating formality of a court. I think it is a damn good thing that to some extent courts should be intimidatory. My experience in practice is that witnesses are a bit over-awed by the look of a court and perhaps this is no harm. It makes them slower to tell the lie they would tell in any other kind of setting. When they do tell a lie it is easily detected by the sixth sense of even a dull advocate. I have no objection to that slightly over-awing dimension of a court, although I do not mean it to intimidate poor, simple people. On the contrary, it is the gougers and the scroungers who deserve to be intimidated. This is why it is a good system.

I want to make a suggestion to Mr Mills for saving himself from that fate, which will break his heart if it descends on him, and the heart of his staff also. He would give great example by spending as little as possible and ignoring the appeals which, I am sorry to say, came from my own benches, for unlimited State expenditure on offices, equipment and staff. There is no need for him to build an empire; but what he could do, with even a fairly skeleton apparatus to serve him, is to hold as many press conferences and explanation sessions as he can. They will be glad to have him on RTE programmes for a certain time and it is only thereafter that bodies like An Coimisiún Dumpála decide they have to spend £1,000 buying four square inches of space in the daily papers because no one is interested in having An Coimisiún Dumpála on "The Late Late Show", or whatever. For a while he will have instant access to publicity and he should use it. This is well meant advice. He should try to damp down expectations of what he can do and explain to the public that there are things he cannot do and that, if one or other office has repeatedly said that a claimant is not entitled to something and if Deputies and Senators and so on have also said so, there is no use coming to him because perhaps in only one case in 10,000 will he get a different answer.

Departments which do not provide adequate explanations for some step which they have taken, which is, in essence, as step of a kind they are perfectly entitled to take, could be challenged and asked to provide an adequate explanation. The simple instance here is the telephone billing system. I know that a Department would suffer a rush of blood to the head if they were personified here as having anything wrong with their billing system. However, the other day I received a letter from the man in charge of the money at a boy's school. It was an account of his differences with the Department of Posts and Telegraphs in regard to the telephone bill. He was so uneasy about the billing that he had a private monitoring system inserted into his own telephone to monitor the number of units consumed and the discrepancy disclosed between what the Department were trying to charge him at the end of the quarter and what his own monitor had recorded as 10,000 units. It is a big busy school and undoubtedly the telephone is heavily used. I think I observe some activity here on my right in writing down that figure. But I want to stress that I am not accusing the Department of being wrong. Perhaps the Department are right in sending him that bill and maybe his monitor is at fault; but it is wrong that he should have to go to the rounds of writing to a deputy, getting the Deputy to make photocopies of the correspondence, sending it in and even then perhaps not getting a satisfactory explanation. That case has nothing to do with the group called Telephone Protest who exist for no other reason than to extract some sense from the Department in regard to their billing processes. That is something the Ombudsman might go into and get his teeth into and not relinquish them until he has broken whatever is causing the trouble in that Department.

In my constituency — it may be that in Deputy Nealon's constituency there are other problems; I know they have telephones now — there is no single matter I get more post about then telephone grievances. I am referring to real grievances, such as complaints from people who have paid deposits on the undertaking that they will get something within a certain number of months. The Department have their £60, £80, whatever figure, but they do not have a telephone and there is no question of paying interest on the money held by the Department either. We all know that the telephone system here is the source of the most universal grievance and anything which would withdraw that from the Ombudsman's purview would take a lot of use from the Ombudsman as far as my constituency is concerned.

People talk as though people in Dublin suburbs do not have any right to call themselves part of the country, but they are Irish also. Many of them come from the constituencies represented by the two gentlemen behind me. They pay their taxes and are entitled to the same considerations as any other citizen. Their votes, funny enough, are just as good as the votes of Mayo or Sligo in putting a Government in or putting one out. They are entitled to expect that, when they are going to have to pay for the apparatus of an Ombudsman, that Ombudsman would not only be permitted but encouraged to put his nose, as a first priority, into the telephone service to see what is going on. We have poured millions into that system and we are entitled to know what has happened to it.

I am sorry if I have struck a different note to the other speakers and that I have gone on longer than I intended. I wish Mr Mills every possible success. I have had an opportunity to convey that wish to him earlier. I know I speak for every Member when I say that anything any of us can do in an unpartisan way to help or advise him will be willingly at his disposal. I should like to congratulate him on being the first holder of an office I hope will develop. He has a chance to make it into a most important and valuable office, an office which will be a friend to liberty and decent Government.

Interrogation of Bishops at the New Ireland Forum, 9 February 1984

There are two points I would like to put to the delegation. One of them is suggested by his use of the word "constituents". Every Dáil Deputy around this table — some of us have more than others — have constituents who are not Catholic. Why, in the context of a united Ireland should Protestant people north of the Border have more rights in this regard, more liberties which are reconcilable with their conscience than constituents of mine have here, or constituents of any other deputy around the table? How would that be a new Ireland? It seems to me to be one setting up a new set of grievances.

Dr. C. Daly: I think that the possible models for a new Ireland are very various. We have no model for a new Ireland presented to us as yet. Therefore, we are being asked to answer a question totally without context. It seems to me that the context of the question has to be precisely framed before the question itself becomes meaningful or possible to answer.

Deputy Kelly: The difficulty is that those of us on the political side of this conference have to deal with concrete realities and sections and sub-sections. That is how we have to see the thing, rather than in generalities. I would like to connect what has been just said with what you said a little while ago, and also with what was in the earlier submission: and that is that the law cannot go too far above the level of the ethos, that the gap between law and majority ethos cannot be too wide. Surely the perception that a legal system is going to mirror the majority ethos is the very thing that the Northern minority have complained about for 60 years. Admittedly, they have not had to complain about a legal system tailored denominationally. It has been tailored, if you like, ethnically and put into practice on a basis of ethnic discrimination. Nonetheless it could be said in defence of that system that it was one which corresponded with the majority ethos. In fact, one of their Prime Ministers did not put a tooth in it when he described it as "a Protestant State for a Protestant people". That has always seemed to us very offensive. Nonetheless, if we now adopt the idea that our laws cannot run too far ahead of the Catholic ethos, merely because a huge majority of our people are Catholic, are we not in danger of becoming a target for the same kind of criticism?

Dr. C. Daly: I was not talking of the ethos of the Catholic population of this country alone. We have tried to make it clear from the very beginning that there are two traditions, two communities, and pluralism should surely mean that each one of them would be recognised in its diversity.

Deputy Kelly: But, with respect that is a generality that all of us could sign, but when it comes to putting it into the practice of an statute what are we to do? I think the delegation would accept that no politician around this table sees divorce as an easy question. Many of us, as individuals, would have great difficulty in making our minds up about it, quite apart from religious allegiance; but we are the ones stuck with the responsibility of leading the people, first of all, to accept a change — if we decided to do that — in the Constitution which at the moment outlaws divorce; and then to put our heads together and try to devise the appropriate criteria for creating a divorce jurisdiction because it will not spring, fully created, out of the ground. There never was such a thing here. We, therefore, have to work with concrete elements and not with generalities; and while we respect and share the generality that one has to accommodate minorities, how is that going to look in the black and white of the statute? Are we going to have a divorce jurisdiction, which no Catholic will be compelled to resort to, naturally, or are we not? We naturally do not take, and as legislators cannot seek, instructions from any Church on that; but we would be glad to have all views on it, and we are finding, I think, some difficulty in extracting a clear answer on a point of this kind.

Dr O'Mahony: I am sure that at this point in time there is an absolutely clear answer except to say that as legislators one must take into account all the considerations — (1) the minority rights, the fact that there are people here in the south who believe that in certain circumstances they have a right to divorce; (2) obviously one has to take into account the effect on the North of Ireland, even though we should not be making a plea to the North; and (3) one has to take into account the social consequences of divorce legislation and also, I would believe, to seriously consider alternative ways of dealing with marital breakdown. In other words, you have to take all these things into consideration and decide what is in the overall interest then for the good of our people, for the good of our country, for peace, for reconciliation and so on. I do not think one could expect us to answer that question.

Mrs McAleese: I think it may be slightly unfair, in one sense, although I understand perfectly the legitimacy of the question, to expect the Church to give you an answer to a dilemma that clearly you as legislators have. We have expressed the point , time and again, that you have a job to do and it is entirely up to yourselves to do it. The church wants no hand or part in making the decision. It is your decision. The only right the Church reserves is like any group in a democracy the freedom to have its say on the issue if the issue happens to be divorce and to have that taken into the balance. At the end of the day it is up to you how you weight that view.

Deputy Kelly: I hope I have not given the impression — I tried to give the opposite impression — that whoever governs this country is going to seek authority from anybody for doing their duty as they see it. I am glad we established a consensus about this across both sides of the conference; but I would like to put to the delegation a perception which was articulated by Bishop Cathal Daly earlier today when he said it was a matter of Christian duty to respect the conscience of others. I would like to have the delegation's view on how, in practice, we are going to see the Church behave where a voter, asked perhaps to vote on a constitutional amendment on divorce, will be looking for guidance as to how he is to reconcile his duty to be fair to minorities who disagree with him — or perhaps even fair to some Catholic neighbour of his who may agree with him, but who is desperate to get out of an impossible marriage — to be fair to these people while, at the same time, respecting the teaching of his own church. that is a ticklish question and I would be glad to have some hint as to how the Church would see itself dealing with it.

Mr. C. Daly: I know you will argue that there is a lot of experience of divorce legislation and its implications and its consequences right around the world so I should have though that there is a very good case to be made for feeling that this need not be the way, may not be the best way, and that, in fact, on grounds of compassion alone one could feel compassion for those whose marriages would be threatened and the children, whose future would be jeopardised, by certain kinds of legislation. Surely there is experientially a built-in multiplier in divorce legislation which, however, restricted it may wish to be at the beginning, becomes impossible to contain until you arrive, as in every legislation virtually in the western world at the present time, at the simple no fault divorce situation. Nobody foresaw that when it started. Nobody wanted that when it started but people are caught on a kind of moving staircase that carries them far beyond where they wanted to go, by the sheer momentum built into the legislation itself. It has not been possible to maintain restrictions. It is a very complex issue and it is easy to think that divorce is the only way. What we are pleading is that other ways have not been looked at and that people should be be left with any illusions about the consequences which not merely may, but from the experience of other countries, will follow from divorce legislation.

Deputy Kelly: I do not want to go back over ground we have covered but I think both Bishop O'Mahony and Professor McAleese admitted, very fairly, a few minutes ago that the only visible alternative, namely an up-dated and generously extended nullity jurisdiction, would not help more than a small fraction of the people whose marriages are on the rocks. So, I think that answer alone will not get us a great deal further. Could I ask a slightly different question? In order to have such a thing as a divorce jurisdiction here, there would have to be two stages. The first stage would be the removal, by referendum — it cannot be done otherwise — of the constitutional bar inhibiting the passage of any law providing for the dissolution of marriage. A quite separate second stage, which might be separated from the first by years, would be the construction of an appropriate divorce process, the elaboration of appropriate criteria and so on. A great deal of responsible thought and agonizing reflection would have to go into this, and that would really be the important stage. Could I ask whether we can take it for granted that the Church would at least not throw its weight into the scale if there were a move to carry through the first stage, in other words, to bring the Constitution of this country back to what it was in the years 1922 to 1937 when there was no constitutional bar on such an enactment, and years in which it can scarcely be argued the country was less Christian than it is now?

Dr. C. Daly: I am afraid, with every great respect, I would feel that that is a political question which is not appropriate for us to answer.

Deputy Kelly:It is not a political question, but I do agree that it is probably the first time since St. Patrick arrived that the representatives of the Hierarchy were asked to think on their feet.

Dr. E. Daly: May I just say that there have been bishops in this Castle before, facing tribunals? Bishops have their decisions to make too. Difficult decisions, unpopular decisions. They have to make them in conscience. they have to make them on the basis of long discussion and then stand by those decisions which they believe in conscience to be true. Anybody, in any position of responsibility or authority, has to make difficult decisions from time to time and live with those decisions. Admittedly, bishops perhaps have the advantage that they do not have to face an electorate every few years but at the same time anyone in authority must make difficult decisions and suffer the pain of making them. All of us have our own particular views. Our views may be diverse, but I think we must have the courage to take decisions and make decisions and in political situations particularly to go to the electorate and put the case as strongly and as sincerely as one can and then ultimately it is the electorate who make the decision.

Dr. C. Daly: I certainly would not wish to have been thought to cop out of the question by saying that this is a political judgment. I sincerely feel that the Church should be expected to say whether there should or should not be a constitutional amendment on abortion, I mean divorce.

Deputy Kelly: Everyone here will recognise that perhaps it is unfair to press you too hard on a point of this kind, but might we hope that that is the equivalent of saying that the Church would maintain absolute neutrality on this question should it arise?

Dr. C. Daly: The Church will face that situation, as it has tried to face other difficult situations, when it is confronted with it but it is legislators who have to confront us with that situation. That is their responsibility, that is their right and that is their duty. Some may have thought that my slip earlier was a Freudian slip. It was a slip of the tongue but there is nothing Freudian about it as far as I am aware, although I have not been psychoanalysed. In fact, we did not give any guidance to our people about the amendment which people have in mind until a specific proposal was formulated by Government and proposed to the people by the Oireachtas. That will be our position with regard to any other proposed constitutional amendment. It is, first of all, the duty of the Oireachtas to formulate a specific proposal for constitutional amendment and then, if this has moral implications, if this has consequences, as we see it, for the moral quality of life in society then, as pastors, we would express our view but we would respect the consciences both of legislators and of the electorate in doing so.

Dr O'Mahony: It is good to hear you speak because it gives us some insight into your own particular concerns and anxieties.

Deputy Kelly: Would the point of view which Bishop Cathal Daly expressed not be more applicable to the second stage of a possible process, if we ever inaugurate such a process, namely to the stage of constructing a divorce process? The first stage, namely removing the relevant section from the Constitution, would be merely bringing our basic law back to the stage at which it was when William T. Cosgrave and Eamon de Valera were successively Presidents of the Executive Council in the early days of this State. There would be no other strings to it. There would be no question of formulating a proposal. The proposal, if it were there at all, would be a purely negative one of deleting something which is there.

Dr. C. Daly. Certainly, I do not wish to be in any situation where I would seem to be saying that this or that period of the constitutional history of Ireland was preferable. I am sure you are not suggesting that. I just have to reiterate what I said before. It is the function of both Houses of the Oireachtas to formulate a proposal for constitutional amendment and when this is formulated we have to take our moral and pastoral decisions in respect of it and give the moral guidance which our people look to us to receive on it with full respect for their consciences and with full realisation that our pastoral guidance is not the only criterion and that ours are not the only values used and principles that have to be respected in the voting.

Family Planning Bill, Dáil, 19 February 1985

I was quoted in a newspaper recently as saying something at a Fine Gael party meeting which I did not bother to contradict, partly because meetings are supposed to be in private and partly because it was a trivial thing anyway. I got so many people writing to me saying that they understood I had said this and that they heartily agreed with it, that I want to explain what I would have meant had I said it. I was reported as saying that there was no public demand for this Bill. There is a certain amount of truth it that. I have heard of no demand for anything of the kind but the reason why there is a no strong public demand for it is that the present law is a farce and it is disobeyed wholesale. People can do without the law one way or the other in this area. A former student of mine wrote to the paper the other say to contradict what he had seen attributed to me as an opinion though in fact I had never said it and he said that all that Deputy Kelly need to do was stroll 500 yards from his office to find a huge demand which is actually being supplied. that demand is supplied so far as I am aware in defiance of the law. That is what I mean by an unworkable law — one which the State does not mean to police and cannot police. The State does not give a damn whether is will ever be policed but it enables it to sit smugly back with its hands folded over its stomach and say "We have done our duty by the youth of this Country". That is the kind of law we had here five years ago and if the Minister did nothing else but show that up I would support him for it.

Though it has not been emphasised in the House, until 1935 we had no such law on our Statute Book; and in the childhood of Deputy Oliver Flanagan and even in the lifetime of Deputy O'Hanlon, it was no offence in Mountmellick or in Carrickmacross to import contraceptive devices for one's own use or for sale to others, whatever the person's marital status. That is an amazing thing. "We never knew that", people will be saying. "That is a new one on us. I thought we always had a strict law about this".

We had not. We did not have a strict law about these things until 1935, and that law skulked through the House, almost because Deputies were afraid to say anything in favour or against it in case they might have to use a word which was unacceptable according to the standards of the time. All we are doing — we are not even doing that because up to then the thing was subject to almost no regulation at all except that advertising contraceptives was prohibited by the 1929 Censorship Act — is bringing the law back part of the way to what it was when the older generation now were first frisking around the Irish Free State.

I would ask if it is therefore the case that we should picture the Irish free State in the years before 1935 as a scene of the horrors Deputy Flanagan portrayed here the other day, and likely to emerge if the Bill becomes law. Was the Irish Free State the scene of licentiousness as gross as we have been led to apprehend? Of course, I will be told that is a disingenuous and rhetorical question because we all know the world has changed and that Ireland has changed since 1935.

Indeed it has, but that has a lesson for us because if Ireland has changed since 1935 it has done so in spite of the most complete zareba, in spite of a Maginot Line of the most defensive legislation ever to appear in Western Europe, with the possible exception of Portugal or Spain. One could lump in with the whole of North Europe a large part of the rest of the world. Ireland has changed in spite of the laws against contraception and on censorship. The latter were so ludicrous in their operation that even Fianna Fáil finally found the courage to amend them. Ireland has changed despite the constitutional prohibition on divorce.

I do not need to labour the point that Ireland was not a hotbed of licentiousness before the 1935 Criminal Law (Amendment) Act closed the floodgates. We all know that is not the case and if it looks like becoming the case now it is because all that has taken place despite all the ingenuity of legislation to stop it. I do not want to be taken as avoiding a point that could be made against me at this juncture. Although we are not doing so in this Bill, we might appear to be running ahead, to be winching down the gates a little faster than the flood is building up on the outside.

270

I should like to echo something which my former colleague, Mr Richie Ryan said yesterday — the suggestion made in recent weeks that the Catholic bishops are somehow wrong in speaking their minds on this point, or even in concerting an orchestrated sequence of pronouncements is a suggestion which never should he heard in a democratic State. The bishops, I think, have the wrong end of the stick in assuming that the State should legislate by means of the criminal law in this area. I think they are wrong about that. But they are absolutely entitled to speak their minds. I cannot understand how anyone can begrudge a Catholic bishop something he would not begrudge to a Protestant bishop, would not begrudge to a communist, would not begrudge to a newspaper editor, would not begrudge to anyone else in the country. I cannot understand that.

I disagree with them about this, I think they have got the wrong end of the stick. I think — as I shall hint in a moment — they are imprudent in taking the line they have taken if it is not an impertinence for me to offer a view like that. But their right to do all this is absolutely clear. The question whether it is sensible for them to have entered into this controversy in the form and with the intensity that they have is a separate question. It is not really a political question, I suppose, but let me just say a word about it. I do not think that the Catholic church in this country is the same organisation that it was when I was a student when the mother and child scheme was being debated and even later when the Fethard-on-Sea boycott was taking place and things like that were happening. It is an organisation which undoubtedly commands a huge and reverential following in this country. Perhaps that is because the people can see no other organ in the State for which they feel the faintest regard or respect. It is easy to lame them for taking what bishops say seriously when they have so little reason to take seriously much of what they hear in here? But their standing no longer depends on authority in the old fashioned sense. It no longer depends on belting people with croziers. It may once upon a time have depended on that.

Once upon a time it was the case that it was dangerous for a politician to step too far out of line with what the Catholic Church required. Those days have utterly passed away. I know there may be corners of the country where that is not apparent. I will not expand on this but there are corners of the country in which it is not apparent that the institutional authority, in the hardest sense of the word, of the Church has not yet dissolved. However, I believe, broadly speaking, that it has dissolved and it does not require any courage to dissent from the bishops these days and no courage to attack them. It may require a lot of courage to defend them, and at times they require defence. Their position with the people no longer depends on the crozier or authority, still less on anything like spiritual tyranny; it depends on the respect and the affection which the Church here has earned over the years, the decades and the centuries.

If I may voice the respectful view of a very low grade Catholic, I think they would be much wiser to depend on that affection and respect for their pastoral effects rather than on what might be interpreted as the exercise of authority.

The Irish Language, Dáil, 26 June 1985

I heard Deputy Noonan talking about our unique heritage and our unique cultural heritage and our unique Irish language. I do not mean to point at him in particular but he was the person who mentioned it. In my years in the House I rarely heard him open his mouth in any language but never in Irish. I do not know what his grip of the thing is or how much interest he has in it. I am willing to suppose he has not less then anybody else but that is not a lot. What is a Dutch man to make of his complaint that Irish has not been made one of the Community's official languages? The Dutchman, if he is the Dutchman I have met, will say: "Where is it in your personal scale of priorities? Do you speak it yourself? Say a few words for us in Irish that will not just be the Our Father or the Apostles Creed that you have learned off in school. Translate the conversation we had about the abominable meal we had in the railway station in Milan into Irish off the top of your head like a good man until I hear what the thing sounds like." I do not believe that he, like a lot of other Members, would be glad to be asked such a thing. Why then does he expect the Dutchman or a Greek to take seriously pleas of that kind? It would not have crossed my mind to mention that, were it not for the fact that I heard this bit of 1927ish flim-flammery float across the House from a man who must have heard it when he was a small child from Dev who at least believed this stuff.

Dev at least believed what he was saying and went to some lengths to practise it, but they did not extend to forcing his followers to do so. He was willing to put up with the most perfunctory observance from them. As I said, he believed what he said and went to some length to practise it, and it rubbed off on the young Deputy Noonan. I can see him in his short trousers, with the wind whistling across the square of Newcastle West listening to Dev speaking from the back of a lorry and saying to himself that if he wanted to get on in politics he would occasionally have to take off his cap to the Irish language and refer to its status as a unique, cultural asset and inheritance.

That is the kind of talk no one outside these shores can understand because it does not come across as serious talk. The stranger judges us by what we do. What he sees when he comes to Ireland on holiday or on a business trip is the cultural situation. I mean "cultural" in a general sense and not just the language we speak but the way we live which, to his eyes, is barely distinguishable from what happens in England. There are the same boring rows of boring semi-detached houses, the same interests, the same sports, the same slang and jargon. We use expressions like "no way" and "hopefully", which nobody used 15 years ago, because the English do. He will see the same type of clothes, the same manners, the same places to go on holiday, the same standards of everything.

Where is this priceless heritage? I mention this only as an example of the awful isolation which our geographical situation forces on us. The sooner we get integrated in Europe and send streams and cycles of our young people to live there the better. Eventually some of them will come back bringing with them skills and experience and, above all, a scale of values, a tariff of the importance of things, not necessarily taking over holus bolus from a German or a Greek, but a tariff which will at least represent a modification of this peculiar Irish mentality in which sanctimonious hypocrisy, unreality, the willingness to know one thing but to believe, or pretend to believe, are such significant parts. That form of mentality works detrimentally to us in industry, agriculture, industrial relations and in politics.

The more we can integrate with people who will give us a standard to measure our own way of doing things, which will enable us to see when we are talking seafóid, which will enable us to understand that we have been preaching something that is not a viable proposition, that will provide some standard by which we can measure our own beliefs, and perhaps modify them, the more we will benefit from it intellectually and even spiritually but certainly industrially, commercially, agriculturally and politically.

Labour Party proposals for a divorce referendum, Dublin, 8 November 1985

I believe a referendum held now would lead to a defeat as crushing as that suffered in 1968 by Mr Lynch's Government in the second PR Referendum.

This defeat, moreover, would be sustained by a government just entering a general election period. We would be fighting that election with a divided and demoralised organisation, and with a serious reverse fresh in the public memory.

Needless to say, Fianna Fáil know all this perfectly well, and must be hugging themselves with the hope that the Government will adopt the Labour proposal. Surely the Labour Party is not so tired of life as to want to throw away the chance of being still on the Government benches after the next election.

There is another consideration which I presume ought to count heavily with people who favour the introduction of a divorce jurisdiction. Public opinion on this matter is clearly changing; and it may easily be that, in a few more years, it will show a clear and constant majority in support of a change in our Law. But a solid defeat now of a referendum on Article 41 would probably mean that no Government would be anxious to put the matter to the test again for a far longer period. Surely the proponents of change must see that everything can be gained by waiting, and possibly a great deal lost by not doing so.

Finally, there is the question of the huge extra burden on Government and Dáil time, the hugh extra distraction from other urgent business, which a divorce referendum must involve (as the horrible abortion referendum did in fact involve). The Bill must be debated and passed in both Houses, and Fianna Fáil can be counted on to spin out this process to its maximum length.

Probably it could not reach the people earlier than next summer; and in the meanwhile every Government Minister and Deputy will be knee-deep in cantankerous circular, petitions, urgings, warnings, political threats, and lobbies of all degrees of malignance and unscrupulousness from both sides. There are times when this cannot be avoided and should not be shirked; but the last 18 months before a general election is not the moment to deliberately invite such a thing.

The effect of this distraction on the Government itself could be disastrous. In fact this Government can point to several substantial achievements — victory over inflation, a good trade balance, large falls in interest rates which have benefited every mortgaged householder as well as industry — and can, if it keeps its mind on its main job, improve on those achievements over the next year and a half so as to reverse the trend of the current opinion polls and win the election. That it could even think of turning aside at this juncture and engaging in a year-long cat-fight about divorce is enough to make its friends despair.

Tenth Amendment of the Constitution (Divorce), Dáil, 15 May 1986

Laying down the law on moral issues or on issues of a social kind which are conditioned by moral considerations is peculiarly suspect and to many people peculiarly hateful in a politician. Politicians are a hissing and a byword to many people, wrongly so, no doubt. Perhaps the public do not understand the motives which drive people into it, the bug which gets into them, or the psychological deficiencies which force them to try to make up in this arena what they lack in others. They may not have enough sympathy. All they see are a lot of fat cats or people who ride along enjoying a high profile and getting a lot of coverage and publicity on what they think is a lot of unearned money. That is undoubtedly a false and unfair criticism. I would say that no matter who was in office. If there were a crowd of Marxists or Balubas in office and forced to go through the hoops which everybody here on both sides has to go through every week of the year, I would still say it.

Rightly or wrongly, the public perception and regard for politicians are not very high. The last straw to the ordinary member of the public is to be pontificated to about his marriage, or about how he should run his sexual existence, by a crowd of fellows who do not mind robbing the State blind, because that is how he sees it, who do not mind running us into war if they could, because that is how he sees it, who makes excuses for murderers, because that is how he sees it, who palliate crimes for which he would be sent to prison a hundred times over, because that is how many citizens see it.

The last straw to him is to be lectured, to be whinged and whined at by someone in this House about how he should run his marriage, about whether he should control fertility by an artificial or mechanical means, whether he should as I heard — I do not think it would be right to name him but anybody who looks back over the record will recall him — a Fianna Fáil frontbencher who spoke here today say when we were debating one of the very minimal extensions of the contraception law in 1979, resort to a urine dipstick as a means of calculating the fertile cycle of a woman in matrimony. Matrimony, relations between man and a woman. He really thought we might reach the day when technology would allow us to decide matters of this kind and run a marriage with a urine dipstick.

That stinks to ordinary people. Anyone expressing his or her views here on a matter like this is running the risk of incurring the contempt of many of the people who elected them. No one here should be arrogant or positive about matters of this kind. I have said how I am going to vote in my own ballot box even if I am not required to vote here, but I am not going to campaign to get anyone else to do so. I feel too unsure about what I am going to do. I hope I am not making a mistake and I hope I am not doing more harm than good. I will not ask anybody else to vote that way, nor will I knock on doors, nor will I ballyrag or arm-twist anybody to follow my example. I feel I am discharging my duty, and it is a hell of a sight more than some Deputies in this House will have done by the time the debate ends, by saying what I propose to do.

I agree with Deputy Cowen and some other Deputies on both sides who spoke in pleading that the next six weeks should not be an acrimonious period. I must say that one of the reasons why I was very much against holding this at all on this side of the election was that I dreaded the stinking cat-fight which we had here in 1983 on the abortion referendum. I felt we were going to get a repetition of that. I must frankly tell the House I am agreeably surprised that that has not turned out to be the case.

In that connection I want to say one other thing in regard to lobbying and sending of post and circulars and letters threatening electorate disaster unless I vote this way of that way. We all have to live dangerously or if we do not, we are not earning our keep. If anyone is not willing to say what he thinks in here, he is not earning his salary. We have to live dangerously and take the risk of electoral disfavour by this or that route. I know that many people who have voted for me are going to vote "no" in this referendum. I am sorry to offend them and I hope I will not lose their support. I have to take the risk that I will.

Let us look back at the history of the State. the former Constitution — and I am a great admirer of it — was a secular Constitution. Not alone was religion not mentioned in it apart from a brief reference to everybody's freedom of worship but God was not mentioned in it anywhere. There was a brief invocation in the Act to which the Constitution was scheduled but the Constitution was entirely secular. It contained the specific prohibition on retroactive penal sanctions but it did not contain a prohibition on the enactment of divorce legislation. Did morality fall to pieces under William Cosgrave who was President of the Executive Council or Taoiseach for the first ten years of the State or under Eamon de Valera who was Taoiseach during the remaining five years of that Constitution's existence? Did we have the bacchanalia that I have heard being predicted by Deputies on both sides at a time when the Constitution contained no prohibition of any kind on the enactment of this kind of legislation? I am not going to make pretences about the period 1922-37. There was no divorce legislation enacted. At that time the only way one could have dissolved a marriage was by an Act of the Oireachtas. In Ireland there never had been a divorce jurisdiction. Under British rule there never was a divorce jurisdiction here under which the courts could dissolve a marriage. The early Irish, under the Brehon laws, had divorce very freely available — it was freely available to both sexes and there were a large number of humane grounds on which a wife was empowered to free herself from her husband. I will not entertain the House by reciting the instances.

Many people, particularly women, get married in their early twenties. They are taking an awful risk as well as throwing away options in life which they may later regret not having exercised. Suppose a person aged 20 or 21 falls in love and marries, the strong statistical likelihood is that they will be in love two or three further times in their life with a lot of people. What will they do then? The Church's answer is that they will have to put up with it. it is easy to say that, but the flesh is very weak. It is not just the flesh because there are dimensions in the attractions of the sexes which far transcend the carnal.

Early adulthood should be a period of liberty, gathering experience and understanding oneself. One's heart must be twisted if one refuses to help those who marry in their twenties and find that they know themselves better later on and cannot make out with their partner. The earlier in their twenties they marry the truer that is. I cannot vote against this. I have always felt strongly on this subject. I do not want to use a word which may seem offensive to others who think otherwise, but it is terribly harsh to say to people of 22 or 23 years of age and who find that they have made a mistake; "That is it. You had your chance.You must stay in this human situation which you made for yourself, immature though your judgement may have been, and little though your knowledge of yourself may have been, for the rest of your life, be it 60 or 70 years." It may be perfect heroic morality, but I cannot bring myself to believe the State should adopt that attitude.

Since the State has done nothing about nullity the only course open to me is not to vote against this proposal but to support it with the strong misgivings which I have outlined. I heard Deputies Flanagan, Glenn and Flynn in the course of their contributions yesterday predict that it would be defeated. If it is, I beg this Government or whatever other Government may be in power to do something quickly about nullity by extending the criteria for it along the lines I have suggested. This could be done within the Constitution without going to the people.

The last theme I wish to embark on is the performance of the Opposition in regard to this issue. I went into the Members' Bar yesterday evening. When I got to the door I could hear happy shouts of laughter. I thought perhaps there was an old Marx Brothers movie on television. I was not far wrong. It was Deputy Brian Lenihan explaining to the people of Ireland his party's position and explaining why his Leader was not here to make the case for himself. The laughter was as cheerfully joined in by a couple of his own colleagues in the bar as by the rest of us. I understand Deputy Haughey's position all too well. He has to keep in with everyone. I recognise the ethos of his party. It was trenchantly put by the man who was then Fianna Fáil Chief Whip, Deputy Ahern. I do not know if he realised he was being reported at a meeting for Fianna Fáil women. In *The Irish Times* there is a headline: Bertie Tells FF Women Sell Your Soul. I shall read two paragraphs from the article:

> The Flurry Knox of Irish politics laid it on the line. Keep your balance. Keep well in with everybody. Say hello to your local TDs and Councillors even if you hate them and you might get nominated at your local convention.

Further on he says:

> You have to walk the line. Take the middle ground. You may hate your TDs but you must do what is required. We all have to swallow humble pie and I have been doing it for years. But if you keep at it —
> — this unremitting diet of humble pie —
> — you can break through and get selected at the convention. If you do it the other way —
> — in other words speak your mind like a free citizen of a Republic —
> you haven't a chance.

That is Deputy Ahern's opinion. He did not take it from the wind. It is the political ethos in which he was brought up. If getting there means selling your soul a little bit, well there is not a profession in the world where you do not have to change your principles. If you play it right and keep your balance you can get to the convention. What an ambition — to submerge and extinguish every feeling and every instinct of truth and straightness if necessary. For what? To save your soul? No, to get through the convention. That is the priority in the party he belongs to. I understand his Leader accepts that priority. He has to keep in with all kinds of people if he is to sit on this side of the House again. He has to keep in with the Ballyscullion vote on the one hand and the Lower Leeson Street vote on the other which by all accounts is strongly represented in his party. It is not easy to do that on this issue.

It is easy for the Taoiseach to do the right thing. There are Deputies on the far side of the House, whose sincerity I do not question, who have said what they will do. The Taoiseach is supported by many people who belong to the Ballyscullion side of the world as well. I take it for granted he understands that he will be switching off a certain number of these by introducing this legislation. However, he is doing it because he believes it is right. That is not the ethos which was offered to the Fianna Fáil women in the Gresham Hotel by Deputy Ahern, presumably with the imprimatur of his Leader. He must keep in with both Lower Leeson Street and Ballyscullion. It is true the Ballyscullion people are dropping off the perch with the passage of years and the Lower Leeson Street people are becoming more numerous. Deputy Haughey would have looked around him at the Fianna Fáil Ard Fheis and would have seen enough gleaming pates among his audience to tell him that there was a bit of life left in Ballyscullion yet.

I sympathise with his position. He is caught between his hillbillies and *Hot Press*. The cute thing for him to do is to lie low like Brer Fox. We suffered for a long time from absentee landlords, but we are now suffering from an absentee warlord — a man who likes being photographed from about 45 angles below so that the cock of the chin will be sufficient, caught in a pose which I thought went out of fashion in 1945 but which has been revived in this context at least. He likes being photographed at Bodenstown and in striking stances at the Forum. I am singling him out only because he has singled himself out as the Leader of a party. No one asked him to be that. I suppose he put himself forward, but we need not go into that. If any other member of that party had acted in the same way I would say the same thing. That is not the conduct of a leader.

It was stated in *The Irish Times* that the Fianna Fáil Leader was having meaningful dialogue in Strasbourg. I presume it is in relation to intervention matters and pollution. He refused to say what his personal view was on the campaign to introduce divorce.He said his opinion was not relevant to this matter. Since when have we had this modesty — which would have suffered to have St. Francis of Assisi canonised — from the Leader of Fianna Fáil? Since when have we had this modesty from the Leader of Fianna Fáil? Since when has he been slow to offer an opinion if he thought that he would get Ballyscullion and Lower Leeson Street both behind it?

Suppose we had a referendum here, for example, to delete Article 3 from the Constitution — another of the mementos which Mr. de Valera has left us with and which will, I suppose, take a little while longer to do away with — would he be as diffident about expressing an opinion on that? Can we suppose that if that were promoted here by this Government — and they would have very good, substantial reasons connected with Northern affairs for doing so — he would be in Strasbourg that week and would he keep away from that issue on the grounds that his view is not relevant? Which of his views are relevant? Would be make a list of the ones which are relevant for the people and of the ones which are not relevant and which he will allow us to overlook and ignore? He is very fond of awarding himself certificates for being mature and responsible when somebody takes him up on something he has said. He says: "No; that was a mature and responsible statement of mine."

I would like to hear his mature and responsible opinions on this matter. Maybe he will turn up here — I know there are a few more hours left in the debate, and possibly he will, and I suppose I will then feel abashed at having dined richly off his absence. But if he does show up here and speak, I hope we will hear from him something more than we heard from his young colleague, Deputy Cowen, last night who delivered an excellently put together but intensely professorial treatment of the subject of divorce, and what would happen in this jurisdiction if it ever came in. He left us as wise as when he started in regard to how he personally is going to vote. I hope if Deputy Haughey does turn up, if his urgent duties contracted six weeks ago to Europeans permit him, he will actually tell us what he himself proposes to do.

I have nothing but contempt for that kind of attitude on the part of a political party, pretending to be neutral. That is the public official stance, although it is a contemptible stance from an alternative Government on a matter of this kind. As far as I can make out from their performance in here, their Deputies are all around the country visibly campaigning against this thing because they calculate that, by declaring themselves officially neutral, they will not lose much face if it is passed. But by busily working against it, if it is defeated, they can call on the Taoiseach to acknowledge that he has made a mistake so serious as to warrant his removal from office and an instant election. Those are only two sides of their position. If it was possible to take more than two sides, and of course it is but I do not want to hold the House up by expanding on it, they would take up as many as there were.It is not a case just of Tadhgín, na dá thaobh, it is a case of Seamaisín na sé taobh, and Seáinín na seacht dtaobh, and sleeveen gach uile thaobh. When I see that kind of thing in a party which once upon a time stood for something, whether it was right or wrong, I am reminded of the words from what Mr Paisley would call the Good Book: "Since thou art neither hot nor cold, I will spit thee forth from my mouth".

Education Vote, Dáil, 13 June 1986

I am in no way trying to decry the teaching of French, which is a well established and important part of our curriculum, but I urge the Minister to take this problem by the throat and settle it once and for all. I am thoroughly tired of hearing each year in this House the perfunctory few words about foreign language teaching but nothing ever seems to happen. Although CII in their anxiety to promote an interest in German almost make it appear to be the case, it is not the case that this is the only problem on the language front. There are immense markets opening up in the world with teeming, exploding populations — not falling populations as in the case of Germany — and with exploding purchasing power, particularly in the Far East. In China they cannot even count the millions of inhabitants. The astronomical population of that country will have trebled their individual purchasing power by the end of the century, but as far as I know not one student in this country is learning Chinese. There are a few people tucked away in some rookery in Trinity or in UCD learning oriental languages but they are doing that more for artistic, literary or purely cultural reasons than for economic reasons. I hope I do not need to tell anyone I do not decry that, but we need to get to grips with the problems that face Irish industry, and particularly when we have a huge unemployed population, with neither side in this House having the faintest clue of how to find jobs for them.

I do not want to get into a political discussion about this. Everyone here knows that if the sides were to change, as Deputy O'Rourke delicately suggested they might sooner or later, the opposite side of the House would be just as much stuck with a six figure unemployment rate as we would. No doubt throwing money at the problem for a few years might knock a few thousand off the unemployment lists, as Dr O'Donoghue did in 1977 and 1978, but it leads to a worse problem later on. On one knows how to solve this problem in the short term but there is one way to solve it, namely, by increasing Irish products, exports and markets. However, it cannot be done by going around the world and expecting everyone else to learn English in order to buy our products. We are not serious about the problem if we imagine that will happen.

I wish to make a concrete suggestion, namely, that the discussions mentioned by the Minister as taking place in an informal committee in regard to the future of Carysfort College should be brought to a conclusion quickly by a firm decision to create on the Carysfort campus — which I agree should not be closed or wound down — an institute for the teaching of foreign languages. I do no mean teaching those languages purely in the literary or cultural sense but with an eye to providing us with a corps of people capable of promoting Irish industry and goods abroad.

I realise that is not what Cardinal Newman meant by education and it was not what I was brought up to believe was the point of education. At one time I would have been horrified to hear myself speak like this. I was brought up to think of education as essentially an egghead pursuit at all levels and particularly at the level after 18 years of age. That kind of thinking is a luxury I have dropped. I suppose I have a job that could be regarded as a luxury job — teaching jurisprudence and Roman law to students, which if they had their way few of them would opt to learn. I am not trying to disparage the source from which I hold my job but we need to get rid of the idea that the only national importance of education is what I might call the Newman importance of developing and unfolding the human personality. Of course that has to be done but I cannot believe that is not possible while, at the same time, providing the country with the level of training in linguistic skills that it needs.

Exporting Irish Food, Dáil, 28 May 1987

I remember, and I have mentioned in here more than once, a deputation of Irish food exporters going to a food fair in, I think, Berlin a few years ago and coming back very deflated, saying that the level of variety, of quality, of attractiveness, of inventiveness in the food products they saw from the rest of the world in Berlin depressed them. They measured these products against the shapeless doorsteps of cheese which is our contribution to the European supermarket and said to themselves, "we have not yet arrived at the fair". That is something which will take more than the appointment of a Minister of State to remedy.

The reason Ireland has not arrived at the fair in the food industry is that Irish people have not sufficient acquaintance with the outside world. Their acquaintance with the outside world in too many cases, apart from a quick run to the sun in Spain or the Canary Islands, tends to be in the English-speaking states which are not distinguished in regard to food. In America a great proportion of the food is uneatable and certainly unenjoyable to the European palate. In Britain where I lived for years and where I still visit frequently the position is not much better. The standards of what one might call the food in the street, the ordinary common or garden restaurant, in both of those countries are lamentably low by the standards of continental Europe. Until Irish people instinctively understand from personal acquaintance the standards which are taken as automatic, as natural and as self-understood in Holland, Germany, Belgium, France and Italy, we will not arrive at the fair about which these exporters spoke.

As I said, I visit Britain quite often. I sometimes work there under my academic hat and sometimes I shop there. When I visit English supermarkets the only Irish products I ever see, and I always buy them of course, are Kerrygold butter, of which I eat very little but I go through the motions of buying it anyway, and Irish cheddar cheese. There is no other Irish food of any kind, animal or vegetable, to be found in the average English supermarket. I also visit Germany a good deal for the same purpose and I shop there. In that country there are no Irish products of any kind to be found except a dusty bottle of Irish whiskey peeping shyly from behind a row of Scotch.

It is not simply a question of ensuring hygiene with regard to the very limited range of products we have. It is a matter of making sure that a whole cohort, almost a whole garrison, of Irish people in the food production area have enough experience of living, which means eating and drinking, abroad in the countries into which we are trying to sell out products. They understand that what we take as being food will not interest the foreign palate.

I have seen printed and I have heard foreigners say, although not in quite the same compact language, that if you want to eat well in Ireland you would have to eat three breakfasts a day. The level of food is very nutritious, it is of the highest possible quality, bursting with proteins and carbohydrates and all sorts of good things but it is not very enjoyable.

The amount of innovation, inventiveness and variety shown with regard to Irish products is exceedingly narrow. That is the reason the home market is being taken over by foreign produce. It is not because we are not buying Irish. If you are spoiled enough as to want a certain variety of food and drink you will not be able to find enough Irish products as we have not got the range of products you would like to indulge in. I am not speaking as an epicure or as somebody who makes a god of his stomach. I do not do so and I am by no means an expert on this, but I know from even the most casual expeditions into supermarkets here, in Britain, in Germany and also in Italy, that that is so. The average consumer abroad, even somebody who is not in a very high income bracket, has a far larger range of indigenous choice in food and drink in his own country than we have here. Until that is understood by Irish food producers there is no use whingeing and whining about us not supporting native industry and about import substitution being of high priority.

Lenihan and Emigration, Dublin, 13 October 1987

After twenty-five years of reckless spoofing, Mr Lenihan has at last decided to tell the bare truth as he sees it; and it is poor encouragement to the rest of his party to follow his reforming example that he should be assailed from all sides for his completely sensible remarks on emigration.

I would not myself adopt all the perspectives which he did in his *Newsweek* interview; for example, I think Government policy should be based on trying to switch the migration emphasis away from America and towards the continental E.E.C.

But apart from this what fault is there to find with Mr Lenihan's view that emigration today is not comparable with emigration as it was in the miseries of the 19th century? Or that many young Irish people actually want to go away and learn about the outside world, and that this is something positive? or that the more the work ethic of dynamic foreign industrial societies can be transplanted back here by returning emigrants, the better?

We need to clear our minds in this country of the cant and old cod which passes for national wisdom and national consensus on such matters. Mr Lenihan gets a beating from every politician and newspaper in sight for saying "we can't all live on a small island"; but he is obviously right if what he means, as I presume he does, is that we can't all live here and have the standard of living and the level of public services we aspire to; or at any rate, not until we have grown out of the half-hearted work ethic and shed the destructive industrial relations attitudes we think are a fundamental constitutional right, and got to grips with the problems presented by a market with tastes quite different from those we have ourselves.

The real point, however, and the most interesting aspect of Mr Lenihan's interview seen as a political marker, is that the consequences of what was absolutely certain to happen as soon as our explosive population expansion ran up against a recession in the world economy were visible and predictable all along. But politicians on every side, instead of warning people what was coming, pretended — with the words of the 1977 Manifesto — that there were "tens of thousands of jobs just waiting to be created", and blamed their political opponents' incompetence and malice for the failure of those jobs to materialise.

Mr Lenihan has at last thrown up the windows and opened the doors of the smoke-filled rooms of which, in popular folklore, he is the archetypal occupant. Instead of shouting him down, his critics would be better occupied drawing some sensible implications, above all in the field of education policy, from the plain facts he has opened to public view.

The National Lottery, Dáil, 9 February 1988

The worst financial device of the whole lot, something which my own party introduced, is the national lottery. Deputy Haughey, who likes to be associated with success or what he perceives as success, is up front, not quite on the Champs Elysées but at some more humble address in order to announce the first annual results of the national lottery. The national lottery had exceeded expectations. That is the Government's position on it. I have to say in justice to Deputy Haughey that had there been a Fine Gael Minister there I do not expect he would have acted any differently. I consider it a gross shame that a national lottery exceeds expectations. While I did not care for the way he used to hold the pistol to the heads of the last Government and would say that he would not vote for them any longer unless he got a scheme costing God knows how many millions which would have torn the heart out of the city of Dublin, I have to agree fully with what the former Deputy Liam Skelly said about the national lottery. I must not be taken as adopting this insulting phrase not can I even vouch for its authenticity. He quoted the great President of France, George Clemenceau, as saying that a lottery was a tax on imbeciles. I do not know whether Clemenceau said that and I would not wish to use language like that in any case about people who play a lottery. I think that language is far too insulting and gross to use about what may be only a small flutter. Nevertheless, I think for a Republic to stoop to a method like this for raising revenue is contemptible and shameful. I am glad to see Deputy Higgins nodding his head. I am amazed. I am beginning to wonder whether I should have studied my brief a bit better before leaving myself open to the charge that he has agreed totally with me about something. I do regard it as shameful if only because it psychologically perpetuates among ordinary people the crock of gold at the end of the rainbow mentality.

Even though Deputy Higgins is looking at what he may think is a smooth rock face of unchallengeable material with which he completely agrees in hearing me say these words, I hope he will not find that I am giving him a toe hold when I admit, to what may be a middle class admission that is, that with one exception, I personally have not bought a lottery ticket. I did once buy one in Italy because the old man selling them appeared to be so miserable and it seemed to cheer him up so much when I bought a couple of tickets from him. I have never bought a lottery ticket with the intention or hope or prospect of winning something. I know no one in my family has and I know, but I better not be too positive, that none of my friends or relations have bought tickets. Going into the post offices in the city, as I have to buy stamps and so forth, I do notice people buying lottery tickets and while they span a fair spectrum of the population and they are not all the same type of people, my impression, and I hope I am not offending anybody in saying so, I would not be doing my job here if I did not give my impressions whether they were right or wrong, is that the lottery tends to be patronised by people who have the least to spare. I have not checked this and perhaps I should have done so before coming in here to speak about it but I suspect that the big end of the lottery business is done on the days when social welfare payments are made. I think it is a scandal that this State should think of financing necessary services, because that is what it is doing, through this course.

I think it is a scandal that in the late 20th century we in this Irish Republic should choose to pick this means of raising revenue from the poorest, not only from them but certainly preponderantly from the less provident sections of the community in order to provide services which we should have been providing out of ordinary revenue.

Budget Debate, Dáil, 2 February 1989

The Minister eloquently exhorted the Irish people to patience. I was the first of the Irish people to hear his exhortation and I must confess to feeling fairly impatient at the terms in which he expressed this pious desire. He said that in the seventies and eighties we as a people were unwilling to wait until our economy could afford to provide the standard of living and social services we observed in wealthier countries. The poor old people of Ireland have to take the blame for the prodigality of those years. The old sow has to get another lash across its back for sinking to its knees under the burden of debt laid on it in those years. Who were to be seen, photographed shaking hands with, clapping on the back, flattering, sluthering and pandering to every section and group who wanted a few extra quid during those years but members of the Fianna Fáil Party when they were out of office? Now they are in and we are all to be patient. When they were out there was no talk of patience. If a Fine Gael Minister spoke about patience or restraint he was told he was a Thatcherite, obsessed with book-keeping. In the interests of a dead ideology he was planting his foot on the neck of the Irish people and destroying the hopes of the younger generation. That is the kind of language we heard from the far side.

I hope it will be seen to the credit of this party — I suppose it is a vain hope because in politics there is no gratitude — that at least the Government are not getting that kind of talk from us this time. We are not identifying with every pressure group who come to the door, agreeing with them that the Government should produce a few more million and that they are Thatcherite and book-keeping obsessed to refuse it. We do not flatter them. I had an intimidatory group of teachers on my doorstep — I call them that not because of their manners, which were impeccable, but because of their excessive numbers, in the region of 30 or 40. This did not happen when Fine Gael were in Government but rather when the Minister opposite and his colleagues were in office. I did not give them one inch, nor did any of my colleagues. I fought the Government's battle for them. I said I considered the Government had done all the country could afford at that time and that I did not consider they should go any further. I refused to go into the lobby against my own party merely to embarrass a Government who, for once, were trying to do the right thing. When did a Fianna Fáil Deputy ever treat people on his doorstep like that? When did he ever tell them the truth, although he probably had the same kind of insight about the conditions of the mid-seventies or the mid-eighties when he was out of Government.

Such considerations go to the wall when it is a question of doing down the other side, getting them out and getting one's own party in. That is the kind of village pitch and toss school of political morality which, if we are not very lucky, will leave this country in the hands of the Cubans before we are finished.

We are back on the old budget debate again. I have often complained about the budget fetish which, needless to say, is due solely to the fact that the English have it. The Chancellor of the Exchequer in the old days used to show up with his silk top hat, his spats and his striped pants and his battered despatch box. It was a lady's day in the spring. Spring breezes fluttered the silks and muslins of the ladies as they crowded through the visitors' entrance at Westminster. Naturally, the Irish Free State and the Irish Republic when it followed on the heels of that polity had to ape the same manners. There is not a battered despatch box but no doubt if Ministers leave it behind for their successors it will become battered in time. The current Minister for Finance and his predecessors are not above the old fetish concerning budget secrets in a little box which will have to wait until the afternoon. The gallery is filled with their families, the ladies not wearing silks and muslin at the beginning of the year but certainly dolled up for the day. It is a big occasion because the English treat it as a big occasion. No other country in Europe has this absurd fetish of budget day when the entire Government programme in fiscal terms has to be put on paper and delivered in the course of a speech. It is an idiotic fetish which we should get rid of.

Not a single measure announced in the budget could not as easily be announced on any other day of the year, including Christmas Day, as far as the law of the State is concerned. There is not a single financial resolution imposing excise duties which could not be imposed on any other day of the year. In the past such resolutions have frequently been imposed. No law and no clause of the Constitution prevents an infinite number of Finance Bills, one amending or modifying the other, introducing changes in income tax, VAT rates or any of the financial measures which require a legislative basis. These could be spread through the year and we would not be brought here for this big occasion on budget day when people fight for tickets to hear a dull speech for an hour and a half. The most recent was as dull as I have ever heard. They have all been dull, from both sides, since I became a Deputy almost 20 years ago.

I heard our Deputy Noonan make an excellent speech delivered at no notice in response to the budget. He talked about a commentator — I knew immediately who he meant — who is a great admirer of the Taoiseach and has been shouting "hurrah" for him for the last 20 years. This commentator gave the last Government an unmerciful lashing day in day out because of their presiding over a sinking economy and so on, and who is chiefly remarkable and notable in the literary sense for having documented the decline of an Irish town back in the fifties.

Only a couple of days before our Deputy Noonan made his speech, I had read articles — as it turned out he had also read them — which ran for two or three days in *The Irish Times* about the human desolation in the eastern parts of County Mayo at present. I am rather out of touch with rural Ireland living where I do but my colleagues in the party tell me that it is the same everywhere else. There is a great silence over the place and Knock Airport is used mostly for returning emigrants and for funerals. The big hospitality dispensed by the publicans in that area is to funeral parties. The remains of loved ones are brought in from abroad. I am not producing this as a stick with which to beat the Government. I am quite certain that the underlying causes were there in our times too, but if that is so, we should try to understand why it is so. It is not all because of financial economic necessary.

I can quite understand it where you suddenly get a factory closure and the people in the district have been conditioned to expect employment only in terms of being found a place in a factory. Naturally, there will be devastation, human as well as everything else, and naturally the only thing people can think of, if they cannot easily get another job, is to emigrate. The descriptions of the awful rushing and clambering to try to get any kind of a little job in whatever other little business might be nearby are heart-rending. I am sure the Minister had the same reaction if he read the articles. However, it is not at all like that.

I saw the response of the Conference on Major Religious Superiors to the budget. It was a very disappointed response and they assert — I do not question their sincerity — that the big end of emigration is involuntary emigration. I question that, I am not contradicting it because I do not have the facts necessary to do so authoritatively. The truth is that nobody really knows why this or that percentage of people emigrate. My two elder sons, in their early and mid-twenties, are abroad, one in London and one in America. They were not driven out of the country by economic necessity and neither of them ever looked for a job in Ireland. The temperament of one is such that he finds it more exciting, interesting, amusing and promising to live in London while the other is pursuing further studies in America which he cannot pursue here. These are two perfectly ordinary boys who are not distinguishable from tens of thousands of others of their age but they are not involuntary emigrants. I hope that one or other of them will come back. If they do not return they must be counted as emigrants but no one has driven them out.

What then leads to such people leaving the country? That is the sort of question the Government should ask themselves. It is not simply a matter of putting a factory at the end of every boreen so that every mother can have each of her sons home for tea but rather of delivering a country which is exciting, interesting and open enough, with frontiers within itself which recede into the distance, which will excite young people and get them to see that this is a country which has a buzz of a different kind from that in England or America.

If our young people want to look abroad I think they should look towards continental Europe where they can go as of right. We do not have to skulk around Germany or Holland as illegals waiting for someone to make up ballads such as the one about the illegals of 1988 which, incidentally, has a grand truculent ring to it. We do not need to skulk around Europe as illegals as we are entitled to go there but who thinks along those lines? If one were to visit a school they could say statistically, that between 30 per cent and 40 per cent of the leaving class will be abroad in Baltimore or in Camden Town in 12 or 18 months' time. If one were to ask the students why they do not think in terms of going to Eindhoven or Frankfurt, natural politeness would prevent them from saying this, but they would think that one was taking leave of their senses.

A Government should try to discover what exactly it is that makes people leave as in most cases it is not economic necessity and they should ask themselves whether a silent judgment is not being passed on the style and atmosphere of the society over which they so smugly preside and see whether something can be done about it at that level. People find this country boring, which it does not have to be and which it is not for those who have been lucky to find a fulfilling niche, occupation or profession but for many it is. Why is it boring and what can a Government do to enlighten themselves about what they are doing wrong, and about the way in which they are steering their society and presiding over it?

There is another dimension which the Government ought to address. There is a resistance to anything which is not employment of a kind in which you do what you are told or of a kind which traditionally is of the middle class, white collar professional sort. No Government have ever made a serious attempt to bring forward a tradition of craftwork, of skilled and highly individual work done by hand. I am not talking about the making of souvenirs but rather about the whole range of individualised craftwork on which the modern world is placing an increasing importance. The Waterford Glass enterprise is the one big exception to the rule but what is happening with that company? Their order books are full and their customers are angry and disappointed because they cannot get deliveries. That company do not seem to be able to get their act together. I am aware that there are other crystal factories but there should be 100 such different trades and specialised, individualised enterprises. The modern world is becoming homogenised, everybody now uses the same makes of sports equipment, listens to Walkman radios and drives the same types of car. This is something that the human spirit rebels and revolts against. When people have any discretionary income they are willing to spend it on things which are not homogenised and they value something which is individual and produced by hand.

At the beginning of January I spent three weeks in Germany. I have an old Aran sweater which one of my sons gave me. It is now getting a bit seedy and run down as it has been washed and worn so often but I wear it when I am working. More than one German spotted me wearing it — it was dilapidated in the sense that perhaps they would not be seen dead in it — but they recognised it as being hand made and that gave it a value quite independent of its calorific or aesthetic qualities. It was the work of an individual human eye and hand and this raised it above the homogenised level of industrial products. That is a perception which was documented about 15 years ago by Dr Kieran Kennedy who was then head of the ESRI in an absolutely marvellous report on the Danish economy. In many respects the Danes have to contend with some of the peripheral problems we have to contend with but they have thrived as a result of concentrating on what was individual, small scale and high quality. They are associated in people's minds with those values and that is a large part of the secret of their success.

An Irish Government ought to put their minds to that matter seriously and in doing so they should run their eye around the things in this country which prosper and which get written about in the inflight magazine, *Cara*, such as the making of harpsichords in some out of the way place, or making an unusual kind of sheep's cheese. Such activity may be easy to sneer at and laugh at but these are the high qualify products which mean prosperity. More than likely they are being made by foreigners — an English woman running a hotel, a German raising a herd of deer, a Canadian running a shell fish farm or a couple of Belgians producing quality woollen products. Very rarely will it be a person of native Irish blood who sees an opportunity such as that and makes the most of it. This is not because we are worse than anybody else or are defective in any way but rather that we are not trained or encouraged to think like that and are shy about inviting people in, as we should do and which is what many countries have done in the past, to show us how these things are done. A Government who are struggling — I suppose the Government with their awful record in creating the problem must be struggling — with the problems of unemployment and emigration ought to ask themselves wither there is a level in the Irish psychology which needs to be addressed and to see, as a consequence, whether our education system, including linguistics education and industrial education, needs to be, in a crash programme, rapidly overhauled before we have the social and psychological infrastructure on which a healthy economy can be built.

In half an hour I am by no means able to draw up a complete list of the things I think are important to mention but perhaps most damaging of the items is our idiotic complacency, the formal official complacency of the Irish. We are not, as individuals, complacent. Talking over a drink or in conversation with our friends or family we are not complacent but we feel publicly and officially that we have to be complacent.

There is an awful lot of second to noneism in this country. Publicly we say that everything here is second to none. We say that the streets of Dublin are second to none. About three years ago I remember making a very disparaging speech about the vile, dilapidated and run down condition of this city which is certainly the scruffiest between here and Calcutta, and I was attacked by a colleague of mine in my own party, a member of Dublin Corporation, who said that Deputy Kelly was an elitist and spends too much of his time abroad in the university cities and does not understand that Dublin is second to none in this, that and the other.

I know that it is not second to none and as long as the public keep me here in the Dáil I will go on saying it and perhaps somebody will have the modesty to say no, it is not second to none. We ought not to run millennia when we are a public reproach and when one cannot walk 100 yards in any direction from O'Connell Bridge without seeing something which would make one cry with shame and which ought to make a city councillor hang himself with shame. We ought not to be running millennia when that is still true, but the complacency, the second to noneism, does not allow us to look at it like that.

At the other end of the scale we had an example here of a miniature but very illuminating thing two days ago. In mentioning the Minister, Deputy Reynolds, I do not want to single him out because I am certain he did only what he was recommended to do by his officials or what another Minister in his position would have done. I put a question down here about the leprous conditions of the bank notes, particularly £1 notes. Let me show the House what I got in change in the restaurant of Leinster House this afternoon. Look at that. That is the place where they sell food. Look at that £5 note. I sometimes get a bundle of £1 notes into my hand and I can smell them and I am perfectly certain, though everybody else here in the House may be laughing at it, I am only repeating an experience everybody else here has had. Do you know the answer I got from the Minister, Deputy Reynolds? He rejected my use of the word "insanitary" to describe the banknotes. He said they are circulated more now than they used to do. That is perfectly true, but he would not use the word "insanitary". What word would he use when banknotes smell up at you from your hand? They stink from your hand. What kind of impression can that create on tourists when they come in and produce a glittering, clean German 100 DM note and get a filthy leprous, crawling pile of these horrible little filthy rags into their hands in exchange? But no, we are second to none. Our currency is second to none and if any consideration is being given to improving the matter it will be all the better when the consideration is complete. They are thinking now of a £1 coin. It is harder to make a coin more permanently filthy than piece of porous paper. They are thinking of it because the English, of course, have a £1 coin. We should be thinking ahead of them; we should be thinking of £2 and, yes, £5 coins because that is where we are going to end at the rate of the depreciation of currency.

Many people will think that is just eccentric elitism once again. It is not. It is a scandal that a Minister could pretend or think it was his job to pretend that our currently is not a reproach to us. Let me add as a footnote to this complacency that it is backed up and made worse by a streak of mandarinism, official and ministerial. I put that question about the banknotes down in this form: "To ask the Minister for Finance if he has noticed the increasingly insanitary condition of the paper currency." When the question appeared on the Order Paper that had been changed to read: "To ask the Minister for Finance if his attention has been drawn to the increasingly insanitary condition of the banknotes". Therefore, a Minister is not allowed to notice. The silly ass solemnity which is part of this complacency is such that somebody feels it his job not to allow a Minister to notice things. He is not supposed to touch currency himself. He is like old Queen Mary in England or another of the Royal Family who would saunter up through Harrods or Marshall and Snelgrove's picking up an umbrella here, a reticule there, and ten steps behind went a detective discreetly paying. He had the banknotes in his pocket. The Queen, naturally, must not be allowed to touch or even see money; or, as is the case in this country, to smell it, and the Minister must not be allowed to notice it. He has to have it at best drawn to this attention. That is the kind of silly ass solemnity and complacency I want us to get away from, and until Government go into retreat and examine their consciences about the psychology from which we all spring and which we all have to fight — I the same as everybody else — and ask about our level of imperviousness to proper standards of cleanliness, punctuality, delivery, of being at a place when you say you will be there, keeping something tidy, we need not be amazed when tourism does not explode or explodes only in terms of returning emigrants.

That is nothing like all I have to say but it is all I have time to say. The budget debate is useful enough and I have no objection to the overall effort of